Corporate Capture
of Development

Corporate Capture of Development

Public-Private Partnerships, Women's Human Rights, and Global Resistance

Edited by
Corina Rodríguez Enríquez &
Masaya Llavaneras Blanco

BLOOMSBURY ACADEMIC
LONDON · NEW YORK · OXFORD · NEW DELHI · SYDNEY

BLOOMSBURY ACADEMIC
Bloomsbury Publishing Plc
50 Bedford Square, London, WC1B 3DP, UK
1385 Broadway, New York, NY 10018, USA
29 Earlsfort Terrace, Dublin 2, Ireland

BLOOMSBURY, BLOOMSBURY ACADEMIC and the Diana logo
are trademarks of Bloomsbury Publishing Plc

First published in Great Britain 2023

Cover design by Louise Dugdale
Cover photo © wyattheiberg / Unsplash

A catalogue record for this book is available from the British Library.

Library of Congress Cataloging-in-Publication Data
Names: Rodríguez, Corina, editor. | Llavaneras Blanco, Masaya, editor.
Title: Corporate capture of development : public-private partnerships,
women's human rights, and global resistance / edited by Corina
Rodríguez Enríquez & Masaya Llavaneras Blanco.
Description: London, UK ; New York, NY : Bloomsbury Academic, 2023. |
Includes bibliographical references and index.
Identifiers: LCCN 2022060675 (print) | LCCN 2022060676 (ebook) |
ISBN 9781350296688 (hardback) | ISBN 9781350296671 (paperback) |
ISBN 9781350296695 (epub) | ISBN 9781350296701 (pdf) |
ISBN 9781350296718 (xml)
Subjects: LCSH: Public-private sector cooperation–Developing countries. | Women's
rights–Developing countries. | Economic development–Developing countries.
Classification: LCC HD3872.D44 C67 2023 (print) |
LCC HD3872.D44 (ebook) | DDC 338.6–dc23/eng/20230208
LC record available at https://lccn.loc.gov/2022060675
LC ebook record available at https://lccn.loc.gov/2022060676

ISBN: HB: 978-1-3502-9668-8
          PB: 978-1-3502-9667-1
        ePDF: 978-1-3502-9670-1
      eBook: 978-1-3502-9669-5

Typeset by Integra Software Services Pvt. Ltd.

To find out more about our authors and books visit www.bloomsbury.com
and sign up for our newsletters.

Contents

List of figures   vii

List of maps   viii

List of tables   ix

Notes on contributors   xi

Foreword   xv

Acknowledgements   xvii

List of abbreviations   xix

Introduction: A feminist critique of PPPs rooted in the global South
Corina Rodríguez Enríquez and Masaya Llavaneras Blanco   1

Part 1   The narrative, political and economic environment of PPPs

1   Medical equipment leasing in Kenya: Neocolonial global
    finance and misplaced health priorities *Crystal Simeoni and*
    Wangari Kinoti   19
2   PPPs meet the developmental state: The case of Ethiopia
    Netsanet Gebremichael   45

Part 2   Normative and institutional labyrinths of PPPs

3   PPPs, corporate responsibility and women's human rights
    in Senegal's finance for development model: The case of the
    Dakar-Diamniadio motorway *Marème Ndoye*   67
4   Opaque practices and substandard health service delivery:
    The case of La Red Asistencial Sabogal de EsSalud in Peru
    Bethsabé Andía Pérez   87

Part 3   Impact of PPPs on human rights: Building resistances
         at national level

5   PPPs in the Isthmus of Tehuantepec Corridor: Megaprojects,
    opacity and women's resistance *Isabel Clavijo Flórez and*
    Julieta Lamberti   119

6   PPPs in publicly funded health insurance schemes: The case of
    PMJAY in India, or how women bear the brunt while the private
    sector expands *Sulakshana Nandi*   143
7   PPPs in agro-energy and their impact on women's rights: The case
    of Addax Bioenergy Sierra Leone *Hussainatu J. Abdullah*   167

Part 4   Impact of PPPs on human rights: Building resistances at
         local level

8   A feminist human rights approach to Ghana's public market PPPs:
    The case of the dome market *Gertrude Dzifa Torvikey and
    Sylvia Ohene Marfo*   201
9   PPPs in the Parirenyatwa Group of Hospitals in Zimbabwe:
    Institutional precarities and piecemeal solutions *Nyasha Masuka*   223
10 Unhealthy partnerships: PPPs in Fiji's Lautoka and Ba hospitals
    Lice Cokanasiga   249

Conclusion: Corporate capture of development in times of exacerbated
crises: Implications for democratic governance, rights and global
inequality *Corina Rodríguez Enríquez and Masaya Llavaneras Blanco*   279

Further reading   292
Index   326

Figures

1.1   Mean OOP payments in Kenya as a share of total household
      expenditure separated by income quintiles, in 2018   26

4.1   Sector-wise distribution of PPP investments (million USD)
      in Peru   115

4.2   Number of PPPs in Peru, organised by sector   115

5.1   PPP modalities in Mexico   121

5.2   Areas of environmental relevance in the Isthmus of Tehuantepec 129

Maps

1.1   Geospatial spread of women in Kenya's marginalised areas
who did not visit health facilities between 2014 and 2015   36

6.1   Location of the Chhattisgarh state in India   144

Tables

1.1   Comparison of African Union Agenda 2063 and SDG Policy
Frameworks   20

1.2   A Timeline of Kenya's Health Financing Policies up to 2010   24

1.3   Leasing Companies Involved in Kenya's MES Programme   30

1.4   Kenya's Healthcare Budget Allocation in FY2015–16   33

2.1   Energy Sector PPPs Reported in Ethiopia's Print Media,
April 2018–May 2020   59

4.1   Classification of PPPs as per Peru's Regulatory Framework   91

4.2   Summary of Agreements in Addendum 2 of the Barton PPP   94

4.3   Remarks on the Minimum Standards and Indicators in the
Barton PPP   98

4.4   Satisfaction Indicators That Do Not Meet Goals in the
Barton PPP   99

4.5   Quality Indicators That Do Not Meet Goals in the Barton PPP   99

4.6   Outcome Indicators That Do Not Meet Goals in the Barton PPP   100

4.7   PPP Projects in Peru's Health Sector as of 2020   112

4.8   National System for Private Investment Promotion in Peru   114

5.1   Projects under the Isthmus of Tehuantepec Development
Programme   123

5.2   Main Beneficiary Companies of the FIT Rehabilitation   126

5.3   Indigenous Population in the Isthmus   131

7.1   Donor Support for Sierra Leone's Public-Private Partnership
Unit, 2013–15   170

7.2   Tax Incentives for Agribusinesses and ABSL   177

7.3   Current PPP Projects in Sierra Leone   192

7.4   DFI Co-financing of Addax Bioethanol Sierra Leone   196

8.1   PPPs with Financial Closure in Ghana, 1999–2019   204

8.2   Institutions, Actors and Mandates in Ghana's PPP Framework   206

9.1   Registered Health Facilities by Ownership in Zimbabwe in 2020   228

9.2   Public-Private Engagement Typology   229

9.3   Modes of Contracting Out to Private for-Profit Providers in
       Zimbabwe in 2009   230

10.1 Apollo Group's Proposed 44 million USD Hospital PPP
       in Fiji, 2007   253

10.2 Aspen Medical's Obligations in the Lautoka and
       Ba Hospitals PPP   255

10.3 Fiji Government's Case for the Lautoka and
       Ba Hospitals PPP   258

10.4 Australia Health and Overall Aid Spending Cuts in the
       Pacific Islands   275

Notes on contributors

Editors

Masaya Llavaneras Blanco is an Assistant Professor of Development Studies at Huron University College at the University of Western Ontario, in Canada. Her research and advocacy centre on issues of care, human mobility and the rights of people on the move in the global South. She holds a Master's in women's studies from the Universidad Central de Venezuela and a PhD in global governance from Wilfrid Laurier University–Balsillie School of International Affairs, Canada. She has been collaborating with DAWN in various capacities since 2010 and joined DAWN's Executive Committee in 2020.

Corina Rodríguez Enríquez is a feminist economist. She is a researcher at the Consejo Nacional de Investigaciones Científicas y Técnicas (Conicet) and the Centro Interdisciplinario para el Estudio de Políticas Públicas (Ciepp) in Buenos Aires, Argentina; Executive Committee Member at DAWN; and Co-director of the PhD programme on political economy at the Interdisciplinary School of Social Studies (IDAES). She holds a Master's in public policy from the Institute of Social Studies (The Hague, the Netherlands) and a PhD in social sciences from Facultad Latinoamericana de Ciencias Sociales (FLACSO).

Authors

Hussainatu J. Abdullah is an independent researcher with research and consultancy experiences in Eritrea, Nigeria, Liberia and Sierra Leone. She has provided consultancy services to the African Development Bank, African Union and the Millennium Challenge Corporation. She holds a PhD in sociology and social anthropology from the University of Hull.

Lice Cokanasiga is a researcher and campaign assistant with the Pacific Network on Globalisation and an alumnae of the DAWN GEEJ Network. Her work revolves around monitoring, tracking and critiquing the Blue Economy agenda in the region and its impact on indigenous peoples' environment in the Pacific Islands. She conducts research on trade liberalisation and its impact on extractive industries in the Pacific, and tracks what donor financing means for the corporate capture of public policy spaces.

Isabel Clavijo Flórez is a sociologist and a researcher on extractivism, corporate state capture and human rights at the Project on Organizing, Development, Education and Research (PODER). Her area of work focuses on conflicts and territorial advocacy processes in the Latin Américan region (México-Colombia). She holds a Master's degree in regional development from El Colegio de la Frontera Norte.

Netsanet Gebremichael is a researcher at the Institute of Ethiopian Studies at the Addis Ababa University. She holds a Master of Arts degree in contemporary cultural studies from the Institute and a PhD in social studies from Makerere University, Uganda. She has served as Directress of Addis Ababa University's Gender Office for two years.

Wangari Kinoti is a feminist activist engaged in global policy advocacy against structural violence and economic justice for women. Over the last sixteen years, she has campaigned and implemented programmes on women's political participation, women's land and natural resource rights, corporate accountability, women's paid and unpaid labour, gender-responsible public services and violence against women, through civil society and societal justice organisations. She is currently working with other African feminist activists to document histories of feminist organising on the continent.

Julieta Lamberti is a feminist and human rights defender who is currently Director of Research in the Project on Organization, Development, Education and Research (PODER). She has directed research on human rights violations due to the Sonora River spill, AMLO's megaprojects and the New Mexico City International Airport. She has been a member of the implementation team of the first community-led Human Rights Impact Assessment of a mining project in the Sierra Norte de Puebla. She has a Master's in social sciences from FLACSO-México and a PhD in sociology from Colegio de México.

Sylvia Ohene Marfo is a PhD candidate in the University of Ghana's Department of Sociology where her thesis is on the sociology of food and agriculture, and specifically on the role of foodways in identity construction. She has extensive qualitative research experience in girls' education, gender, migration, food and agriculture. She holds a Bachelor of Arts in sociology and philosophy and an MPhil in sociology.

Nyasha Masuka is a Special Service assignment holder in the health systems strengthening department at the World Health Organization in Zimbabwe. He holds two Bachelor's degrees in medicine and surgery from the University of Zimbabwe and a Master's in public health – health systems management and policy from the Prince Leopold Institute of Tropical Medicine in Antwerp, Belgium. The findings and conclusions of the chapter he has authored in this book is based entirely on his research and do not reflect the views of any organisation he has worked for in the past or is currently a part of.

Sulakshana Nandi is the State Convener of Public Health Resource Network (PHRN), Chhattisgarh, and a founding member of Chaupal, a tribal resource agency that supports community-based organisations working on the right to food and health, forest rights, and gender and tribal rights. She is involved in research, capacity building and advocacy on issues related to health equity and access, and public policy and programmes for health and nutrition, with a focus on gender and vulnerable communities. She is co-chair of the People's Health Movement, Global, and holds a PhD in public health from the University of Western Cape, South Africa.

Marème Ndoye holds a Doctorate of State in economic sciences from the Cheikh Anta Diop University of Dakar, Senegal. She is a CAMES (African and Malagasy Council for Higher Education) Assistant Professor in the Faculty of Economic Sciences and Management at the same university. She teaches and carries out research around development economics, decentralised funding systems for analysis and project evaluation. Since September 2020, she is a monitoring evaluation and economic analysis lead at the Millennium Challenge Account.

Bethsabé Andía Pérez is a feminist activist with more than twenty years' experience promoting the rights of women at non-profit institutions and in the public sector. She is an economist with Master's degrees in gender, population and development from the Universidad Nacional Mayor de San Marco (UNMSM) and in business administration from the Escuela de Administración de Negocios para Graduados (ESAN).

Crystal Simeoni is an Atlantic Fellow on Social and Economic Inequality at the London School of Economics. She is a Pan-African feminist and works to inculcate Pan-African feminist narratives into macroeconomic policy processes and spaces at different levels.

Gertrude Dzifa Torvikey is the Programme Officer for the *Feminist Africa* journal based at the Institute of African Studies, University of Ghana. She teaches gender courses at the Centre for Gender Studies and Advocacy (CEGENSA) at the same university. Her research interests include agrarian livelihoods, gender and migration. She holds a PhD in development studies from the University of Ghana's Institute of Statistical, Social and Economic Research (ISSER).

Foreword

Human Rights and the Search for Economic Truth

Juan Pablo Bohoslavsky

Independent Expert on Foreign Debt and Human Rights,
UNHRC (2014–2020)

It has been said that neoliberal economic ideas – among them public-private partnerships (PPPs) – are dangerous because they remain immune to empirical refutation. But this immunity is explained by political and social factors that allow the few who benefit from PPPs to keep on enriching their coffers at the expense of those most heavily hit by this financial infrastructure – in particular, the most vulnerable groups. This is not a natural phenomenon, and it can be changed.

A number of human needs for social reproduction are unmet, paralleled by a colossal failure of the state to ensure economic and social development for all. As this book demonstrates, the response has been more power to corporations and more liabilities to states. In practice, this works like a state insurance system ensuring profitability to corporations at any cost over the realisation of human rights. How could PPPs deliver promised social goals based on those conditions?

In 2015, the Addis Ababa International Conference on Financing for Development endorsed PPPs as a miraculous developmental tool. The 2011 United Nations Guiding Principles on Business and Human Rights (Principle 4) had established that states must ensure that business enterprises that they own, control or are associated with, respect human rights. This is why a Third World Approach to International Law (TWAIL) to legally analyse PPPs does not really demand the creation of new obligations in international law, but rather the enforcement of existing ones.

This is not a book on recent economic history. While most of the chapters of this book tell us about PPP projects that have already been implemented, and their negative impacts on women's rights, neither past experience nor the pandemic have changed PPP promoters' minds. In 2020, the World Bank (WB) deployed a multibillion dollar financial initiative, through its Health, Nutrition and Population Division, to support private actors in key sectors highly sensitive to human rights, including public health. These multilateral loans are channelled through the International Finance Corporation (IFC) – the WB's private financing arm – despite its lack of experience in developing public health systems. The implications of PPPs in the health sector are highlighted and explained in several chapters of this book.

This book is meant to operate at both the epistemic and political levels. It provides concrete, solid and representative evidence and explains the pertinent causal mechanisms that help us understand how and why PPPs too often negatively affect women's human rights. The book contributes to dismantling the spillover fallacies[1] that the promoters of PPPs try to sell – and have actually sold – around the world. Human rights activists know it well: truth is compelling for political mobilisation.

Note

1   By spillover fallacies we mean all the positive (direct and indirect) effects that PPPs might have, from the point of view of their promoters.

Acknowledgements

This book has been made possible thanks to the commitment, dedication and hard work of all the authors. Our deep thanks to Hussainatu J. Abdullah, Lice Cokanasiga, Isabel Clavijo Flórez, Netsanet Gebremichael, Wangari Kinoti, Julieta Lamberti, Sylvia Ohene Marfo, Nyasha Masuka, Sulakshana Nandi, Marème Ndoye, Bethsabé Andía Pérez, Crystal Simeoni and Gertrude Dzifa Torvikey for joining the project, and for their effort and patience throughout the process.

This book is the result of several years of work in which DAWN has been critically analysing, from a feminist perspective, the process of corporate capture of states and of global governance. We would, therefore, like to thank those who have contributed with their analysis, research and activism throughout this process.

Our thanks to the participants of the February 2018 workshop in Cape Town, especially Hibist Kassa and colleagues from the Southern Africa Rural Women's Assembly.

Thank you to Zenebewerke Tadesse, who made substantive contributions early on in the project, and to the participants of the Addis Ababa workshop in May 2019, who provided evidence and reflections specific to the African context.

Many thanks to Fatou Sow, host of a workshop we held at an early stage of the process in the city of Dakar. Thanks also to Viviene Taylor, Sue Godt and Takyiwaa Manuh for their comments on draft versions of the chapters and for invaluable inputs.

Thanks to Gita Sen and María Graciela Cuervo for their support and guidance as DAWN's General Co-coordinators. We are also grateful to everyone from DAWN's Executive Committee and Global Board, who provided useful comments and inputs at different moments of the project.

The final manuscript would not have been possible without the daily work, dedication and patience of Sala Weleilakeba and assistance from Damien Gock and Sharan Sindhu. We are grateful to both Chris Engert, who undertook the preliminary editing of chapters, and Sohel Sarkar, who finalised the editing and prepared the manuscript. Thanks also to DAWN's communications team, who continue to disseminate parts of the research that is reflected in this book.

We wish to record our sincerest gratitude for the support extended to DAWN by the Hewlett Foundation at every stage of the project – from the research, the analysis, the writing to the final publication.

For us this project and this book has been an immense learning process. We are grateful for having had the opportunity to work together and for being able to keep up the spirit since the onset of Covid.

Finally, our gratitude to the communities and relations who sustain our work with their labour, kindness and affection.

Corina Rodríguez Enríquez and
Masaya Llavaneras Blanco

Abbreviations

A4D	Agriculture for Development
AB-PMJAY	Ayushman Bharat-Pradhan Mantri Jan Arogya Yojana (rough translation: Healthy India-Prime Minister's People's Health Scheme)
ABSL	Addax Bioenergy Sierra Leone Limited
ACHPR	African Charter on Human and Peoples' Rights
ADB	Asian Development Bank
AFD	Agence Française de Développement (French Development Agency)
AfDB	African Development Bank
AFDZEE	Autoridad Federal para el Desarrollo de las Zonas Económicas Especiales (Federal Authority for the Development of Special Economic Zones)
AFRC	Armed Forces Revolutionary Council
AIBD	Aéroport international Blaise Diagne (Blaise Diagne International Airport)
AICA	Áreas de Importancia para la Conservación de las Aves (Relevant Areas for Birds Conservation)
AICD	Africa Infrastructure Country Diagnostic
AIDI	African Infrastructure Development Index
AITF	Agribusiness Investment Task Force
AJS	Association des jurists sénégalaises (Senegalese Women Lawyers Association)
ALVF	Association de lutte contre les violences faites aux femmes (Association for the Fight against Violence against Women)
ANC	Antenatal Coverage

ANSD	Agence nationale de la statistique et de la démographie (National Statistics and Population Agency)
AOG	Addax and the Oryx Group Limited (CH)
APC	All People's Congress
APDD	Autoroute à péage de Dakar-Diamniadio (Dakar-Diamniadio Toll Motorway)
APEC	Asia-Pacific Economic Cooperation
APIX	Agence pour la Promotion des Investissements et Grands Travaux Sénégal (National Agency for the Promotion of Investment and Major Works Senegal)
APIX	L'agence pour la promotion des investissements et grands travaux (National Agency for the Promotion of Investment and Major Works)
APROFES	Association pour la promotion de la femme sénégalaise (Association for the Promotion of the Senegalese Woman)
ARD	Agence régionale de développement (Regional Development Agency)
AU	African Union
AUD	Australian Dollar
Austrade	Australian Trade and Investment Commission
BANOBRAS	Banco Nacional de Obras y Servicios Públicos (National Bank of Public Services and Works)
BfA	Bread for All
BID (IDB)	Banco Interamericano de Desarrollo (Inter-American Development Bank)
BIO	Belgian Investment Company for Developing Countries
BIT	Bilateral Investment Treaty
BKPS	Bo-Kenema Power Service
BM (WB)	Banco Mundial (World Bank)

BNDE	Banque nationale pour le développement économique (National Bank for the Economic Development)
BOP	Business Operating Permit
BOT	Build Operate Transfer
BPL	Below Poverty Line
BWI	Bretton Woods Institutions
CAS	Contrato de Asignación de Servicios (Administrative Services Contract)
CEA	Clinical Establishments Act
CEDAW	Convention on the Elimination of all forms of Discrimination against Women
CEDEAO	Communauté économique des États de l'Afrique de l'Ouest (Economic Community of West African States (ECOWAS))
CEDEF	Convention sur l'Élimination de toutes les formes de discrimination à l'égard des Femmes (Convention on the Elimination of all Forms of Discrimination against Women (CEDAW))
CEFP	Centro de Estudios de las Finanzas Públicas (Centre for Public Finance Studies)
CEHAT	Centre for Enquiry into Health and Allied Themes
CEMDA	Centro Mexicano de Derecho Ambiental (Mexican Centre for Environmental Law)
CENAGAS	Centro Nacional de Control de Gas Natural (National Centre for Natural Gas Control)
CEO	Chief Executive Officer
CESCR	Committee on Economic and Social and Cultural Rights
CESOP	Centro de Estudios Sociales y de Opinión Pública (Centre for Social Studies and Public Opinion)

CET	Construction-Exploitation-Transfert (Construction-Operation-Transfer)
CFE	Comisión Federal de Electricidad (Federal Electricity Commission)
CGTP	Confederación General de Trabajadores del Perú (General Confederation of Workers of Peru)
CNAPPP	Comité national d'appui aux partenariat public-privé (National Committee for Support to Public-Private Partnership)
CNDH	Comisión Nacional de los Derechos Humanos (National Human Rights Commission)
CNEL	China New Energy Limited
CNH	Comisión Nacional de Hidrocarburos (National Hydrocarbons Commission)
CONABIO	Comisión Nacional para el Conocimieto y Uso de la Biodiversidad (National Commission for the Knowledge and Use of Biodiversity)
CONEVAL	Comisión Nacional de Evaluación de la Política. de Desarrollo Social (National Council for the Evaluation of Social Development Policy)
CONFIEP	Confederación Nacional de Instituciones Empresariales Privadas (National Confederation of Private Business Institutions)
COPASA	Sociedad Anónima de Obras y Servicios (Limited Company of Works and Services)
COPRI	Comisión de Promoción de la Inversión Privada (Commission for the Promotion of Private Investment)
COSEF	Conseil sénégalais des femmes (Senegalese Council of Women)
Covid-19	Coronavirus Disease 2019
CP	Contrat de partenariat (Partnership Contract)

CPIP	Comité de Promoción de la Inversión Privada de EsSalud (Committee for the Promotion of Private Investment of EsSalud)
CPISS	Comité de Promoción de Infraestructura y Servicios de Salud (Committee for the Promotion of Infrastructure and Health Services)
CRD	Chronic Renal Disease
CSO	Civil Society Organization
D.L.	Decreto Legislativo (Legislative Decree)
D.S.	Decreto Supremo (Supreme Decree)
DACF	District Assembly Common Fund
DASP	Direction de l'appui au secteur privé (Private Sector Development Department)
DAWN	Development Alternatives with Women for a New Era
DDSP	Direction du développement du secteur privé (Private Sector Support Department)
DEG	Deutsche Investitions-und Entwicklungsesellschaft (German Investment Corporation)
DESC	Derechos Económicos Social y Culturales (Economic, Social and Cultural Rights)
DFI	Development Financial Institutions
DfID	Department for International Development (UK aid)
DFPPP	Direction des financements et des partenariats public-privé (Public-Private Partnerships Financing Department)
DHIS	District Health Information System
DMD	Debt Management Division
DoHFW	Department of Health and Family Welfare
DPES	Document de politique économique et sociale (Economic and Social Policy Document)

DS	Developmental State
DSDEF	Document de stratégie pour le développement de l'entreprenariat féminin (Strategy Document for the Development of Female Entrepreneurship)
DSP	Délégation de service public (Public Service Delegation)
DSRP	Document stratégique de réduction de la pauvreté (Strategic Poverty Reduction Document)
EAIF	Emerging Africa Infrastructure Fund
EDFI	European Development Finance Institutions
EDSA	Electricity Distribution and Supply Company
EEP	Ethiopian Electric Power
EF	Economía y Finanzas (Economy and Finance)
EPG	Eminent Persons Group
EPRDF	Ethiopian People's Revolutionary Democratic Front
EPS	Entidades Prestadoras de Salud (Healthcare Providers)
EQUINET	Regional Network for Equity in Health in East and Southern Africa
ERC	Equal Remuneration Convention
ESAM	Enquête sénégalaise auprès des ménages (Senegalese Household Survey)
ESHIA	Environmental, Social and Health Impact Assessment
EsSalud	Seguro Social de Salud (Social Health Insurance) (formerly IPSS)
ETB	Ethiopian Birr
EU	European Union
Eurodad	Red Europea sobre Deuda y Desarrollo (European Network on Debt and Development)
EVD	Ebola Virus Disease

FAFS	Fédération des associations des fédérations féminines du Sénégal (Federation of Women's Associations of Senegal)
FAO	Food and Agriculture Organization
FBO	Farmer-Based Organization
FCFA	Franc CFA (CFA Franc) (Originally, the Franc of the French colonies in Africa, after independence, it became the Franc of the Financial Community of Africa)
FDI	Foreign Direct Investment
FDP	Farmer Development Programme
FED-CUT	Federación Centro Unión de Trabajadores del Seguro Social de Salud del Perú (Federation Workers' Union Centre of the Social Health Insurance of Peru)
FEMNET	The African Women's Development and Communication Network
FGD	Focus Group Discussion
FIAS	Foreign Investment Advisory Services
FIT	Ferrocarril del Istmo de Tehuantepec (Tehuantepec's Istmo Railway)
FJD	Fijian Dollar
FMI (IMF)	Fondo Monetario Internacional (International Monetary Fund)
FMO	Netherlands Development Finance Company (NL)
FNA	Fiji Nursing Association
FNPF	Fiji National Provident Fund
FOMIN (MIF)	Fondo Multilateral de Inversiones (Multilateral Investment Fund)
FONGIP	Fonds de garantie des investissements prioritaires (Priority Investments Guarantee Fund)

FONSIS	Fonds souverain d'investissement stratégique (Sovereign Strategic Investment Fund)
FOROSALUD	Foro de la Sociedad Civil en Salud (Civil Society Forum on Health)
FPIC	Free, Prior and Informed Consent
FSS	Forum for Social Studies
G7	Group of Seven, which includes the advanced economies of Canada, France, Germany, Italy, Japan, UK, United States and the European Union
G20	Group of Twenty: Argentina, Australia, Brazil, Canada, China, France, Germany, India, Indonesia, Italy, Japan, Mexico, Russia, Saudi Arabia, South Africa, South Korea, Turkey, UK, United States and the European Union
GADN	Gender and Development Network
GBP	Great Britain Pound (Sterling)
GDP	Gross Domestic Product
GE	General Electric
GELD	Projet Équité de genre dans la gouvernance locale (Gender Equity Project in Local Governance)
GHG	Greenhouse Gas
GHS	Ghanaian Cedi
GII	Gender Inequality Index
GIZ	Deutsche Gesellschaft für Internationale Zusammenarbeit
GNI	Gross National Income
GoSL	Government of Sierra Leone
GoZ	Government of Zimbabwe
GREFELS	Groupe de recherches sur les femmes et les lois au Sénégal (Research Group on Women and Laws in Senegal)

GST	Goods and Service Tax
GW	Gigawatt
HDI	Human Development Index
HDP	Health Development Partners
HEC	Hyundai Engineering Company Limited
HIPC	Heavily Indebted Poor Countries
HSSF	Health Sector Services Fund
HWC	Health and Wellness Centre
ICA	Infrastructure Consortium of Africa
ICF	Investment Climate Facility
ICT	Information and Communications Technology
ICU	Intensive Care Unit
IDC	Industrial Development Corporation (ZA)
IDE	Investissements directs étrangers (Foreign Direct Investment)
IDG	Indice de développement de genre (Index Gender Development Index (GDI))
IEA	Institute for Economic Affairs
IFC	International Finance Corporation
IFC-PS	International Finance Corporation-Performance Standards
IFI	International Financial Institution
IGV (GST)	Impuesto General a las Ventas (General Sales Tax)
IKM	Iseme, Kamau and Maema
ILO	International Labour Organization
IMA	Indian Medical Association
IMF	International Monetary Fund
IMR	Infant Mortality Rate
INEGI	Instituto Nacional de Estadística y Geografía (National Institute of Statistics and Geography)

INPI	Instituto Nacional de los Pueblos Indígenas (National Institute of Indigenous Peoples)
IPO	Initial Public Offering
IPRESS	Instituciones Prestadoras de Servicios de Salud (Health Service Providers)
IPSS	Instituto Peruano de Seguridad Social (Peruvian Institute of Social Security) (became EsSalud with Law No. 27056, of 1999)
ISDS	Investor State Dispute Settlement
ISE	Indice Institutions sociales et égalité homme-femme (Social Institutions and Gender Index (SIGI))
IT	Information Technology
ITC	International Trade Centre
JICA	Japan International Cooperation Agency
JSA	Jan Swasthya Abhiyan (People's Health Movement)
KES	Kenyan Shilling
KHSSP	Kenya Health Sector Strategic and Investment Plan
KII	Key Informant Interviews
LATINDADD	Red Latinoamericana por Justicia Económica y Social (Latin American Network for Economic and Social Justice)
LICs	Low-Income Countries
LLP	Limited Liability Partnership
LPS/PME	Lettre de politique sectorielle des petites et moyennes entreprises (Sector Policy Letter for Small- and Medium-Sized Enterprises (SPL/PME))
MCE	Municipal Chief Executive
MDAs	Ministries, Departments and Agencies
MDB	Multilateral Development Bank

MEF	Ministerio de Economía y Finanzas (Ministry of Economy and Finance)
MES	Managed Equipment Services
METEC	Metals and Engineering Corporations
MFD	Maximizing Financing for Development
MIA	Manifestación de Impacto Ambiental (Environmental Impact Statement)
MIA-R	Manifestación de Impacto Ambiental Modalidad Regional (Environmental Impact Statement)
MDGs	Millennium Development Goal
MINSA	Ministerio de Salud (Ministry of Health)
MMDAs	Metropolitan, Municipal and District Assemblies
MMM (MMF)	Marco Macroeconómico Multianual (Multi-year Macroeconomic Framework)
MMR	Maternal Mortality Ratio
MoF	Ministry of Finance
MoFEP	Ministry of Finance and Economic Planning
MoH	Ministry of Health
MoHCC	Ministry of Health and Child Care
MoHMS	Ministry of Health and Medical Services (Fiji)
MoU	Memorandum of Understanding
MP	Member of Parliament
MPTF	Multi-Partner Trust Fund
MSBY	Mukhyamantri Swasthya Bima Yojana (Chief Minister's Health Insurance Scheme)
MSF	Multi-Stakeholder Forum
MTP	Mid-Term Plan
MW	Megawatt

NaBCO	Nation Builders Corps
NAC	National Airport Corporation
NACO	Netherlands Airport Consultants
NAFTA	Tratado de Libre Comercio de América del Norte (North American Free Trade Agreement)
NBE	National Bank of Ethiopia
NCD	Non-Communicable Disease
ND	No Date
ND	Sin Fecha (No Date)
NDA	National Democratic Alliance
NGO	Non-Governmental Organization
NHA	National Health Authority
NHM	National Health Mission
NHS	National Health Strategy
NHSRC	National Health Systems Resource Centre
NIP	National Infrastructure Plan
NITI	National Institution for Transforming India
NLP	National Land Policy
NPA	National Power Authority
NPP	New Patriotic Party
NRHM	National Rural Health Mission
NSADP	National Sustainable Agriculture Development Plan
OC	Operating Company
OCDE	Organisation de coopération et de développement économiques (Organisation for Economic Co-operation and Dévelopment (OECD))
OCI	Órgano de Control Interno (Internal Control Body)
ODA	Official Development Assistance
ODD	Objectif du développement durable (Sustainable Development Goal (SDG))

OECD	Organización para la Cooperación y el Desarrollo Económicos (Organisation for Economic Co-operation and Development)
OMS (WHO)	Organización Mundial de la Salud (World Health Organization)
ONP	Observatoire national de la parité (National Observatory of Parity)
ONU	Organisation des Nations Unies (United Nations Organization (UNO/UN))
OOP	Out-of-Pocket
OPC	Office of the President and Cabinet
OPS (PAHO)	Organización Panamericana de la Salud (Pan-American Health Organization)
PAP	Plan d'action prioritaire (Priority Action Plan)
PAR	Plan d'action de réinstallation (Resettlement Action Plan)
PAS	Programmes d'ajustement structurel (Structural Adjustment Programme (SAP))
PAU	Project Advisory Unit
PDIT	Programa para el desarrollo del Istmo de Tehuantepec (Programme for the Development of the Isthmus of Tehuantepec)
PE	Public Enterprise
PEMEX	Petróleos Mexicanos (Mexican Oil)
PFA	Project and Financial Analysis
PFHI	Publicly-Funded Health Insurance
PFSD	Private and Financial Sector Development
PGH	Parirenyatwa Group of Hospitals
PHBG	Parirenyatwa Hospitals Board of Governors
PHC	Primary Healthcare
PHM	People's Health Movement

PHRN	Public Health Resource Network
PIAPPEM	Programa para el Impulso de Asociaciones Público-Privadas en Estados Mexicanos (Programme for the Promotion of Public-Private Partnerships in Mexican States)
PIB	Produit intérieur brut (Gross Domestic Product (GDP))
PICES	Poverty Income Consumption Expenditure Survey
PID	Public Investment Division
PIDIREGAS	Proyectos de Infraestructura Diferidos en el Registro de Gasto (Deferred Infrastructure Projects in the Expenditure Register)
PIFS	Pacific Islands Forum Secretariat
PMDC	People's Movement for Democratic Change
PME	Petites et moyennes entreprises (Small- and Medium-Sized Enterprises (SMEs))
PNIC	Plan Nacional de Infraestructura para la Competitividad (National Infrastructure Plan for Competitiveness)
PNUD	Programme des Nations Unies pour le développement (United Nations Development Programme (UNDP))
PODER	Proyecto sobre Organización, Desarrollo, Educación e Investigación (Project on Organization, Development, Education and Research)
PP	Partnership Platform
PPA	Power Purchase Agreement
PPDA	Public Procurement and Disposal Act
PPIAF	Public-Private Infrastructure Advisory Facility
PPP	Public-Private Partnership/Asociación Público-Privada/Partenariat Public-Privé
ppp	Purchasing Power Parity

PPPPP	Public-Private-Professionals-People-Partnership
PPPU	Public Private Partnership Unit
PPS	Proyectos para Prestación de Servicios (Project for Provision of Services)
PPTE	Pays pauvres très endettés (Heavily Indebted Poor Countries)
PROINVERSIÓN	Agencia de Promoción de la Inversión Privada (Private Investment Promotion Agency)
PRS	Poverty Reduction Strategy
PSDI	Private Sector Development Initiative
PSE	Plan Sénégal Émergent (Emerging Senegal Plan)
PSI	Public Services International
Pty	Proprietary Limited Company
PVTG	Particularly Vulnerable Tribal Group
PwC	Pricewaterhouse Coopers
R&D	Research and Development
RABI	Remove Administrative Barriers to Investments
RAMSI	Regional Assistance Mission to the Solomon Islands
RAN	Registro Agrario Nacional (National Agrarian Registry)
RCH	Reproductive and Child Health
RED	Renewable Energy Directive
RGE	Recensement général des entreprises (General Business Census)
RPI	Retribución por Inversiones (Remuneration for Investments)
RPO	Retribución por Operaciones (Remuneration for Operations)
RPS	Retribución por el Servicio (Remuneration for Service)
Rs	Indian Rupee

RSB	Roundtable on Sustainable Biomaterials
RSBY	Rashtriya Swasthya Bima Yojana (National Health Insurance Scheme)
RSE	Responsabilité sociétale de l'entreprise (Corporate Social Responsibility)
SA	Société Anonyme (Public Limited Company)
SADC	Southern Africa Development Community
SAP	Structural Adjustment Programme
SCA	Stratégie de croissance accélérée (Accelerated Growth Strategy)
SCP	Smallholder Commercialisation Programme
SCs	Scheduled Castes
SCT	Secretaría de Telecomunicaciones y Transporte (Ministry of Telecommunications and Transportation)
SDE	Sénégalaise des Eaux (Senegalese Water Board)
SDG	Sustainable Development Goal
SEGOB	Secretaría de Gobernación (Secretariat of Government)
SEI	Stockholm Environment Institute
SEMARNAT	Secretaría de Ambiente y Recursos Naturales (Secretariat of the Environment and Natural Resources)
SENER	Secretaría de Energía (Secretariat of Energy)
SEZ	Zonas Económicas Especiales (Special Economic Zones)
SHCP	Secretaría de Hacienda y Crédito Público (Ministry of Finance and Public Credit)
SHRC CG	State Health Resource Centre, Chhattisgarh
SiLNoRF	Sierra Leone Network on the Right to Food
SINAMES	Sindicato Nacional de Médicos de EsSalud (Doctors' National Union of EsSalud)
SINAMSSOP	Sindicato Nacional Médico del Seguro Social del Perú (National Medical Union of Social Security of Peru)

SINESSS	Sindicato Nacional de Enfermeras del Seguro Social de Salud (National Union of Nurses of the Social Health Insurance)
SISTRANGAS	Sistema de Transporte y Almacenamiento Nacional Integrado de Gas Natural (Integrated National Natural Gas Transport and Storage System)
SLIEPA	Sierra Leone Investment and Export Promotion Authority
SLPP	Sierra Leone People's Party
SNA	State Nodal Agency
SNDES	Stratégie nationale de développement économique et social (National Strategy for Economic and Social Development)
SNEEG	Stratégie nationale pour l'équité et l'égalité de genre (National Gender Equity and Equality Strategy)
SNPIP	Sistema Nacional de Promoción de la Inversión Privada (National System for the Promotion of Private Investment)
SOE	State-Owned Enterprise
SONES	Société nationale des eaux du Sénégal (Senegalese National Water Company)
SRL	*Società a Responsibilità Limitata* (Private Limited Company)
SSA	Sub-Saharan Africa
STs	Scheduled Tribes
SUTACAS	Sindicato Unido de Trabajadores Asistenciales Callao Salud (United Union of Healthcare Workers Callao Salud)
TARSC	Training and Research Support Centre
THL	Tina Hydropower Limited
TPA	Third Party Administrator

TSP	Transitional Stabilisation Programme
TWAIL	Third World Approach to International Law
UEMOA	Union économique et monétaire ouest-africaine (West African Economic and Monetary Union)
UHC	Universal Health Coverage
UIT	Unidad Impositiva Tributaria (Tax Unit)
UMI	Upper-Middle-Income
UN	United Nations
UNDP	United Nations Development Programme
UNICEF	United Nations International Children's Emergency Fund
UNOPs	United Nations Office for Project Services
UPA	United Progressive Alliance
USAID	United States Agency for International Development
USD	United States Dollar
VAT	Impuesto al Valor Agregado (Value Added Tax)
VGGT	Voluntary Guidelines on the Responsible Governance of Tenure of Land, Fisheries and Forest
VVG	Village Vegetable Garden
WB	World Bank
WBG	World Bank Group
WHO	World Health Organization

Introduction

A feminist critique of PPPs rooted in the global South

Corina Rodríguez Enríquez and
Masaya Llavaneras Blanco

This book deals with some recurring development issues. On the one hand, it talks about the need for countries, mainly – but not only – across the global South, to expand the provision of social services to their populations in order to guarantee the most basic human rights such as health, education and decent standards of living. It also emphasises the need for countries to improve and expand their infrastructure, in part to achieve the above goals and in part to improve opportunities for economic development, which would better equip them to guarantee people's rights.

On the other hand, the book deals with the structural challenges that states face in order to finance public policies aimed at expanding and strengthening economic and social infrastructure and the provision of social services. The scope of the book thus lies squarely within debates and discussions on 'financing for development'.

The volume also addresses inequalities which are at the heart of development. It deals with inequalities between countries that turn a community's needs and development aspirations into business opportunities for an elite minority in the global North and, in some cases, in the global South. The corporate capture of development also deepens inequalities within countries by reproducing the marketisation of the public sphere and transforming citizens and denizens into consumers. In particular, the book explores the ways in which some dimensions of inequality, such as those based on gender, are exacerbated by the very solutions that propose to tackle them.

To this end, the book presents a series of case studies on public-private partnerships (PPPs) in countries across Africa, Asia, the Pacific and Latin America. It uses a feminist framework to analyse these cases, seeking to contribute to the debate on the benefits and challenges of the PPP model in addressing development needs.

Role of the private sector in the discourse and making of development

In the current phase of concentration and financialisation of global capital, private corporations have increasingly gained a position of power over other actors. In many regions of the global North and South, they are able to impose their own agendas, driven by the constant search for ever-greater profits. Private actors have increasingly come to subordinate public and collective interests, diminishing the capacity of the state to regulate them, threatening human rights, and challenging labour, environmental and other laws and regulations.

Indeed, powerful private interest groups and their partners have gained excessive influence over policy making, thereby eroding both human rights and democratic processes. This corporate capture of the state has systemic and long-standing influence, and is backed by narratives arguing that (1) states, through processes of 'rent-seeking', are inherently economically inefficient; and (2) policy issues are of such technical complexity that ordinary people cannot understand, and therefore should not (or need not) engage with them. The disingenuous inference often drawn from these assertions is that private corporations operate in public interest; what is good for corporations is claimed to be self-evidently good for the state and those that live in its territory, including citizens.

The current avatar of the corporate capture of the state is the PPP model. The relentless pressure on states, in both the global North and South, to implement fiscal compression policies underpins the emergence of PPPs as the vehicle of choice for development programmes and the circulation of investment finance. PPPs, as defined by the Global Campaign Manifesto, 'are essentially long-term contracts, underwritten by government guarantees, under which the private sector builds (and sometimes runs) major infrastructure projects or services traditionally provided by the State, such as hospitals, schools, roads, railways, water, sanitation and energy'.[1] PPPs have a long history in the global North and a relatively shorter one in the South. More recently, they have been promoted by regional development banks and international financial institutions as a way to secure financing, first for the United Nations' Millennium Development Goals (MDGs) and currently for the Sustainable Development Goals (SDGs).

Governments and funders frame the PPP model as a silver bullet that facilitates the building of large infrastructure projects and the provision of public services; solves the problems of inadequate public financing, technology and skilled human resources; and improves efficiency and effectiveness. These partnerships are also seen as a great model for the private sector. Since most PPP projects are backed by sovereign guarantees from the state, they present institutional investors, including Northern pension funds, with high-return, low-risk investment opportunities. For this reason, a growing critique of PPPs revolves around their role in reinforcing the corporate capture of the state. This critique also challenges their lack of effectiveness, and poor transparency and accountability. It understands PPPs as an extension of the corporate capture of multilateral governance systems in regional, national and local policy spaces. The role of states in multilateralism has been gradually diluted since the inclusion of business interests in processes such as Rio 92 in the early 1990s. The insertion of corporate interests in the UN system, for example, became clearer in the early 2000s and was reinforced in the post-2015 development agenda and the expansion of multistakeholderism. PPPs are a concrete manifestation of how corporate powers have permeated governance processes at the global, national and local levels, undermining long-term and universal approaches (Adams and Martens, 2015; People's Working Group on Multistakeholderism, 2021; Pingeot, 2016).

A brief introduction to PPPs

As defined in the Global Campaign Manifesto, PPPs are 'essentially long-term contracts, underwritten by government guarantees ....' They are arrangements that involve some form of risk sharing between the public and private sectors (Romero, 2015). What differentiates PPPs from public procurement is that, in a PPP, a private company is responsible for raising the upfront costs of investment which are then paid back by the taxpayer, either directly or through the state, over the course of the contract by which the private company builds, maintains and operates (or delivers some agreed variant of) the service. In return, the private company expects a guaranteed profit on its investment.[2] A PPP is different from 'informal or loose collaborations between different actors, including multi-stakeholder partnerships and short-term outsourcing arrangements for the delivery of goods and the provision of services, for instance, in health or education. It also excludes privatisation schemes, by which previously publicly-owned services and facilities are fully transferred (by sale) to the private sector' (Romero, 2015: 11).

The analysis of PPPs in health and education needs a more flexible and broader definition since, in many cases, such projects involve not only corporations but also funders and philanthropic organisations (although the latter are sometimes linked to corporations). Nonetheless, the core issue remains the role of the private sector in the functioning of the state.

The varied definitions of PPPs that countries currently include in their regulatory frameworks share some common characteristics:

1. These are medium- or long-term but finite contracts between the public sector (at the national or local level) and a private sector company or consortium.
2. There is a private finance component, sometimes through a complex network of diverse participants, which must be repaid by the public sector or the users.
3. Private actors often have a relevant role in different stages of the project (design, implementation and financing).
4. The public partner's main tasks include setting the objectives to be achieved in public interest, overseeing the quality of the proposed services and the price policy, and ensuring the achievement of the stated objectives.
5. In the event that the contract is not renewed, the ownership of the asset is transferred to the public sector upon its completion (Romero, 2015; Unión Europea, 2004). Contracts, however, can be extended for long periods, in which case, service provision remains in private hands (Hall et al, 2013).

Risks that are meant to be shared under PPPs include those associated with construction, such as design problems, building cost overruns and project delays; performance risks, such as the availability of an asset, and the continuity and quality of the service provision; and demand risks, such as the ongoing and future need for the service/asset which can impact project value and revenues. There are also macroeconomic risks related to factors which affect financing costs, such as inflation, interest rates and exchange rates. Finally, there are political and regulatory risks that include changes in regulations and political decisions, such as tax policy changes or new environmental rules, which affect the project (Romero, 2015).

Private sector partners may recover their investment in one of two ways:

1. PPPs in which users pay. The private partner is allowed to charge the public for using the facility, generally by levying a fee, which can be supplemented by subsidies paid by the government; or
2. PPPs in which the government pays. The private sector company provides and administers the infrastructure or services for the public

authority and receives regular payments from the public partner based on the level of service provided (Eurodad et al., 2019).

The cases presented in this book illustrate a combination of the different features of PPPs. They point to the commonalities among them, but also the specific complexities that arise in different sectors and jurisdictions.

Role of IFIs in the promotion of PPPs in the SDG era

The current promotion of PPPs has been framed within the implementation of the 2030 Agenda for Sustainable Development and the Addis Ababa Agenda for Action on Financing for Development. Under these frameworks, it was agreed that the mechanisms used to generate the capital required to deliver the 2030 Agenda would need to go beyond international aid[3] to include finances available to governments directly as well as through private sector investments. At the same time, the World Bank (WB) announced a new strategy called Maximizing Finance for Development (MFD), which the bank claimed would 'leverage solutions' and connect and coordinate the public and private sectors: 'The MFD approach insists that nothing should be publicly financed if it can be commercially financed in a sustainable way. If commercial financing is not forthcoming for a project, a country must promote a more investment-friendly environment and/or provide private sector guarantees, risk insurance and other inducements' (Alexander, 2018: 7).

In 2017, this approach was also adopted by the G20 via the Hamburg Principles[4] which apply to various multilateral development banks (MDBs). The approach is based on the belief that traditional methods of financing are not sufficient to achieve the SDGs. Accordingly, it emphasises the importance of 'attracting private solutions' (The Equality Trust, 2019).

As Alexander (2016) has argued, these infrastructure plans involve a new paradigm described in a 2015 report entitled 'From Billions to Trillions', and is built on the following three pillars:

1. The use of public money (i.e. taxes, user fees, guarantees, etc.) to leverage or catalyse private sector investment, particularly long-term institutional investment (i.e. pension and insurance funds, sovereign wealth funds, private equity funds, etc.);
2. A commitment to create 'pipelines' of 'bankable' projects, with an emphasis on megaprojects[5] (initially in four sectors: transportation,

energy, water and sanitation, and information and communications technology (ICT)); and

3. Mechanisms to replicate PPPs rapidly through standardised clauses in PPP contracts, information disclosure requirements, procurement, risk mitigation, etc., as well as by updating the legal and financial regulations of countries (i.e. land acquisition, investor protections, etc.) to attract private investment.

From the private sector perspective, the profitability (or 'bankability') of projects is crucial for these plans to make sense. Depending on the sector and location, PPPs represent an attractive business opportunity for companies, especially those in construction and engineering; service providers, such as those in healthcare; and financial institutions, such as banks and institutional investors. They present an opportunity for those investors who hold trillions of dollars and are looking for attractive returns and seeking to diversify their portfolios in order to reduce the risks to their investments (Romero, 2015).

More recently, the G20 Eminent Persons Group (EPG) proposed that securitising on a large scale across the MDB system would, in effect, create new asset classes and attract a wider range of investors. In this way, the EPG seeks to engage the private financial sector not only for financing investment projects, but also for securitising future revenue streams from existing project pipelines and bundling them into tradeable assets in the financial markets (Alexander, 2018).

The Draft Guidance on PPP Contractual Provisions, formulated by the WB and published in February 2019, open for public consultation to capture inputs and recommendations by all relevant stakeholders, is one way to facilitate the replication of PPP projects.[6] However, civil society organisations (CSOs) have stressed the need to review this Draft Guidance in order to avoid imbalances in the way risks and rewards and rights and responsibilities are allocated between private sector partners and the public sector contracting authority. In April 2019, a large number of CSOs supported a joint submission by Foley Hoag LLP, legal experts from the International Institute for Sustainable Development (IISD) and the Observatory for Sustainable Infrastructure, who made a number of critical observations.[7] In their view, the Draft Guidance, for the most part, is fixated on getting the PPP agreement signed by motivating the private partner at the expense of the host country and its people. The latter are urged to accept the negative consequences that may befall them as a result of these contractual provisions as the cost of attracting infrastructure investment. This approach maximises the profit margin of the private partner while potentially creating large contingent liabilities for the host country.

An updated version of the Draft Guidance seems to have responded to this critique by adding three new chapters that can potentially assist in the negotiation of balanced contractual provisions, and recognise the local law as the appropriate tool to govern PPP contracts. The rest of the document, however, retains earlier biases in favour of the private sector, leaving the Draft Guidance without a broader sustainable development perspective. Among other things, the Guidance emphasises the principle of value for money, according to which a public service should be provided by a private entity that can offer higher quality results at a certain cost or the same quality at a lower cost. The private sector bias notwithstanding, the value for money principle recognises that the efficient use of public resources and the management of fiscal and financial risks are paramount. Yet, the management of the non-financial risks of PPPs arising from environmental, social and governance factors find little or no mention in the WB's document.

PPPs in practice

The organisations that promote PPPs have made all possible efforts to demonstrate their positive impact, but have not been able to avoid acknowledging the pitfalls entirely. A study from the WB's own Independent Evaluation Group (IEG) confirms that there is little evidence of the positive impact of PPPs (IEG-WB, 2012). Critical empirical analysis[8] shows that PPPs are controversial, at least when taking into account cost, efficiency, equity, community access to services, environmental justice, transparency and accountability. More crucially, a feminist analysis of PPPs, which is central to this volume, sheds light on some lesser discussed aspects, namely, their negative implications for gender equality and women's human rights.

The first possible downside of PPPs stems from their financial cost. In many cases, these projects have proven costlier for governments in the long run than traditional public investments. This is because the conditions outlined in PPP contracts usually imply heavier financial costs than those arising from direct government borrowing. The cost is even greater in developing countries where investors expect higher returns to compensate for the presumed higher risks.

The biggest potential financial cost stems from the possibility of contingent liabilities due to poor project design, whereby obligations that had not been calculated before are imposed on the state. This is worsened by few pre-existing transparency mechanisms within states, the lack of government guarantees in tax accounting registries and limited capacity to manage the initial contracts or renegotiations (Alarco Tosoni, 2015;

Pessino, 2016). The fiscal implications of PPPs result either from (1) direct liabilities, which are payment terms set in the contract (e.g. capital contributions to ensure that a project that is economically desirable, but not commercially viable, can proceed); or (2) from contingent liabilities, which are payments required from governments if a particular event occurs (e.g. if the exchange rate of the domestic currency falls or the demand plummets below a specified level).[9]

The second controversial aspect of PPPs has to do with efficiency, understood in terms of its classic definition of achieving a goal in the least costly way. According to the IEG-WB (2012), an in-depth, though not statistically representative, evaluation of twenty-two PPPs indicated that the results were mixed when it comes to improvements in efficiency. The most positive outcomes were observed in countries that have consolidated frameworks to manage PPPs, that is, where the state already has strong institutions and well-developed capacities, thus undermining the argument that the private sector necessarily improves efficiency.

Third, PPPs have the potential to restrict people's access to services and lower their quality, thereby threatening and weakening people's rights. This is usually the case when the financing of PPPs includes user fees, making access to services costlier or unaffordable for large sections of the population (Romero, 2014). Besides, as profit-led ventures, PPPs are rarely developed in sectors that are unprofitable for the private partner, even when there are social inequities and gaps that need to be addressed.

Fourth, poor regulation of PPPs has caused serious social and environmental damage. Poor planning, lack of ex-ante impact assessments, flawed normative frameworks as well as weak state capacity to monitor the process serve to increase the risk of negative impacts on natural resources and people's livelihoods.

Fifth, PPPs are highly controversial when it comes to transparency and accountability. Often, these projects do not go through the normal procedures of procurement, and contract details remain unpublished. There are few or no mechanisms for conducting proper consultations with communities at the project development stage. Thus, PPPs restrict democratic accountability and increase the scope for corruption as negotiations remain mired in commercial confidentiality.

More recently, feminist critiques have begun to raise serious concerns as PPPs expand into areas that are central to women's lives and livelihoods: exploitation of natural resources, energy, infrastructure and social services. Existing analyses have highlighted the impact of corporate power on women and historically marginalised communities, as well as the risks posed by PPPs to gender equality. These risks arise from:

1. Fiscal constraints, as PPPs are expensive and transfer risks to the state and society, thereby limiting the resources available to deliver gender-transformative infrastructure and social provisions;
2. A 'race to the bottom' in terms of working conditions, as PPP projects often fail to meet labour standards or provide social protections;
3. Restricted access to social services, due to rising costs associated with PPPs;
4. The lack of participation in project selection, design and monitoring of PPPs, and the absence of transparency or accountability mechanisms;
5. The loss of access to land, water, and other private and common resources, which are taken over in the name of PPPs with the full support of governments, thus reducing women's ability to provide for their own and their families' subsistence and even resulting in destitution; and
6. The perpetration of greater violence, including the sexual violence, when women resist or demand justice.[10]

Organisation of this book

Existing gender analyses of PPPs have, however, largely drawn on studies that were not specifically meant to evaluate the gender dimension. In other cases, insufficient information has meant that the conclusions are reasonable but hypothetical. The initial findings thus point to the need to deepen the analysis of PPPs from an intersectional feminist perspective embedded in the global South.

This book aims to fill this gap by building on existing analyses through a series of case studies that explore PPP projects in sectors such as health, energy, local market infrastructure, transportation and other large infrastructure.

The case studies undertake a multidimensional analysis of PPPs:

1. They examine the context in which the projects are developed, envisaging how they fit into global financing for development strategies, how they account for geopolitical and economic interests, and how they align (or not) with national discourses on development strategies for the improvement of living conditions.
2. They pay attention to the power relations between the main actors involved in the projects, including multilateral organisations, corporations, national governments, and social and women's organisations.

3. They review existing legal and regulatory frameworks for PPPs.
4. They examine specific projects by locating them in the national path dependency, ongoing processes of privatisation, and governmental and private sector strategies.
5. They analyse the gender and human rights' impact of the implementation and functioning of PPPs.
6. They review the transparency and accountability mechanisms (or the lack thereof) for monitoring PPPs.
7. Finally, they provide an overview of the existing forms of resistance to these processes and to concrete PPP projects.

The book is organised into an introduction chapter, four parts and a concluding chapter. The first part focuses on the narrative, political and economic environment of PPPs in the global South. It includes a chapter on **Kenya** in which Crystal Simeoni and Wangari Kinoti analyse the country's specialised medical equipment leasing scheme to explore broader questions of the neocolonial imposition of private financing models by international finance institutions and other players in the global financial architecture, and the extent to which these impact the social contract between the state and its citizens. The authors examine the central question of priority setting through a series of related inquiries: what informs the decision to spend on one healthcare need *versus* another, what does 'making it' look like, and which stakeholders are involved and consulted in decision-making processes? The chapter argues for greater Pan-African and feminist resistance against prevailing orthodox macroeconomic policies increasingly centred on private finance and calls for an intensification of the connected struggles against neoliberal and neocolonial systemic oppression across the continent.

The second chapter in the first part puts forth the case of **Ethiopia**. Netsanet Gebremichael describes and analyses Ethiopia's engagement with a PPP model of development financing in the context of a political transition from the ideological orientation of a developmental state to market-led liberalisation. The chapter shows how the political understanding of what constitutes the public itself underwent a substantive change as the country transitioned from a public enterprises model, in which the state had a hegemonic role in the economy, to public-private ownership of public assets in the form of PPPs. It focuses on PPPs in Ethiopia's energy sector and examines the shifting political dynamics by looking into the politics of such partnerships, drawing from media narratives, expert opinions and historical analysis.

The second part of the book talks about the normative and institutional labyrinths that accompany PPPs. It includes a case study of **Senegal** in which

Marème Ndoye explores the construction of a toll motorway outside Dakar against the backdrop of the Plan Sénégal Émergent (Emerging Senegal Plan) or PSE which made it possible to implement priority economic reforms and investment projects across the country. As the chapter illustrates, even as Senegal relied on an attractive regulatory and institutional framework to make PPPs a privileged means of financing, the system could not counter the inefficiencies of private actions, respect women's human rights or safeguard the environment. The chapter demonstrates the limits of the PPP model by highlighting the relatively high cost of infrastructure, the loss of human lives and the displacement of people, especially women. It also points to the additional efforts required to reduce the risks and negative impacts associated with PPPs.

The second chapter in this part presents the case of **Peru**, written by Bethsabé Andía Pérez. It analyses the PPP for the Alberto Barton-Callao Hospital and the primary care centre of the healthcare network La Red Asistencial Sabogal de EsSalud (the National Healthcare Insurance). It locates the case within the privatisation processes underway in Peru since the 1990s and looks at the institutional system developed with the advice of international organisations to promote PPPs as the solution to the country's infrastructure deficit. The author argues that this complex project was not adequately negotiated, resulting in vaguely defined services, follow-up mechanisms and modifications. The case thus ably illustrates the lack of transparency, avoidance of social monitoring and the growing risk of corruption associated with PPPs. In particular, it demonstrates how this specific project affected women's access to health and infringed on their labour rights. Finally, it elaborates on trade union and social movements that continue to resist the implementation of PPPs and the privatisation of public services in Peru.

The third and fourth parts of the book focus on the impact of PPPs on women's human rights as well as on the ongoing resistance to them at the regional, state and provincial levels, and at the local and micro levels, respectively.

In the chapter on **Mexico**, Isabel Clavijo Flórez and Julieta Lamberti analyse the Interoceanic Corridor of the Isthmus of Tehuantepec, a megaproject of the Mexican government aimed at the construction of infrastructure and energy projects, including the rehabilitation of the Isthmus Railway, and the construction, maintenance and operation of the Jáltipan Salina Cruz gas pipeline. While the project is supposedly based on a development model that meets social needs, it reproduces relations of domination over the territories in question by prioritising economic growth linked to extractive production. As the chapter illustrates, this type of growth not only generates negative environmental and social impacts, but also accentuates the discrimination, marginalisation and invisibility experienced by women in the region. The author shines a light on the women defenders of the Isthmus who not only resist these projects, but also simultaneously develop their own notion of well-being and propose an agenda that centres their right to health, education, food, water and environmental protection.

The chapter on **India,** authored by Sulakshana Nandi, presents the case of Ayushman Bharat-Pradhan Mantri Jan Arogya Yojana (AB-PMJAY). Considered the largest PPP initiated by any Indian government to date, the AB-PMJAY was meant to expand (in terms of population and annual amount coverage) an earlier publicly funded health insurance (PFHI) scheme known as the National Health Insurance Scheme. The study assesses the impact of PFHI schemes in general, and the PMJAY in particular, on women in India, with special reference to the state of Chhattisgarh. It reveals the serious implications of such schemes for women's health and access to healthcare, especially those belonging to socio-economically vulnerable sections. Women are forced to incur additional (illegal) out-of-pocket payments when utilising PFHI schemes, especially in the for-profit private sector. Even during the Covid-19 pandemic, the PMJAY failed to provide the requisite financial protections. On the contrary, the scheme has meant that funds that could have been used to improve the public sector, which provides more equitable health services and caters to more women, are diverted to the private sector, which is concentrated in urban centres and engages in unethical practices. Whilst women are most affected by these schemes, they have no formal role in their functioning. However, as in the other case studies, people's health movements and women's collectives have put up resistance against the PMJAY.

In the chapter on **Sierra Leone**, Hussainatu J. Abdullah analyses the case of Addax Bioenergy Sierra Leone Limited (ABSL) to argue that PPPs have failed to promote social development, including women's rights and gender equality. Premised on generating profits from the provision of social services, the PPP model is at odds with the long-term change that social activists advocate, the author suggests. The chapter details how IFIs, led by the WB, shaped Sierra Leone's PPP process, providing technical assistance for the development of a PPP framework. Despite the backing of these development finance institutions, ABSL's operations failed woefully, evident in the casualisation of labour; the suspension of social programmes; violation of the principle of free, prior and informed consent (FPIC), and social and environmental standards; inadequate compensation to land leasers and involuntary resettlement of residents. In particular, ABSL reinforced gender-based discrimination at its operational site by refusing to employ women in adequate numbers in its factories and to adopt an employment quota that would guarantee work to women. Other gender-specific losses included the displacement of people, and the loss of access to fertile land, food security and clean water, which collectively increased women's workload.

The chapter on **Ghana**, written by Gertrude Dzifa Torvikey and Sylvia Ohene Marfo, focuses on the construction of lockable shops and open sheds, under a PPP framework, at the Dome Market in the Ga East Municipality in the Greater Accra Region. Their research shows that the projects, which were arbitrarily conceived and implemented by the financiers and the Ga East Municipal Assembly, dispossessed traders and failed to allocate alternate trading spaces. The design and implementation of the PPP exacerbated existing class differences among the traders and reproduced structural inequalities between men and women. The PPP also deepened power struggles in the market leadership structure by weakening the position of the women traders and their collective bargaining platforms. In response, women traders put up strong resistance, employing various strategies such as demonstrations, political threats and complaints. Their protests convinced the state to suspend the PPP and take over the remaining construction work in the market.

The chapter on **Zimbabwe** focuses on the case of the Parirenyatwa Group of Hospitals as author Nyasha Masuka argues that the PPPs being implemented in the country's health sector do not actively mainstream gender equality. These PPPs have not been consistently guided by any regulatory framework. When such a framework did exist, the PPP implementation processes did not necessarily abide by it or take into account human rights and/or gender equality. For example, while Zimbabwe exempts pregnant and lactating women from paying user fees when accessing health services, there is no legislation in place to enforce this policy. There have been instances where women have either been denied such care or detained in maternity wards for failure to pay user fees. Women cannot access care in the private wings of public hospitals or buy medicines from the private pharmacies in public hospitals because of prohibitive costs. In line with the other case studies, the lack of transparency and accountability resulted in acts of resistance from healthcare professionals, legislators and denizens in Zimbabwe, ultimately leading to the cancellation of all PPPs in public hospitals.

Finally, in the chapter on **Fiji**, Lice Cokanasiga analyses the first PPP in the country that involved private financing of two public hospitals, undertaken with guidance from an MDB. The contract was for the redevelopment of one public hospital and the construction of a new wing at another. The author depicts this PPP as a controversial venture, so much so that the Fiji Nursing Association (FNA) challenged the government over it. Australian medical firm Aspen Medical, the private entity involved in the PPP, partnered with the Fiji National Provident Fund (FNPF) in order to bid for the contract. The FNPF, a statutory body that manages a compulsory savings scheme for all Fijian employees and offers members the option of lifetime superannuation or pensions upon retirement, risked the pension funds of members to invest in this PPP. No consultations took place either with FNPF members or the people from the city of Lautoka, the town of Ba as well as the rest of the western division who would access health services at the two public hospitals involved in the PPP. No feasibility studies or impact assessments on health, environment or gender are available to recommend the proposed PPP, and Fiji's economy is too small to absorb the associated risks.

The analysis put forth in these chapters is firmly rooted in a Southern intersectional feminist perspective. Each of the ten case studies present strong evidence of the negative consequences of PPPs for women's livelihoods and human rights as well as their impact on other forms of inequality. In documenting these cases, we hope the book will enrich ongoing debates on the role of public and private sectors in financing development. It is also our endeavour, through this book, to contribute to the improvement of regulatory and transparency frameworks and, most crucially, to strengthen the struggle for democratic development and the feminist resistance against global corporate capture.

Notes

1   See 'Public-Private Partnerships: Global Campaign Manifesto', 13 October 2017. Available at: https://www.eurodad.org/ppps-manifesto.
2   'Public-private partnerships are also referred to as private finance initiatives (PFI) in the UK, and as "blended finance" or "blending" by the UN and multilateral development banks (MDBs) such as the World Bank and the International Monetary Fund (IMF) when they also raise financing for the project and add the financing costs to the contractual payments to governments.' (The Equality Trust, 2019: 7).
3   However, the UN insists that '[o]fficial development assistance is still necessary to help the countries most in need, including the least developed countries, to achieve sustainable development'. Available at: https://www. un.org/sustainabledevelopment/development-agenda.
4   The Principles of MDBs' Strategy for Crowding-in Private Sector Finance for Growth and Sustainable Development (henceforth the Hamburg Principles) provide a common framework for multilateral development banks to increase levels of private investment in support of development. The principles include: (1) recognising the primacy of country ownership; (2) creating

an investment-friendly environment; (3) expanding and standardising credit enhancement; (4) prioritising commercial financing; (5) blending concessional resources and private capital; (6) reviewing incentives for crowding-in private sector resources. (World Bank – IMF, 2017, Annex 1).

5 Since 2010, the G20 has worked with development banks in Africa and Asia, in particular, to strengthen existing infrastructure project preparation facilities (PPFs) to fill the 'pipelines' with megaprojects.

6 Similarly, other frameworks are being discussed and accepted, such as the UNECE Guiding Principles for People First PPPs as well as the UNCITRAL Legislative Guide on PPPs.

7 'Joint Submission to the World Bank on the Draft 2019 Guidance on PPP Contractual Provisions', 30 April 2019. Available at: https://d3n8a8pro7vhmx.cloudfront.net/eurodad/pages/614/attachments/original/1594042848/Joint_submission_World_Bank_PPP_guidance.pdf?1594042848.

8 Eurodad (2018) presents a summary of these analyses from various countries across continents.

9 Contingent liabilities can be explicit, which are the most common public guarantees, such as those related to the risk of inflation, exchange rate instability, etc., or implicit, which depend on the expectations by the public or pressure by interest groups and are triggered by cases of underperformance where the public sector ends up bailing out the project (or even worse, bailing out the private sector company) (Romero, 2015).

10 Some of these findings are analysed in Eurodad, FEMNET, G&DN (2019) and DAWN (2015).

References

Adams, B., and J. Martens (2015), *Fit for Whose Purpose? Private Funding and Corporate Influence in the United Nations*, New York: Global Policy Forum.

Alarco Tosoni, G. (2015), *¿Negocio Público o Privado? Ventajas y desventajas de las APPs en América Latina*, Lima: Latindadd. Available at: http://www.latindadd.org/wp-content/uploads/2018/08/NEGOCIO-PUBLICO-PRIVADO-VENTAJAS-Y-DESVENTAJAS-DE-LAS-APP-EN-AMERICA-LATINA.pdf (accessed 1 February 2021).

Alexander, N. (2016), *Infrastructure Investment and Public Private Partnerships*, Washington DC: Heinrich-Böll-Stiftung.

Alexander, N. (2018), *The Hijacking of Global Financial Governance?*, Washington DC: Heinrich-Böll-Stiftung.

DAWN (2015), 'Public-Private Partnerships and Gender Justice in the Context of the 3rd UN Conference of Financing for Development'. Available at: https://dawnnet.org/wp-content/uploads/2015/03/Ffd3_Public-Private-Partnerships-and-Gender-Justice.pdf (accessed 1 February 2021).

The Equality Trust (2019), 'Finance Development not Dividends. Challenging the Rise of PPPs'. Available at: https://equalitytrust.org.uk/sites/default/files/finance-development-not-dividends-2019-03-v4.pdf (accessed 1 February 2021).

Eurodad (2018), *History Repeated. The Failures of PPPs*, Brussels: Eurodad.

Eurodad, FEMNET, G&DN (2019), *Can Public-Private Partnerships Deliver Gender Equality?*, Brussels: Eurodad.

Hall, D., Lobina, E., and Terhorst, P. (2013), 'Re-municipalisation in the Early Twenty-first Century: Water in France and Energy in Germany, International', *Review of Applied Economics*, 27 (2): 193–214. Available at: 10.1080/02692171.2012.754844 (accessed 1 February 2021).

IEG-WB (2012), *World Bank Group Support to Public-Private Partnerships: Lessons from Experience in Client Countries*, Washington DC: World Bank.

People's Working Group on Multistakeholderism (2021), *The Great Takeover: Mapping of Multistakeholderism in Global Governance*, Amsterdam: The Transnational Institute.

Pessino, C. (2016), 'Tratamiento de pasivos contingentes', Presentación en el Seminario *Espacio Fiscal y Proyectos de Inversión. El Rol de las APP*, Lima: Banco Interamericano de Desarrollo.

Pingeot, L. (2016), 'In Whose Interest? The UN's Strategic Rapprochement with Business in the Sustainable Development Agenda', *Globalizations*, 15 September. Available at: 10.1080/14747731.2015.1085211 (accessed 1 February 2021).

Romero, M. J. (2014), 'Where Is the Public in PPPs? Analysing the World Bank's Support for Public-Private Partnerships', 29 September. Available at: http://www.brettonwoodsproject.org/2014/09/public-ppps-analysing-world-banks-support-public-private-partnerships (accessed 1 February 2021).

Romero, M. J. (2015), 'What Lies Beneath? A Critical Assessment of PPPs and Their Impact on Sustainable Development', 9 July. Available at: https://www.eurodad.org/what_lies_beneath (accessed 1 February 2021).

Unión Europea (2004), 'Libro verde sobre la colaboración público-privada y el derecho comunitario en materia de contratación pública y concesiones', 30 April. Available at: https://op.europa.eu/en/publication-detail/-/publication/94a3f02f-ab6a-47ed-b6b2-7de60830625e/language-es (accessed 1 February 2021).

World Bank – International Monetary Fund (2017), 'Maximizing Finance for Development: Leveraging the Private Sector for Growth and Sustainable Development', 19 September. Available at: https://www.devcommittee.org/sites/dc/files/download/Documentation/DC2017-0009_Maximizing_8-19.pdf (accessed 1 February 2021).

Part One

The narrative, political and economic environment of PPPs

Medical equipment leasing in Kenya: Neocolonial global finance and misplaced health priorities

Crystal Simeoni and Wangari Kinoti

Introduction

Access to quality, universal, gender-responsive and affirming healthcare remains a fundamental challenge for Africa and its citizens. For women, healthcare provisions are critical for reasons beyond their personal health. Failing healthcare systems mean additional hours spent caring for the sick and elderly, leaving less time for other pursuits such as decent paid work, education, political participation or leisure. Women's unpaid labour thus subsidises collapsed public health systems. Globally, 70 per cent of health and social care work is performed by women, and one in five women are employed in the care sector (WHO, 2019). National and local healthcare delivery, therefore, not only drives health outcomes, but also determines time poverty, paid and unpaid labour, livelihoods and access to human rights.

Never have the intersections of multiple crises and inequalities been clearer than during the ongoing Covid-19 pandemic. Now more than ever, it has become critical to dismantle the failed global systems that fuel such crises, and replace them with co-created, sustainable, equitable and just systems.

This chapter contributes to the ongoing feminist analyses of macroeconomic policies in general, and public-private partnerships (PPPs) in particular, with regard to the healthcare sector by examining how they impact women and their communities. We are particularly committed to interrogating and challenging the persistence of neoliberal policies imposed on and embraced by African governments to the detriment of the African people, while remaining cognizant of the skewed, ever-evolving and complex nature of global finance and governance.

Setting the scene: Emergence of health sector PPPs in Kenya

Health as a global right

The right to health is recognised as an inalienable human right in a number of global and regional frameworks. The African Union's Agenda 2063,[1] a shared strategic framework for the socio-economic transformation of the continent, articulates a number of goals relevant to healthcare. The first includes a high standard of living, quality of life and well-being for all, covering income, jobs, education, health and transformed economies. Another goal aims at healthy and well-nourished citizens, and expanding access to quality healthcare services, especially for women and girls. African states have also committed themselves to implementing the United Nations' Sustainable Development Goals (SDGs). Agenda 2063 and the SDG framework converge on several points (see Table 1.1).[2]

Crucially, health as a right is inclusive of other rights. The Committee on Economic, Social and Cultural Rights (CESCR), responsible for monitoring the International Covenant on Economic, Social and Cultural Rights (ICESCR), includes safe food, safe drinking water and sanitation, adequate nutrition, adequate housing, healthy working and environmental

Table 1.1 Comparison of African Union Agenda 2063 and SDG Policy Frameworks.

African Union Agenda 2063	Priority areas	SDGs
A high standard of living, quality of life and well-being for all citizens.	Incomes, jobs and decent work; Poverty, inequality and hunger; Social security and protection, including for persons with disabilities; Modern, affordable and liveable habitats and quality basic services.	1. No poverty; 2. Zero hunger; 8. Decent work and economic growth; 11. Sustainable cities and communities.
Healthy and well-nourished citizens.	Health and nutrition.	3. Good health and well-being.

Source: African Union Commission (2015), 'Agenda 2063: The Africa We Want'. Available at: https://au.int/sites/default/files/documents/36204-doc-agenda2063_popular_version_en.pdf (accessed 18 February 2020).

conditions, health-related education and information, and gender equality as 'underlying determinants of health' (Office of the United Nations High Commissioner for Human Rights, 2008: 3). The CESCR also elaborates on the entitlements contained in the right to health, including equality of opportunity to enjoy 'the highest attainable standard of physical and mental health', and the participation of the population in health-related decision-making at both national and community levels (Office of the United Nations High Commissioner for Human Rights, 2008: 1). Article 12 of the Convention on the Elimination of all forms of Discrimination against Women (CEDAW), which Kenya ratified in 1984, requires states to take measures to ensure that women and men have equal access to healthcare. Kenya has also ratified the Protocol to the African Charter on Human and Peoples' Rights (ACHPR) on the Rights of Women in Africa (commonly known as the Maputo Protocol) which commits member states to make provisions for 'adequate, affordable and accessible health services, including information, education, and communication programmes for women, especially those in rural areas'.[3] Article 19(b) of the Protocol explicitly guarantees women's right to sustainable development and compels states to ensure that women participate at all levels of decision-making, implementation and evaluation of development programmes. The impact of PPPs on Kenya's health sector should be examined in light of the explicit commitments the country has made by ratifying these and other global and regional human rights and development frameworks.

Interactions between governance and development visions

Kenya's 2010 Constitution, which replaced the Independence Constitution of 1963, significantly altered the distribution of power in the country by moving from a centralised to a devolved system of national government, characterised by forty-seven elected counties. Ten years later, the objectives of devolution, such as promoting democratic and accountable exercise of power, allowing communities to manage their own affairs, and providing proximate and easily accessible services, are far from realised.

Yet, Kenya has an impressive framework for health decentralisation and delivery – essential services are the responsibility of county governments while health policy and management of national referral health facilities are left to the national government. In 2017, President Uhuru Kenyatta announced the Big Four Agenda aimed at fulfilling Kenya's third Medium Term Plan (MTP) and progressing towards its ambitious Vision 2030 development blueprint for industrialisation and attainment of middle-income status (Kenya, Ministry of Planning and National Development, 2007). The agenda included food security, affordable housing, manufacturing and affordable healthcare for all through Universal Health Coverage (UHC). Two years prior to this, the government had launched the Managed Equipment Services (MES) programme – the subject of this chapter – describing it as 'a flexible, long-term contractual arrangement that involves outsourcing the provision of specialised, modern medical technology and equipment to private sector service providers' (Parliament of Kenya, The Senate, 2018: 1).

The programme came at a time when Kenya's life expectancy at birth stood at 66.3 years and the poverty rate at 36.1 per cent (UNDP, 2019). In 2018, the Human Development Index (HDI) put Kenya in the medium human development category with a rank of 147 out of 189 countries, a position it shared with Nepal (UNDP, 2019). Kenya is ranked 134th out of 162 countries on the Gender Inequality Index (GII) which reflects gender inequalities in reproductive health, empowerment and economic activity (UNDP, 2019).

History repeating itself: Structural adjustment, health financing and debt

With a current gross national income (GNI) per capita of 1,620 US dollars (USD), Kenya has been classified as a lower-middle-income country since 2015. The Brookings Institution (2019) observed that, as countries move from low- to middle-income status (with GNI per capita between 1,026 USD and 3,995 USD), they experience a big shift in the composition of public and private spending on health. This is because their eligibility criteria for concessional development assistance change, and with it foreign health aid and technical assistance decline. This, coupled with a global shift towards private development finance, creates the perfect entry point for the private sector and PPPs.

From the time Kenya gained independence from Britain in 1963 up to 1993, it introduced six measures in a series of healthcare reforms: (1) harmonisation, (2) decentralisation of medical care, (3) expansion of preventive health services such as family planning, (4) introduction of a national medical insurance scheme, (5) selective integration of traditional medicine, and (6) introduction of user fees (applied at each point of service and paid directly by health seekers to access that service) (Mwabu, 1995).

Kenya removed user fees in public health facilities in 1965, reversing a discriminatory colonial imposition. However, in the next major policy shift that came thirty-four years later – via the 1989–93 Development Plan – the government reiterated a commitment to reintroduce user fees in public health facilities. The government had made this commitment in the earlier 1983–5 plan, but had not implemented it due to public outcry. In December

1989, user fees were reintroduced under the guise of 'cost sharing' after 'considerable pressure from donors' (Mwabu, 1995, 245–55). They were subsequently suspended in 1990, and reintroduced between 1991 and 1992. Kenya's health sector has since relied on out-of-pocket (OOP) payments for most levels of care.

These changes were primarily the result of the structural adjustment programmes (SAPs) introduced by Kenya in the 1980s at the behest of the World Bank (WB) and the International Monetary Fund (IMF) in exchange for financial resources. These neoliberal measures, which included huge cuts in government expenditure, had devastating effects on the delivery of public services. The impact of the SAPs was felt particularly acutely by women. The collapse of publicly delivered social services and infrastructure increased their unpaid care and domestic work burdens; low-skilled public-sector jobs, which mainly employed women, were lost; and user fee payments were borne primarily by them.

> Health facilities were previously on average six to seven kilometres away from most households [...] many of them closed down while those that remained open lack[ed] basic amenities. At Nakuru District Hospital, for example, expectant mothers [were] required to buy gloves, surgical blades, disinfectants and syringes in preparation for childbirth. In addition, they [had] to bribe hospital personnel in order to be attended to. This [was] usually too expensive for many women and they opt[ed] for traditional birth attendants.
>
> (Parsitau, 2008: 195)

Over the years, some exceptions were made to the imposition of user fees. In 2004, they were abolished and replaced by a one-off registration fee in the lowest-level health facilities (dispensaries and health centres). Some groups, including children under five years of age, malaria and tuberculosis patients, and pregnant women giving birth in public facilities, are currently exempt from paying user fees. However, adherence to these progressive policy changes is low due to cash shortages and other challenges (Chuma and Okungu, 2011). Table 1.2 outlines health financing policies between the colonial period up to 2010, and their impact on equity.

For the financial year 2015–16, Kenya's total health expenditure stood at 3.46 billion USD, or 5.2 per cent of the gross domestic product (GDP). Expenditure on health accounted for only 6.7 per cent of the government's total expenditure, which was approximately 36 per cent of the GDP (Ministry of Health, Kenya, 2019). This fell short of the 2001 African Union Abuja Declaration target of spending at least 15 per cent of a country's annual budget on health sector improvement (WHO, 2011).[4]

Table 1.2 A Timeline of Kenya's Health Financing Policies up to 2010.

Years	Policy	Equity impact
Colonial period	User fees in all public facilities.	Discriminatory policy against Kenyans imposed by colonial government.
1963–5	User fees continued for two years after independence.	Negative impact on affordability and utilisation of healthcare services.
1965	User fees removed in all public health facilities. Health services provided for free, funded predominantly through tax revenue.	Potential for equity, provided there are mechanisms to ensure that the poor benefit from the tax-funded system.
1989	User fees introduced at all levels of care.	Negative impact on healthcare demand, especially among the poorest; decreased utilisation, including essential services such as immunisation.
1990	User fees suspended in all public health facilities.	Increase in utilisation patterns, confirming previous reports that user fees are a barrier to access.
1991–2003	Phased reintroduction of user fees in 1991, starting from hospital level. Children under five, special conditions/services such as immunisation and tuberculosis exempted from payment. User fees continue to exist in Kenya at all levels of care.	User fees major barrier to access, resulting in high OOP payments and negative implications for equity.
2004	User fees abolished in dispensaries and health centres (lowest levels of care), and registration fees of 10 and 20 KES introduced, respectively. Children under five, the poor and special conditions/services such as malaria and tuberculosis exempted.	Utilisation initially increased by 70% and later settled at 30% higher than before user fee removal. Adherence to policy low due to cash shortages.
2007	All fees for deliveries/childbirth abolished in public health facilities.	No data on extent to which policy was implemented, no evaluation.

| 2010 | A health sector services fund (HSSF) that compensates facilities for lost revenue associated with user fee removal introduced. Dispensaries and health centres receive funds directly into their bank accounts from the treasury. | Possible positive impacts on adherence to fee removal policy and equity |

Source: Chuma, J., and V. Okungu (2011), 'Viewing the Kenyan Health System through an Equity Lens: Implications for Universal Coverage', *International Journal of Equity in Health*, 10 (22). Available at: https://doi.org/10.1186/1475-9276-10-22 (accessed 18 February 2020).

A study of health spending by twelve counties in 2014–15 found that, on average, households were the biggest spenders at 37.3 per cent, followed by county governments at 36.4 per cent, and donors and corporations at 16.3 and 10.1 per cent, respectively.[5] The bulk of household health spending was in the form of OOP payments defined as 'direct payments made by individuals to healthcare providers at the time of service use' (WHO, n.d.). This put pressure on household budgets which could have otherwise been used for food and other basic necessities, increased household-debt risk and placed severe limits on whether poorer households could access or afford quality healthcare. It is typically the poorest households that carry the heaviest health spending burden (see Figure 1.1). Women's OOP expenditure is 'systematically higher than that of men at least in part because of the high financial burden related to and paying for delivery care and other reproductive services' (Ravindran, 2012). High OOP expenses also mean that more women have unmet health needs than men (Ravindran, 2012). At 27.7 per cent, Kenya's OOP health expenditure is higher than many African countries, including that of Rwanda which stands at 6.4 per cent (Institute of Economic Affairs, 2020a).

Any discussion on Kenya's public health spending must also address its debt crisis. ActionAid International pegs the country's external debt servicing for 2019 at a staggering 36 per cent of its national budget. Between 2017 and 2019, its debt payments tripled.

… as much money goes into paying debt as the total spending on education and health combined. If that figure was reduced to 12 per cent through cancellation, rescheduling, or other methods, Kenya would have had an extra 4.4 billion US dollars available for spending on public services. At the same time, if a 15 per cent share of the potential 4 billion dollar excessive debt servicing was freed up, this could also raise another 13 dollars per person to be spent on health. In a country which is spending around 30 dollars per person this could boost spending.

(ActionAid, 2020: 47–8)

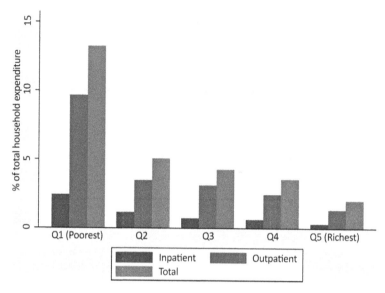

Figure 1.1 Mean OOP payments in Kenya as a share of total household expenditure separated by income quintiles, in 2018.

Source: Salari, P., et al. (2019), 'The Catastrophic and Impoverishing Effects of Out-of-Pocket Healthcare Payments in Kenya, 2018', *BMJ Global Health*, 4 (6): E001809. Available at: https://gh.bmj.com/content/bmjgh/4/6/e001809.full.pdf (accessed 18 February 2020).

PPP architecture, policy and legal frameworks

Kenya's Ministry of Health (MoH) evidently prioritises private sector engagement in the delivery of quality healthcare to citizens. The Cabinet Secretary for Health, speaking on behalf of the President at an African Union summit, said:

> The healthcare market in Africa was worth 35 billion US dollars in 2016 and is set to grow to 65 billion US dollars by 2022. Kenya, and many other African countries are open to private sector investment in healthcare.

In his statement to the UN General Assembly, the President stated his commitment to 'introduce innovative financing models that reorient private capital, create new instruments and modalities that strengthen regulatory framework to de-risk investments'.[6]

These statements from the country's top officials encapsulate Kenya's view of healthcare as a key component of economic growth, and the private sector as the largest contributing factor to achieving these targets. They also replicate the WB's language of de-risking investments.

The MES programme was conceived against this backdrop, under the 2014–18 Kenya Health Sector Strategic and Investment Plan (KHSSP) that lays the foundation for PPP coordination in the sector (Ministry of Health, Kenya, 2014). It includes capacity-building programmes for policymakers and private sector players, and sets out clear objectives about promoting private sector participation in health financing through PPPs and other mechanisms, and increasing private sector investments in health service provision through infrastructure development.

More broadly, Kenya's Public Private Partnerships Act (2013)[7] has established a PPP Committee that approves PPP projects, authorises allocations from the PPP fund, and oversees the monitoring, evaluation and fiscal accountability of projects. Its secretariat and technical arm is the Public Private Partnerships Unit (PPPU), whose mission is 'to introduce and communicate PPP policy, to develop PPP practice and take a key role in the sustainable delivery of PPP projects in Kenya'.[8] PPP contracts are guided by the Public Private Partnerships Regulations,[9] and petitions or complaints are heard by the Public Private Partnerships Petition Committee, which sits as a tribunal within the judiciary.

When it comes to the country's PPP architecture, it is difficult, at least from the outside, to see where the WB ends and the government starts, and where the space for public participation actually lies. Kenya's PPP programme is supported by the Infrastructure Finance and Public Private Partnerships Project of the WB and has close to forty listed bilateral and multilateral development partners.[10] The WB-funded PPPU is strategically placed in government and has direct reporting lines to the PPP Committee and the National Treasury (World Bank Blogs, 2015). The director of the PPPU sees the unit as the 'guardian of the integrity of the PPP process' that ensures 'effective engagement' with other public sector parties and the market. More crucially, its role is envisaged as that of 'an equal third party that is emotionally invested in the safe delivery of an impending birth [PPPs] and its eventual development into childhood, troublesome teenage years, settling into adulthood and the eventual passing on/re-birth' (World Bank Blogs, 2015). Several top advisors to the president have had long and illustrious careers with the WB prior to joining the government.

In providing the background to its establishment, the PPPU cites Kenya's Africa Infrastructure Country Diagnostic (AICD) Report. The AICD was implemented by the WB and funded by the UK's Department for International Development (DfID), the Agence Française de Développement (AFD), Germany's KfW Development Bank, the European Commission and the PPP Advisory Facility of the World Bank Group (WBG). The PPPU reiterates the AICD's estimation that Kenya's infrastructure deficit would require sustained expenditure of approximately 4 billion USD per year over the next decade (presumably between 2008 and 2018). Based on this estimate, Kenya 'made infrastructure development through PPPs a priority as a mechanism that can help it address the major infrastructure gaps in the country'.[11]

The Kenya SDG Partnership Platform, established in 2017 with the objective of achieving SDG 17 on 'partnerships for the goals', is a high-level collaboration between the government and the UN system in Kenya, whose main function is to 'unlock significant private-public collaborations and investments'.[12] Finally, there is the SDG Partnership Platform Multi-Partner Trust Fund in Kenya, which works as the main instrument to mobilise financing through contributions from multilateral and bilateral foundations, and the private sector.[13]

The MES programme: Leasing specialised medical equipment via a PPP

Overview of the programme

The MES programme was launched in 2015 through contracts signed between the health ministry, county governments and private sector providers. The contracts, worth approximately 432 million USD, would run for seven years with the possibility of a three-year extension.

As of 2020, the stated objective of the programme was to guide the supply and installation of specialised medical equipment to two hospitals in each of the forty-seven counties as well as four national referral hospitals, thus covering a total of ninety-eight hospitals (Ministry of Health, Kenya, 2016). It is designed to cover the key healthcare areas of dialysis, emergency, maternal and child health, basic and advanced surgery, critical care and imaging services. The programme provides specialised, modern and state-of-the-art operating theatre equipment, sterilisation equipment, renal dialysis equipment, intensive care unit (ICU) equipment, and X-Ray and other imaging equipment, and also contributes to the upgrading of hospitals (Korir, 2018). The rationale provided for the MES programme was that it would allow the government to spread its healthcare budget over several years by deferring capital outlay.[14] This would make Kenya 'arguably the first country, not only in Africa but possibly globally, to enter into one of the largest sustainable healthcare projects' (Olotch, 2018: 4).

The key actors

Multilateral governance institutions

Kenya's MES programme fits perfectly into WB's Maximizing Finance for Development (MFD)[15] approach, which seeks to ensure the realisation of the SDGs by bridging, through the private sector, the funding gap created by the inability of traditional, aid-heavy financing models to meet goals set by countries.[16] This 'cascade approach' recommends that reforms be attempted first, before subsidies and public investments are considered (WBG, 2018). Accordingly, this approach is underpinned by accelerated financialisation, described as the increasing importance of financial markets, financial motives, financial institutions and financial elites in the operation of the economy and its governing institutions, both at the national and international levels (Epstein, 2006). A major driver of financialisation is the G20, with the G7 controlling the IMF and many multilateral development banks (MDBs). Jason Hickel (2019) describes this phenomenon as a 'global apartheid' in the global governance system. Hickel calculates that, for every vote that the global North has at the WB, sub-Saharan Africa has 0.17th, measured in income per capita. This leads to an obscene imbalance of decision-making powers in favour of the wealthy global North countries.

Hoping to 'reset' its role in the global financial architecture, the G20, through its Eminent Persons Group (EPG), has pushed for a set of proposals to promote financialisation, devolving this agenda to the international financial institutions (IFIs).[17] This 'coup', as some critics call it (Heinrich Böll Stiftung, 2018), gives the G20 immense power over development finance, including pushing for privatisation and PPPs. The MFD approach requires the MDBs to reshape the financial systems of developing countries, forcing them to align with global finance (Inter Press Service, 2019). The G20 also accords the private sector a decision-making role in the MDBs, either as 'adjunct' non-voting members on their board and/or board committees, or as members of advisory panels on investments (Heinrich Böll Stiftung, 2018).

Neither these proposals nor the global finance architecture, more broadly, makes room for civil society, labour unions or the voices of ordinary citizens, despite their sustained multilevel organising against globalised neoliberalism and harmful macroeconomic policies. For years now, these groups have decried the impact of privatisation, 'flexibilisation' of regulations (especially in the labour market) and other global finance policies on the lived realities of people and communities, particularly in the global South.

The financialisation of development lending, under the MFD approach, relies on the increased use of securitisation markets. This carries huge risks, including the extensive promotion of privatisation and PPPs, both of which have a poor track record when it comes to costs borne by taxpayers. This was evident in popular actions across the globe aimed at the re-nationalisation and re-municipalisation of public services and infrastructure (Heinrich Böll Stiftung, 2019).

Private sector entities

As per official, publicly available documentation, Kenya's MES programme has five international leasing companies: Shenzhen Mindray Bio-Medical Limited (China), Esteem Industries (India), Bellco SRL (Italy), Philips Medical Systems (the Netherlands) and General Electric (United States) (see Table 1.3).

There are provisions to subcontract local private companies solely to supply consumables to support core functioning of the equipment. However, media reports show that local companies, such as Megascope Health (K)

Table 1.3 Leasing Companies Involved in Kenya's MES Programme.

Country	Company	Value of contract (billion KES)
China	Shenzhen Mindray Bio-Medical Ltd.	4.5
India	Esteem Industries	8.8
Italy	Bellco SRL	2.3
The Netherlands	Philips Medical Systems	3.6
United States	General Electric East Africa Services	23.8

Source: Parliament of Kenya, The Senate (2018), 'The Managed Equipment Service (MES) Project, Brief and Suggested Questions'. Available at: http://www.parliament.go.ke/sites/default/files/2018-11/ MES%20Brief_Nov%202018%20%285%29_%20With%20Suggested%20Questions%20.pdf (accessed 18 February 2020).

Limited,[18] have been subcontracted by Shenzhen Mindray Bio-Medical Limited to not only supply but also install and commission core equipment for the MES programme (The Star, 2019). Other reports associate Sysmex Europe GMBH with a 2.9-billion Kenyan shillings (KES) contract (The Standard, 2020).

General Electric (GE) East Africa signed a Memorandum of Understanding (MoU) with the Kenyan government to develop projects in key sectors, including healthcare, and plays a leading role in a long list of public and private health-related projects.[19] Lauding the MES as a great example of a PPP in Africa, the company reports that it has deployed 585 units of various types of medical equipment across all ninety-eight hospitals covered under the programme (GE Healthcare, 2019). Elsewhere, a senior GE executive notes that the company's 'mission to transform Kenya's healthcare system is still in its infancy within the wider context of the Kenyan government's transformation plans, but already what it has achieved serves as a powerful illustration of how an established risk sharing procurement model such as a PPP can be adapted to create a new type of partnership to successfully address the healthcare challenges faced by governments and Ministries of Health' (World Bank Blogs, 2017). Another GE executive, in a published opinion on 'what to consider when pursuing a public-private partnership', highlights two key factors – 'a government that fully embraces private sector collaboration' (also described as 'progressive thinking') and 'clear budget allocations and aligned stakeholders' (GE Healthcare, 2019). Conspicuously absent is any reference to public interest.

In a report on upgrading and equipping the ICU at Nyeri County Referral Hospital, Philips claims that it has transformed this local unit into a 'world class facility' with increased capacity to treat patients, reduced operating costs and a staff motivated by improved workflow and regular training.[20]

It is important to note that both Philips and GE are mentioned in an August 2019 media report concerning a probe into suspicious sales of medical equipment to the Brazilian government (Reuters, 2019). The probe concerns activity that dates back to 2010, with allegations of payoffs to secure government contracts. Investigations by Brazilian authorities have reportedly prompted similar investigations by the United States Federal Bureau of Investigations, the Department of Justice and the Securities and Exchange Commission.

There is not much information available online on Shenzhen Mindray, Esteem Industries and Bellco SRL beyond their lists of products and suppliers.

The MES companies are from China, India, Italy, the Netherlands and the United States. Kenya had a bilateral investment treaty (BIT)[21] with Italy, but it was terminated in 2014. Its BIT with China has been signed but is yet to come into force. It has a treaty with the Netherlands that came into force in 1979. In addition, Kenya has entered into negotiations for a free trade agreement with the United States, which would also subject it to the Investor State Dispute Settlement (ISDS) mechanism. This poses an even greater risk for Kenya and other African countries when it comes to engaging with global private finance for development outcomes. Already, investor claims have resulted in the African region losing large amounts of resources which could have otherwise filled the healthcare provision gaps that private sector players are purportedly plugging. Between 2013 and 2019, African states had 109 recorded investment treaty arbitration claims. This six-year period accounted for 11 per cent of all known investor-state disputes globally. These legal claims have cost Africa an estimated 55.5 billion USD since 1993, and this is from only 54.7 per cent of the total number of cases (Barigaba, 2019).

Legal advisors

Iseme, Kamau and Maema (IKM) Advocates[22] provide legal services to the MES programme. IKM staff have written blogs for the WB, one of which was ranked among the bank's top twelve blogs for 2017.[23] IKM's experience lies in dispute resolution, projects and infrastructure, public procurement and PPPs, and tax issues. These areas have been major sites of struggle against neoliberal and neocolonial agendas in the African continent, be they in the fight for tax justice, resistance to mega infrastructure projects or dispute resolution in trade agreements that incur heavy settlement payments.

Gender and human rights impact of the MES

The implementation of the MES programme prompted a huge public outcry in Kenya, forcing the Senate to form an ad-hoc committee to investigate it. The think tank Institute for Economic Affairs (IEA) conducted an in-depth value for money assessment aimed at determining the cost-effectiveness of the scheme and determining whether it would result in better health outcomes (Institute of Economic Affairs, 2020b). These and other processes have raised several concerns which can be placed under two categories: (1) lack of transparency in contracts, costing and allocation; and (2) the broader question of gaps in priority setting.

Lack of transparency in contracts, costing and allocation

The Senate document lists the lack of full disclosure by the health ministry on the MES contracts as one among several concerns about the project. The document states that some facility heads were not fully aware of the exact equipment they expected to benefit from as part of the programme. As such, some MES providers are suspected to have supplied incomplete sets of equipment to facilities (Institute of Economic Affairs, 2020b). Indeed, in writing this paper, we have found it incredibly difficult to obtain official information on the programme.

In the absence of such information, budgets are the easiest way to tell what governments are prioritising, as they will allocate resources to these items. The third biggest allocation in Kenya's healthcare budget in 2016–17 was to the MES, next only to the allocations for the country's two biggest referral hospitals. The budget allocations also demonstrate a de-prioritisation of preventative public healthcare which is critical to ensuring a healthy population (see Table 1.4).

Table 1.4 Kenya's Healthcare Budget Allocation in FY2015–16.

Allotments	Billion KES	Million USD
Kenyatta National Hospital	8.8	81.4
Moi Teaching and Referral Hospital	5.8	53.7
Lease of Medical Equipment [MES]	**4.5**	**41.7**
Free Maternal Healthcare	4.3	39.8
Kenya Medical training college	3.5	32.4
Doctors/Clinical Officers/Nurses Internship	3	27.7
Kenya Medical Research Institute	1.7	15.7
Roll out of Universal Health Coverage	1.4	12.9
Free Primary Healthcare	0.9	8.3
Health Insurance Subsidy	0.7	6.5
National Aids Control Council	0.6	5.5

Source: Ministry of Health (2019), Kenya National Health Accounts FY 2015/2016. Nairobi: Government of Kenya. Available at: http://www.healthpolicyplus.com/ns/pubs/16339-16616_KenyaNHAmainreport.pdf. (accessed 18 February 2020).

Healthcare is the biggest budget item for county governments, accounting for approximately 25 per cent of their total budgets. Approximately 5 per cent of county health budgets went to the MES (Institute of Economic Affairs, 2020b). Yet, county governments were not given access to the contracts that the national government entered into on their behalf with the private sector (Institute of Economic Affairs, 2020b). With all health functions, except health policy, devolved to the county level, the lack of transparency linked to health-related contracts and procurement is a major concern, more so, because Kenya's Constitution upholds the tenets of public participation.

Kenya's Auditor General raised similar queries in his audit of county accounts for the 2015–16 and 2017–18 fiscal. The audit found that 'the lawfulness and accuracy of expenditure of 4.57 billion KES (41.7 million USD) on the MES could not be verified due to lack of supporting documents' such as contracts, legal opinions on contracts from the Attorney General, and procurement and progress reports which were not made available (Institute of Economic Affairs, 2020b: 16).

Payments for the MES programme were deducted at source by the National Treasury from allocations made by the national government to the counties. In mid-2018, counties which previously expected to pay 95 million KES annually (approximately 950,000 USD) found that the deductions increased to 200 million KES (1.9 million USD), more than double the amount agreed upon (Parliament of Kenya, The Senate, 2018). However, no official explanation was given.

The government and private sector argue that leasing of medical equipment is better value for money, given the cost of maintenance and servicing (Parliament of Kenya, The Senate, 2018). However, at one of the Senate hearings, a representative of Shenzhen Mindray admitted that Kenya would have saved massive amounts of resources if it had made direct purchases (The Star, 2019).

Edward Ouko, Kenya's former Auditor General, has called the MES programme 'a betrayal of trust of the Kenyan taxpayers', adding that the 'funds would have been better spent on expanding basic healthcare' and that 'more midwives and more clinics might have saved more lives in a country where 342 women die from pregnancy complications per 100,000 live births' (Reuters, 2020).

Gaps in priority setting

One of the most common complaints raised by county governments before the Senate committee was the fact that they were not involved in discussing health needs and service delivery priorities (The Council of Governors,

2019). The lack of due diligence and consultations between the national and county governments on what equipment was needed in which county meant that some counties received equipment that was not top priority for them, or that they had already received earlier from other government schemes (Parliament of Kenya, The Senate, 2018). Besides, in at least twenty-nine of the forty-seven counties, many of which are located in geographically remote and marginalised areas, the equipment delivered remained unused due to the lack of requisite staff to operate them as well as inadequate water and electricity supply (Parliament of Kenya, The Senate, 2018).

A year after the MES programme was launched, Kenyan doctors went on a 100-day nationwide strike – the longest in the country's history – culminating in the jailing of the doctors' union leadership (The East African, 2017). The strike was to demand fairer remuneration and better working conditions. On an average, there is only one doctor for every 6,355 Kenyans (Africa Check, 2018), but stark inequalities in distribution mean that the capital city of Nairobi, which accounts for only 8 per cent of Kenya's population, has 32 per cent of its doctors (Kenya Health Workforce Report, 2015).

Fraym's geospatial data (see Map 1.1)[24] shows that only 65 per cent of women in Kenya in 2015 had visited a health facility in the past year. The women who did not visit any health facilities during this time were concentrated in marginalised areas that have fewer doctors and health centers.

Amplifying these obvious gaps in prioritisation is the fact that the prevailing philanthro-capitalist and developmental assistance continues to weaken African health sectors. The current approach is predominantly vertical and skewed towards support for single issues or perceived needs, such as specialised infrastructure, taking up large percentages of working budgets. At the same time, public and primary health strategies have fallen off the priority lists of governments and into the hands of bilateral agencies (such as USAID) – a phenomenon Dr Richard Ayah, Director of the Africa Centre of Excellence for Non-communicable Diseases at the University of Ghana, describes as '... our best public health infrastructure [as] foreign owned' (Ayah and Ndii, 2020). Without a robust public and community health infrastructure owned and managed by the state, it becomes next to impossible to implement interventions that will keep the population healthy. The Covid-19 crisis has shown how detrimental the disproportionate focus on vertical health interventions at the expense of horizontal interventions can be. There can be no healthy population without access to safe water and hygiene, adequate nutrition, access to vaccines and so on. It is people and community interventions, not financialisation, that must be at the heart of policy making.

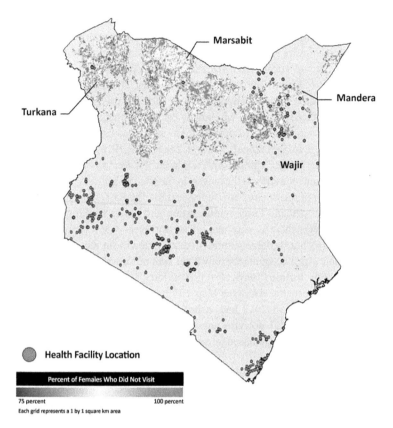

Map 1.1 Geospatial spread of women in Kenya's marginalised areas who did not visit health facilities between 2014 and 2015.

Source: Women's Access to Health Facilities in Kenya (2019). Available at: https://fraym.io/womens-access-to-health-facilities-in-kenya (accessed 18 February 2020).

Gaps in women's access to health services

The absence of a robust health infrastructure disproportionately impacts women. Because of their lower incomes, women predominantly rely on public health facilities for maternity care and primary healthcare for their children, especially in countries like Kenya. An excessive focus on funding 'non-essential' specialised equipment directs resources away from accessible and affordable primary healthcare, thus limiting the health service provisions that women can turn to. Because services under PPPs are usually offered for a fee, women are less likely to be able to afford specialised equipment even if they were up and running with water, electricity and doctors.

Besides, the public sector has historically played a crucial role in providing work opportunities for women. In fact, women constitute a greater proportion of the workforce in health and education. Any diversion of resources away from these sectors may affect the allocation available for the wage bill, thus reducing women's access to work. These findings in the Kenyan context are similar to those highlighted in a briefing by Eurodad, the Gender and Development Network (G&DN) and the African Women's Development and Communications Network (FEMNET) (2019).

Mapping the resistance

Since the signing of the MES in 2015, there have been numerous and continuous calls for transparency and accountability, as well as widespread criticism of the underlying logic and processes of the programme. The resistance has principally been led by county governors whose budget allocations were deducted at source to finance the programme and pay for equipment that most counties are not even using. The pushback is linked not only to how the deductions were made, but also to how the sum deducted has been increasing without consultations on the original contract. The Senate probe and the hearing by the Senate Health Committee which started in the last quarter of 2019 was an outcome of the county governors' objections coupled with public pressure.

Thus far, there has been no known responses from the Kenya women's rights movement, possibly due to its limited coordinated engagement with macro-level economic policy. However, macroeconomic issues are feminist issues and must be central to the Pan-African feminist struggle.

Our aim in writing this chapter was not so much to zero in on the details of the MES programme as to shine a spotlight on the wider question of what lies at the heart of development decisions and who is part of that process. Publicly funded and universally delivered services were, and continue to be, in a state of collapse. An unequal, undemocratic and extractive global economic governance system lies at the heart of this collapse, but these issues often seem too abstract to be linked to a local hospital that is in a state of disrepair.

In conversations we have had with young women born in the mid- to late 1990s, the reality of little to no living memory or knowledge of public services has been striking. This comes as no surprise. In fact, it is safe to assume that a vast majority of Kenyans, three quarters of whom are under thirty-five years of age, see few alternatives to private finance in solving public problems.

Conclusion

The imposition of user fees for health services was a colonial project. Now, the neocolonial project continues to keep poorer countries in a private finance chokehold with poor people bearing the brunt. Healthcare becomes a 'market', citizens become 'customers' or 'clients', and their rights are trampled on as governments clamber for private investments to achieve the ultimate goal of economic growth.

As feminist activists invested in the co-creation of alternative futures for Africa, our primary concern is to understand the impact that a faulty, misplaced and artificially imposed development policy has on women and their communities. PPPs are demonstrably costlier than publicly funded services, lack transparency and are driven by bottom lines and profit margins, with virtually all risk relegated to the public purse. Yet, governments continue to pursue them. The impact on the public is not just financial. There are also major flaws in the government's priority setting on public health – who benefits from it and where the biggest investments are made. Alongside these are concerns about the lack of public participation and agency in policy making, and the absence of women's voices despite the direct negative impact of these policies on their everyday lives.

A government's ability to provide quality universal healthcare relies on a combination of factors. There needs to be an understanding of local community priorities, meaningful investment in co-created community health strategies and reliance on local expertise.

Although the labelling and iterations of macroeconomic interventions change through the years, the basic neoliberal and neocolonial spirit and intentions remain the same. There is the perception that the feminist struggle to reject these notions is new, when in fact, this struggle goes back decades. In reimagining feminist futures, we need to revisit and build upon this existing knowledge, apply it to our current contexts and be more intentional in connecting seemingly disparate struggles.

Notes

1   'Our Aspirations for the Africa We Want'. Available at: https://au.int/en/agenda2063/aspirations.
2   Ibid.
3   Protocol to the African Charter on Human and People's Rights on the Rights of Women in Africa (Maputo Protocol Text). African Union, 2003, available at: https://www.un.org/en/africa/osaa/pdf/au/protocol_rights_women_africa_2003.pdf.

Also see: African Charter on Human and Peoples' Rights (Article 16.2), available at: https://www.achpr.org/legalinstruments/detail?id=49#:~:text=The%20African%20Charter%20on%20Human,freedoms%20in%20the%20African%20continent.

4   Abuja Declaration on HIV/AIDS, Tuberculosis and Other Related Infectious Diseases, Abuja, Nigeria, 24–27 April 2001. Available at: https://au.int/sites/default/files/pages/32904-file-2001_abuja_declaration.pdf.

5   'Health Policy Project Kenya County Health Accounts: Summary of Findings from 12 Pilot Counties', April 2016. Available at: https://www.healthpolicyproject.com/pubs/7885_FINALSynthesisreportoftheCHA.pdf.

6   President Uhuru Kenyatta's statement to the United Nations General Assembly in 2019. Available at: https://www.president.go.ke/2019/09/25/statement-by-his-excellency-hon-uhuru-kenyatta-c-g-h-president-of-the-republic-of-kenya-and-commander-in-chief-of-the-defence-forces-during-the-general-debate-of-the-74th-session-of-the-united-nat.

7   Republic of Kenya, Public Private Partnerships Act 2013. Available at: http://pppu.redhousestage.com//wp-content/uploads/2017/11/ppp-act-2013-2.pdf.

8   Public Private Partnerships Unit, 'About PPPU'. Available at: http://www.pppunit.go.ke/about.

9   Republic of Kenya (2014), 'Public Private Partnerships Regulations 2014'. Available at: http://pppu.redhousestage.com//wp-content/uploads/2017/11/PPP-Regulations-2014.pdf.

10 The National Treasury, 'Public Private Partnership / Development Partners'. Available at: https://www.treasury.go.ke/public-private-partnership/development-partners.html.

11 Republic of Kenya (2014).

12 Kenya SDG Partnership Platform. Available at: https://kenya.un.org/en/15284-sdg-partnership-platform.

13 Ibid.

14 https://blogs.worldbank.org/ppps/transforming-kenya-s-healthcare-system-ppp-success-story.

15 World Bank (n.d.), 'Maximizing Finance for Development'. Available at: https://www.worldbank.org/en/about/partners/maximizing-finance-for-development.

16 Ibid.

17 G20 EPG (2018), 'Making the Global System Work for All: Report of the G20 Eminent Persons Group on Global Financial Governance', October. Available at: https://www.globalfinancialgovernance.org/assets/pdf/G20EPG-Full%20Report.pdf.

18 Megascope Healthcare home page. Available at: https://megascopekenya.com/.

19 General Electric, 'Kenya'. Available at: https://www.ge.com/africa/content/kenya.

20 https://www.philips.com/c-dam/corporate/newscenter/global/case-studies/
     nyeri-county-referralhospital/nyeri-county-referral-hospital-customer-
     partnership.pdf.
21 The United Nations Conference on Trade and Development defines
     a bilateral investment treaty as an agreement between two countries
     for promotion and protection of investments made by investors from
     these countries in each other's territory, subject to the ISDS mechanism
     (UNCTAD, 2007).
22 IKM website. Available at: http://www.ikm.co.ke.
23 World Bank (2017), 'Year In Review: 12 Top Blogs of 2017'. Available at:
     https://blogs.worldbank.org/ppps/year-review-12-top-blogs-2017.
24 Women's Access to Health Facilities in Kenya (2019). Available at:
     https://fraym.io/womens-access-to-health-facilities-in-kenya.

References

ActionAid (2020), 'Who Cares for the Future: Finance Gender Responsive
     Public Services! Full Report', 13 April. Available at: https://actionaid.
     org/sites/default/files/publications/final%20who%20cares%20report.pdf
     (accessed 18 February 2020).
Africa Check (2018), 'As Help from Cuba Arrives, Is There Only One Kenyan
     Doctor for Every 16,000 People?', 19 June. Available at: https://africacheck.
     org/reports/as-help-from-cuba-arrives-is-there-only-one-kenyan-doctor-
     for-every-16000-people (accessed 18 February 2020).
Ayah, R., and D. Ndii (2020), 'An Insider's Take on Kenya's Public
     Health System', 28 April. Available at: https://www.youtube.com/
     watch?v=BZK3IU0kyqs (accessed 18 February 2020).
Barigaba, J. (2019), 'Civil Society Seeks Reforms to Stem Trade Suits Losses', *The
     East African*, 7 December. Available at: https://www.theeastafrican.co.ke/
     news/ea/Civil-society-seeks-reforms-to-stem-trade-suits-losses/4552908-
     5376918-p4x360z/index.html (accessed 18 February 2020).
Brookings Institute (2019), 'What Happens to Health Financing during the
     Middle-Income Transition?', 16 December. Available at: https://www.
     brookings.edu/blog/future-development/2019/12/16/what-happens-
     to-health-financing-during-the-middle-income-transition (accessed
     18 February 2020).
Chuma, J., and V. Okungu (2011), 'Viewing the Kenyan Health System through
     an Equity Lens: Implications for Universal Coverage', *International Journal of
     Equity in Health*, 10 (22). Available at: https://doi.org/10.1186/1475-9276-10-22
     (accessed 18 February 2020).
The Council of Governors (2019), 'Senate Proceedings on the Medical Equipment'.
     Available at: https://cog.go.ke/component/k2/item/184-senate-proceedings-on-
     the-medical-equipment (accessed 18 February 2020).

The East African (2017), 'Kenyan Doctors, Govt Agree to End Strike', 14 March. Available at: https://www.theeastafrican.co.ke/news/Kenyan-doctors-end-strike/2558-3849516-view-printVersion-rf46rez/index.html (accessed 18 February 2020).

Epstein, G. A. (2006), *Financialization and the World Economy*, Cheltenham: Edward Elgar Publishing.

G20 EPG (2018), 'Making the Global System Work for All: Report of the G20 Eminent Persons Group on Global Financial Governance', October. Available at: https://www.globalfinancialgovernance.org/assets/pdf/G20EPG-Full%20 Report.pdf (accessed 18 February 2020).

GE Healthcare (2019), 'Opinion: What to Consider When Pursuing a Public-Private Partnership', by F. Fezoua, 11 October. Available at: https://www. gehealthcare.com/article/opinion-what-to-consider-when-pursuing-a-public-private-partnership (accessed 18 February 2020).

Health Policy Project (2016), 'Kenya County Health Accounts: Summary of Findings from 12 Pilot Counties', April. Available at: https://www. healthpolicyproject.com/pubs/7885_FINALSynthesisreportoftheCHA.pdf (accessed 18 February 2020).

Heinrich Böll Stiftung (2018), 'The Hijacking of Global Financial Governance', by N. Alexander. Available at: https://us.boell.org/en/2018/04/23/hijacking-global-financial-governance (accessed 18 February 2020).

Heinrich Böll Stiftung (2019), 'From the Washington Consensus to the Wall Street Consensus', by R. Rowden. Available at: https://us.boell.org/ en/2019/10/11/washington-consensus-wall-street-consensus (accessed 18 February 2020).

Hickel, J. (2019), 'Apartheid in the Global Governance System', 5 January. Available at: https://www.globalpolicyjournal.com/blog/05/01/2021/ apartheid-global-governance-system (accessed 18 February 2020).

Institute of Economic Affairs (2020a), 'Kenya's Comparison of Out of Pocket Expenditure on Health with Its Peers'. Available at: https://www.ieakenya. or.ke/number_of_the_week/kenyaa-s-comparison-of-out-of-pocket-expenditure-on-health-with-its-peers (accessed 18 February 2020).

Institute of Economic Affairs (2020b), 'Leasing of Medical Equipment Project in Kenya: Value for Money Assessment', by J. Mutua and N. Wamalwa. Available at: https://www.ieakenya.or.ke/publications/research-papers/ leasing-of-medical-equipment-project-in-kenya-value-for-money-assessment (accessed 18 February 2020).

Inter Press Service (2019), 'World Bank Financialization Strategy Serves Big Finance', by J. K. Sundaram and A. Chowdhury, 9 April. Available at: http://www.ipsnews.net/2019/04/world-bank-financialization-strategy-serves-big-finance (accessed 18 February 2020).

International Finance Corporation (2020), 'A Letter from Jim Yong Kim, World Bank Group President'. Available at: https://www.ifc.org/wps/ wcm/connect/CORP_EXT_Content/IFC_External_Corporate_Site/

Annual+Report+2017/2017-Online-Report/Leadership-Perspectives (accessed 18 February 2020).

Kenya Health Workforce Report (2015), 'The Status of Healthcare Professionals in Kenya, 2015'. Available at: https://taskforce.org/wp-content/uploads/2019/09/KHWF_2017Report_Fullreport_042317-MR-comments.pdf (accessed 18 February 2020).

Korir, M. (2018), 'Managed Equipment Services: The Kenyan Story: Good Intentions Aren't All That's Needed for a Successful Medical Program', *The Pathologist*, 16 March. Available at: https://thepathologist.com/outside-the-lab/managed-equipment-services-the-kenyan-story (accessed 18 February 2020).

Ministry of Health, Kenya (2014), 'Transforming Health: Accelerating Attainment of Universal Health Coverage'. Available at: https://www.health.go.ke/wp-content/uploads/2016/03/KHSSP-BOOK.pdf (accessed 18 February 2020).

Ministry of Health, Kenya (2016), 'Demystifying the Managed Equipment Service Scheme (MES) Project in Kenya', Brochure. Available at: http://publications.universalhealth2030.org/uploads/MES-BROCHURE.pdf (accessed 18 February 2020).

Ministry of Health, Kenya (2016), 'Transforming Health: Accelerating Attainment of Universal Health Coverage'. Available at: https://www.health.go.ke/wp-content/uploads/2016/03/KHSSP-BOOK.pdf (accessed 18 February 2020).

Ministry of Health, Kenya (2019), Kenya National Health Accounts FY 2015/2016, Nairobi: Government of Kenya. Available at: http://www.healthpolicyplus.com/ns/pubs/16339-16616_KenyaNHAmainreport.pdf (accessed 18 February 2020).

Ministry of Planning and National Development, Kenya (2007), 'The Vision; Seeing the Vision Through'. Available at: http://vision2030.go.ke (accessed 18 February 2020).

Mwabu, G. (1995), 'Healthcare Reform in Kenya: A Review of the Process', *Health Policy*, 32 (1): 245–55.

Ngumi, N. (2018), 'Health for All: A Reflection on the Current State of Healthcare in Kenya', *The Elephant*, 16 August. Available at: https://www.theelephant.info/features/2018/08/16/health-for-all-a-reflection-on-the-current-state-of-healthcare-in-kenya (accessed 18 February 2020).

Office of the United Nations High Commissioner for Human Rights (2008), 'The Right to Health', Fact Sheet no. 31. Available at: https://www.ohchr.org/Documents/Publications/Factsheet31.pdf (accessed 18 February 2020).

Olotch, C. (2018), 'Managed Equipment Services (MES) – Healthcare for Development: The Kenya MES Experience'. Available at: https://docplayer.net/57372467-Managed-equipment-services-mes-healthcare-for-sustainable-development-the-kenya-mes-experience-cynthia-olotch.html (accessed 18 February 2020).

Parliament of Kenya, The Senate (2018), 'The Managed Equipment Service (MES) Project, Brief and Suggested Questions'. Available at: http://www.

parliament.go.ke/sites/default/files/2018-11/MES%20Brief_Nov%20
2018%20%285%29_%20With%20Suggested%20Questions%20.pdf (accessed
18 February 2020).

Parsitau, D. S. (2008), 'The Impact of Structural Adjustment Programmes
(SAPs) on Women's Health in Kenya', in: M. Sama and V. Nguyen (eds),
Governing Health Systems in Africa, Dakar: CODESRIA.

Ravindran, T. K. S. (2012), 'Universal Access: Making Health Systems Work for
Women', *BMC Public Health*, 12 (S4). Available at: https://bmcpublichealth.
biomedcentral.com/articles/10.1186/1471-2458-12-S1-S4 (accessed
18 February 2020).

Reuters (2019), 'Exclusive: Philips, under Investigation in U.S. and Brazil, Fired
Whistleblower Who Warned of Graft', by B. Brooks, 21 August. Available at:
https://www.reuters.com/article/us-brazil-corruption-healthcare-exclusiv/
exclusive-philips-under-investigation-in-u-s-and-brazil-fired-whistleblower-
who-warned-of-graft-idUSKCN1VB0BJ (accessed 18 February 2020).

Reuters (2020), 'Leaders Cheered as Kenya Binged on Medical Equipment. Did
Patients Get Help?', by M. Fick, 14 February. Available at: https://af.reuters.
com/article/idAFKBN2080RV-OZATP (accessed 18 February 2020).

Salari, P., et al. (2019), 'The Catastrophic and Impoverishing Effects of Out-
of-Pocket Healthcare Payments in Kenya, 2018', *BMJ Global Health*, 4 (6):
E001809. Available at: https://gh.bmj.com/content/bmjgh/4/6/e001809.full.
pdf (accessed 18 February 2020).

The Standard (2020), 'Report: Billions Wasted in State Medical Project',
by F. Sunday and P. Thoronjo, 14 February. Available at: https://www.
standardmedia.co.ke/article/2001360362/report-billions-wasted-in-state-
medical-project (accessed 18 February 2020).

The Star (2019), 'Chinese Firm in Medical Gear Probe Says Leasing Expensive',
by J. Otieno, 7 November. Available at: https://www.the-star.co.ke/
news/2019-11-07-chinese-firm-in-medical-gear-probe-says-leasing-
expensive (accessed 18 February 2020).

UNCTAD (2007), 'Bilateral Investment Treaties 1995–2006: Trends in
Investment Rulemaking'. Available at: https://unctad.org/en/Docs/
iteiia20065_en.pdf (accessed 18 February 2020).

UNDP (2019), 'Human Development Report 2019 – beyond Income, beyond
Averages, beyond Today: Inequalities in Human Development in the
21st Century'. Available at: http://hdr.undp.org/sites/default/files/hdr2019.pdf
(accessed 18 February 2020).

WBG (2018), 'Optimizing Finance for Development', by T. Cordella, Policy
Research Working Paper 8320, January. Available at: http://documents1.
worldbank.org/curated/en/859191517234026362/pdf/WPS8320.pdf
(accessed 18 February 2020).

WHO (n.d.), 'Out-of-Pocket Payments, User Fees and Catastrophic
Expenditure'. Available at: https://www.who.int/health_financing/topics/
financial-protection/out-of-pocket-payments/en (accessed 18 February
2020).

WHO (2019), 'Delivered by Women, Led by Men. A Gender and Equity Analysis of the Global Health and Social Workforce'. Available at: https://cdn.who.int/media/docs/default-source/health-workforce/delivered-by-women-led-by-men.pdf?sfvrsn=94be9959_2 (accessed 18 February 2020).

WHO (2011), 'The Abuja Declaration: Ten Years on'. Available at: https://www.who.int/healthsystems/publications/abuja_report_aug_2011.pdf?ua=1 (accessed 18 February 2020).

World Bank (n.d.), 'Maximizing Finance for Development'. Available at: https://www.worldbank.org/en/about/partners/maximizing-finance-for-development (accessed 18 February 2020).

World Bank Blogs (2015), 'Kenya's 3 Keys to Success: How to Create an Effective Public-Private Partnership Unit', by S.K. Kamau, 17 December. Available at: https://blogs.worldbank.org/ppps/3-keys-success-public-private-partnership-ppp-unit-kenya-and-5-lessons-share (accessed 18 February 2020).

World Bank Blogs (2017), 'Transforming Kenya's Healthcare System: A PPP Success Story', by M. Patolwala, 24 May. Available at: https://blogs.worldbank.org/ppps/transforming-kenya-s-healthcare-system-ppp-success-story (accessed 18 February 2020).

PPPs meet the developmental state: The case of Ethiopia

Netsanet Gebremichael

Introduction

Between 2015 and 2018, massive anti-government protests erupted across Ethiopia against the then ruling party, the Ethiopian People's Revolutionary Democratic Front (EPRDF), in response to human rights violations and economic strife linked to corruption and large-scale dispossession of land, which was being transferred from farmers to investors. The protests, which challenged the exclusion of Ethiopian citizens from the benefits of economic growth achieved by the developmental state (DS), were spearheaded by young people in the Oromia and Amhara regions. The state's primary response was a massive crackdown, including imprisonment and killing of protesters during the frequent government-mandated states of emergency. The other response was a rhetorical promise of radical reform and an anti-corruption culture within the state. The popular protests continued despite these promises and eventually led to a leadership change in the EPRDF in April 2018. Former Prime Minister Hailemariam Dessallegn[1] resigned, and Abiy Ahmed Ali took charge.

Abiy Ahmed's speech, on the occasion of the transition, promised hope and change, and a plan for reform (The Guardian, 2018). In his speech, the new prime minister recognised the crucial role played by his mother and wife in his public and private achievements (Ali, 2018). Using their support as an example, Abiy Ahmed lauded all Ethiopian women as hard-working and resilient, responsible for carrying the nation on their backs, and deserving of acknowledgement, respect and celebration. This narrative framed women as moral-economic subjects of the nation, presenting them as 'good citizens', and obedient and apolitical subjects who stood in direct contrast to the protesters. It dehistoricised and depoliticised the political subjectivities of women.

The progressive aspects of Abiy Ahmed's speech, which recognised the invisible contributions of women to national politics and his own individual ascension, needs to be contextualised by examining the gendered aspects of both the nation's and his own individual success story. This reactionary stance that depicts women as passive 'good citizens' needs to be challenged through a feminist empirical and theoretical intervention. This chapter offers precisely such an intervention by illustrating the omission of women from the promotion and introduction of public-private partnerships (PPPs) in Ethiopia.

It examines whether and how women and popular demands are included in the macroeconomic policies forged in Ethiopia's DS politics by analysing the introduction of PPPs in the infrastructure sector. The chapter casts a critical lens at how PPPs are unfolding in the country's contemporary political landscape and explores how the Ethiopian media, between 2018 and 2020, shaped the narrative of PPPs as an alternative finance model for development infrastructure. The chapter is divided into four sections. The first section historicises the shift towards PPPs by situating it against a backdrop of the DS model in Ethiopia and the African continent. Section 2 examines the ways in which the narrative on PPPs is constructed in Ethiopia's print and broadcast media. This media analysis helps illuminate who is understood as the 'public' in the discussion on PPPs, and takes this conversation forward through three related enquiries: how are PPPs presented in Ethiopia, who narrates what they are, and to what end? To answer these questions, the chapter analyses twenty-one primary sources, including newspaper articles, online material, and public debates and dialogues, as well as eight secondary sources. Section 3 presents the two predominant ways in which scholars and macroeconomic policy advisers debate PPPs in Ethiopia. Section 4 focuses on the PPPs implemented in the country's energy sector, and provides an overview of how these are framed in the media. The chapter concludes by foregrounding the possibilities for rethinking PPPs by drawing on the tensions between the old and the new mode of financing infrastructure.

All sources consulted and analysed in the chapter lie within a two-year timeframe between April 2018 and May 2020. Each category of source material is analysed separately, substantively and thoroughly in order to illuminate the specific input made by each.

Prior to 2018, contemporary media and official narratives in Ethiopia promoted a dominant critique of the DS, depicting this model as the culprit that saddled the country with a huge debt and a reduced repayment capacity. The solution being proposed now is to liberalise the economy and enable both foreign and local private sectors to play a leading role in the economic life of the country. In media coverage, PPPs are mentioned in the larger context of economic liberalisation which includes the privatisation of state-owned enterprises (SOEs).

The transition from DS to PPPs

The concept of development has served as a permanent ideology and a source of legitimacy of the modern Ethiopian state. The state hitherto has been framed as a hegemonic actor monopolising development management and excluding the public. Despite mass organisations for women, peasants, urban dwellers and the youth being established in different regimes, the state has remained dominant when it comes to the management of development (Rahmato, 2008). State developmentalism, therefore, is the norm, rather than the exception, in Ethiopia. The form of DS in place since the 1990s is a relatively recent addition that displaced the previous socialist developmentalism.

In Ethiopia, state developmentalism implies subsidising and protecting the public, mainly the poor, against the heavy 'invisible hands' of the global market. Even though any control by international financial institutions (IFIs) has been contested, there has been little resistance against what is perceived as the state's historical mission to foster social transformation in Ethiopia. The DS of Ethiopia is a new articulation of this enduring trend of state-society relations.

There is ample literature on the DS, and contestations on the subject between scholars and policy practitioners. Conceptually, there is an agreement on what differentiates the DS from other state forms (mainly the liberal and neoliberal-oriented states). Among other factors, the *ideology-structure nexus* places the DS apart from other types of state. Ideology informs the state's mission to enforce development, defined as accumulation and industrialisation. Structure denotes the capacity of the state to keep development independent of social forces (Mkandawire, 2001). The DS in Ethiopia, as in many other countries, was born out of a clear understanding of the 'role of an activist state in the process of catching up, a role further necessitated by the strong determination and vision to develop Ethiopia' (Oqubay, 2015: 4).

Theories on the DS describe it as a leviathan which stands above society. According to Jostein Hauge and Ha-Joon Chang (2019), there are five elements that define the DS. First, most of the literature points to Japan and the Asian Tigers as the origin of the model. However, as Thandika Mkadawire (2001) argues, other regions such as Africa had DS projects before the era of structural adjustments. Second, the DS is not a monopoly over development management by the state. Rather, it is a project that involves 'private ownership with heavy state intervention' (Berhe, 2020), meaning that the partnership between the private sector and the state is not based on symmetrical power relations. According to Mulugeta Gebrehiwot Berhe, the Ethiopian state is 'at the centre of rent collecting and [is] using it to guide the private sector while being independent from it' (Berhe, 2020). This means that 'the state should control the commanding heights of the economy (banks, utilities and some key production sectors including the public ownership of land) and be able to lead the private sector' (Berhe, 2020). Third, the ideological apparatus of the DS and its emphasis on industrialisation make it different from other forms of the state. Fourth, the DS uses development gains as a source of legitimacy. Fifth, it operates using professional bureaucracy (Hauge and Chang, 2019).

While it is debatable whether the DS originated in Japan and East Asia, most analyses about the model are drawn from these regions. However, using these analyses as universal blueprints amounts to overlooking or flattening historical experiences elsewhere, including in Africa (Ashine, 2018). At the same time, there are very few studies which explore a DS evolving in a specific historical place and context. In understanding the Ethiopian DS, one must take into account 'Ethiopia's rich history of independence and civilisation and its mimetic interest in finding East Asian role models […] as sources of inspiration' (Oqubay, 2015: 75). An insightful example of the peculiar historical conditions that led to the evolution of Ethiopia's DS is offered by Hauge and Chang (2019), who show how the country took inspiration from the East Asian model but also departed from it in many aspects. The authors explain the structural deviation of the Ethiopian model as follows:

> Another deviation from the East Asian DS model is the lack of power and independence of the bureaucracy and the small size of the domestic private sectors in manufacturing industry. Most 'industrial policy power' in Ethiopia lies in the hands of the ruling party, the EPRDF. The dominant actors in the Ethiopian economy are SOEs [state-owned enterprises, exemplified by metals and engineering corporations (METEC)] and foreign firms. There is therefore not much of a basis for the existence of an 'alliance' or a 'symbiotic' relationship between the bureaucracy and the 'productive' domestic private sector, which characterized the East Asian DS model.
>
> (2019: 835)

SOEs became the exceptional feature of the Ethiopian DS during the eras of socialist developmentalism and modernising emperors. Through them, the state took a hegemonic and active role in the management of development. However, that is not the case in the current iteration of the Ethiopian DS.

Critical works on the politics of transition in Ethiopia have exposed the irony of 'anti-privatization protests' becoming 'the primary vehicle for an unprecedented program of economic liberalization' (Zeleke, 2019: 179). As three years of protests piled on the pressure to 'reform', the new leadership that came to power in April 2018 used corruption charges against the military-run industrial conglomerate METEC as a justification to introduce liberalisation and full and/or partial privatisation of SOEs. This process also included privatising the most successful SOEs, including Ethiopian Airlines, Ethio Telecom (ETC) and electric power production and distribution companies. These strategic sectors had been historically controlled by the state; control over these sectors defined the *ethos* and *praxis* of the Ethiopian state.

The Grand Ethiopian Renaissance Dam is a good example of the political nature of development in Ethiopia. The dam is seen by both the state and the general public as 'a reflection of and contributor of strong transformative economic growth under tight macro-economic constraints and a symbol of the government's recognition of the political imperative of transformation' (Oqubay, 2015: 4). Such megaprojects where the state plays an active and hegemonic role depict a top-down nation-building project.

In contrast, the ongoing liberalisation process in Ethiopia centres the rationale and language of PPPs. What is new in this transition is not the invitation to the private actor to participate, but the process of eroding the presence of the state by privatising the SOEs that define the Ethiopian DS. As mentioned earlier, the autonomy of the DS is explained by the power asymmetry between the private sector and the state, with the state historically having the upper hand. But whether this asymmetry will persist in the new political economy of PPPs remains, for now, an open question. The current government's official discourse also introduces a new notion of the 'public', replacing the 'relative autonomy' of the state as a central feature of the DS. In the past, the ideological social base of the Ethiopian DS was a peasantry 'mobilized for development and social transformation' (Berhe, 2020). The new political economy of PPPs now raises the obvious questions of who would represent its new social base, and who would constitute the 'public' in the PPP model? Development in Ethiopia has been, and still is, seen primarily as a political process. This invites the additional question of what would be, or what is, the new politics in PPP-constituted Ethiopia. The next section attempts to answer these questions by critically exploring media narratives of PPPs as the new language and ideology mediating state-society relations in Ethiopia. The section approaches the notion of the 'public' in two intertwined ways:

1. The public refers to the wider population – citizens whose resources are negotiated to be developed under the PPP framework. In this context, the public is constituted by the end users of development projects whose intersectional interests are supposedly represented by the government; and
2. The constitution of the public is also understood in light of its omissions, namely whose interests are accounted for and whose interests are omitted in the way PPPs are being introduced in Ethiopia. The answer to this question highlights the political significance of PPPs.

Media narratives on PPPs between 2018 and 2020

Most local Amharic and English newspapers discuss PPPs in Ethiopia in the context of ongoing economic reforms, and the support that this process receives from IFIs such as the World Bank (WB) and the International Monetary Fund (IMF). These discussions are intertwined with the political transition underway in the country since April 2018. While PPPs as a form of public investment are used to highlight the beginning of a change within the Ethiopian DS model, the new ruling elite overseeing this transition is represented by both local and international media as the bearers of change. Furthermore, the shift from state-led macroeconomic policies to the opening up of development finance to local and foreign private actors is praised as a positive move without any critical examination of its impact. PPPs are framed as part of the process of expanding the role of the private sector in financing public development, and Ethiopia is presented as the private international market's next frontier. In concrete terms, adopting the PPP model of development financing in Ethiopia entails the liberalisation of the economy and the privatisation of its SOEs, both for local and foreign private actors.

The newspaper reports reviewed as part of this study seem to suggest that the government was forced to introduce macroeconomic schemes to halt the depletion of foreign exchange reserves, and reduce internal and external debt accumulated by unprofitable and inefficient public enterprises (Fortune, 2019). But the same reports are silent on how the government plans to host public deliberation and debates on these reforms. More often than not, the public appears as a mere demographic promise for an expanding market, without any corresponding discussion on how to protect the public from the potential negative consequences of private sector incursions. The private sector, according to these media reports, is consulted as the primary stakeholder in economic liberalisation, and some of these consultations are held behind closed doors (Fortune, 2019).

A number of policy recommendations from international and non-governmental organisations[2] emphasise that Ethiopia needs to undergo political, legal and macroeconomic policy reform to lay the groundwork for PPPs. The WB and IMF, for instance, recognise the economic achievement of the DS model in Ethiopia (The Reporter Ethiopia, 2018b). However, both institutions simultaneously push for economic liberalisation and privatisation of SOEs under the PPP model of development financing (UNDP, 2015). This means less state intervention and opening up the economy to grant a key role to the private sector. What is lacking in these recommendations is an analysis of the historical macroeconomic and political significance of SOEs that goes beyond their economic logic.

Media coverage mirrors the omissions of international and non-governmental organisations by neglecting to mention how the transition to PPPs affects power relations between the state and the private sector, and places limits on the state's ability to control 'the commanding heights of the economy' and 'lead the private sector', a phenomenon that once characterised the *ethos* of the Ethiopian DS (Berhe, 2020). Instead, these narratives point to the macroeconomic and legislative reforms as necessary steps in moving towards the PPP model (Fortune, 2019). In particular, the media is calling for a reform of the investment law. In a November 2019 article titled 'Bill to Liberalise Investment Laws Reaches Councils of Ministers', *Addis Fortune,* one of the foremost business newspapers in the country, explained that a special committee, comprising seventeen experts, had revised the law to 'allow public private partnerships in the areas of manufacturing of military weapons, international airport transport service, import and export, power distribution through the integrated national grid system' (Fortune, 2019). The new revision, according to *Addis Fortune,* would open the door to foreign involvement in the financial sector. The report states that, since 1974, the year known for the eruption of the Ethiopian Revolution, there has been no legal framework to support opening up the economy to foreign capital (Fortune, 2019).

While the macroeconomic reforms are reported as a new chapter for the country, the ideological, structural and political significance of state-led macroeconomic policy, and its political rationalisation of development and developmentalism as the state's leading ideology and its source of legitimacy, is rarely discussed and simply taken for granted. The political significance of, or the stakes involved in, the constitution of the new 'public' under the

PPP framework is also rarely discussed. Rather, the transition is presented as a purely technical move – an implementation of macroeconomic legislative reforms on the recommendation of national and international experts (The Reporter Ethiopia, 2018b).[3]

Together, these media narratives frame the move towards PPPs in post-2018 Ethiopia as a necessary shift. More often than not, this shift is positioned as inevitable, leaving out ideological contradictions. The reports echo the views of experts from the World Bank Group (WBG) who described the country's 2018 political reforms as a 'structural reform process' and affirmed the transition from a state-led economic policy to the PPP model as a necessary part of economic reforms (The Reporter Ethiopia, 2018b). The WBG characterised Ethiopia's DS model simultaneously as a success story as well as a necessary and enabling factor for transitioning to the PPP model:

> While the model [DS] had been undeniably successful in delivering development outcomes for the country in the past, the Bank believes, it is approaching its inevitable limit as a prudent economic strategy for Ethiopia. According to Mathew Verghis, macroeconomic expert with WBG, as successful as the state-led economic model has been, thus far, the time has come for a major rebalancing through an extensive participation of the private sector. While official announcement from the GoE [Government of Ethiopia], so far, has been about the planned partial privatization of the some of the government monopolies in sectors like telecom, logistic and air transport, Mathew and his team, on the basis of the discussions they have conducted with the authorities, are convinced that the reform drive is much more bigger [*sic*], and that it encompasses opening up these sectors for foreign and domestic competition.
>
> (The Reporter Ethiopia, 2018b)

What is intriguing about the above review is that it conceptualises the DS model both as a successful endeavour and as a precondition for the adoption of PPPs. The underlying logic is that state-driven economic infrastructure development eventually has to give way to private sector intervention. The transition is also described in ahistorical terms, devoid of any mention of the country-wide mobilisations against the economic strife and the exclusion of the people from the fruits of economic growth. Such an omission ignores the complexity of the shift from the DS to PPPs and positions the latter as the only available policy option.

Besides, media coverage has not addressed the political nature of the role played by national and international experts who are spearheading Ethiopia's shift towards the PPP model of development financing. The political aspect of this macroeconomic transition and its significance in constituting who is assumed to be the new 'public' in the PPP model remains obscured in mainstream discussions.

The use of macroeconomic rationalisation alone to describe the shift from state-led infrastructure development to the PPP model fails to account for the impact on the government's accountability to its citizens. It also fails to recognise the socio-economic impact of giving profit-seeking actors a central role in carrying out macroeconomic reforms. The increasing pre-eminence of the private sector, foreign private actors and international monetary institutions reflects changes in the *ethos* of Ethiopia's modern state, diminishes the legitimacy of the masses and treats as inevitable the introduction of a PPP model which necessarily entails the privatisation of SOEs, a policy supported by the IFIs.

A case in point is the public support offered by Nataliya Mylenko, the task team leader for the Growth and Competitiveness Operation of the WB, for the various reforms initiated to ease the introduction of PPPs in the country. *The Report Ethiopia* quotes Mylenko, who at the time was working for the WB, advocating for IFI support to Ethiopia in response to its 'reform of the energy and telecom sectors, reforms in business licensing regulations [...] expected reforms in business competition law and in reviewing investment proclamation, impending reform in the civil society proclamation, and significant reforms in the regulation of State-owned Enterprise[s]' (The Reporter Ethiopia, 2018b). These reforms have facilitated the current government's access to technical and financial aid in the form of long-term loans and technical support from the WB and the French government. According to *The Reporter Ethiopia*, this was the first support Ethiopia received from the WB in fifteen years (The Reporter Ethiopia, 2018b).

Macroeconomic reforms have not only enabled the government to acquire financial aid and loans, but also boosted its political legitimacy among the IFIs. But how these reforms have affected the government's accountability to the masses, whose protests were among the reasons that triggered the regime change, has not been considered by international organisations such as the UNDP, the IMF and the WB that keep pushing for a shift towards the PPP model. This omission illustrates the failure of international organisations and their proposed economic reforms to account for the local political significance of macroeconomic reform. The fact that Ethiopia's macroeconomic reforms have been heralded by external non-state actors can be seen as a form of state capture by international business organisations and is reflective of the underlying economic logic of international monetary organisations.

Furthermore, state capture can be observed in the way in which international business organisations and funding institutions are presented at the forefront of media coverage on PPPs. International corporations are the target audience of this coverage as well as the central actors, and PPPs are almost always mentioned in relation to loans received or promised by IFIs. The media thus plays a significant role in carrying out an unofficial public relations campaign in favour of PPPs. Media coverage is also replete with profiles of international private actors as potentially or actually interested in investing in Ethiopia (Capital Ethiopia, 2019c). By profiling corporations in this way, the media contributes to a shift in the role of the DS which used to mobilise news of development projects to bolster its local social base. Instead, the new state appears to be sending out invitations mainly to international business organisations by promoting their profiles in the national media.

When addressing the reasons for the shift towards PPPs, media narratives point to three prominent reasons: (1) to expand public development, (2) to increase efficiency and reduce project delays and (3) to reduce the existing national debt (Capital Ethiopia, 2019a). However, much of the critical scholarship in this area argues that, conceptually and empirically, PPPs are more beneficial to the private sector than to citizens and/or their respective governments. Eurodad's Maria José Romero writes that 'private finance only provides about 15–20 per cent of total infrastructure investment' (2015: 10). In the same report, she suggests that infrastructure PPPs can actually be more expensive for developing nations.

The Ethiopian DS model is illustrative of the hegemonic role of the nation-state in planning and implementing the country's macroeconomic life. Development projects allow the state to derive legitimacy for itself and simultaneously displace the active participation of the masses to the periphery. Through such deliberate exclusion, the state seeks to imply that people are not active owners in the planning, implementation and ownership of state-led development projects. It is worth asking, therefore, how the transition to the PPP model would allow meaningful political participation for instrumentalised and disenfranchised citizens of the DS. How are citizens a part of the shift in the role of the state and the liberalisation of the economy? How are the citizens' interests and infrastructure development needs represented? How is the public in the PPP model protected from the possible hegemonic role of the private sector, both local and international, whose primary interest is profit extraction? What is the political role and accountability of the local and international experts who take part in transposing and recommending the shift to PPPs? These questions require a dialogue that analyses the shift towards PPPs not merely as an *economic* move, but rather, as one which has *political* significance at both the national and global levels.

Such a debate *has* been taking place, albeit peripherally, with public intellectuals such as Ato Kebour Ghenna and the macroeconomic analyst and scholar Alemayehu Geda, whose views on the full and/or partial privatisation of some of Ethiopia's SOEs are in stark contrast to the mainstream narrative. This debate was also played out in a Public Dialogue Forum put together by the civil society organisation Forum for Social Studies (FSS) in April 2019.

Debating privatisation of SOEs: Two views from intellectuals

The FSS is an independent non-profit organisation known for hosting public policy dialogues and debates on contemporary issues. On 19 September 2019, the FSS held a public debate to bring together opposing views on the privatisation of SOEs as part of the broader macroeconomic reforms being undertaken by the contemporary Ethiopian state.[4] Brook Taye, who is currently serving as a Senior Advisor to the Ethiopian Ministry of Finance (MoF), argued in favour of the PPP model, while Ato Kebour Ghenna, an entrepreneur and a public intellectual, presented a critical view.

The PPP promise: Minimise debt, increase efficiency and generate capital

According to Brook Taye, PPPs can help reduce Ethiopia's spiralling external debt, increase the efficiency of its various sectors and expand its public service. He points to three key factors that have influenced the Ethiopian state's decision to carry out macroeconomic reforms via full and partial privatisation of SOEs.[5]

1. Most SOEs have accumulated debt and are unprofitable, thus becoming a fiscal burden for the government. Public enterprises (PEs), Brook Taye notes, hold 48 per cent of the foreign loans that the central government acquired between 2014 and 2019. The energy sector and sugar corporations have 400 billion Ethiopian Birr (ETB) of debt in commercial loans;
2. Delays in project completion and poor performance of SOEs have, in turn, led to delays in debt repayments and over-indebtedness; and
3. Most SOEs lack the capital to carry out further infrastructure development in their respective sectors.

Regardless of these challenges, the government has not decided to terminate the services offered by SOEs, Brook Taye points out, but rather continues to subsidise them due to the social relevance of their services. For example, the government has not cut power supply even though the public sector enterprise Ethiopian Electric Power (EEP) has paid neither its international nor its national debt. Instead, the government is subsidising it temporarily. How are Ethiopian SOEs to continue accumulating such massive amounts of debt and still remain profitable, Brook Taye asks. With current assessments by the MoF showing most SOEs as unprofitable for the public and the government, Brook Taye argues that PPPs can be used to finance SOEs in a way that even covers their past debts.

In an interview to *The Reporter Ethiopia* on 19 December 2019, he described Ethiopia's current economic model as 'pragmatist'. When questioned by journalist Birhanu Fikade on 'the core agenda behind privatization', Brook Taye responded:

> I don't see it as a privatization agenda that the government is working on, rather it is more of a SoE reform agenda. But in the discussion panels that I have attended and the argument I heard from some people completely misses the mark. When you talk about the sugar sector privatization, the attempt made so far to make sure that Ethiopia is both self-sufficient and hard currency generating country from export of sugar has not been successful. […] *government, as a regulator, work[s] with private players in a very transparent way and generate[s] revenues from those properties to utilize that finance on other infrastructure."*
>
> (The Reporter Ethiopia, 2019c) (emphasis mine)

For Brook Taye, a pragmatic economic model means redefining the role of the state by limiting it to being a regulator with partners in the private sector. However, the terms and goals of this partnership are vague. In the same interview, when asked about the life span of the new economic reforms, he said:

> Most of the SoEs were created during the time of His Majesty Haile Selassie in the 1940s. They need to be recalibrated and they need to know what they have at their warehouses. *I think this all relies on what individuals could do. If we really work hard and dedicate ourselves to make sure that it is a reality, three years is a lifetime.*
>
> (The Reporter Ethiopia, 2019c) (emphasis mine)

A fundamental assumption behind the new economic reform agenda is that there is a need for a dedicated individual to make it a reality. But a reality for whom, and to what end? PPPs are being pushed by IFIs through incentives given and promised by international monetary institutions and foreign private companies. It is curious that involving profit-seeking PPPs in SOEs is seen as the solution to the macroeconomic challenges of high debt, inefficiency and a lack of capital for infrastructure investments.

Defining the state as a regulator that operates with private actors and dedicated individuals to alleviate macroeconomic ills implies a passive public that has been rendered both analytically and politically absent (The Reporter Ethiopia, 2019c). This even as critical literature on PPPs urges government bodies to pay attention to the adverse history of this model of development financing as its operational and financial impacts may linger for many generations (Romero, 2015). With the failure of a PPP, the public sector will likely have to carry the debt burden. Brook Taye's promise of the positive impact of PPPs ignores these possibilities. In fact, an overwhelmingly positive tone seems to be a shared feature of the introduction of PPPs across developing countries. As Romero argues, 'all too often PPPs suffer from an "optimism bias"' (Romero, 2015: 7). This, she explains, is a consequence of 'weaker incentives for rigorous analysis on both the private and the public sector sides' (Romero, 2015).

Cautionary voices can initiate further public debates and dialogue on PPPs and their potential positive and adverse impacts on Ethiopia's economy and politics. Ato Kebour Ghenna is one of them.[6] He has been a vehement critic of the country's economic reform agenda. At the FSS public debate, Ghenna contested Brook Taye's views and was critical of the proposal to privatise Ethio Telecom. He pointed out that the institution had been monopolised by the Ethiopian state for over four decades, and that for developing countries like Ethiopia, strengthening PEs was a matter of national sovereignty. Denationalising them would jeopardise that sovereignty. For most developed nations, Kebour Ghenna noted, the privatisation of SOEs was a matter of local-national policy. For developing nations, however, the same process is being driven by IFIs with the aim to facilitate foreign and local investors' access to national public enterprises as sites for profit making.

It is a mistake on the part of the current government to view profitability as the exclusive domain of private entities, Kebour Ghenna asserted. SOEs are not only profit-making enterprises but also sites where the public can access services subsidised by the state. Once these are privatised, the public will no longer be able to claim a subsidised price for the services used, leaving them to enter into profit-driven market relations. Besides compromising national sovereignty, privatising SOEs will affect the right of the public to access and receive services from these institutions and hold them accountable. Turning SOEs into private entities, fully or partially, will thus transform the nature of social relations between them and the public, Kebour Ghenna noted. This would also alter the historical function of the state, assigning a hegemonic role to the private sector and imposing a profit-making *ethos*. For Kebour Ghenna, once privatisation kicks in, there is no going back; all alternative options to tackle debt must, therefore, be exhausted *before* resorting to privatisation.

An alternative way to resolve internal and external debt, lack of foreign currency reserves and poor economic performance would be to make use of remittances worth 3 billion US dollars that Ethiopia receives annually, Kebour Ghenna suggested.[7] Addressing the crucial issue of public accountability, he questioned whether the government's mandate to privatise SOEs was a unanimous decision. The special advisory council which manages the privatisation process has thus far not produced any public study or report. For Kebour Ghenna, this is a signal that, for the government, accountability is a matter of rhetoric rather than a practice of transparency.

Energy for sale

In his interview with *The Reporter Ethiopia*, Brook Taye raised the case of the EEP, the country's most indebted SOE, while discussing the role of the PPP model of financing in the restructuring of public enterprises. The restructuring of EEP is being driven by two intertwined expectations: (1) to reduce the SOE's debt and (2) to enable it to expand electricity supply to underserved and unserved sections of the country. In other words, EEP is adopting the PPP model in order to expand.[8] According to the government, EEP's past debts and future investments are up for sale. The sale of various energy typologies is expected to ease EEP's past national and foreign debts, and build the SOE's capacity to invest in future expansion projects.

Treating this merely as a macroeconomic policy shift is the major shortcoming of the current reform process. The government has provided no indication of whether and how the general public, which will be affected either positively or adversely by the privatisation of EEP, has been consulted during the process. A similar pattern of leaving the public out of consultations is revealed by a broader analysis of media reports on the energy sector. This analysis simultaneously illustrates the ways in which the sector is being promoted to be sold through PPPs. Media coverage is directed at the private sector in order to attract potential buyers. Multinational companies, international advisors and government officials appear as key actors in this coverage while public and public interests remain absent. Table 2.1 summarises how energy sector PPPs are presented in newspapers and social

Table 2.1 Energy Sector PPPs Reported in Ethiopia's Print Media,
April 2018–May 2020.

Energy type	Aggregate amount, the sum total of all energy projects related to one type of energy	Location of the project	Public institutions involved	All IFIs promoting the given energy type and foreign national states
Wind power	11	Afar and Somali regions	Ministry of Finance	Denmark, Ministry of Foreign Affairs of Denmark
Solar energy	24	Afar and Somali regions, Debire Birhan and Dire Dawa	Ministry of Finance	1. The state of Saudi Arabia; 2. International Finance Corporation; 3. World Bank Group
Geothermal	Not mentioned	Afar and Somali regions, Debire Birhan and Dire Dawa	Ministry of Finance	Denmark, Ministry of Foreign Affairs of Denmark
Hydro power	1	0	Ministry of Water and Irrigation	World Bank Group and World Bank Energy Specialist

Source: Prepared from data compiled by author.

media coverage. The main actors are government institutions, IFIs and
foreign investors who have expressed interest in buying and selling different
forms of energy in specific regions. Energy users, as a category, remain in
the background, and their interests are assumed to be represented by the
government. Moreover, the potential significance of these energy projects
is rarely framed in terms that refer to ordinary citizens who use energy
provided by these services.

In the mainstream media narrative, accountability is linked not to
communities or energy users, but to governments and profit-making

corporations. This is why it is necessary to highlight the invisibility of the public and its potential substitution by a few government offices as sellers. Most energy sector PPPs are in the promissory stage of identifying what is up for sale, which projects have gained the attention of international private companies and what kind of external support the sector is gaining from IFIs. Table 2.1 mentions the public institutions that are involved in developing regulatory frameworks and negotiating with foreign investors. In contrast, consumers and end users of public goods and services are rarely mentioned in the reviewed media coverage. Among local actors, only officials at the MoF and EEP are cited in the media. That the public part of PPPs is taken for granted is evident in the ways in which these partnerships are represented in media narratives, where government officials and the private sector are depicted as the key actors who will address the macroeconomic problem of debt and future investments.

Besides, the local aspects of the economy only find mention in discussions on potential sites of operation or when potential consumers are described as market niches. For example, *The Reporter Ethiopia* only mentions the Afar and Somali regions as sites where two solar energy projects under PPPs are located (Fikade, 2019a). Why were these two locations chosen for these specific types of energy, who will consume the energy generated and to what end are questions that remain unanswered.

The peripheralisation of the general public from consultation and debate, the negotiation/negation of the public for/from societal equity issues in the ongoing process of policy transformation and deciding *on behalf of the public* under the guise of economic growth are shared features of the DS and PPPs in Ethiopia. The earlier DS paradigm, in which the state had a hegemonic role over both the private sector and the general population, witnessed a period of rapid economic growth (Oqubay, 2017). Yet, the benefits of this growth were not available to the masses. Rather, growth was achieved by relegating the masses to the periphery through massive land eviction programmes for investment, resulting in human rights abuses by authorities and culminating in waves of protests throughout the country. These protests, which started in 2015, resisted the logic of economic growth that does not benefit the general public and eventually led to a change in the government leadership in 2018.

These protests hold a lesson for the current macroeconomic reforms process – that short-term gains in economic growth or even debt relief may not address the structural contradictions that constrain growth over the long term. To address these structural contradictions, we have to start by asking the question: who decides what resources are to be used and towards what end? On this, the so-called pragmatism of the PPP model offers no answers.

Conclusion: Uncertainties as generative sites for resisting PPPs in Ethiopia

Although the discussion on PPPs in Ethiopia currently denotes a shift away from the DS, the transition is not devoid of the previous model's hangover. This trend is particularly evident in the constitution of the PPP Board (The Reporter Ethiopia, 2018a). Populating the Advisory Council on PPPs with government-assigned personnel shows that there is a less substantive shift from the DS to PPPs. The politics of representation of the public has not changed despite the powerful protests prior to 2018. The protests called attention to growing economic and political marginalisation, were marked by gendered, ethnic and regional inequalities, and were fuelled by economic growth for the 'masses of peasants' model of the Ethiopian DS. The new leadership's response was to promote PPPs as an opportunity to reduce Ethiopia's external debt, without paying sufficient attention to public interest. A democratic model of inclusion demands that the public be protected from profit-led market relations dominating the logic and practice of the public service sector which has allowed the entry of foreign and local private actors. Without sufficient public engagement, the implementation of PPPs may lead to state capture by the private sector and IFIs.

There needs to be a thorough debate about the implementation of PPPs. It is necessary to discuss whether PPPs are the only available option to finance the public sector's current spending, past debts and future investments. The current Ethiopian government is wholeheartedly embracing the push from the WB and the IMF to open up the economy, privatise SOEs and reduce national debt, but it also needs to account for how this new model will change the country's political and social fabric.

There is also a need to scrutinise reports by IFIs and comments by high-ranking IFI officials which simultaneously praise Ethiopia's 'unorthodox'[9] DS model and push for economic liberalisation. With both these models reproducing the marginalisation of the public, it may be worthwhile to adopt a critical perspective and slow down the process of economic reforms in order to investigate and rethink options to finance public service provision and infrastructure development.

The uncertainties on PPPs in Ethiopia emerge from the lack of public accountability as the current government continues to take measures without fully engaging with the public.[10] The macroeconomic shift takes a top-down approach and, thereby, disguises the potential impact on people's daily lives. Are citizens' interests being considered in this reform process? The answer is overwhelmingly negative. Citizens' perspectives are rarely analysed except by a few critical local experts whose voices are marginalised by both private and government media houses.

Notes

1   The naming convention used in Eritrea and Ethiopia does not have family names, and typically consists of an individual personal name and a separate patronymic. Children add the given names of their father and paternal grandfather consecutively to their own given name. The grandfather's given name is taken as a family surname. We have used bold type for family names in this chapter. See https://en.wikipedia.org/wiki/Naming_conventions_in_Ethiopia_and_Eritrea. Similar rules apply to the authors cited in this document.

2   The state of infrastructure in many developing countries tends to be poor and inadequate to meet the rising demand. This reveals the constraints that governments in developing countries and especially in sub-Saharan Africa (SSA) face in terms of scarcity of funds, corruption, poor planning and project formulation, as well as inefficient capacities. PPPs have emerged as one of the ways to overcome these constraints. By tapping into private sector finance and ingenuity, governments are able to finance critical infrastructure, improve project preparation, execution and management and deliver efficient services to the citizens. (UNDP, 2015: 1).

3   Although the sector was finally opened to local private players in 1994, the government continued to insist that the regulatory capacity of the National Bank of Ethiopia (NBE) was not developed enough to regulate foreign financial firms. In the event of legislation, opening up the financial sector will signal one of the first significant economic reforms in line with the recommendations of financial institutions such as the World Bank.

4   Available at: https://www.fssethiopia.org/index.php/2019/09/23/public-dialogue-on-privatization.

5   Available at: https://www.youtube.com/watch?v=-SVC9amFVrw.

6   Available at: https://www.youtube.com/watch?v=-SVC9amFVrw.

7   Available at: https://www.fssethiopia.org/index.php/2019/09/23/public-dialogue-on-privatization.

8   Available at: https://www.capitalethiopia.com/capital/investors-ask-to-shed-light-on-solar-project/2/2.

9   Available at: https://www.youtube.com/watch?v=tPKMUd_3nnk.

10 Available at: https://www.youtube.com/watch?v=o5TVk48Z194.

References

Ali, A. A. (2018), Full English Transcript of Ethiopian Prime Minister Abiy Ahmed Ali's Inaugural Address. Available at: https://www.opride.com/2018/04/03/englishpartial-transcript-of-ethiopian-prime-ministerabiy-ahmeds-inaugural-address (accessed 20 February 2020).

Ashine, Y. (2018), 'When Theory Misses History', A Review of *State and Economic Development in Africa: The Case of Ethiopia* by A. Tesfaye, *African Review of Books*, under CODESRIA, 14 (1): 10–12. Available at: https://www.researchgate.net/publication/335570979_vol14_n1_yonas_ashine_when_theory_misses_history/link/5d6e288f92851c853888a0d7/download (accessed 20 February 2020).

Berhe, M. G. (2020), *Laying the Past to Rest: The EPRDF and the Challenges of Ethiopian State-Building*, London: Hurst & Company.

Capital Ethiopia (2019a), 'Public-Private Partnership in Store for Addis Rail Line', by D. Astatike, 10 June. Available at: https://www.capitalethiopia.com/featured/public-private-partnership-in-store-for-addis-rail-line (accessed 20 February 2020).

Capital Ethiopia (2019b), 'Investors Ask to Shed Light on Solar Project', by M. Yewondwosssen, 9 September. Available at: https://www.capitalethiopia.com/capital/investors-ask-to-shed-light-on-solar-project (accessed 20 February 2020).

Capital Ethiopia (2019c), 'Workshop Advances Food Fortification', by E. Tilahun, 25 November. Available at: https://www.capitalethiopia.com/capital/workshop-advances-food-fortification (accessed 20 February 2020).

Ethiopian Energy & Power Business Portal (2018), 'Denmark and Ethiopia Expand Cooperation on Wind Energy', 28 October. Available at: https://www.ethioenergybuz.com/en/?option=com_content&view=article&id=239&catid=26 (accessed 20 February 2020).

Ethiopian Energy & Power Business Portal (2020a), 'Ethiopian Council of Ministers Approved the Power Purchase Agreement with CORBETTI Geothermal', 15 June. Available at: https://ethioenergybuz.com/en/renewables/geothermal/596-ethiopian-council-of-ministers-approved-the-power-purchase-agreement-with-corbetti-geothermal.html (accessed 20 February 2020).

Ethiopian Energy & Power Business Portal (2020b), 'Ethiopian Ministry of Finance Approves Five Wind Farm Projects for PPP Investment', 23 April. Available at: https://ethioenergybuz.com/en/renewables/wind/546-ethiopian-ministry-of-finance-approves-five-wind-farm-projects-for-ppp-investment.html (accessed 20 February 2020).

Ethiopian News Agency (2019), 'Gov't Speeding up Procurement of 17 PPP Projects', 18 June. Available at: http://www.ena.et/en/?p=8306 (accessed 20 February 2020).

Fortune (2019), 'Bill to Liberalise Investment Laws Reaches Council of Ministers', by G. Samuel, 23 November. Available at: https://addisfortune.news/bill-to-liberalise-investment-laws-reaches-council-of-ministers (accessed 20 February 2020).

Forum for Social Studies (2019), 'Public Dialogue on Privatization'. Available at: https://www.fssethiopia.org/index.php/2019/09/23/public-dialogue-on-privatization (accessed 20 February 2020).

The Guardian (2018), 'Ethiopia: "These Changes Are Unprecedented": How Abiy Is Upending Ethiopian Politics', by J. Burke, 8 July. Available at: https://www.theguardian.com/world/2018/jul/08/abiy-ahmed-upending-ethiopian-politics (accessed 20 February 2020).

Hauge, J., and H. Chang (2019), 'The Concept of a "Developmental State" in Ethiopia', in: F. Cheru, C. Cramer and A. Oqubay (eds), *The Oxford Handbook of the Ethiopian Economy*, 824–41, Oxford: Oxford University Press.

Mkandawire, T. (2001), 'Thinking about Developmental States in Africa', *Cambridge Journal of Economics*, 25 (3): 289–314.

Oqubay, A. (2015), *Made in Africa: Industrial Policy in Ethiopia*, Oxford: Oxford University Press.

Oqubay, A. (2017), 'Breaking Down Ethiopia's Fast-Growing Economy', *Bloomberg QuickTake*. Available at: https://www.youtube.com/watch?v=o5TVk48Z194 (accessed 20 February 2020).

Rahmato, D. (2008), *The Peasant and the State: Studies in Agrarian Change in Ethiopia 1950s–2000s*, Addis Ababa: Addis Ababa University Press.

The Reporter Ethiopia (2018a), 'Major Power, Highway Projects Valued at USD 6.5 bln Approved for PPP', by B. Fikade, 27 October. Available at: https://www.thereporterethiopia.com/article/major-power-highway-projects-valued-usd-65-bln-approved-ppp (accessed 20 February 2020).

The Reporter Ethiopia (2018b), 'Departure from Developmental State', by A. Seyoum, 17 November. Available at: https://www.thereporterethiopia.com/article/departure-developmental-state (accessed 20 February 2020).

The Reporter Ethiopia (2019a), 'PPP Approves Six Solar Projects Worth USD 800 Mil', by B. Fikade, 19 January. Available at: https://www.thereporterethiopia.com/article/ppp-approves-six-solar-projects-worthusd-800-mil (accessed 20 February 2020).

The Reporter Ethiopia (2019b), 'Saudi Energy Firm Awarded First Solar Project under PPP', by Y. Abiye, 14 September. Available at: https://www.thereporterethiopia.com/article/saudi-energy-firm-awarded-first-solar-project-under-ppp (accessed 20 February 2020).

The Reporter Ethiopia (2019c), 'Interview: Economic Pragmatist', by B. Fikade, 14 December. Available at: https://www.thereporterethiopia.com/article/economic-pragmatist (accessed 20 February 2020).

Romero, M. J. (2015), 'What Lies Beneath? A Critical Assessment of PPPs and Their Impact on Sustainable Development', Brussels: Eurodad. Available at: https://www.eurodad.org/what_lies_beneath (accessed 20 February 2020).

UNDP (2015), 'Prospects of Public-Private Partnership (PPP) in Ethiopia – Development Brief', UNDP Ethiopia No, 1/2015. Available at: https://www.undp.org/content/dam/ethiopia/docs/Public%20Private%20Partnership%20jan2015updated.pdf (accessed 20 February 2020).

Zeleke E. C. (2019), *Ethiopia in Theory: Revolution and Knowledge Production, 1964–2016*, Leiden: Brill.

Part Two

Normative and institutional labyrinths of PPPs

PPPs, corporate responsibility and women's human rights in Senegal's finance for development model: The case of the Dakar-Diamniadio motorway[1]

Marème Ndoye

Introduction

Development requires a reduction in inequalities alongside economic growth. Since 2014, growth rates in Senegal have exceeded 6 per cent, but entrenched and deepening poverty has undermined poverty reduction programmes and called official statistics into question. The difficulty of reconciling growth efforts with development and poverty reduction can be attributed to persistent social inequalities and the consequent lack of social inclusion and optimal resource distribution.

Since the 2000s, development strategies in Senegal have emphasised the importance of putting in place reliable infrastructure as a means of attracting investments, jumpstarting production and, thereby, driving economic growth. However, the country's socio-economic situation, its fragile financial fabric and a recurring budget deficit have posed significant challenges to the financing of infrastructure development projects and programmes.

Financial globalisation since the mid-1980s, marked by a surge of capital flows between countries, has made it possible for states to finance their infrastructure needs. At the same time, the twin processes of liberalisation and privatisation have meant that states have taken a backseat when it comes to the financing and execution of such projects, allowing private sector actors, whose sole aim is profit maximisation, to take over (Rodríguez Enríquez, 2019). External financing may have arguably improved the profitability of public infrastructure projects, but with states unable to regulate private players, these projects have often led to unintended consequences. They have negatively impacted human rights and social inclusion, and intensified existing socio-economic inequalities, especially in developing countries. As this chapter demonstrates, women have been particularly disadvantaged by the inefficiencies produced by private sector incursions.

Development Alternatives with Women for a New Era (DAWN) has highlighted some of the ways in which the private sector undermines women's human rights. This could be through the push for competitiveness and greater productivity which worsens women's working conditions; the ambiguous discourse on corporate social responsibility (RSE), which encourages little or no faith that companies are (or will be) gender sensitive; or tax evasion and lobbying by companies which limit public revenue and the space for political action (Rodríguez Enríquez, 2017). In Senegal, the involvement of the private sector in public infrastructure development has led to the displacement of women, hindered their access to essential services and disrupted their livelihoods.

The process of upgrading public infrastructure coincided with the liberalisation of the economy oriented towards public-private partnerships (PPPs) as an infrastructure financing mechanism. According to their proponents, PPPs can help cushion the state's limited financial resources; reduce inefficiencies in the design and implementation of projects; and foster the integration of innovation, technology transfer and capacity building. For these reasons, they are promoted as the most appropriate means of financing development projects. In reality though, PPP financing can often prove costlier than bank borrowing or bond issuance, more so in developing countries where additional returns are required to offset presumed higher risks (Romero, 2015). They can also exacerbate inequalities and harm the environment.

Faced with some of these challenges, Senegal, in 2004, introduced a legislative framework to supervise the construction and operation of public infrastructure through PPP financing. However, the new framework did not consider the gender-specific impacts of PPPs or their repercussions on human rights and social inequalities. The consequences of these omissions were especially evident in the Dakar-Diamniadio toll motorway project, which was executed using PPP financing and was marked by a high cost of infrastructure, loss of human lives and the displacement of people, especially women. The project thus demonstrated the limitations of the PPP model in upholding human and gender rights.

This chapter is particularly interested in understanding how PPP projects undertaken in Senegal have impacted women's human rights. The first section outlines the socio-economic backdrop and the gender policies in the country, the second and third sections examine the regulatory framework and implementation of PPPs in the country, and the final section analyses their impact on women's human rights through a case study of the Dakar-Diamniadio toll motorway project.

The socio-economic and policy backdrop

Senegal is located in the western part of the African continent, south of the Sahara. More than 50 per cent of its population of 16.2 million inhabitants are women. The capital city of Dakar covers 0.3 per cent of the country's total surface area but is home to nearly 23 per cent of its people (ANSD, 2019).

Its geographic location gives Senegal a strategic advantage in international trade and fishing. Its relative socio-political stability – the country has witnessed two political changes of power without major tension – has also made it a favoured investment destination. The first change of power in 2000 ushered in a liberal regime which centred the private sector in its development strategies. Recent years have seen healthy growth but challenges remain in the form of poor human development metrics. In 2019, Senegal ranked 166th in the world and 33rd in Africa in the United Nations Development Programme's (UNDP) human development index.[2]

Measuring quality of life, mapping the economy

Following its independence in 1960, Senegal experienced a period of economic stability that was interrupted by an economic crisis in the 1970s. This crisis was used to justify the imposition of structural adjustment programmes (SAPs) to improve the economic situation and plug the budget deficit. It was only in the decade following the 1994 currency devaluation that some macroeconomic indicators began to improve. The gross domestic product (GDP) rose 5 per cent against an average contraction of more than a per cent in the previous decade. However, this was not accompanied by any visible improvement in the perception of poverty. According to data from the Senegalese Household Surveys (ESAM), poverty[3] fell from 67.9 per cent in 1994–5 to 57.1 per cent in 2001–2 (ANSD, 1994; 2001).[4] A decade later, this figure declined to 46.7 per cent, according to estimates from the 2011 Poverty Survey. But for most Senegalese households (53.3 per cent), the economic situation during this time deteriorated compared to the previous years (ANSD, 2013).

The Plan Sénégal Émergent (Emerging Senegal Plan) or PSE came against this backdrop. A long-term development programme launched in 2014 during the term of President Macky Sall, its stated aim is to turn Senegal into an emerging economy by 2035 by implementing priority economic reforms and investment projects, clearing the way for growth and preserving the economy and debt sustainability. The plan is divided into three strategic axes: (1) inclusive growth through a structural transformation of the economy; (2) human development by strengthening human capital, social protection and sustainable development; and (3) good governance to ensure peace and security.

Following the implementation of the PSE, Senegal's growth rate rose to 6.5 per cent in 2015, the highest since 2003, and to 6.8 per cent in 2018. The projected growth for 2019 was roughly the same. Besides agriculture, the main engine of job creation in the country, these rates were attributed to major infrastructure investments undertaken under the PSE (World Bank, 2018). The bulk of the growth, however, came from services which accounted for nearly 61 per cent of total value added over 2014–18.

The budget deficit shrunk to an estimated 3.5 per cent in 2018 from 5.4 per cent in 2011. At the same time, external debt, while bearable, gradually increased, justifying the turn to PPP financing. This period was also marked by an unequal distribution of resources, with the richest 20 per cent owning 46.9 per cent of the country's wealth in 2011 (World Bank, 2019).

Social inclusion remained a fraught issue. Job creation failed to keep pace with internal migrations and a rising economically-active population. Most paid work was, and continues to be, informal, resulting in low wages, underemployment and limited social protections.

Since 2005, three generations[5] of development policy documents on poverty reduction and good governance strategies sought to take gender into account, but failed to achieve the desired objectives. The resultant disparities were reflected across gender inequality indices. In 2012, the OECD Social Institutions and Gender Index (SIGI) ranked Senegal 41st out of eighty-six countries, with a value of 0.23 (with zero representing equality). The Gender Development Index (GDI), calculated based on the quality of life, ranked Senegal 124th out of 149 countries globally, and third among the Economic Community of West African States (ECOWAS). The index pegged the quality of life for men at 0.52 and women at 0.449 (Ministère de la Femme, de la famille et de l'enfance, 2015).

Gender policies and the fight against social inequalities

Inspired by colonial models, independent Senegal established extension programmes for women (*'animation' féminine*) dedicated only to domestic tasks (hygiene practices, childcare, etc.), especially in the rural areas. It took several years (notably the World Decades for Women, 1975–95) and increasing awareness of women's struggles in the world and Africa for Senegal to transform and strengthen its women-oriented programmes.

Since 1976, under pressure from women's movements, the government has introduced specialised structures (Secretariat for the Status of Women, various ministries of women, social development, family, gender, etc.) and reforms aimed at improving the legal status and political participation of women. It has ratified most international conventions, including the 1979 Convention on the Elimination of All Forms of Discrimination Against Women (CEDAW) and the African Charter on Human and Peoples' Rights (ACHPR) initiated in 1981 by the African Union[6] and enforced in 1986. This Charter, however, committed signatories 'to [take] into account the virtues of their historical traditions and the values of African civilization', factors which are often used to justify violations of women's rights. Legal duality (colonial and customary law), inherited from colonialism, persists in many African legislative systems and fails to take into account the rights of women specified in several international documents, notably the Beijing Platform (1995). Women's movements, therefore, pushed for the adoption of the Protocol to the African Charter on Human and Peoples' Rights on the Rights of Women in Africa, commonly known as the Maputo Protocol, which Senegal ratified in 2004.

Gender equality emerged as a pressing issue in Senegal under the influence of international and Pan-African feminist debates, especially since the 2000s. In 2001, the revised Senegalese Constitution stipulated that men and women have equal rights to the possession and ownership of land, ownership of patrimony and personal management of property, and education.[7] The abolition and criminalisation of female genital mutilation in 1999 marked an important milestone. In 2005, the adoption of the law on reproductive health allowed women control over their fertility, thus meeting the guidelines of the Maputo Protocol. Legislative provisions in 2008 promoted women's access to the military, the gendarmerie and the police. The year 2010 also saw the adoption of the law on parity, resulting in a 43 per cent representation for women in the National Assembly. Finally, the 2013 nationality law eliminated discrimination based on gender (Ministère de la Femme, de la famille et de l'enfance, n.d.). Senegal's gender policies have also been marked, in recent years, by stronger social protection systems, with particular emphasis on women (family grants given to the poorest families, free caesarean sections, etc.).

As far back as 2004, Senegal's Ministry of Women, Family and Children adopted the National Strategy for Equity and Gender (SNEEG) to implement gender equality issues between 2005 and 2015. This included promoting the empowerment of women and young girls through capacity building of institutions and local communities, and integrating gender into public policies for inclusive growth. Thereafter, in 2015, the Ministry updated the SNEEG framework with the aim 'to make Senegal an emerging country in 2026 with a united society in a rule of law, without discrimination, where men and women will have the same opportunities to participate in its development and enjoy the benefits of its growth' (Ministère de la Femme, de la famille et de l'enfance, n.d.). The 2016–26 SNEEG has synergies with the objectives of the PSE and takes into account the United Nations' Sustainable Development Goals (SDGs) on improving the quality of life and reducing gender inequalities.

Policies that addressed gender and social inequalities were included in the Priority Action Plans (PAP) associated with the PSE. For instance, PAP1 (2014–18) and PAP2 (2019–23) assign points against certain parameters that count towards a score system that, in turn, is used to select which policies receive funding. PAP1 attributed a score of 10 out of 100 to PSE policies for their inclusion of social equality indicators in general, without specifying gender equality. Thus far, PAP2 has assigned scores of 5 and 7 out of 100 to policies that addressed the reduction of gender and social inequalities, respectively (Ministère de l'Économie et des finances, 2014; 2019). Moreover, 11 per cent of the cost of the PSE PAP2 strategy is dedicated to reducing all forms of inequality, including the consolidation of peace and security; the promotion of the fundamental principles of the rule of law, human rights and justice; the promotion of equity and gender equality; the reform of the state and the strengthening of public administration, regional planning and territorialisation of policies; and strategic, economic and financial governance.

Since March 2013, a circular from the Prime Minister's Office has enshrined Senegal's gender policy with the creation of a gender unit at the level of each ministry, and the implementation of a gender action plan. The objective is to systematically take the gender dimension into account in all current interventions. However, this has not been implemented in certain ministerial departments such as the ministry in charge of infrastructure, which is of interest to this study. The constraints include the lack of relevant and competent personnel and ineffective application of laws protecting women.

Gender issues should also be integrated into programmes being implemented at the local level and extended to the regional development agencies (ARD) which support local development. There is little local capacity across Africa to design and implement gender-sensitive programmes and projects, but with international cooperation and through many non-governmental organisations (NGOs), the work of raising awareness on sexual abuse of women is well underway in several local communities. Actions initiated under the Gender Equity Project in Local Governance (GELD) confirm that these interventions have improved the conditions of women and advanced the achievement of gender equality (Ministère de la Femme, de la famille et de l'enfance, 2015).

More girls than boys are enrolled in primary and middle school, but the trend is reversed in secondary school when girls are forced to abandon their education and get married. This impacts individual job performance. Young men dominate the national employment numbers, although urban and rural areas show divergent trends. In the cities, 41.1 per cent of young men have jobs against 35.3 per cent of young women, while in rural areas, a higher percentage of young women (64.7 per cent) are employed compared to young men (58.9 per cent). Despite a directive calling for the integration of equity and equality in the actions of sectoral ministries, it is clear that efforts still need to be made towards effective gender integration and equality in development and poverty reduction strategies.

Traditional means of financing development policies

Senegal is characterised by a strong dependence on tax and customs revenues and a relatively weak financial base. The banking system fails to meet the financial needs of the government and individuals. The financial market, until recently, was relatively small. Like other developing countries, Senegal has, therefore, resorted to external debt and official development assistance (ODA) to finance development, making it heavily dependent on external aid. Public debt has been the main source of funding for development projects and programmes. This has resulted in high debt ratios and a structural budget deficit.

Since 1985, the SAPs have forced the government to expose the country to international market competition. Although protectionist measures have always been an important source of revenue for Senegal (Diagne, 2006), successive programmes now include measures aimed at lowering tariffs and removing non-tariff barriers. At this level, two major constraints deserve attention. The first is that the domestic private sector has limited capacity to meet expectations due to difficulties in accessing financial services, the lack of skills, and the informal nature of economic activities which constitute an obstacle to public procurement. Secondly, the nature of certain goods or services justifies the intervention of the government. These include public goods and services such as roads, health, education, infrastructure and public utilities.

Until the 2000s, ODA was one of the most viable options available to countries to finance their economic development. But a changed landscape has since subjected traditional development aid to tight budgetary conditions and thrown up new tools and players to replace older forms of financing. In particular, the slowdown in official aid and concessional lending has led to the increased use of private instruments such as the international financial markets (Genre, 2016). Since 2015, with the advent of the SDGs to reduce poverty, the issue of financing has become even more acute. Indeed, the cost of investments necessary to achieve these goals is quite high, making it difficult to reconcile the ambitious pursuit of SDGs with the budgetary rigour demanded by donors.

Since 2012, Senegal's return to indebtedness has increasingly worried development actors. Even if the argument of a still sustainable debt rate is served (at 47.7 per cent, it is lower than the community standard of 70 per cent), its rapid growth is worrisome, and the risk to budgetary balances and the threat to future generations are real. Against this backdrop, private financing presents an alternative with two main arguments in its favour: the private sector is supposedly more efficient, and private financing helps manage public debt and relieve the state budget.

Emergence of the PPP Model in Senegal

In 1985, with the implementation of the SAPs, Senegal opened up its economy and expanded the role of the private sector. At this stage, it made private sector participation contingent on the financial viability of the sector, goods or services targeted.

The dynamics of the rise of the private sector

Thereafter, in 2000, Senegal created the National Agency for the Promotion of Investment and Major Works (APIX) to encourage and facilitate business creation and investment promotion in the country. Since then, all economic policy documents made the private sector a priority axis for reducing poverty by improving the business climate. In 2010, these efforts earned Senegal a rank of 157 out of 190 countries in the World Bank's (WB) Ease of Doing Business index. By 2020, the country climbed to the 123rd position. The progress was partially offset by a slowdown in the implementation of certain reforms between 2012 and 2014.

Despite an overall improvement in the business climate, the national private sector faced several constraints, including an early mortality rate (around 60 per cent of Senegalese companies disappear in the first year of creation), the predominance of the informal sector and the lack of professionalism, limited access to public procurement, weak production of financial information and difficulty in accessing bank financing adapted to small- and medium-sized enterprises (SMEs), which constitute 99.8 per cent of Senegalese companies (ANSD, 2017a). These shortcomings paved the way for foreign expertise, particularly in the form of PPPs.

Through the PSE, the state made PPP financing the preferred route for implementing infrastructure projects. Under PAP1, to bridge a financing gap of 30 per cent, Senegal counted on the participation of the private sector, which eventually covered around 37 per cent of this gap. This strategy was made possible through the active promotion of PPPs.

In 2007, the government created the Directorate of Support to the Private Sector (DASP) – it was later renamed the Directorate of Private Sector Development (DDSP) – to consolidate the experiences of all ministerial departments in charge of the economy and supervise the optimal management of businesses. The Directorate also strengthened the technical and financial support system for the private sector, allowing companies to access appropriate financial services and increase their participation in wealth and job creation.

PAP2 of the PSE sought to capture additional financial flows by increasing the participation of the local private sector and attracting more foreign direct investments for capital-intensive sectors and strategic projects. Under PAP2, projects have to adhere to a strict technical and financial structure in order to garner the maximum possible private capital while being implemented as a PPP. This is how the private sector is currently being invited to take majority stakes in promising markets such as infrastructure. In turn, the state is expected to formulate attractive and operational regulatory frameworks for PPPs that guarantee access to relevant information on private investment opportunities as well as on the structuring and support of projects.

The Unintended Consequences

PPP financing has also been introduced in other African countries confronted with over-indebtedness and constrained with adhering to the debt ratio criteria. The Heavily Indebted Poor Countries (HIPC) initiative, formulated to cope with indebtedness, reflects the difficulties in accessing equity financing for public goods and services. Under certain conditions relating to the cost of access to resources, recourse to external financing has been deemed more profitable. This, in turn, has driven profitability of projects and programmes.

However, financial profitability has not translated into economic, social and/or environmental benefits. On the contrary, the proliferation of PPPs in

Senegal since the 2000s has also given rise to much controversy, including litigation related to adverse environmental impacts and exacerbation of social inequalities. Originally promoted as financing instruments that would reduce poverty and inequalities, and avoid negative impacts on the environment, PPPs now face significant challenges (Romero, 2015), with the private sector itself contributing to inefficient management of financial, material and human resources. As the private partner concerns itself solely with defending financial profitability, it is left up to the public authority to defend the moral, financial and economic interests of citizens, and ensure equity. This is precisely why PPP financing should allow risk sharing between the public and private sectors, and be accountable to both public officials and the population through, among other things, consumer associations.

Legal and institutional framework for PPPs

Given the potential negative fallouts, the utilisation of PPP financing in public infrastructure projects requires an appropriate regulatory framework to tackle the associated challenges and risks. Such a framework was created by Senegal in 2004 (Gouvernement de la République du Sénégal, 2017). Two institutions attached to the Ministry of the Economy, Planning and Co-operation currently supervise PPPs in the country. These are the Department of Financing and Public-Private Partnerships (DFPPP), set up under the former Ministry of Investment Promotion and Partnerships, and the Development of State Teleservices. Acting in technical and legal capacities, the two institutions define and put in place the Senegalese government's PPP policy. They participate in the development of state policies, guidelines and instructions, and the dissemination of best practices on the financing, design, implementation and management of PPP projects. They also counsel and assist ministerial departments, local authorities and authorised entities in the preparation, implementation and monitoring of PPP contracts. In addition, the National Support Committee for Public-Private Partnerships (CNAPPP), established in 2014, validates the preliminary assessments of PPP projects; supports public sector entities in their preparation, negotiation and monitoring; and popularises and promotes PPPs.

Contracting authorities wishing to set up a PPP (public procurement contract) in Senegal must comply with the provisions of applicable laws and regulations[8] which, depending on the contract, could include (1) the Code of Obligations of the Administration which governs public contracts and public service delegations, and (2) the Public Procurement Code which defines leases and concession contracts, and the law on partnership contracts.

Currently, the same type of contract is covered by different laws and regulations. Depending on the sector in question, it is also necessary to refer to the specific sectoral legal provisions which may influence the contractual provisions of a given PPP project. All these laws/regulations and their implementing decrees make it possible to set up in all sectors of the country, excluding those subject to specific regulations, either a public service delegation (DPS) or a PPP. In both cases, the implementation of a PPP project must fit into the institutional framework dedicated to the chosen contract (Saware, 2019).

Limitations of the PPP model in addressing social balance

Since the full realisation of the country's economic potential is often beyond the scope of the domestic private sector, public authorities are turning to the international private sector for know-how and financial capacity. However, the allure of private sector participation can hide irregularities. This creates the scope for PPPs to produce negative spillover effects on society. They can impact public finances either directly, if the project implementation is tainted with irregularities, or indirectly, through tax concessions which are granted and justified as a means of attracting investors. PPPs can also harm local communities and vulnerable groups, trigger popular uprisings and result in litigations (Saware, 2019).

Examples of such litigations include the International Chamber of Commerce's directive to the state of Senegal to pay Kumba Resources Limited 400 billion Franc CFA (FCFA) for abusive breach of a mining agreement, and cases of corruption and underinvestment noted by the Court of Accounts and the General State Inspectorate in the concession for a container terminal at the Autonomous Port of Dakar.

Uncertainties and information asymmetries explain the gap between expected performance of and actual results produced by PPPs. In the pre-contractual phase, uncertainty dominates and is reinforced by changes in the rules of the game. Policy performance is affected if the public official in charge is not supported by experienced human resources. The selection of the project awardee may be hampered by the complexity and heterogeneity of the criteria to be considered, making it difficult to compare tenders. These criteria respond to certain legal, accounting and financial logics which are not necessarily those used by the public institution (Campagnac and Deffontaines, 2012).

The search for social balance is particularly incumbent on the concerned public official, and the difficulty of arbitrating in favour of public interest feeds the asymmetry of post-contractual information. When community interests are not included in the selection criteria, the execution of the contract can lead to conflicts with the population and impose additional costs that are then borne by the community.

PPPs can potentially worsen social and economic inequality, hinder access to essential services and promote corruption, all for the sake of profitability. Their human rights impact may include violations of economic and social rights such as access to basic social services (healthcare and education), the right to decent work and equitable access to land.

The intervention of private partners can also lead to certain forms of exclusion. Disadvantaged categories of the population can be excluded from certain infrastructures due to high prices. Because of their profit motives, PPP projects are concentrated in the capital and big cities, thus depriving rural populations. In light of these findings, the state must have a means of ex-post control over PPP activities in order to improve economic efficiency.

PPPs in practice

The first PPP was introduced in Senegal in 1996 with a lease-type contract between the Senegalese Water Board (SDE), the private operator exclusively responsible for drinking water facilities, and the Senegalese National Water Company (SONES), a public body responsible for asset management and quality control of this public service. The initial ten-year contract has since been extended by various additional clauses. Following a controversial call for tenders,[9] SDE was replaced by the French company SUEZ in January 2020.

PPP contracts in infrastructure

The need for new infrastructure in the country has been prompted by difficulties related to land (almost exhausted in Dakar), decentralisation and decongestion policies in the capital city, and tourism-related issues. As mentioned earlier, the limitations of domestic companies have meant that PPPs in the infrastructure sector are increasingly being deployed through foreign investment.

Under the PSE, Senegal plans to implement, by 2023, a set of structuring projects and reforms with high value-added content and job creation. These projects will rely on the legal and institutional framework established in 2004 with the aim of striking a balance between the state and private operators when it comes to PPPs.

The introduction of new innovative financing schemes for infrastructure projects presents short- or medium-term risks for all stakeholders – the public sector, users and private operators. As a first-level institutional response to these risks, Senegal has established an Infrastructure Council whose objectives include building broad and lasting consensus in the field of infrastructure, establishing an independent and qualified watch to assess the consistency of approaches and attitudes of stakeholders, and ensuring wide dissemination of its observations. The Council comprises three personalities appointed by the President of the Republic from a list of six persons proposed by institutions for the defence of human rights and the preservation of the interests of users.

The Infrastructure Council is entrusted with the selection of the project operator and the preservation of balances that condition the sustainability of contractual relations. It is important to ensure transparency in the selection of the project operator, a process that is governed by the competitive tendering procedures established by the law on CET contracts. Registered in the long term and operating in sectors subject to frequent technological adjustments, these contracts expose contracting parties to legal risks.

The balance of projects designed to meet strategic needs may be threatened by changes in regulations in the socio-economic environment or technologies. The risk exposure is higher when the degree of maturity of the legal and institutional framework calls for substantial reforms. The major stake lies in consolidating the sustainability of projects while guaranteeing that state policies and administrative decisions will be subject to independent review. The review results should be published periodically to ensure transparency (Journal officiel de la République du Sénégal, 2004).

The optimism surrounding the PSE during 2014–18 was dampened by weakening private financing in PPP projects. Of the 1,111 billion FCFA expected, about twenty PPP projects worth 397.8 billion FCFA were executed, particularly in the areas of infrastructure, energy, tourism, industry, agriculture and health. The shortfall was on account of the delay in establishing the legal framework for a new PPP law (that Senegal implemented in March 2021) and non-availability of feasibility studies for several targeted projects. Going forward, the Infrastructure Council will need to adapt to changes in the legal framework while integrating the balance of contractual relationships (Journal officiel de la République du Sénégal, 2004).

The Dakar-Diamniadio Toll Motorway

To date, only two major infrastructure projects in Senegal have used PPP financing: the Dakar-Diamniadio toll highway (APDD), known as 'the highway of the future', and the Blaise Diagne International Airport at Ndiass

(AIBD). The APDD is the first highway in Senegal to be executed under the legal regime of PPPs set up in 2004.

The capital city of Dakar is home to 85 per cent of the country's economic activities and accommodates nearly 23 per cent of the population. Entering and leaving Dakar thus poses a real problem of congestion. To address this issue, the Dakar-Diamniadio highway project was first introduced in the 1970s under the presidency of Léopold Sédar Senghor, the first President of the Republic of Senegal. He planned to establish a highway from Dakar to Thiès via Diamniadio. A comprehensive study was carried out by the then Ministry of Public Works, Urban Planning and Transport. However, the economic situation at the time delayed the implementation of the project which was finally resurrected in 2002. At this point, financing for the project was secured through a PPP mechanism with the concession option. It made the use of the motorway chargeable, which was not the initial plan.

Work on the motorway began in 2009 and was undertaken in three phases: the stretch between Dakar and Diamniadio was inaugurated in 2013, the section between Diamniadio and the airport was launched in October 2016 and, finally, the stretch between Sindia and Mbour was inaugurated on 22 January 2019. Work on this last section was due to be completed in 2016 but was delayed by lengthy negotiations on compensating property owners.

The first 35-kilometre phase of this highway was co-financed by the WB, the French Development Agency (AFD) and the African Development Bank (AfDB) to the tune of 52.5 billion FCFA, 40 billion FCFA and 33.2 billion FCFA, respectively (Faye, 2018). A private company SENAC SA, which is 100 per cent owned by the Eiffage Group,[10] obtained the concession for a period of thirty years. The second seventeen-kilometre phase cost a total of 92.2 billion FCFA; of this, 69.2 billion FCFA came from the state and 23 billion FCFA from SENAC SA. The 55-kilometre AIBD-Sindia stretch was built at a total cost of 200 billion FCFA. This section is part of the AIBD-Mbour highway and received funding from Exim Bank of China and the state.

The APDD is part of a general policy on upgrading infrastructure, land use planning and sub-regional integration. The project had to restructure unserviced and flood-prone neighbourhoods that lay in its route. It developed and built fully serviced residential houses over a 165-hectare resettlement area. The project had also planned to close and move the Mbeubeuss waste dump which lay on the route of the motorway and would have harmful effects on the surrounding population. Later, studies carried out for the construction of a technical landfill centre for waste identified a risk of producing dangerous biogas that would have affected residents in the resettlement area. The centre was eventually not operationalised due to the reluctance of the population.

Impact of the toll motorway project on gender and human rights

Although SENAC SA is fully owned by the Eiffage Group, it consists mostly of local staff, thus contributing to job creation and adding value to the economy. However, the project had several negative impacts. The motorway crossed a total of ten municipalities, including six on the first section (Pikine-Diamniadio) and four on the second (Diamniadio-AIBD). These included residential areas, market gardening in the Thiaroye area, the Mbao classified forest, areas under fruit production and other agricultural activities, and small businesses (mechanics' workshops, restaurants run by women who are also active in the sale of iced water, juice, etc., and other services run by young girls).

Due to the potential negative consequences – the displacement of families and commercial activities, the nuisance caused by the work, and the environmental impact linked to the motorway's passage through the classified forest of Mbao – the project was classified under Category 1, which requires a comprehensive environmental and social impact study. A Resettlement Action Plan (PAR) was then initiated, under which a total of 3,350 families were affected. Seventy per cent of the families were relocated to resettlement areas while the rest opted for monetary compensation.

Gender as a category was not taken into account either in the survey of the population affected by the project or in the choice of resettlement areas. Women who were impacted by the project faced difficulties in carrying out their primary activities of production and reproduction, and in recreating neighbourly ties. The people resettled in Tivaouane Peulh were affected by the remoteness of the area. Even though a market was built for them, they had no customers. Those resettled could also no longer count on the mutual support of neighbours. Some women had access to additional support meant for vulnerable groups – the elderly, people with disabilities and those below the poverty line. Most women were farmers and the support provided to them took the form of donation of seeds, fertilisers and small agricultural equipment as well as training. However, there was no list of beneficiaries that could be used to monitor the distribution of aid.

SENAC SA introduced a gardening project directly targeting women in the affected municipalities. This was carried out under the company's corporate social responsibility (RSE) policy. Along with other actors concerned by the highway project, SENAC SA also set up a socio-economic and environmental observatory to supervise the effective implementation of the RSE policy (Eiffage, 2017). The observatory was aimed at identifying and assessing major changes that were related, directly or indirectly, with the project. Another corporate policy directed towards women was the creation, in 2016, of an association of Eiffage women in Senegal to conduct humanitarian actions with the support of corporate management.

Despite these efforts, the toll motorway project was widely contested. There were multiple complaints against it, including a case that was referred to the League of Human Rights. The project led to the loss of lives and resources, which was attributed to the company's non-compliance with project commitments. The main disputes and complaints can be summarised as follows:

1. The motorway is said to be one of the most expensive in the world, both in terms of the investment cost and the user fee. The average cost per kilometre was estimated at 2 billion FCFA.[11] The high user fees charged on the AIBD-Mbour axis were later renegotiated lower on the instruction of the President of the Republic. The high cost of infrastructure put pressure on public finances, and the high user fees led to exclusion and price discrimination. In its response to these concerns, Eiffage noted that for every 1,000 FCFA paid at the toll, 300 FCFA went to the state, 400 FCFA was directed towards the reimbursement of the investment, and only 300 FCFA went to the licensee.

2. Contrary to pre-specified conditions of the project, only toll areas of the highway were lit. The lack of lighting led to an increase in the number of accidents. Public anger was especially evident following the accidental death of a famous musician on the motorway. A petition challenging the poor conditions of the motorway collected over 25,000 signatures and a large demonstration was organised at the site of the musician's accident. The company was declared responsible and ordered to pay 44 million FCFA to the victim's family. A case lodged following another fatal accident resulted in an order of conviction against the company by the League for Human Rights. These accidents, which often occurred at night, were attributed to both the private party which did not comply with project specifications in the interest of cost minimisation and the public party for its laxity and lack of ex-post control.

3. Eiffage's policy on promoting road personnel was non-compatible with Senegalese labour law and put women at a disadvantage. Labour laws in Senegal, relating to women and pregnant women, prohibit night work in factories, manufacturing activities, mines and quarries, construction sites (especially roads and buildings), and workshops and their outhouses. In promoting road personnel based on night shifts, Eiffage's corporate policy discriminated against women workers.

4. According to complaints voiced by a Koranic School and relocated tenants, the damage suffered due to displacement greatly exceeded the compensation received. Additional social assistance will be allocated to this group.

Conclusion

Budgetary pressure and debt challenges have supported the mainstream narrative that presents the use of PPPs for financing development projects and programmes as an imperative. However, PPPs have also raised several concerns. Competition between private and public interests has made the power of the private partner evident. PPPs have proved to be more expensive compared with the budgetary source of financing. In the case of the Dakar-Diamniadio motorway, the loss of human lives, the displacement of affected people and the project's failure to take into account the needs of displaced persons have revealed the limits of the legal and institutional framework for PPPs, which is more interested in creating attractive and secure outcomes for private actors, rather than addressing gender and social needs. The lack of respect for the environment has often been the basis for protests against PPPs. Even if this is factored into compensation standards, much remains to be done in communicating information about the compensation process and its distribution.

The private company's RSE policy has addressed some of these inequalities by focusing on vulnerable groups, especially women. It thus constitutes a first step towards integrating human and women's rights into the corporate system. However, limits in the institutional and legal framework in relation to information asymmetries and the absence of effective control over the execution of contracts are obstacles to achieving equity, and upholding human rights and gender equality. Although PPPs in Senegal have evidently had negative impacts on women, the associated regulatory frameworks and policies did not take gender aspects into account, either in the census of PAPs or in the choice of resettlement areas in the Dakar-Diamniadio toll motorway project. It is thus essential to strengthen the system to adhere to equity and equality in all instances of implementation and monitoring of PPP contracts.

Going forward, Senegal's PPP pipeline includes new projects in the field of maritime transport infrastructure and services, such as the Ndayane port project, to be implemented under PAP2 of the PSE. For these projects to be completed efficiently and sustainably, it is critical that lessons learnt from the Dakar-Diamniadio toll motorway be taken into account.

Notes

1   Most acronyms used in this chapter are abbreviated from the original French terms/names.

2   The protests in Senegal in March 2021 demonstrate the persistence of these problems and growing political tensions. See here: https://www.hrw.org/news/2021/03/12/senegal-respect-free-expression-assembly.

3   Here, poverty is measured from an income threshold that allows the acquisition of a basket of food worth 2,400 kilocalories per day, per adult, increased for non-food expenses.

4   Senegalese Household Survey is a nationwide survey on household consumption and expenditure. The first survey was carried out in 1994–5 (ESAM I) with a sample of 3,300 households and the second (ESAM II) in 2001–2 with 6,600 households.

5   This is the Strategic Poverty Reduction Document (DSRP II) launched in 2007. During 2011–15, the Economic and Social Policy Document (DPES), known as the third generation DSRP, had taken over. The DPES was replaced in 2012 by the National Strategy for Economic and Social Development (SNDES). The PSE was born in 2014 from the merger of the SNDES, the Accelerated Growth Strategy (SCA) and the Yoonu Yokuté Programme (the path to emergence) of President Macky Sall.

6   Former Organization of African Unity (1963–99) with headquarters in Addis Ababa (Ethiopia). The new union was born in 2002.

7   These rights are enshrined in Articles 7, 15 and 19 of Senegal's Constitution.

8   On the regulatory level, the PPP framework is split into two axes. The first axis is constituted by two laws passed by Senegal in 2004. The first law 2004–13 of 1 February 2004 aims to promote PPP financing relating to contracts for the construction-operation-transfer of infrastructure (CET Contracts Law). It was subsequently amended by laws No. 2009–21 of 4 May 2009, No. 2011–11 of 28 April 2011, No. 2014–09 of 20 February 2014 and No. 2015–03 of 12 February 2015. Then Law No. 2004–14 of 1 March 2004 on the Infrastructure Council was promulgated. In 2010, this system dedicated to CET contracts was reinforced by Decree No. 2010–489 of 13 April 2010, setting out the specific terms and conditions for awarding of CET contracts by local authorities, authorising them to formulate PPP contracts (Journal Officiel de la République du Sénégal, 2014, 2015; République du Sénégal, 2014). The second axis of the legal framework concerns Law No. 2006–16 of 30 June 2006, amending Law No. 65–61 of 19 July 1965 on the Code of Obligations of the Administration which governs public contracts and public service delegations. The latter has transposed into domestic law Directive No. 04/2005 / CM / UEMOA on Procedures for the Award, Execution and Settlement of Public Contracts and Public Service Delegations in the UEMOA and Directive

No. 05/2005 / CM / UEMOA on the Control and Regulation of Public
Contracts and Public Service Delegations in UEMOA.

9   SDE challenged the award of the contract to SUEZ in the Supreme Court,
asserting it had made the lowest bid.

10   Eiffage is a French concession and construction group.

11   'Le pays où les autoroutes sont les plus chères au monde', *Seneplus*, opinions, by
Mamadou Oumar Ndiaye, 28 May 2018. Available at: https://www.seneplus.
com/opinions/le-pays-ou-les-autoroutes-sont-les-plus-cheres-au-monde.

References

ANSD (Agence Nationale de la Statistique et de la Démographie) (1994),
'Enquête sénégalaise auprès des ménages'.

ANSD (Agence Nationale de la Statistique et de la Démographie) (2001),
'Enquête sénégalaise auprès des ménages'.

ANSD (Agence Nationale de la Statistique et de la Démographie) (2013),
'Deuxième enquête de suivi de la pauvreté au Sénégal (ESPS-II 2011)'.

ANSD (Agence Nationale de la Statistique et de la Démographie) (2017a),
'Rapport global du recensement général des entreprises 2016'.

ANSD (Agence Nationale de la Statistique et de la Démographie) (2017b),
'Enquête nationale sur l'emploi au Sénégal deuxième trimestre'.

ANSD (Agence nationale de la statistique et de la démographie) (2019),
'Violences basées sur le genre et pouvoir d'action des femmes', Publication
réalisée dans ce cadre du partenariat entre ONU FEMMES et l'ANSD pour
la mise en œuvre du Projet (*Publication produced in partnership with UN
Women and ANSD as part of the project 'Support on Gender Statistics'*).
Available at: https://www.ansd.sn/ressources/publications/Rapport-VBG_
ANSD-2019.pdf (accessed 15 February 2020).

Campagnac, E., and G. Deffontaines (2012), 'Une analyse socio-économique
critique des PPP', *Revue d'économie industrielle*, 140: 45–79. Available at:
https://journals.openedition.org/rei/5474 (accessed 15 February 2020).

Diagne, A. (2006), 'Politiques commerciales, intégration régionale et
distribution des revenus au Sénégal', *Mondes en développement*, 3
(135): 101–29. Available at: https://www.cairn.info/revue-mondes-en-
developpement-2006-3-page-101.htm (accessed 15 February 2020).

Eiffage (2017), 'L'Observatoire'. Available at: https://www.autoroutedelavenir.sn/
fr/lobservatoire (accessed 15 February 2020).

Faye, O. A. (2018), 'Baisse des tarifs de l'autoroute à péage'. Available at: http://
reussirbusiness.com/actualites/baisse-des-tarifs-de-lautoroute-a-peage
(accessed 15 February 2020).

Genre, V. (2016), 'Les nouveaux visages du financement du développement en
Afrique Subsaharienne: risques et opportunités', *Techniques financières et
développement*, 123 (2): 15–25.

Gouvernement de la République du Sénégal (2017), 'Unité PPP-Partenariats Public-Privé'. Available at: https://www.sec.gouv.sn/unit%C3%A9-ppp-partenariats-public-priv%C3%A9 (accessed 15 February 2020).

Journal officiel de la République du Sénégal, 1 mars 2004.

Journal officiel de la République du Sénégal, 25 mars 2014.

Journal officiel de la République du Sénégal, 19 février 2015.

Ministère de l'Économie et des finances (2014), 'Plan d'actions prioritaires 2014–2018'.

Ministère de l'Économie et des finances (2019), 'Plan d'actions prioritaires 2019–2023'.

Ministère de la Femme, de la famille et de l'enfance (2015), Stratégie nationale pour l'équité et l'égalité de genre (2016–2026).

Rodríguez Enríquez, C. (2019), 'Corporate Accountability and Women's Human Rights: An Analytical Approach to Public-Private Partnerships (PPPs)', DAWN. Available at: https://dawnnet.org/wp-content/uploads/2021/04/DAWN-Discussion-Paper-31_-PPPs-analytical-framework.pdf (accessed 15 February 2020).

Rodríguez Enríquez, C. (2017), 'Corporate Power: A Risky Threat Looming over the Fulfilment of Women's Human Rights', in: *Civil Society Reflection Group on the 2030 Agenda for Sustainable Development. Spotlight on Sustainable Development 2017. Reclaiming Policies for the Public*. Berlin, FES. Available at: https://www.socialwatch.org/node/17687 (accessed 15 February 2020).

Romero, M. J. (2015), 'What Lies Beneath? A Critical Assessment of PPPs and Their Impact on Sustainable Development', *European Network on Debt and Development*. Available at: https://www.eurodad.org/what_lies_beneath (accessed 15 February 2020).

Saware, A. (2019), *L'encadrement des partenariats public-privé par la régulation et les unités de PPP en Afrique: le cas de l'Union économique et monétaire ouest-africaine (UEMOA)*, Paris, France: Édilivre.

UNDP (2019), 'Human Development Report'. Available at: http://hdr.undp.org/sites/default/files/hdr2019.pdf (accessed 15 February 2020).

World Bank (2018), 'Vue d'ensemble, 2018'. Available at: https://www.banquemondiale.org/fr/country/senegal/overview (accessed 15 February 2020).

World Bank (2019), 'Base de données, 2019'. Available at: https://data.worldbank.org/country/senegal (accessed 15 February 2020).

Opaque practices and substandard health service delivery: The case of La Red Asistencial Sabogal de EsSalud in Peru

Bethsabé Andía Pérez

Introduction

In 2008, the Peruvian government entered into a public-private partnership (PPP) to design, build, operate and maintain the New Alberto Barton Hospital III at Callao and its primary care centre, the Alberto Leonardo Barton Thompson Polyclinic. The hospital and the polyclinic would be part of the La Red Asistencial Sabogal de EsSalud (Sabogal Healthcare Network of EsSalud),[1] increasing the number of health service provider institutions (IPRESS) under the network, which offers different levels of care. EsSalud is the equivalent of Peru's social security programme, while the Red Asistencial is the decentralised body that represents the social health insurance programme in an assigned geographical area, and is tasked with providing comprehensive health services to the insured population in that area by coordinating the operations of the various IPRESSs.

This chapter analyses the Alberto Barton PPP through an intersectional feminist lens. It demonstrates that the contract is marked by weak quality indicators and standards, vague follow-up mechanisms and a lack of transparency. Besides, the addenda to the contract bear serious indications of corruption. These factors are detrimental to EsSalud and negatively impact the quality of health services provided to all users, and to women in particular. As the majority of the healthcare workforce, women are also at the receiving end of the Barton PPP's failure to uphold labour standards. The PPP was initiated amid an already precarious health sector in Peru[2] that jeopardises the health rights of women, making such an analysis critical.

The first part of the chapter reviews the backdrop, and the policy and legal framework for PPPs in Peru, especially with regards to the health sector. The second part focuses on the characteristics of the Barton PPP, its implementation and its impact on the human rights of women. Finally, the chapter analyses the resistance mounted in response to the PPP.

Background and policy framework for PPPs

Latin American countries adopted a market-based economic system in the early 1990s, implementing macroeconomic stabilisation programmes and structural reforms. These measures were aimed at generating conditions for sustained economic growth based on private investment and reintegration of the countries of the region into the international financial market. In Peru, these measures were implemented by the Alberto Fujimori government (1990–2000). The stabilisation programme, introduced in August 1990, was followed by structural reforms in March 1991 which lifted restrictions on foreign investments, opened the economy up to international trade, deregulated markets and privatised public enterprises.

Privatisation 'was conceived as a tool through which the state would transfer the productive and entrepreneurial initiative to the private sector' and supposedly achieve greater efficiency in the allocation of resources and the production of goods and services (Ruiz Caro, 2002: 10). The new Constitution of Peru, adopted in 1993, allowed the state a subsidiary role, meaning it would 'only carry out subsidiary business activity, directly or indirectly, when authorised by express law for reasons of high public interest or of manifest national convenience' (Article 60). In effect, privatisation led to the withdrawal of the state from important productive sectors and its reduced participation in others. The creation of various instruments, such as law contracts, allowed the state to establish guarantees and provide security for investors, thereby facilitating private investments.

A decade after privatisation was set in motion, it became clear that 'some [state-owned entities] were sold at undervalued prices, that in certain cases privatisation was not justified, that it was poorly conceived and that the resources obtained from their sale were not used properly' (Ruiz Caro, 2002: 9). Besides, the principle of efficiency that was used to justify privatisation had not been achieved in most sectors (Ruiz Caro, 2002). However, successive governments continued with the policy – with a particular emphasis on investments linked to the concession of infrastructure works and public services – and perfected the legal instruments to facilitate its implementation.

One of Peru's main public policy instruments, the National Policy for the Promotion of Private Investment in PPPs and Asset Projects, formulated at the end of Ollanta Humala's administration (2011–16), promotes private sector participation in public infrastructure in order to improve the scope and quality of public services, energise the national economy, generate productive employment and, thereby, achieve a competitive economy (MEF, 2016).

Similarly, policy guidelines set out in the Multi-year Macroeconomic Framework (MMF) 2020–3,[3] aim to achieve sustained economic growth by boosting investment, competitiveness and productivity (MEF, 2019a). The National Infrastructure Plan for Competitiveness (PNIC), one of the pillars of the MMF, prioritises fifty-two infrastructure projects worth 30,060 million US dollars (USD) and proposes to make 66 per cent of this investment through the PPP modality (MEF, 2019c).

In addition, rules have been approved to improve the regulatory framework for PPPs and tax works, and monitoring committees have been set up to ensure the implementation of large investment projects. The Private Investment Promotion Agency (PROINVERSION) has been implementing measures to encourage private investment, such as legal stability agreements, tax refunds and early recovery of General Sales Tax (GST) (MEF, 2019a).

PPPs in the health sector

Health reforms in Peru started in the 1990s with the formulation of the Health Policy Guidelines 1995–2000 (PAHO, 2002), which mandated basic health services to be guaranteed by the state as a 'social responsibility' and jointly undertaken by the public and private sectors (MINSA, 1998: 31). The policy thus reoriented the state-civil society relationship towards one of complementarity, spurring competition between state health services, social security and private health services. It emphasised 'pluralism and competitiveness, removing anachronistic regulations that reduce the productive potential of the sector and building new financing, management and service provision models to achieve equity, efficiency and quality' (MINSA, 1998: 43). The reform process was managed by Peru's Ministry of Health (MINSA) and 'supported by the IDB [Inter-American Development Bank], the World Bank, the Public Treasury and international technical cooperation' (PAHO, 2002: 5).

Two laws established the legal framework for the health sector in 1997. The General Health Law (Law 26842) made the state responsible for the provision of public health services and the promotion of universal and progressive health insurance. The Law for the Modernization of Social Security in Health (Law 26790) introduced new forms of care for the beneficiaries of social security through the participation of private providers. Under the second law, 'Health Care Provider Institutions [EPS] are understood to be public or private companies and institutions, other than the IPSS[4] whose sole purpose is to provide health care services, with their own infrastructure and that of third parties (Article 13).' This law also granted employers who provide health coverage to their active workers, either through their own services or through health plans or programmes contracted with the EPS, a credit with respect to their contributions.

Other strategies for private sector participation in healthcare included outsourcing and intermediation of services, and hiring private health service providers under the Framework Law on Universal Health Insurance (Law 29344, 2009). In this context, PPPs have been used as a mechanism to expand service coverage. Currently, there are four PPP projects in operation in the health sector, three managed by EsSalud and one by the health ministry (see Annex 1, Table 4.7).

Legal and regulatory framework for PPPs

Up until 2008, the regulatory framework put in place during the Fujimori administration also served as the legal framework for PPPs. Thereafter, Peru adopted the Decreto Legislativo (D.L.) 1012 which is the framework law for PPPs, specifically allowing for private sector participation in the operation of public infrastructure and the provision of public services.

D.L. 1012 classifies PPPs as self-sustaining and co-financed. Self-sustaining PPPs are those that demand a minimum or no guarantee by the state, and whose non-financial guarantees have a minimum or no probability of demanding the use of public resources. Co-financed PPPs require the granting or contracting of financial guarantees, and their non-financial guarantees have a significant probability of demanding the use of public resources (Article 4). Depending on the financing modality and origin of the initiative, PPPs are further classified into four types (see Table 4.1). Four principles – value for money, transparency, competition and adequate risk allocation – guide project development under the PPP modality (see Annex 2).

The Fifth Final Complementary Provision of D.L. 1012 states that EsSalud is empowered to promote, process and sign PPP contracts with the purpose of incorporating private investments and management in health services provided to the insured. The law was in force during the signing of the Barton PPP contract.

Subsequently, other regulations have been issued to strengthen the promotion of private investments. These include the Legislative Decree of

Table 4.1 Classification of PPPs as per Peru's Regulatory Framework.

Types of PPP Projects	
Origin State initiative/Self-financed	State initiative/Co-financed
Private initiative/Self-financed	Private initiative/Co-financed

Source: Legislative Decree No. 1012 (2008), Framework Law on Public-Private Partnerships for the Generation of Productive Employment and Establishes Regulations for Expediting the Processes of Promoting Private Investment, *Official Gazette El Peruano*, 13 May.

the Framework for the Promotion of Private Investment through Public-Private Partnerships and Projects in Assets (D.L. 1224, 2015) and its Regulations (D.S. No. 410–2015-EF), and D.L. 1362 (2018) on Public-Private Partnerships and Projects in Assets. D.L. 1362 created the National System for the Promotion of Private Investment (SNPIP), which was formed by public entities belonging to the non-financial public sector (Article 2). It included all public entities of the national, regional and local governments as well as non-financial public enterprises.

While these legislations have been perfected to increase private investments at all levels of government, they contain no mechanisms to monitor PPPs; understand whether they perform better than traditional public investment; and evaluate their impact on the environment, social rights and gender gaps. The principles attached to these laws are declaratory since there are no mechanisms to enforce them. Furthermore, exceptions are made that often weaken the implementation of these laws.

The weaknesses of the organisations charged with managing the processes and deficiencies of the regulatory framework have, in turn, made PPPs breeding grounds for corrupt practices, at great economic and political cost to society (Alarco Tosoni, 2015; Alarco Tosoni and Salazar, 2019; Baca, 2017; Benavente et al., 2017). At the same time, there are no mechanisms to incorporate the opinions of communities and people impacted by PPPs, or provisions that allow them to monitor PPP implementation. Rather, it is against their rights. The procedural rules of D.L. 1362 permit only public entities, which are title-holders of projects executed under the PPP modality, to 'initiate early on the process of identification, acquisition, clean-up, and expropriation of the lands and necessary and supportive areas for the execution of the project, as well as the release of interferences under responsibility'. They are also authorised to carry out 'relocation or resettlement that allow the release and clean-up of lands and areas for the implementation of the project' (Article 30). (For more on the role of the main actors involved in Peru's PPP projects, see Annex 3.)

Characteristics of the Barton PPP

Key objectives

The objective of the Barton PPP is to design, build, operate and maintain the New Alberto Barton Hospital III at Callao and the primary care centre of the Sabogal Healthcare Network of EsSalud. Together, these two entities are meant to provide 250,000 insured persons in that geographic area with a range of white coat services,[5] including emergency treatment, outpatient consultation, hospitalisation, obstetrics and surgical centres, and critical care units.

Implementation process

In 2008, EsSalud approved its Strategic Plan 2008–11 and Strategic Investment Plan, performed a cost-benefit analysis to decide the investment modality, and opted for a PPP.[6] However, the principle of value for money was not applied in its analysis. The projected investment of the Barton PPP was 39.9 million USD, and according to D.L. 1012 regulations (D.S. No. 146-2008-EF), the public-private comparator – the numerical expression for the value for money principle – had to be applied only to projects worth over 100,000 UIT (Tax Units) (112 million USD in 2008 terms).

When it comes to public initiatives, the state has defined the characteristics of the goods and services that can be offered by interested parties. For the Barton PPP, EsSalud used the modality of private initiative through which private proponents are requested to present proposals under a set of requirements. One consortium, BM3 SALUD, consisting of four Spanish companies – Ribera Salud S.A., Mensor Consultoría y Estrategia S.L., BM3 Obras y Servicios and Exploraciones Radiológicas Especiales ERESA – expressed interest and developed a proposal that met the technical requirements established in the Bases and Draft Contract.

The EsSalud board declared the consortium's proposal in public interest and invited third parties to submit their expressions of interest for the execution of the project along with a letter of guarantee within ninety days. Only the BM3 SALUD consortium submitted a tender and was awarded the contract by the EsSalud board on 10 February 2009.

Contract and participants

The contract was signed on 31 March 2010 between EsSalud and Callao Salud S.A.C., the company established by the BM3 SALUD consortium to execute this contract (EsSalud, 2010a).

As mentioned earlier, EsSalud is the decentralised public organisation attached to the Ministry of Labour and Employment Promotion, and tasked with providing coverage to the insured and their beneficiaries by granting benefits that correspond to the Social Security in the Health Contribution System (Law 27056, 1999). It is authorised to enter into all types of contracts and/or agreements permitted by Peruvian law, including contracts for the realisation of medium- or long-term investments and services, as established in its Strategic Investment Plan (D.S. No.025-2007-TR).

Callao Salud S.A.C., hereafter the operating company (OC),[7] is constituted by seven Spanish companies – BM3 Obras y Servicios S.A., Ribera Salud S.A., Mensor Consultoría y Estrategia S.L., IBT Health, BM3 Iberosalud S.L., Exploraciones Radiológicas Especiales S.A. and Ibérica de mantenimiento S.A. Its majority shareholder, IBT Salud, is a member of the IBT Group that specialises in the development and execution of public works, equipment projects and concessions (Callao Salud SAC, 2016).

Amendments to the contract

In February 2011, the OC requested certain amendments to the contract, which were approved by the Central Office for the Promotion and Management of Investment Contracts in April 2011. These amendments, which benefit the OC and harm EsSalud and the Peruvian state, included the transfer of ownership so as to exempt the OC from paying a temporary tax on net assets, provisions for the OC to demand reimbursement for improvements made, provisions for the OC to be recognised for general expenses and investments in the event of any termination scenario, and a reduction in the size of the land on which the work would be built without a corresponding reduction in infrastructure costs (EsSalud, 2011).

The second addendum came after EsSalud moved to terminate the contract when the OC failed to prove that it had the necessary financing to undertake the infrastructure construction mandated under the project. The contract was extended through a direct treatment process – that does not involve a public tender – and signed on 28 March 2012 (EsSalud, 2012). Once again, the OC stood to benefit from the addenda, shifting the onus of investments onto EsSalud (see Table 4.2). At no point during the formulation and implementation of the PPP were actors within and outside EsSalud (trade unions, civil society organisations, citizens) allowed to participate and critically examine the agreements.

Table 4.2 Summary of Agreements in Addendum 2 of the Barton PPP.

Commitments of the OC	Benefits that the OC receives from EsSalud	Remarks
Haemodialysis centre and 60,000 sessions per year. Outpatient care.	Updating equipment plan (implies an investment by EsSalud, every three years for Group II and every ten years for Group I).	The equipment plan was $11,449,870 in Group I and $1,375,240 in Group II. This could mean an investment greater than the services received. The objective of the PPP changes, such that EsSalud must invest to keep the PPP operational.
Diagnostic tests to be made available for the non-affiliated population once demand from the affiliated population is met.		Such conditionality means tests may eventually not be carried out. The increased use of equipment for diagnostic tests means EsSalud would have to keep updating equipment.
	Corporate purchases. The OC can outsource services.	If the OC lowers costs, quality control of services may become difficult.

Source: EsSalud (2012), 'Addendum No. 2. Asociación Público Privada Nuevo Hospital III Alberto Barton – Callao'. Available at: http://www.essalud.gob.pe/asociacion-publico-privada-contratos-vigentes (accessed 21 September 2020).

Key aspects of the contract

The terms

The contract is to be executed over thirty-two years, including two years for construction and thirty years for operation. The construction was scheduled to begin after the financial closure. As this process alone took two years, the terms were extended from 2010, when the contract was awarded, to April 2014, when operations finally started.

Payments and costs

Typically, white coat projects can be based on per capita payment or payment for services. The Barton PPP uses the per capita model. Under the project, EsSalud has assigned the healthcare of 250,000 insured persons to the OC, and allotted a per capita amount for each insured person. Regardless of the services used, the per capita amount is calculated based on an accident rate and the medical procedures to be performed (Bravo, 2013). The total income thus accruing to the OC comprises a Remuneration for Investments (RPI) and a Remuneration for Operations (RPO). This total monthly remuneration that EsSalud must pay is called Remuneration for Service (RPS). Payments to the OC by EsSalud also factors in deductions for penalties and adjustments.

Investment and operating resources

The projected referential investment for the Barton PPP in the economic proposal was 39.92 million USD, which was updated through Addendum 2 to 48.45 million USD, excluding GST. This is a 21 per cent increase over the initial proposal (EsSalud, 2018b). Consequently, the RPI rose from 6.9 million USD per year prior to Addendum 2 to 8.6 million USD.

The operating cost at the time of signing the contract was 65.8 million USD, much higher than the amount stated in an earlier study comparing the costs of hospital services. This study determined that the public sector operated at 60 million USD per year compared with the PPP operator's offer of 45 million USD per year (Bravo, 2013), making room for potential savings. In the end, however, the cost of the PPP was much higher. The higher investment and cost of operation as well as the adjustments that EsSalud had to make call into question the effectiveness of the Barton PPP.

Supervision of contracts and operations

EsSalud exercises its administrative competences by itself and/or through a third-party supervisor. The PPP Contract Execution Monitoring Office verifies the OC's compliance with project obligations on behalf of EsSalud. In turn, EsSalud must hire a supervisor responsible for carrying out legal, financial and economic audits as well as technical audits on the indicators and standards defined on the date of commencement of operations. As mentioned, there are no mechanisms for the participation of trade unions, citizens or other civil society entities in the supervision process.

EsSalud can also review initially defined standards and ratios of operation of services (for instance, the number of medical professionals available for a certain number of citizens) and adapt them to the reality of the healthcare network at any point in time. However, the contract does not indicate how often and the mechanisms through which the review will take place.

The contract itself is marked by several inconsistencies. The minimum requirements for the development of the private initiative project were defined for a Level-III hospital – which typically offers the most complex medical and surgical health services – as shown in Annex X of the contract (EsSalud, 2010b). However, the service indicators and minimum standards of care detailed in Annex 1–3 of the contract correspond to those of a Level-II hospital (EsSalud, 2010b). Such inconsistencies necessitate continuous discussions with the OC and generate inefficiencies that harm the insured (EsSalud, 2019). The permanent tension between the interests of the OC, looking to maintain or increase its profitability, and EsSalud, responsible for upholding the interests of the insured, is detrimental to the quality of health services provided.

Impact of the Barton PPP on human rights and gender equality

Economic repercussions

Higher investments and operating costs of PPPs also impact the coverage and quality of healthcare in general by reducing the possibility of investments in other health services. This is exacerbated by the costs of supervision of contracts and operations.

There are additional costs generated by corruption. In the Barton PPP, the initial bid was for the development of a Level-III hospital and a primary care centre. But, according to the newspaper *El Comercio* (2018), the audit report of EsSalud's Internal Control Body (OCI) found that the Committee for the Promotion of Infrastructure and Health Services (CPISS) approved the winning proposal 'without observing that the equipment and infrastructure plans did not consider the minimum services corresponding to a category III-1 hospital', thus failing to comply with the terms of the bid.

By allowing the Barton PPP to proceed with equipment and services corresponding to those of a Level-II hospital, EsSalud, in effect, favoured the OC since only low and medium complexity patients with lower care costs are referred to it. The unions have criticised the fact that the PPP charges 300 million soles annually[8] but only assists in cases of simple pathologies (SINAMSSOP, 2017; SINESSS, 2017).

The OCI audit report also states that the CPISS approved a modification in the cost of medicines at the request of the consortium. This, coupled with the Level-II categorisation, affected care capacities and caused Barton's haemophilia patients to be transferred to Alberto Sabogal Hospital. This generated an expense of 576,499 soles[9] which was transferred from Barton to Sabogal (El Comercio, 2018). Transfers of patients with similar complex ailments can have potentially fatal consequences.

Coverage and quality of services

Although the Barton PPP contract specifies contractual penalties, the description of penalties in the operations phase established in Annex VI of the contract *does not include non-compliance with the service indicators and minimum standards of care*. This is why four years after operations began, the Arbitration Court of the Lima Chamber of Commerce made an acknowledgement of the mechanisms for applying penalties imposed by EsSalud through awards issued on 12 July and 15 August 2018 (EsSalud, 2018a). In the same year, three internal procedures – applying hospital penalties, granting compliance to reports of supervision of hospital operation contracts and verifying penalties of hospital operation contracts – were approved and implemented to improve the management of the Barton PPP (EsSalud, 2018a).

In any case, minimum standards of care and related indicators do not guarantee better quality of service or even services at par with other EsSalud facilities. These standards and indicators have lower goals than those formulated by MINSA or EsSalud (see Table 4.3), and even these lower goals were not met by the OC (see Tables 4.4, 4.5 and 4.6). Of the thirteen quality and outcome indicators that do not meet their goals, six directly affect women's health (these are marked with an asterisk in Tables 4.5 and 4.6). The realisation of these goals is far less than proposed targets, deepening the health gaps that affect women.

Table 4.3 Remarks on the Minimum Standards and Indicators in the Barton PPP.

Type/name	Remarks
Minimum standard	
Outpatient medical consultation, 5 patients per hour	The standard of the MINSA is 3–4 according to specialty (MINSA, 2013).
User Satisfaction Indicators	
Percentage of complaints	The PPP contract limits the possibility of filing complaints by asking for evidence or verifiable information.
Quality indicators	
Percentage of patients with deferrals of first appointments for outpatient clinic and/or diagnostic and therapeutic procedures. Greater than 5 days	Protocols should be established according to the type of symptoms; in certain cases, 5 days may be too much.
Percentage of patients with deferrals of follow-on appointments for outpatient clinic and/or diagnostic and therapeutic procedures. Greater than 10 days	The MINSA (2001) standard is less than 7 days.
Percentage of patients with surgery deferrals greater than 30 days	Protocols should be established according to the type of illness; in certain cases, 30 days may be too much.
Use of protocols and clinical practice guidelines, target 90%	The use of protocols is a contractual commitment so it should have a goal of 99%.
Outcome indicators	
Early diagnosis of breast cancer and cervical cancer, goal >60%	The indicator should not be static; progressive targets should be set as MINSA (2017) does.
PAP screening coverage, target >60%	The standard for EsSalud standard (2016) is 70%; here too, progressive targets should be set.
Mammography screening coverage in women over 40, target >60%	PAHO recommends mammography screening for women aged 50–69 years, and screening in a context of rigorous research, monitoring and evaluation for women aged 40–49 (2015).
Caesarean section rate less than 38%	MINSA's (2013) standard is 20–25%.

Source: EsSalud (2010b), 'Annexes. Asociación Público Privada Nuevo Hospital III Alberto Barton – Callao'. Available at: http://www.essalud.gob.pe/asociacion-publico-privada-contratos-vigentes (accessed 21 September 2020).

Table 4.4 Satisfaction Indicators That Do Not Meet Goals in the Barton PPP.

Indicator name	Result (%)	Goal (%)
Overall user satisfaction	83.46	90
For surgical services	88.85	90
For clinical services	64.04	90
For diagnostic services	83.64	90

Source: EsSalud (2017), 'Hospital Alberto Leonardo Barton Thompson: Publicación de indicadores contractuales (July-September 2017)', Gerencia Central de Promoción y Gestión de Contratos de Inversiones. Available at: http://www.essalud.gob.pe/transparencia/pdf/publicacion/HOSPITAL_ALBERTO_LEONARDO_BARTON_THOMPSON.pdf (accessed 21 September 2020).

Table 4.5 Quality Indicators That Do Not Meet Goals in the Barton PPP.

Indicator name	Result (%)	Goal (%)
Percentage of patients with deferrals of first appointments for outpatient clinic and/or diagnostic and therapeutic procedures; greater than 5 days	27.60	<5
Percentage of patients with deferrals of follow-on appointments for outpatient clinic and/or diagnostic and therapeutic procedures; greater than 10 days	15.25	<10
Availability of medicines: dispensing indicator	95.67	>99
Percentage of patients with complicated hypertensive pregnancy disease(*)	42.03	<5

(*) Services specific to women and/or girls

Source: EsSalud (2017), 'Hospital Alberto Leonardo Barton Thompson: Publicación de indicadores contractuales (July-September 2017)', Gerencia Central de Promoción y Gestión de Contratos de Inversiones. Available at: http://www.essalud.gob.pe/transparencia/pdf/publicacion/HOSPITAL_ALBERTO_LEONARDO_BARTON_THOMPSON.pdf (accessed 21 September 2020).

Table 4.6 Outcome Indicators That Do Not Meet Goals in the Barton PPP.

Indicator name	Result (%)	Goal (%)
Early diagnosis of breast cancer (*)	33.33	>60
PAP screening coverage (*)	21.28	>60
Mammography screening coverage in women over 40 (*)	16.01	>60
Prostate cancer screening coverage	34.77	>50
Caesarean section rate (*)	41.28	<38
Immunisations – pentavalent vaccine coverage	60.27	>90
Immunisations – polio vaccine coverage	0.25	>90
Immunisation coverage for measles, mumps and rubella	88.88	>90
Prenatal control for pregnant women (*)	47.16	>90

(*) Services specific to women and/or girls

Source: EsSalud (2017), 'Hospital Alberto Leonardo Barton Thompson: Publicación de indicadores contractuales (July-September 2017)', Gerencia Central de Promoción y Gestión de Contratos de Inversiones. Available at: http://www.essalud.gob.pe/transparencia/pdf/publicacion/HOSPITAL_ALBERTO_LEONARDO_BARTON_THOMPSON.pdf (accessed 21 September 2020).

Working conditions and impact on women workers

The Barton PPP contract specifies that the OC should be subject to private sector labour regulations. However, information collected from the social networks of key informants reveals that the PPP implemented an annual compensatory role[10] that infringed on workers' right to a continuous working day and a maximum of 150 hours of work per month for technical nurses and care assistants, and did not account for overtime.

These conditions reduced workers' income, made it impossible for them to reconcile their family time with working hours, and left them with little time to obtain training or supplement their income. Since women constitute a majority of healthcare workers, work overload and poor pay contributed to a widening of the nationwide salary gap between men and women.

Implications for transparency

Although the contract and addenda to the Barton PPP can be accessed on the EsSalud website, the information that supported decision-making and the documents pertaining to the monitoring of the operations phase of the project, such as reports of the contract and operations supervisor, are not available. This means civil society has no information on the PPP's progress and cannot demand, if necessary, a termination of the contract. A lone report on contract indicators was published in 2017. In contrast, the consortium that develops a proposal deemed to be of public interest has access to a lot more information. The D.L. 1012 regulations equip the consortium with prior knowledge of the contract and the project, enabling it to override potential competition.

The continuous modifications to the legal regulations also reduce transparency. Initially, the D.L. 1012 regulations (D.S. No. 146-2008-EF) established that no addenda can be made to any contract in the first three years of project execution. Thereafter, if a proposed addendum resulted in an over 15 per cent increase in the total cost of the PPP project, the concerned government entity could evaluate the convenience of undertaking a new selection process (Article 9). However, this article was modified by D.S. No. 144-2009-EF which established the various grounds on which addenda could be signed during the first three years. The Barton PPP took advantage of this modification, generating cost overruns for the state and creating grounds for corruption.

Resistance to health sector PPPs

For decades, social movements[11] have been resisting the privatisation of public services in general and denouncing the various strategies for the privatisation of social health insurance (EsSalud) in particular. They have argued that PPPs and other modes of outsourcing services are, effectively, ways of privatising the health sector in addition to being sources of corruption.

Internal resistance at Alberto Barton Hospital

When the Barton PPP began its operations, it appeared to comply with the labour rights of workers, but over time, the situation deteriorated. As one worker put it: 'This company started off very well by complying with its workers on everything. However, today everything is upside down for us, the staff. With the annual [compensatory] role, it is terrible to work in these conditions. To come in the morning and return in the evening. To work tired and stressed out from the traffic. Terrible' (Ramirez, 2018).

The OC tried to clamp down on worker agitation by stipulating labour stability as one of the conditions of signing agreements. One worker relates: '... we started with 6-hour rotating schedules and then they imposed a 9-hour schedule on us. They forced us to sign and, so far, we can't return to the schedule at the beginning of the contract' (Polo, 2018).

The United Union of Healthcare Workers Callao Salud (SUTACAS) was formed in March 2018 in response to this situation. The union demanded relief from the annual compensatory role and work overload. In both cases, workers' rights were recognised. Over time, they campaigned against anti-union practices and entered into negotiations with EsSalud and the MINSA to lend legal support to their demands.

Participation of social organisations

Unions expressed their opposition to PPPs in the health sector in various ways. In 2010, the National Medical Union of Social Security of Peru (SINAMSSOP) stated that 'EsSalud commits itself not to implement privatisation or public-private partnerships' (SINAMSSOP, 2010a). However, in the commitment act with EsSalud, it was later clarified that 'they have not reached agreements [...] regarding Public-Private Partnerships and Administrative Contracting of Services'. Stating that PPPs are the basis for the privatisation of EsSalud, the unions also demanded that D.L. 1012 be declared unconstitutional (SINAMSSOP, 2010b).

The General Confederation of Workers of Peru (CGTP) has highlighted this struggle at various platforms. In 2014, it declared: 'Defence of health and public education, increase in budget according to the National Agreement. Defence of social security [EsSalud], [...] without privatisation of its services. No to privatisations through Public-Private Partnerships'. During the national strike of 9 July 2015, the CGTP stated: 'No to privatisations or Public-Private Partnerships of strategic state enterprises and public services' (CGTP, 2015).

In its Master Plan 2013–21, EsSalud (2014) prioritises 'the use of contracting processes of private entities and public-private partnerships for new investments and for the management of health units'. In response, the Alliance for the Defence of the Right to Health and Social Security, formed by nine EsSalud unions to oppose its championing of PPPs, reaffirmed:

> ... the National Public Health System has sufficient installed capacity, in many cases idle, and the state and EsSalud have sufficient budget and

resources to promote a strong investment in repowering the hospitals, polyclinics and assistance centres [...] without the need to count on the participation of the Public Private Partnerships which in the end represent a millionaire business of resources and privileges behind the backs of the people.

(SINAMSSOP, 2014)

The Federation Workers' Union Centre of the Social Health Insurance of Peru (FED-CUT) decried the fact that the Central Manager of Health Benefits had been forced to resign for proposing to review the contracts of the Alberto Barton and Guillermo Kaelin hospital PPPs, considering them to be harmful to EsSalud (FED-CUT, 2015).

In 2015, the Doctors' National Union of EsSalud (SINAMES) published a statement rejecting the fragmented, segmented and underfunded health system that objectifies people and commodifies health. It criticised privatisation as neither equitable nor inclusive, and blamed it for deepening the health crisis.

In 2017, when the Committee for the Promotion of Private Investment of EsSalud (CPIP) was created to carry out private investment projects through PPPs, several institutions took a stand against it. The National Union of Nurses of the Social Health Insurance stated that:

Under the argument of giving coverage to the insured and their beneficiaries, the intention is to leave the health services that are paid for with the money of the insured in private hands. This modality implies a risk, as it leaves the commitment to the healthcare and quality deserved by the insured population in the hands of third parties.

(SINESSS, 2017)

The nurses' union alerted civil society to the cost incurred by EsSalud due to the Barton and Kaelin PPPs as well as the more recent Piura and Chimbote PPPs. This even as no resources are allocated to address the lack of healthcare professionals, the maintenance and acquisition of equipment, and obsolete infrastructure.

In the same year, the Peruvian Medical Association asked EsSalud to demonstrate with technical studies that PPPs are able to produce good results in the health sector, and demanded that the state place limits on the economic profits of the private sector, if such alliances are formed (Sarmiento, 2017). The social security medical union stated that 'there is no need for PPPs in the health sector, since the budget it has is sufficient to build hospitals, buy equipment and hire more doctors' (Sarmiento, 2017).

Similarly, the Civil Society Forum on Health or FOROSALUD, a national movement that centres human rights, gender and interculturality, has criticised the privatisation of health and highlighted the negative consequences of health sector PPPs on the population.

However, despite the consensus among various unions and social movements on the problems and disadvantages of PPPs in public services, Peru is yet to see a unified, solid and alternative movement opposing PPPs.

Conclusion and recommendations

Peru has undergone sustained privatisation of public services and promotion of private investments in public infrastructure projects since the 1990s. During this time, PPP legislations and their continuous modifications have left little room for competition, while the lack of transparency and the absence of mechanisms for civil society participation have led to corrupt practices.

The Barton PPP has resulted in higher costs than traditional public investments, in terms of both investment and operation costs. The increasing and inflexible annual remuneration that EsSalud will have to pay for the next thirty years is not in line with the Level-II services that the PPP provides and compromises the state's ability to invest in other health services. The quality of services and their effective supervision are also hampered by gaps in the contract. The coverage and quality of services are not guaranteed. Besides proffering weak standards and indicators in the contract, the OC has failed to meet its own quality goals and uphold workers' rights.

Given this analysis, this chapter puts forth the following recommendations:

1. Elimination of private initiative PPPs and consideration only of public initiative PPPs that are included within the framework of the National System of Strategic Planning.
2. Generation of mechanisms for the participation of civil society in different phases of projects.
3. Publication of information on indicators, minimum standards and unit costs, thereby allowing civil society to follow up on projects.
4. Generation of the following mechanisms to comply with transparency in information, thus ensuring competition:

   • The public entity's website must have documents that support decision-making with respect to contracts.

- The contract proposal must be published, inviting remarks or suggestions, before it is signed.
- Monitoring and evaluation reports of the contract supervisor must be published.

5. Ex-ante and ex-post evaluations of projects.
6. Ex-ante evaluation should include the evaluation of environmental, gender-based and cultural impacts.
7. Application prior to the consultation processes during the ex-ante evaluation, when dealing with projects that may affect communities.
8. Guarantee of the application of the value for money principle to all projects, and a methodology for applying the public-private comparator.
9. Strict regulation of renegotiations and the use of addenda for contracts, and publication of documents that support these decisions.

The chapter also makes the following recommendations regarding resistance to PPPs:

1. Joint efforts to prevent civil society voices opposing PPPs from being diluted in the face of aggressive promotion strategies by the government.
2. Strategic actions:

   - Demand that no new PPP contracts be made until a transparent evaluation has been carried out.
   - Sustained dissemination campaigns on the SNPIP and the results of PPPs.
   - Dissemination of and follow-up on reports of corruption.
   - Incorporation of all demands based on the law of transparency in information that allow for the follow-up of contracts and, if necessary, have mechanisms to request their resolution.

3. Strengthening:

   - Training programmes on the SNPIP and the PPP legislation.
   - Creation of spaces for the exchange of experiences with regard to follow-up of contracts, dissemination and advocacy campaigns.

4. Transformation of existing knowledge into intellectual capital that generates a current of opinion and strengthens the social movement resisting PPPs and privatisation, and the creation and promotion of new knowledge.

Notes

1 Funded by taxes paid by employers and calculated as a percentage of employee wages, EsSalud covers 25 per cent of the country's population (Instituto Nacional de Estadistica e Informatica, 2019).
2 Peru has a decentralised healthcare system that consists of a combination of governmental and non-governmental coverage. See https://www.who.int/ workforcealliance/countries/per/es/ (accessed 19 January 2021). See also, the official website of EsSalud at: http://portal.essalud.gob.pe.
3 The MMF, the most relevant document in economic matters, contains macroeconomic and fiscal projections, as well as the assumptions upon which they are based, for a period of four years.
4 The IPSS or Peruvian Institute of Social Security, through Law 27056, later became the Social Health Insurance, EsSalud.
5 A Peruvian term for professionals in the health sector (because the people who provide these services, mainly doctors, wear 'batas blancas' or white coats).
6 Neither the investment plans nor the cost-benefit analysis of current PPP contracts is available on the EsSalud website. See http://www.essalud.gob. pe/transparencia/index.html and http://www.essalud.gob.pe/asociacion-publico-privada-contratos-vigentes, both last accessed 21 September 2020.
7 The legal entity constituted by the successful bidder who signs the PPP contract with EsSalud.
8 Approximately 90 million USD (average bank exchange rate for the 2019 period: 3.34).
9 Approximately 173,000 USD (average bank exchange rate for the 2019 period: 3.34).
10 The annual compensatory role adds up the working hours for the entire year and distributes them arbitrarily, not taking into account the legally established daily or monthly working hours.
11 Social movement is 'a process of politicized collective action aimed at fighting against forms of accumulation and colonisation that reproduce injustice and that has an alternative vision of society and development' Bebbington (2008).

References

Alarco Tosoni, G. (2015), '¿Negocio Público Privado? Ventajas y desventajas de las asociaciones públicas privadas (APP) en América Latina'. Available at: http://www.latindadd.org/wp-content/uploads/2018/08/NEGOCIO-PUBLICO-PRIVADO-VENTAJAS-Y-DESVENTAJAS-DE-LAS-APP-EN-AMERICA-LATINA.pdf (accessed 21 September 2020).

Alarco Tosoni, G. (2017), 'Corrupción, neoliberalismo y asociaciones público privadas', *Otra Mirada*, 20 February. Available at: http://www.otramirada. pe/corrupci%C3%B3n-neoliberalismo-y-asociaciones-p%C3%BAblico-privadas (accessed 21 September 2020).

Alarco Tosoni, G., and C. Salazar (2019), *Riesgos Público-Privados: fallas regulatorias en las Asociaciones Público-Privadas y recomendaciones de política para la región desde el caso peruano*, Lima: Latindadd.

Baca, E. (2017), 'Las asociaciones público-privadas en el Perú: ¿Beneficio público o negocio privado?', August. Available at: http://propuestaciudadana. org.pe/wp-content/uploads/2017/09/Estudio-APP.pdf.

Bebbington, A., M. Scurrah and C. Bielich (2008), 'Mapeo de movimientos sociales en el Perú actual'. Available at: https://hummedia.manchester.ac.uk/ schools/seed/socialmovements/publications/reports/Bebbingtonetal_ InformeMapeodeMovimientosSocialesPeru.pdf (accessed 21 September 2020).

Benavente, P., J. Escaffi, J. Távara and J. Segura (2017), 'Las Alianzas Público-Privadas (APP) en el Perú: beneficios y riesgos', November. Available at: https://departamento.pucp.edu.pe/economia/libro/las-alianzas-publico-privadas-app-en-el-peru-beneficios-y-riesgos (accessed 21 September 2020).

Bravo, S. (2013), 'Asociaciones Público Privadas en el sector salud', *Revista de Derecho Administrativo-RDA* 13: 123–41. Available at: http://revistas.pucp. edu.pe/index.php/derechoadministrativo/article/view/13472 (accessed 21 September 2020).

Callao Salud SAC (2016), 'Quiénes somos: Memoria Corporativa 2016. Complejo Hospitalario Alberto Barton'. Available at: https://callaosalud.com. pe/presentacion/quienes-somos (accessed 21 September 2020).

CGTP (2015), 'CGTP Perú' [Facebook], 2 July. Available at: https://es-la. facebook.com/notes/cgtp-per%C3%BA/-plataforma-de-lucha-del-paro-nacional-9-de-julio-cgtp/1726275177599760/?__tn__=H-R (accessed 21 September 2020).

El Comercio (2018), 'Essalud nombra a gerentes investigados por corrupción', 19 June. Available at: https://elcomercio.pe/lima/sucesos/essalud-nombra-gerentes-investigados-corrupcion-noticia-529013-noticia (accessed 21 September 2020).

EsSalud (2010a), 'Contrato. Asociación Público Privada Nuevo Hospital III Alberto Barton – Callao'. Available at: http://www.essalud.gob.pe/asociacion-publico-privada-contratos-vigentes (accessed 21 September 2020).

EsSalud (2010b), 'Annexes. Asociación Público Privada Nuevo Hospital III Alberto Barton – Callao'. Available at: http://www.essalud.gob.pe/asociacion-publico-privada-contratos-vigentes (accessed 21 September 2020).

EsSalud (2011), 'Addendum No. 01. Asociación Público Privada Nuevo Hospital III Alberto Barton – Callao'. Available at: http://www.essalud.gob. pe/asociacion-publico-privada-contratos-vigentes (accessed 21 September 2020).

EsSalud (2012), 'Addendum No. 2. Asociación Público Privada Nuevo Hospital III Alberto Barton – Callao'. Available at: http://www.essalud.gob.pe/ asociacion-publico-privada-contratos-vigentes (accessed 21 September 2020).

EsSalud (2014), 'EsSalud presenta Plan Maestro 2013–2021'. Available at: http://www.essalud.gob.pe/essalud-presenta-plan-maestro-2013–2021 (accessed 21 September 2020).

EsSalud (2017), 'Hospital Alberto Leonardo Barton Thompson: Publicación de indicadores contractuales (July–September 2017)', Gerencia Central de Promoción y Gestión de Contratos de Inversiones. Available at: http://www.essalud.gob.pe/transparencia/pdf/publicacion/HOSPITAL_ ALBERTO_LEONARDO_BARTON_THOMPSON.pdf (accessed 21 September 2020).

EsSalud (2018a), 'Annual Report 2018'. Available at: http://www.essalud.gob.pe/ memoria-institucional (accessed 21 September 2020).

EsSalud (2018b), 'Ficha técnica del proyecto construcción del nuevo hospital III Callao'. Available at: http://www.essalud.gob.pe/transparencia/pdf/ publicacion/ficha_contrato_hospt_callao.pdf (accessed 21 September 2020).

EsSalud (2019), *Hacia la modernización de la seguridad social en el Perú. Libro blanco 2*, Lima: Social Health Insurance.

EsSalud (n.d.), 'Contracts in Force'. Available at: http://www.essalud.gob.pe/ asociacion-publico-privada-contratos-vigentes (accessed 21 September 2020).

FED-CUT (2015), 'Contratos APP son lesivos para ESSALUD y el País. Informativo 06 CDN FED CUT'. Available at: https://issuu.com/fedcut/docs/ informativo_cut_06_2015 (accessed 21 September 2020).

Instituto Nacional de Estadistica e Informatica (2019), 'Acceso a seguro de salud'. Available at: https://www.inei.gob.pe/estadisticas/indice-tematico/ access-to-health-insurance/ (accessed 2 February 2021).

Inter-American Development Bank (n.d.), 'LAC PPP Risk Management Group – LAC PPP RMG'. Available at: https://www.iadb.org/es/lacpppgroup (accessed 21 September 2020).

MEF (2016), 'Politica Nacional de Promoción de la Inversión Privada en APPP y Proyectos en Activos'. Available at https://www.mef.gob.pe/contenidos/ inv_privada/normas/Anexo_PolItica_Nacional_Promocion_Inversion_ Privada_APP_PA.pdf (accessed 21 September 2020).

MEF (2019a), 'Marco Macroeconómico Multianual 2020–2023', 23 August. Available at: https://www.mef.gob.pe/contenidos/pol_econ/marco_macro/ MMM_2020_2023.pdf (accessed 21 September 2020).

MEF (2019b), 'Organization Table'. Available at: https://www.mef.gob.pe/ contenidos/acerc_mins/doc_gestion/organigrama_2019.pdf (accessed 21 September 2020).

MEF (2019c), 'National Infrastructure Plan for Competitiveness'. Available at: https://www.mef.gob.pe/contenidos/inv_privada/planes/PNIC_2019.pdf (accessed 21 September 2020).

MEF (n.d.), 'Statistics'. Available at: https://www.mef.gob.pe/es/asociaciones-publico-privadas/estadistica (accessed 21 September 2020).

MINSA (1998), 'El desafío del cambio del milenio: Un sector salud con equidad, eficiencia y calidad. Lineamientos de política de salud 1995–2000'. Available at: https://www.gob.pe/institucion/minsa/informes-publicaciones/352755-el-desafio-del-cambio-del-milenio-un-sector-salud-con-equidad-eficiencia-y-calidad-lineamientos-de-politica-de-salud-1995-2000 (accessed 21 September 2020).

MINSA (2001), *Manual de indicadoreshospitalarios. Serie herramientas metodológicas en epidemiologia y salud pública N°004*, Lima: MINSA, General Office of Epidemiology.

MINSA (2011), 'Norma Técnica de Salud 'Categorías de Establecimientos del Sector Salud' RM No. 546-2011-MINSA'. Available at: https://www.gob.pe/institucion/minsa/normas-legales/243402-546-2011-minsa (accessed 21 September 2020).

MINSA (2013), 'Indicadores de gestión y evaluación hospitalaria, para hospitales, institutos y DIRESA. Documento de trabajo'. Available at: http://bvs.minsa.gob.pe/local/MINSA/2739.pdf (accessed 21 September 2020).

MINSA (2017), *Plan Nacional para la prevención y control de cáncer de mamas 2017–2021 (RM No. 442-2017-MINSA)*, Lima: MINSA, General Directorate of Strategic Interventions in Public Health, Directorate of Prevention and Control of Cancer.

SINAMES (2015), 'Pronouncing. Diario Uno', 22 March: 7. Available at: https://issuu.com/impresosdiariounoperu/docs/du22032015/14 (accessed 21 September 2020).

SINAMSSOP (2010a), 'Document 2010'. Available at: http://www.sinamssop.org/pliegos-y-acuerdos-anteriores (accessed 21 September 2020).

SINAMSSOP (2010b), 'Statement 008-2010'. Available at: http://www.sindicatomedicoperu.org/pdf/comunicado/C-2010/comunicado008.pdf (accessed 21 September 2020).

SINAMSSOP (2010c), 'Minutes 2010'. Available at: http://www.sinamssop.org/pliegos-y-acuerdos-anteriores (accessed 21 September 2020).

SINAMSSOP (2014), 'Press Release No. 004-2014-UG'. Available at: http://www.sinamssop.org/2014/12/nueve-sindicatos-de-essalud-constituyeron-frente-de-defensa-del-derecho-a-la-salud-y-la-seguridad-social (accessed 21 September 2020).

SINAMSSOP (2017), 'No al ofrecimiento de ESSALUD a empresas británicas APPs'. Available at: http://www.sinamssop.org/2017/04/no-al-ofrecimiento-de-essalud-a-empresas-britanicas-apps (accessed 21 September 2020).

SINESSS (2017), 'Gestión de EsSalud busca traspasar a empresas extranjeras el servicio a la salud por el que pagan millones de asegurados'. Available at: https://sinesss.org/gestion-de-essalud-busca-traspasar-a-empresas-extranjeras-el-servicio-a-la-salud-por-el-que-pagan-millones-de-asegurados (accessed 21 September 2020).

PAHO (2002), 'Análisis de las Reformas del Sector Salud en los Países de la Región Andina. 2nd. edition', July. Available at: https://www.paho.org/hq/dmdocuments/2010/Analisis_Reforma_Sector_Salud-SubRegion_Andina_2002.pdf (accessed 21 September 2020).

PAHO and WHO (2015), 'Documento de posición de la OMS sobre el tamizaje por mamografía. Resumen de recomendaciones'. Available at: https://www.paho.org/hq/dmdocuments/2015/SP-Mammography-Factsheet.pdf (accessed 21 September 2020).

Political Constitution of Peru (2016), *Eleventh Official Edition*, Lima: Ministry of Justice and Human Rights.

Polo, M. (2018), 'United Union of Healthcare Workers Callao Salud', [Facebook], 9 January. Available at: https://es-la.facebook.com/pg/Sindicato-Unido-de-Trabajadores-Asistenciales-De-Callao-Salud-163097324448932/posts/?ref=page_internal (accessed 21 September 2020).

Ramirez, D. (2018), 'United Union of Healthcare Workers Callao Salud', [Facebook], 25 January. Available at: https://es-la.facebook.com/pg/Sindicato-Unido-de-Trabajadores-Asistenciales-De-Callao-Salud-163097324448932/posts/?ref=page_internal (accessed 21 September 2020).

Ruiz Caro, A. (2002), *El proceso de privatizaciones en el Perú durante el período 1991–2002*, Santiago de Chile: ILPES, ECLAC. Available at: https://repositorio.cepal.org/handle/11362/7273 (accessed 21 September 2020).

Sarmiento, M. (2017), 'Alianzas público-privada en el sector Salud desatan cuestionamientos al Ejecutivo', lamula.pe. Available at: https://redaccion.lamula.pe/2017/07/26/alianza-publico-privado-en-el-sector-salud-desata-cuestionamientos-al-ejecutivo/lumasap (accessed 21 September 2020).

Legal regulations of Peru

Laws

Law No. 26790 (1997). Law of Modernization of the Social Security in Health, *Official Gazette El Peruano*, 15 May.

Law No. 26842 (1977). General Health Law, *Official Gazette El Peruano*, 15 July.

Law No. 27056 (1999). Law for the Creation of the Social Health Insurance (ESSALUD), *Official Gazette El Peruano*, 29 January.

Law No. 28424 (2004). Temporary Tax on Net Assets, *Official Gazette El Peruano*, 21 December.

Law No. 29344 (2009). Framework Law for Universal Health Insurance, *Official Gazette El Peruano*, 9 April.

Legislative decrees

Legislative Decree No. 1012 (2008). Framework Law on Public-Private Partnerships for the Generation of Productive Employment and Establishes Regulations for Expediting the Processes of Promoting Private Investment, *Official Gazette El Peruano*, 13 May.

Legislative Decree No. 1224 (2015). Framework for the Promotion of Private Investment through Public-Private Partnerships and Projects in Assets, *Official Gazette El Peruano*, 25 September.

Legislative Decree No. 1362 (2018). Regulates the Promotion of Private Investment through Public-Private Partnerships and Projects in Assets, *Official Gazette El Peruano*, 21 July.

Supreme decrees

Supreme Decree No. 025-2007-TR (2007). It Establishes Provisions Related to Social Security in Health and Social Health Insurance, *Official Gazette El Peruano*, 20 December.

Supreme Decree No. 146-2008-EF (2008). Regulations of the D.L. 1012 That Approves the PPP Framework Law, *Official Gazette El Peruano*, 8 December.

Supreme Decree No. 144-2009-EF (2009). They modify Art.9 of the D.S. No. 146-2008-EF. (Regulations of DL 1012), *Official Gazette El Peruano*, 24 June.

Supreme Decree No. 410-2015-EF (2015). They Approve Regulations of the Legislative Decree No. 1224 Framework Law for the Promotion of Private Investment through Public-Private Partnerships and Projects in Assets, *Official Gazette El Peruano*, 27 December.

Supreme Decree No. 240-2018-EF (2018). Regulation of Legislative Decree No. 1362, Which Regulates the Promotion of Private Investment through PPPs and Projects in Assets, *Official Gazette El Peruano*, 30 October.

Appendix

Annex 1: Table 4.7 PPP Projects in Peru's Health Sector as of 2020.

In charge of management	Name	Type of project	Scope	Year of assignment	Duration of contract #
EsSalud	Callao Hospital and Sabogal Network	Private initiative/ Self-financed	Design, construction, medical equipment and comprehensive care for the assigned population.	2010/2014	30 years of operation + 2 years of construction
EsSalud	H. V. M. T and Rebagliati Network	Private initiative/ Self-financed	Design, construction, medical equipment and comprehensive care for the assigned population.	2010/2014	30 years of operation + 2 years of construction
EsSalud	Network of stores and pharmacies	Private initiative/ Self-financed	Construction of stores, remodelling of hospital warehouses, logistics management of medicines and supplies.	2009/2012	10 years of operation + 3 months for launch
MINSA	Management of the National Children's Institute – San Borja	State initiative/ Co-financed	Maintenance of the building, facilities. Clinical and non-clinical equipment. Operation and maintenance of general services and diagnostic support services. Acquisition of technical assistance service.	July 2014/ Oct 2014	10 years operation + 3 months launch + 15 days to check inventory

Source: Compiled by author with data from EsSalud and MINSA.

Annex 2: PPP Implementing Principles in Peru

Principles under which projects should be developed under the PPP modality:

1. Value for money: A public service should be provided by a private entity that can offer higher quality results at a certain cost or the same quality at a lower cost;
2. Transparency: All quantitative and qualitative information used for decision-making during the evaluation, development, implementation and accountability stages of a project must be made known to the public under the principle of publicity established in Article 3 of the Consolidated Text of the Law on Transparency and Access to Public Information (D.S. No. 043-2003-PCM);
3. Competition: Competition must be fostered and promoted in order to ensure efficiency and lower costs in the provision of infrastructure and public services and to avoid any anti-competitive and/or collusive act; and
4. Adequate risk allocation: There must be an adequate distribution of risks between the public and the private sectors.

Annex 3: Main Actors Involved in Peru's PPP Projects

The main actors in any PPP project are: (1) the state, (2) private enterprises, (3) international organisations and (4) civil society.

1. The state regulates and promotes private investment through PPPs and projects in assets and has generated an institutional framework that cuts across all public entities at all levels of government. The SNPIP is presided over by the MEF which establishes the policy for the promotion of private investment. Its governing body is the General Directorate of Private Investment Promotion Policy, which establishes guidelines and issues binding opinion. In turn, PROINVERSION, as an attached entity, aims to promote private investment through PPPs, projects in assets and 'tax works' for their incorporation in public services, public infrastructure, in assets, projects and state enterprises.

Table 4.8 National System for Private Investment Promotion in Peru.

Central	Ministry of Economy and Finance;	
	The Private Investment Promotion Agency – PROINVERSION;	
	Special Committees.	Other public entities authorised by law.
	The Ministries;	
	Private Investment Promotion Committee-CPIP;	Private Investment Promotion Committee-CPIP.
	Specialised body for project management>300,000 UIT.	
	The Regulatory Agencies.	Specialised body for project management>300,000 UIT*.
	The Comptroller General of the Republic, without prejudice to its autonomy and legal powers	
Regional	Regional Government;	
	Private Investment Promotion Committee-CPIP;	
	Specialised body for project management>300,000 UIT.	
Local	Local Government;	
	Private Investment Promotion Committee-CPIP;	
	Specialised body for project management>300,000 UIT.	

Source: (*) UIT 2020 approx 1,265 USD. Based on the D.L. No. 1362, 2018; D.S. No. 240-2018-EF.

2. Private companies either participate directly in the bidding process or propose projects. The latter process has been marked by corruption. Through business associations, private companies influence the state to formulate policies that favour private investment in PPPs. The National Confederation of Private Business Institutions (CONFIEP) guides investments into particular sectors according to their interests. This has led to the concentration of PPPs in transportation, energy and communications sectors (see Figures 4.1 and 4.2).

3. International organisations like the World Bank (WB), International Monetary Fund (IMF), United States Agency for International Development (USAID) and Inter-American Development Bank (IDB) promote and provide theoretical, technical and financial support to PPPs.

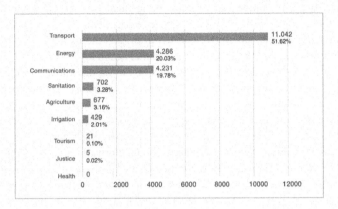

Adapted from MEF's Statistics (n.d.)

Figure 4.1 Sector-wise distribution of PPP investments (million USD) in Peru.

Source: Adapted from MEF statistics (n.d.).

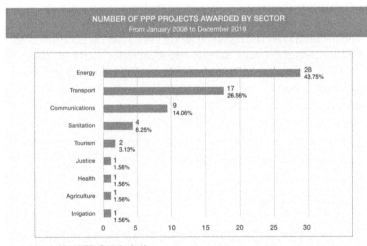

Adapted from MEF's Statistics (n.d.)

Figure 4.2 Number of PPPs in Peru, organised by sector.

Source: Adapted from MEF statistics (n.d.).

In a 1993 report, the WB proposes a three-pronged approach to improve health conditions in developing countries by promoting growth policies, directing public spending on health to low-cost and high-efficiency programmes, and facilitating greater diversity and competition in the financing and provision of health services. The Bank weighed in on EsSalud's Master Plan 2013–21 which prioritises the use of PPPs both for new investments and for the management of health units (EsSalud, 2014).

The IDB considers the benefits of PPPs to be dependent on adequate distribution and management of associated risks. It thus promotes the development of the institutional capacities of governments for the evaluation and management of these risks (IDB, n.d.). Peru is part of the PPP Risk Management Group dedicated to generating a space for exchange and cooperation among specialists in public-private financing. The IDB also promotes and finances the structuring of projects. Under its regional advisory programme, EsSalud has received an allocation for PPP investments to develop a project in the city of Piura (EsSalud, 2019).

In 2014, Peru signed up to the OECD's Country Programme meant to support emerging economies in designing reforms and strengthening public policies. Thereafter, a set of projects were carried out over two years (2015–16) to support Peru in its reform agenda and improve its public policies in key priority areas.

4. Civil society is represented, in part, by academic sectors such as universities and research centres which provide analyses and evidence on the advantages and disadvantages of PPPs as well as information on related corruption cases. Another important sector of civil society is made up of social movements that challenge PPPs and the privatisation of public services.

Part Three

Impact of PPPs on human rights: Building resistances at national level

PPPs in the Isthmus of Tehuantepec Corridor: Megaprojects, opacity and women's resistance

Isabel Clavijo Flórez and Julieta Lamberti

Introduction

In 2019, President Andrés Manuel López Obrador's government in Mexico proposed the Interoceanic Corridor of the Isthmus of Tehuantepec megaproject that has since emerged as a grave threat to communities, territories and ecosystems in the region. The Isthmus of Tehuantepec connects the territories of Oaxaca and Veracruz, and is of historical, geopolitical and economic interest. At its narrowest point, the Isthmus separates the Pacific and Atlantic oceans by barely 200 kilometres. These territories are home to indigenous and peasant populations, and form an ecosystem of great relevance due to their biodiversity and hydrology.

Prevailing development models have considered the Isthmus not as a biological corridor but, rather, as a commercial one, particularly for the energy and hydrocarbon sector. Since the 1970s, the Tehuantepec Isthmus has been configured to emulate the Panama Canal.

This study takes up the most recent interest in this territory, namely, the government's Development Programme for the Isthmus of Tehuantepec whose 'nodal axis' is the Interoceanic Multimodal Corridor. The programme consists of a series of projects, including the renovation of the Isthmus of Tehuantepec Railway, the development of the Jáltipan Salina Cruz gas pipeline and the creation of 'free trade zones'. It aims to identify specific areas in which to set up these projects and attract national and foreign investments under the public-private partnership (PPP) framework.

The programme has met with community resistance as indigenous people assert their right to decide which parts of the territory are to be included and what activities are to be carried out under these projects. Their main concerns include potential negative impacts on the environment and the local economy, and a further consolidation of extractive energy projects that have already harmed the soil, water and wildlife in the region. Women have been central to this struggle, highlighting the repercussions, strengthening organisational processes and developing proposals for the collective well-being of the region.

The chapter begins by explaining the trajectory of PPPs in Mexico and analysing the meaning and prior context of 'free trade zones'. It then reviews the two PPP projects in the Interoceanic Multimodal Corridor, the main actors involved and the community resistance against these projects. Finally, it uses a feminist lens to study the impact of these projects on the territories in question. This research seeks to contribute to the work of the female social leaders in Veracruz and Oaxaca, as well as community organisations currently engaged in a struggle to reclaim territorial autonomy, defend the environment and fight for a notion of well-being that rejects the prevailing development model.

Introduction of PPPs in Mexico

The 1990s saw a surge in PPPs in Latin America in the backdrop of economic liberalisation and privatisation. In the neoliberal worldview, development policies aimed at accelerating economic growth are hindered by the state's regulatory framework, or, as the World Bank puts it, by 'the limitations of public provision' such as the 'lack of technical skills, slow procurement processes and budget constraints' (Michelitsch and Szwedzki, 2017). The proposed solution is to combine public and private capital in the form of PPPs to stimulate growth and introduce efficiency and sustainability in the supply of public goods and services (World Bank, 2017).

The Deferred Infrastructure Projects in the Expenditure Register (PIDIREGAS) was the first PPP model in Mexico. It was created after the 1995 reform of the Budget, Accounting and Public Expenditure Law, as well as through reforms of the General Law on Public Debt and the Federal Law of Budget and Fiscal Responsibility. Under a build, lease, transfer (BLT) model, private companies undertook the execution of the works on behalf of public entities and the state committed to buying the goods and services built (PIAPPEM, n.d.). Many infrastructure projects, including those with prominent participation from the Federal Electricity Commission (CFE) and Petróleos Mexicanos (PEMEX), as well as numerous road projects were implemented under this scheme.

In 2002, Mexico introduced the Projects for the Provision of Services (PPS) scheme intended to increase 'the amount of public resources allocated to other priority areas of social impact' (PIAPPEM, n.d.: 4). Here, private capital was used not just for the construction of roads and infrastructure, but also for health, education, water, security, culture and sports.

In 2012, the Public-Private Partnerships Law unified under a single framework all the regulations that, up until then, were applied through a set of different norms. It provided a broad definition of PPPs and allowed for the involvement of the private sector in meeting social welfare objectives (Chamber of Deputies, 2012). Between 2010 and 2017, almost all states – barring Tlaxcala and Zacatecas – and sub-national[1] entities formulated their own legislations to regulate PPP contracts.

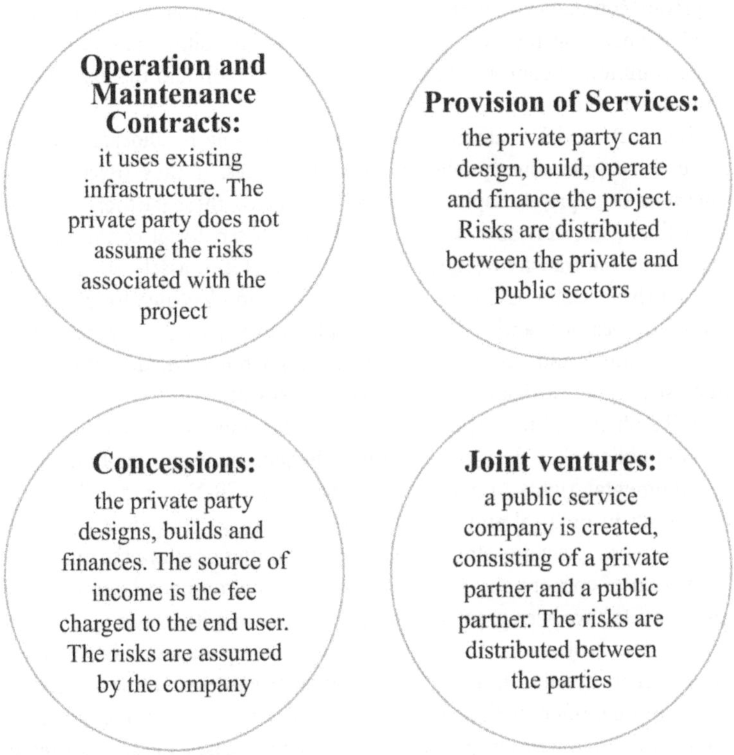

Operation and Maintenance Contracts:
it uses existing infrastructure. The private party does not assume the risks associated with the project

Provision of Services:
the private party can design, build, operate and finance the project. Risks are distributed between the private and public sectors

Concessions:
the private party designs, builds and finances. The source of income is the fee charged to the end user. The risks are assumed by the company

Joint ventures:
a public service company is created, consisting of a private partner and a public partner. The risks are distributed between the parties

Figure 5.1 PPP modalities in Mexico.

Source: Based on information from the Centre for Public Finance Studies. See CEFP (2016), 'Las Asociaciones Público Privadas como Alternativa de Financiamiento para las Entidades Federativas', Chamber of Deputies, June. Available at: https://www.cefp.gob.mx/publicaciones/documento/2016/junio/eecefp0032016.pdf (accessed 1 May 2020).

Most PPPs were undertaken as concessions or PPS (CEFP, 2016). Concessions transfer the responsibility for a productive asset from the public sector to a private company for a period of over ten years (CEFP, 2016), while PPSs are technical-economic actions performed by the private actor to attend to what were originally the state's responsibilities (Government of Jalisco, 2008). PPSs may or may not involve a pre-existing public asset. They 'emerge when a private investor or the government identifies an opportunity, but they do not necessarily respond to fully identified urgent needs' (CEFP, 2007: 12). A key concern with PPSs is that the profit margin required by the private sector is much higher than that of the public sector, thus raising project costs and draining public finances. These long-duration contracts may also be subject to changes in investment strategies and internal reorganisations of private companies as well as their board of directors and owners (CEFP, 2007). Concession and PPSs share similar modalities, although the former is more common in contracts relating to the exploration and the exploitation of natural resources.

The PPP model assumes that the state is unable to allocate adequate resources to guarantee public goods and services. It thus welcomes the intervention of private capital. However, in Mexico, these partnerships have been financially unviable and often resulted in territorial conflicts. PPPs depend on the transfer of rights to public resources or assets, such as land, to the private sector. Conflicts arise when the land identified for projects is owned by peasants and indigenous people, and is part of an autonomous social, cultural and economic space that does not coincide with private interests, triggering dispossession and displacement.

PPPs often lead to corporate capture of the state as the economic elite makes public policy decisions for private benefit, undermining human and environmental rights and common welfare (ESCR-Net, n.d.). They can also result in political and legislative interference as companies pressurise legislatures to 'provide better business opportunities or eliminate or weaken regulation of corporate activities'.[2] In Mexico, environmental authorisation and permits have been granted despite potentially negative consequences for ecosystems. Projects have been authorised to companies that have already caused environmental disasters.[3] Environmental legislation allows companies to determine, often at their own discretion, the mitigation measures and compensation to be awarded for damages. In many cases, these measures are lax, non-existent or unfeasible.[4]

Currently, Mexico is part of the United Nations' 2030 Agenda for Sustainable Development and has formed the National Council that implements it (Consejo Nacional de la Agenda 2030). This agenda has promoted the implementation of PPPs in Latin America, deeming them valid strategies to achieve sustainable development and eradicate poverty.

Isthmus Corridor: A 'historic PPP'

The Isthmus Corridor was officially announced by the Ministry of Finance and Public Credit (SHCP) with the launch of a Development Programme for the Isthmus of Tehuantepec on 17 June 2019.[5] The programme seeks to promote a new model of development; reduce the stagnation caused by the lack of investments; generate jobs; and preserve, restore and increase natural resources and biodiversity (SHCP, 2019). The multimodal and decentralised public body, the Interoceanic Corridor of the Isthmus of Tehuantepec, operates the programme by means of public and private investments (SEGOB, 2019b). This entity has the capacity to enact laws considered necessary to 'promote the region's productive capacity and modernize the physical infrastructure' (SEGOB, 2019b).

The Corridor is an interesting example of how PPPs work. The government justified the project by claiming that it would bring social welfare to a region with high poverty rates. It is composed of several long-term projects (see Table 5.1) that use existing public infrastructures, including the Isthmus railway operated by the state-owned majority holding company, Ferrocarril del Istmo de Tehuantepec S.A de C.V. or FIT (SCT, n.d.), and the Jáltipan-Salina Cruz gas pipeline administered by the National Natural Gas Control Centre or CENAGAS (SHCP and BANOBRAS, n.d.). The railway project has been tendered to six private companies, some of which are in a consortium, and the gas pipeline is in the process of being awarded under the concession

Table 5.1 Projects under the Isthmus of Tehuantepec Development Programme.

Constituting Projects
Construction of a new container terminal in the port of Coatzacoalcos and Salina Cruz. Modernisation of the oil port and construction of an industrial port in Salina Cruz
Rehabilitation of the Isthmus Railway
Construction of the Palomares-Matías Romero trans-Isthmus-trunk extension circuit
Establishment of 6 Welfare Development Areas in the municipalities of Acayucan, Minantitlán, Matías Romero, Ciudad Ixtepec, Coatzacoalcos and Salina Cruz
Construction, operation and maintenance of the Jáltipan-Salina Cruz gas pipeline
Development of wind power plants for electricity generation in the region of Ixtepec in Oaxaca
Maintenance and rehabilitation of the Minantitlán and Salina Cruz refineries

Source: Data from the SHCP and the National Bank of Public Works and Services, Banobras. See (SHCP, 2019), 'Programa para el Desarrollo del Istmo de Tehuantepec', *Conferencia Binacional de Infraestructura.* Available at: https://www.gob.mx/programaistmo/articulos/programa-para-el-desarrollo-del-istmo-de-tehuantepec (accessed 1 May 2020).

scheme. In both cases, private companies will build, maintain and operate these services. In addition, ten industrial parks of 500–1,000 hectares each will be built as part of the project (López Obrador, 2020)

Megaprojects in the multimodal corridor

From special economic zones to free trade zones

The Special Economic Zones (SEZ) Bill (Gaceta Parlamentaria No. 4372-VIII, 2015) was approved and introduced as federal law on 1 June 2016. Thereafter, the Federal Authority for the Development of Special Economic Zones and the Regulation of the Federal Law of Special Economic Zones were created on 30 June.[6]

In its 2013 energy reforms, Mexico committed to safeguarding the private sector by aligning the objectives of national planning with the interests of the sector.[7] The SEZs were part of the package that sustained this government policy. In 2019, however, the current government abolished the decrees creating these economic zones, arguing that none of them had been able to start operations and it was necessary to rethink the conditions that were conducive to development under a policy of austerity and rationality. This left the operation of the SEZS without legal viability (SEGOB, 2019a). Of the original seven SEZs, only two projects – Salina Cruz located in the state of Oaxaca and Coatzacoalcos in the state of Veracruz – remained in place and became part of the Interoceanic Corridor of the Isthmus of Tehuantepec megaproject.

In 2018, Rafael Marín Mollinedo, appointed as the head of the Tehuantepec Isthmus Development Programme, announced the creation of a free trade zone throughout the Isthmus (AFDZEE, 2018d). The format of free trade zones had been decreed in 1981 specifically for the border regions (SEGOB, 1981) and was similar to that of special economic zones. Both the free trade zones and the special economic zones (re)arrange the territory based on a notion of development anchored in economic growth and supported by foreign investments. In both formats, the state guarantees entrepreneurs incentives such as freedom from taxes and tariffs, tax benefits and infrastructure, labour flexibility, and legal security for acquisition and purchase of land.[8] Companies operating in free trade zones enjoy a 30 per cent reduction in income tax, a 16 per cent decrease in value added tax (VAT) and lower fuel prices (SHCP, 2019). The Isthmus Corridor works as a free trade zone that guarantees private actors the support of state and municipal governments, a regulatory improvement that implies procedural diligence in processing applications for concessions, PPSs and legal certainty for investments.

However, free trade zones are not backed by any regulatory framework. Till date, no separate decree has been published for the Isthmus free trade zone. Only the decree creating the Corridor and its statutes have been made public (Corredor Interoceánico del Istmo de Tehuantepec, 2020). Financial and contract information has been published sporadically. Given the lack of operational guidelines, the configuration of the free trade zone in the Isthmus is subject to decisions taken by the Corridor on the general development of the project. This makes it difficult for communities and citizens to obtain clear information and exercise control over the operation of the zone, and leads to ambiguities in the enforcement of agrarian and fiscal environmental regulations. Companies leverage these regulatory gaps to ensure the success of their investments.

Isthmus of Tehuantepec Railway

This project consists of the rehabilitation of the 206-kilometre railway line between Veracruz and Oaxaca. To date, six contracts – to be carried out under the PPS scheme – are known to have been granted for the rehabilitation of 146.3 kilometres of railway line from the entrance of Salina Cruz to the junction of Medias Aguas (FIT, 2020). Table 5.2 shows the main beneficiaries.

There are two Spanish companies with contracts in their name. Although the Hermes S.A de C.V Group is to be in charge of the Ubero-Mogoñe route, the beneficiaries of this contract include a Spanish company, Caltia, which belongs to the Copasa Group, with headquarters in Galicia, whose president and majority shareholder is José Luis Suárez Gutiérrez (COPASA, 2019). This group was in charge of the expansion of the Veracruz port, a project considered to be strategic for the movement of oil products in the region (COPASA, 2016). The port project was challenged by the inhabitants of Veracruz in 2017 for not taking into account its cumulative environmental impact and ignoring the existence of a coral reef in the area (CEMDA, 2017).

The SACMAG Group was charged with the supervision of the work in the Mogoñe-La Mata section, and would participate in the rehabilitation of the stretch from Salina Cruz to Medias Aguas (FIT, 2019b). In 2015, the SACMAG Group, a partner of the Dutch company, Netherlands Airport Consultants BV. or NACO, was among the companies contracted for the New International Airport in Mexico City (Lamberti and Rothstein, 2017).

The Azvi Group, also a beneficiary of the Mayan Train (FIT, 2020),[9] has been contracted to carry out the work on the Medias Aguas-Ubero section of the project.

Table 5.2 Main Beneficiary Companies of the FIT Rehabilitation.

Stretch	Subsidiaries	Parent company	Country of origin	Owners
Medias Aguas-Ubero	Construcciones Urales S.A de C.V. **associated with** Regiomontana de Construccion y Servcios S.A.O.I. de C.V.	Grupo Azvi	Spain	Manuel Contreras Ramos, President
Ubero-Mogoñe	La Peninsular Compañia Constructora S.A de C.V. associated with Caltia Conseciones S.A de C.V., Grupo Emprendedor Caltia S.A.P.I. de C.V. and Ferropartes Industriales del Norte S.A de C.V.	Grupo Hermes	Mexico	Carlos Hank Rhon, Chairman of the Board of Directors
Mogoñe-La Mata	Ferro Maz S.A de C.V. associated with Constructora Torres y Asociados S.A de C.V., Constructor Janus S.A de C.V. and Chiñas Construcciones S.A de C.V.	Ferro Maz Consortium	Mexico	Fernando Able Altamiro Becerra. Data only existing in the Mexican public registry of commerce
La Mata-Colonia Jordan	Comsa Infraestructura S.A de C.V. associated with Grupo Constructor Diamante S.A de C.V.	COMSA Corporación	Spain	Jorge Miarnau Monserrat, President. Miarnau Family owner of 50% of the capital
Technical Supervision of the stretch Mogoñe-La Mata	Coodinación téchnico administrativa de Obras, S.A de C.V. associated with Colinas de Buen S.A de C.V.	Grupo SACMAG	Mexico	Juan José Risoul Rosan, President
Colonia Jordan-Salina Cruz	Construcciones y Maquinaria SEF, S.A. de C.V.	Grupo SEF	Mexico	So far no public information has been recorded

Source: Data from the Ministry of Finance and Public Credit, CompraNet 2020.[10] See FIT (2020), 'Fallo FIT-GARMOP-OP-Z-2019-LP', CompraNet. Available at: https://sites.google.com/site/cnetuc/contrataciones (accessed 1 May 2020).

The SEF Group is known in the Mexican rail industry as one of the main sellers of Ferromex, a company that belongs to the Mexico Group, the fourth largest company in the country.[11] Ferro Maz S.A de C.V. is an open-end stock corporation registered in June 2019 to carry out integral projects for the construction and maintenance of railway lines, among other tasks.[12] It is likely that this company was incorporated to participate in this project as a front for a larger business group.

In 2019, the Auxiliary and Urban Surveillance Corps of the State of Mexico was awarded a contract to provide security and surveillance services in the sections and buildings of the FIT, in addition to the railway lines of Chiapas Mayab (FIT, 2019a). This line could be used to complement the route of the Maya Train. The surveillance company had been questioned, under the previous government, for possible acts of corruption (SinEmbargo, 2020) and violation of the human rights of Central American migrants (CNDH, 2019a).

Between 1 January 2019 and 5 March 2020, the Ministry of the Environment and Natural Resources (SEMARNAT, n.d.)[13] reportedly received only three requests for environmental authorisation for three sections of the railway project. However, these requests do not correspond to the six projects for which contracts have been awarded.[14] These could be additional routes which are currently being undertaken by the FIT. The environmental authorisations of the six contracts for the railway project have not been published to date.

The main objective of the railway track rehabilitation is 'to build a 300 km double-track electric train to connect the two ports in three hours, so that shipping companies save time and money' (CESOP, 2019). The rehabilitation and maintenance of the track fulfil a fundamental objective of the Corridor programme – the guarantee that the intermodal loading terminal Pearson, located in Oaxaca, will perform the work of loading and unloading goods that will be transferred to the ports in Salina Cruz and Coatzacoalcos (SCT, n.d.). At the moment, the main goods transported on this track include cement, iron, non-metallic minerals and wood (CESOP, 2019). The railway project is part of an extractive agenda that aims to consolidate the energy corridor in the south of the country.

Jáltipan-Salina Cruz gas pipeline

Unlike the railway project, no concession has been announced or published till date for the gas pipeline. It is part of the Five-Year Plan for the Expansion of the National Integrated Natural Gas Transportation and Storage System 2015–19. The pipeline is considered a strategic project with the aim of 'extending the coverage of the gasification system and detonating new markets' (SENER, 2015). It is 247 kilometres long and received an estimated investment of 643 million US dollars (USD) by 2019. According to the information available as of June of that year, the pipeline is operating partially, at a capacity of 90 million cubic feet per day (SHCP and BANOBRAS, n.d.). This information has not been modified in its technical file, meaning that if it remains in operation, it would be doing so without an environmental permit. The Mexican environmental authority has not registered authorisation resolutions for the project,[15] and the Ministry of Energy (SENER) has not stated whether it has received or applied for a mandatory social impact evaluation.[16]

The PPP contract is in the form of a twenty-year concession granted through public bidding with greenfield investment (SHCP and BANOBRAS, n.d.), a type of foreign direct investment (FDI) in which the investor controls the production, design and installation of the works. Unless renewed, the works will come under public control and administration upon completion of the contract.[17] According to the Five-Year Plan, the gas pipeline has been planned as a source of natural gas supply for a refinery, a cogeneration plant and a liquefaction plant in Salina Cruz,[18] as well as for export to Central America (SENER, 2015). The project remains in force within the framework of the new Integrated National Natural Gas Transport and Storage System (SISTRANGAS) Five-Year Expansion Plan 2019–24.[19]

According to the National Hydrocarbons Commission (CNH), the gas pipeline aims to ensure the supply of natural gas to the ten industrial estates/parks to be built along the Isthmus Corridor.[20] This means that, once the concession is made, its transport capacity will be increased. In addition, the CNH indicated that the characteristics of operation and industrial and commercial projections of the gas pipeline are aligned with those expected for the Salina Cruz SEZ.[21] The industrial estates/parks that will be installed and supplied with gas will carry out activities pertaining to the electrical, metal-mechanical, textile and agro-industrial sectors. Hydroelectric and geothermal plants will be installed to consolidate a regional energy corridor (AFDZEE, 2018c).

Territorial impact

From biological corridor to commercial corridor

Oaxaca and Veracruz hold the first and third place, respectively, as states with the greatest biodiversity in Mexico. More than half of Oaxaca's territory is covered by forests that are home to unique species of fauna and flora. Two of the most important rivers in the country, the Papaloapan and Grijalva, are also located in this territory (CONABIO, 2018). Veracruz is characterised by diverse altitudes and a great variety of climates that have produced its biodiversity. Its abundant water assets, particularly the Coatzacoalcos river, have some of the most diverse marine life in the state (CONABIO, 2013).

Currently, the main threats to these ecosystems come from the expansion of the agricultural frontier caused by large extensions of monocultures, oil industry activities that contaminate water sources, deforestation generated by the cutting and looting of wood, and 'the opening of roads, oil wells, power lines, and other works that seriously affect biological flows by cutting off connectivity between fragments of vegetation' (CONABIO, 2013: 45). Infrastructure projects that do not consider medium- and long-term mitigation measures cause irreversible damage, as do mining activities that drastically modify landscapes and alter natural biological corridors (El Universal, 2020b). Finally, wind farms that are part of the energy industry affect the routes of birds and bats, erode the soil through the use of spilled oils and solvents, encourage changes in land use for food production and generate conflicts over land (El Universal, 2020a).

The Interoceanic Corridor could further affect the ecosystems of the Isthmus by consolidating such extractive projects and serving as a hub for their operations. Between January 2018 and January 2020,

---

Important Areas for the Conservation of Birds:
Los Tuxtlas (487 species), Sierra Norte (485 species), Uxpanaga (341 species), Chimalapas (432 species), Istmo de Tehuantepec-Mar Muerto (169 species)

Ecoregions:
warm wet rainforests, warm dry forests and temperate mountain ranges. These ecoregions form a large ecosystem that links Veracruz and Oaxaca with other states such as Tabasco, Quintana Roo, Yucatán and Chiapas.

Priority Hydrological Regions:
Papaloapan, Tehuantepec and Oaxaca Coast.

Endemic fauna:
274 species of fauna that only exist in this region and are under the category of high risk and priority for national protection.

Figure 5.2 Areas of environmental relevance in the Isthmus of Tehuantepec.

Source: Based on information from the National Commission for the Knowledge and Use of Biodiversity (CONABIO, n.d.), Semarnat (SEMARNAT, n.d.), FIT MIA and gas pipeline MIA.[22]

SEMARNAT reported eleven Environmental Impact Statements (MIAs) filed by developers seeking environmental permits for wind, electric and hydroelectric power-generation projects in Oaxaca. Five of these have already been authorised. Two MIAs for photovoltaic projects in Veracruz have also been authorised. In the mining sector, of the three MIAs filed for the exploitation of non-metallic minerals – two in Oaxaca and one in Veracruz, two were authorised.[23]

A megaproject without consent

Today, we are told that our peoples will benefit from this railway, but the most urgent thing for us is that there should be drinking water, support for agricultural producers, artisans, small traders and equipped hospitals.

(Agencia de Noticias, 2020)

Ten indigenous communities,[24] comprising 100,962 people, inhabit the region of the Isthmus where the six polygons projected for the Corridor will be developed. The area of influence is made up of seventy-nine municipalities – thirty-three in Veracruz and forty-six in Oaxaca – which are home to Afro-Mexican and peasant peoples. The Isthmus has one of the highest poverty rates in Mexico. In Oaxaca, 66.4 per cent of the population live in poverty, only 16.3 per cent have access to health services, 27 per cent lack access to food (insufficient to lead an active and healthy life) and 58.3 per cent have access to basic housing services. In Veracruz, 67.9 per cent of the population live in poverty, 16.7 per cent have access to health services, 27 per cent lack access to food and only 42.1 per cent have access to basic housing services (CONEVAL, 2018). These issues call for a priority discussion on improving the population's living conditions.

The megaproject, however, did not start from this discussion and, instead, focused on promoting infrastructure and production for extractive sectors. Little wonder then that the programme does not have the consent of communities who inhabit these regions.

Between March and April 2019, the SHCP, together with the National Institute of Indigenous Peoples (INPI), published calls for what they termed 'regional consultative assemblies' on the creation of the Development Programme for the Isthmus of Tehuantepec. But the communities in the region did not consider these legitimate decision-making mechanisms. They argued that the meetings violated their right to procedures carried out in good faith, and in culturally adequate ways that are conducive to free, prior and informed consent (CNDH, 2019b). The National Human Rights Commission requested precautionary measures to assuage the communities'

Table 5.3 Indigenous Population in the Isthmus.

Areas in Veracruz	Municipalities	Population	Total
Acayucan	Acayucan	7,642	49,256
Coatzacoalcos	Coatzacoalcos	16,255	
Minantitlán	Minantitlán	12,300	
	Cosoleacaque	13,059	
Ciudad Ixtepec	Ciudad Ixtepec	11,507	51,706
	El Espinal	6,389	
	Asunción Ixtaltepec	10,613	
Matías Romero	Matías Romero	10,360	
	El Barrio de la Soledad	1,581	
Salina Cruz	Salina Cruz	11,256	
			100,962

Source: Information from the SHCP (SHCP, 2019) and data from the catalogue of indigenous communities (CNDH, 2010).

concerns (CNDH, 2019b). Consultations resumed after the Interoceanic Corridor of the Isthmus of Tehuantepec was established. But, once again, the indigenous peoples denounced this as an irregular measure and filed a constitutional lawsuit challenging the decree that created the Corridor.[25] By overlooking the traditional consultation processes of indigenous communities, the authorities essentially denied the social claims and political struggles against mainstream models of development.

In April 2019, female human rights defenders in Veracruz stated that consultations had been held without providing adequate information to their representatives. The authorities in charge only presented the general objectives of the development programme and declined to go into the details of individual projects, including the railway lines and the gas pipeline.[26] On several occasions, authorities of the Development Programme for the Isthmus of Tehuantepec, the FIT and the gas pipeline have denied knowledge of information, refused to take responsibility for failing to deliver requested information and pinned the blame for such failure on each other, forcing people to make repeated requests. Even as the deadlines for delivery of information were suspended due to the Covid-19 pandemic,[27] decision-making on contracts, budgets and project operations continued unabated.

On 11 June 2020, the Community Assembly, which includes the five Oaxacan municipalities affected by the megaproject, addressed a letter to the Presidency of the Republic, stating that the Covid-19 pandemic is being used to carry out activities related to the rehabilitation of the railway without respecting the views of the community. Citing the danger of contagion, they demanded that such activities be suspended (Agencia de Noticias, 2020).

Resistance and re-existence

The impact of territorial conflicts generated by this megaproject has been felt particularly acutely by women defenders in the region. Historically, poverty coupled with violence and inequalities has prevented most women in these communities from participating in school and/or the labour market (INEGI, 2019). More than half of the women have faced violence relating to employment discrimination, partner/domestic violence and sexual intimidation from strangers (INEGI, 2019). In 2019, Veracruz reported the highest number of femicides among all states (Martínez, 2019). In January 2020, Oaxaca was among the ten states with the most femicides (El Universal, 2020a).

In this backdrop, the women defenders protested the fact that 'the participation of women in the consultative assemblies held by the federal government has not been seen, women have not been included or informed on how the megaproject will affect us' (Mujeres del Istmo, 2019). The exclusion is significant given that at least a fourth of certified landowners in Oaxaca and Veracruz, as of 2019, were women (RAN, 2019). Yet, the community authorities are predominantly men who, besides being inadequately consulted in the PPP processes, were considered the only reference point for community decision-making.

The PPP model – and the configuration of the Isthmus free trade zone – prioritises benefits to companies and promises agility in administrative procedures and attractive tax reductions. It reduces to mere 'formalities' environmental authorisation procedures; indigenous and citizen consultations; and decisions related to land-use planning that require time for elaboration, circulation, information, participation, advocacy, and organisation of space for deliberation and dialogue between citizens and institutions. Such administrative 'agility', however, negatively impacts human, territorial and environmental rights of the communities.

The design of the megaproject fosters and maintains relations of domination over territories and populations, and results in protracted disputes between communities and companies over opposing political, economic and cultural interests.

In the face of such disputes, it is essential to refer to community organisational processes. Currently, the struggles against mining and energy extraction in the Isthmus aim to protect what women defenders in the region call *the corridor of water and life*. The following section is a contribution by the women who make up the Sierra de Santa Marta Articulation Process,[28] a network of organisations that has drawn up an agenda for resistance and a way of rethinking common welfare.

Indigenous and Afro-descendent women defend the Isthmus territory

Over the last decade, indigenous and Afro-Mestizo women of the Oaxacan and Veracruz Isthmus have played a key role in the struggle for territorial defence and resistance against the incursion of wind, mining and hydrocarbon extraction companies. Theirs is a struggle for life, autonomy and sovereignty over their territory. This territory not only provides material support, but also symbolises their history and culture. This is where they have developed a sense of life, belonging and roots.

These women have been leading the resistance at the regional level in Veracruz and Oaxaca, and building alliances at the national and international levels. Some of them are councillors in the Indigenous Council of Government of the National Indigenous Congress, where men and women from all over the country organise and fight to protect Mother Earth, their communities and the indigenous territories.

With the Interoceanic Corridor of the Isthmus of Tehuantepec and the industrial parks/estates to be developed along the railway lines, threats which had once been overcome have resurfaced. It is clear to these indigenous women that the companies are going to dispossess the communities of their territories. The few jobs they may generate will not compensate for the dispossession of the mountain water the companies will require for their operations; the contamination of the water, air and land, and the health hazards that their operations will generate; and the insecurity that will be exacerbated throughout the territories.

The women know that the PPP projects will intensify patriarchal violence, insecurity and crime, as is always the case when money circulates not for people but for corporations, politicians and leaders of organised crime. The companies interfere in decision-making processes in the assemblies meant to defend rights, culture and territories. The resultant conflicts divide communities. On occasion, the divisions between communities culminate into massacres, as with the Ikoots community of San Mateo del Mar, Oaxaca or the burning of city hall vehicles by the Nahua people of Tatahuicapan in southern Veracruz in June 2020.

These women are determined not to give a drop of water to what they regard as 'death projects' and will persist in their efforts towards building autonomy through surveillance tactics, community radio, community generation of electricity, strengthening of community assemblies and planting of food they deem healthy. Their proposed alternatives to the crisis emphasise local control of productive and reproductive processes, access to land tenure, community decision-making, a political commitment to territory that recognises both their rights and the rights of nature as well as transformation of gender relations between men and women.

They challenge the patriarchal, capitalist, racist and colonial vision of the state, big capital and their institutions, as well as the femicidal macho violence of society that considers nature, territory and women's bodies as 'resource' or 'property' that can be appropriated. Despite the gender inequalities that persist in their communities, the indigenous and Afro-Mestizo women reject the status of victimhood; they are rebellious women who resist. They propose and develop negotiation strategies and promote territorial resistance inspired by *women who fight* in other latitudes. They question the traditions and customs that normalise their exclusion and subordination in their communities. They refuse to accept that PPPs can solve the problems that are caused by the very developmental model that proposes them. They are aware of how the PPP model creates a vicious circle that reproduces the same territorial conflicts over and over again, albeit with components that can vary across regions and contexts.

To counter these harms, they propose an alternate agenda that is based on collective well-being and the inalienable right to health, education, food, access to water and environmental protection. Their aim is to break away from a system in which a few powerful actors monopolise resources and put the very processes that regenerate life at risk (Pérez Orozco, 2014).

Conclusion

PPPs have facilitated a corporate capture of the state by allowing private companies to fulfil a public role and, thereby, interfere in political and administrative decision-making. The PPP framework adapted for the Interoceanic Corridor in Mexico has seen private companies replace state functions, especially when it comes to decision-making on the organisation of territory, security, and an economic and productive model for the region.

Decisions of public interest are taken based on considerations of private benefit of those who operate the projects.

The Corridor is structured according to the geopolitical attractions of this region, and seen as a commercial node for energy. Its importance as a trade corridor comes at the cost of a dismissal of the region's ecological relevance. The consequent negative impacts include territorial conflicts and the dispossession of communities. This is currently being challenged by the indigenous Afro-Mestizo and peasant women who are resisting the planned PPP projects and defending their territories through an agenda that centres community well-being and a sustainable life.

Notes

1   Mexico consists of thirty-two states with legal autonomy and their own constitutions.
2   International Network for Economic, Social and Cultural Rights Red-DESC.
3   On 6 August 2014, Buena Vista del Cobre S.A de C.V., a subsidiary of Grupo Mexico, one of the most powerful companies in the mining and infrastructure sector in Mexico, spilled 40 million litres of acidified copper sulphate into the Bacanuchi and Sonora rivers, causing the most serious environmental disaster in the country's mining industry. Yet, in 2016, this company received environmental authorisation to build a new mine tailings dam in the area of the spill. Available at: https://www.projectpoder.org/es/2019/07/observaciones-al-informe-preventivo-del-proyecto-nueva-presa-de-jales-para-buenavista-del-cobre-s-a-de-c-v-26so2013md082.
4   In 2019, Canada's Almaden Minerals, while applying for environmental authorisation to exploit gold and silver in the state of Puebla, indicated that mitigation measures related to the control of leaks or spills and the recovery of fertile soils would be implemented 'only if possible'. Available at: 'Regional Environmental Impact Assessment, with risk analysis. Ixtaca Mining Project, project number 21PU2019M0014', pages VII-6 and VII-7.
5   At the time of writing this chapter, the full programme has not been published.
6   This is a 'decentralized administrative body of the Ministry of Finance and Public Credit, responsible for planning, promotion, regulation and verification of the Zones'. Official Gazette of the Federation, undated.
7   This reform redefined the role of the state and granted powers to the private sector in order to promote a new model of energy production and generation in which *Petróleos Mexicanos* and the Federal Electricity Commission could partner with private capital for the construction and operation of new refineries and finance, install, maintain and operate infrastructure for the provision of electricity transmission and distribution

services. It also provided that the activities of this sector are strategic, of priority interest and public, so they would be prioritised for the occupation of national territory. Available at: https://www.gob.mx/sener/documentos/explicacion-ampliada-de-la-reforma-energetica.

8   SEGOB, 2019b, Article 4-V.

9   Another megaproject of the current government located in the southeast region of Mexico, which will transport fuel and passengers over a distance of 1,500 kilometres. The Isthmus Railway will be connected to this train line.

10 Information on owners and beneficiaries was obtained from the companies' websites and media reports.

11 SEF (n.d.). 'Construcciones y Maquinaria SEF, S.A de C.V', available at: http://www.sefcym.com/index.php/nosotros

12 Information obtained from the Public Registry of Commerce on Commercial Folio No. N-2019047000.

13 Response to the request for access to information on folio number 0001600028720. Keys to the projects for consultation of the Environmental Impact Statements: 20OA2019V0020, 20OA2020V0001, 9/DC-0464/12/19.

14 I. Rehabilitation of railroad track Chivela-Lagunas, Oaxaca km Z213+550 KM Z-226+200. II. Rehabilitation of railroad track Tolosita and Salina Cruz, Oaxaca km 159+270 – 308+200. III. Rehabilitation of railroad track km 96+146 – 213+250 y 226+200 to 241+280 Oaxaca and Veracruz.

15 Project key: 20OA2015G0028. The status of the procedure can be consulted on the website of the Ministry of Environment and Natural Resources, available at: https://apps1.semarnat.gob.mx:8443/consultatramite/estado.php.

16 Response to the request for information made to the SENER, on folio number 0001800031720 on 11 June 2020.

17 (2012) Article 123.

18 Cogeneration is the production of electrical and thermal energy from the use of gas. Liquefaction consists of changing the gas into a liquid state.

19 Response to the request for information made to the CRE, on folio number: 1811100089229 on 11 June 2020.

20 Response to the request for information on folio number 1800100005520 of 23 March 2020, available at: https://www.gob.mx/cenagas/prensa/cenagas-presenta-7-acciones-para-atender-las-demandas-de-gas-natural-en-el-sur-sureste-del-pais.

21 Response to the request for information on folio number 1800100005520. The authority referred to consult the Opinion of the Special Economic Zone of Salina Cruz, available at: https://www.gob.mx/cms/uploads/attachment/file/372131/Dictamen_.pdf.

22 Response to the request for access to information to Semarnat on folio number 0001600028720. Keys to the projects for consultation of the Environmental Impact Statements: 20OA2019V0020, 20OA2020V0001, 9/DC-0464/12/19.

23 Response to the request for access to information to SEMARNAT on folio number 0001600521119, on 28 January 2020.
24 Zapoteco, Mixe, Zoque, Huave, Chontal, Chinanteca, Mazateca, Mixteca, Popoluca, Nahua.
25 Writ of protection 135/2019 filed with the seventh district court of Oaxaca by representatives of the Mixe people. Information consulted in the integral information system at Human Rights Prohd Centre, available at: http://centroprodh.org.mx/sididh_2_0_alfa/?p=60860.
26 Extraordinary Regional Assembly: 'Patriarchal System and Mega-Project of the Isthmus', 27–29 April 2019 in Tatahuicapan, Veracruz.
27 Agreements for the suspension of terms and deadlines, National Transparency Platform, available at: https://www.plataformadetransparencia.org.mx/web/guest/vinculos_acuerdos_estados.
28 It is made up of the Network of Women of the Earth United for a Future and a Better World AC, civil resistance against high electricity rates, the network of community radio stations of the Sierra de Santa Marta, the Bety Cariño Human Rights Centre AC, Tssooka-teyoo of the Sierra AC and Defence of the Territory and Strengthening of the Popoluca People, Jaraneros 'Son Altepe'.

References

AFDZEE (2018a), 'Anexo 4.1 Análisis de mercado y demanda potencial, ZEE de Coatzacoalcos'.
AFDZEE (2018b), 'Dictamen de la Zona Económica Especial de Coatzacoalcos'.
AFDZEE (2018c), 'Dictamen de la Zona Económica Especial de Salina Cruz'.
AFDZEE (2018d), 'Presentación del Programa para el Desarrollo del Istmo de Tehuantepec'. Available at: https://www.gob.mx/zee/es/articulos/presentacion-del-programa-para-el-desarrollo-del-istmo-de-tehuantepec?idiom=es (accessed 1 May 2020).
Agencia de Noticias (2020), 'Pueblos de Oaxaca exigen frenar obra de remodelación del ferrocarril', *Istmo Press*, 11 June. Available at: http://www.istmopress.com.mx/istmo/pueblos-de-oaxaca-exigen-frenar-obra-de-remodelacion-del-ferrocarril (accessed 1 May 2020).
CEFP (2007), 'Proyectos para Prestación de Servicios (PPS)'. Available at: https://www.cefp.gob.mx/intr/edocumentos/pdf/cefp/cefp0192007.pdf (accessed 1 May 2020).
CEFP (2016), 'Las Asociaciones Público Privadas como Alternativa de Financiamiento para las Entidades Federativas', Chamber of Deputies, June. Available at: https://www.cefp.gob.mx/publicaciones/documento/2016/junio/eecefp0032016.pdf (accessed 1 May 2020).
CEMDA (2017), 'Admiten amparo contra ampliación del puerto de Veracruz por violar derecho al medio ambiente sano'. 10 April. Available at: https://

www.cemda.org.mx/admiten-amparo-contra-ampliacion-del-puerto-de-veracruz-por-violar-derecho-al-medio-ambiente-sano (accessed 1 May 2020).

CESOP (2019), 'El proyecto del tren transístmico', Chamber of Deputies LXIV Legislature. Available at: http://www5.diputados.gob.mx/index.php/camara/Centros-de-Estudio/CESOP/Estudios-e-Investigaciones/Carpetas-Informativas/Carpeta-informativa-No.-119.-El-proyecto-del-tren-transistmico (accessed 1 May 2020).

Chamber of Deputies of the Honourable Congress of the Union (2012), 'Ley de Asociaciones Público Privadas', *Diario Oficial de la Federación* [Official Journal of the Federation], 15 June. Available at: http://www.diputados.gob.mx/LeyesBiblio/pdf/LAPP_150618.pdf (accessed 1 May 2020).

CNDH (2019a), 'Sobre el caso de violaciones a los derechos humanos atribuibles a elementos de los cuerpos de guardias y vigilantes auxiliares de la entonces Comisión Estatal de Seguridad Ciudadana del Estado de México; y del acceso a la justicia en su modalidad de procuración', 31 October. Available at: https://www.cndh.org.mx/sites/default/files/documentos/2019-11/REC_2019_98.pdf (accessed 1 May 2020).

CNDH (2019b), 'CNDH Requests the Federal and State Authorities of Oaxaca and Veracruz to Grant Precautionary Measures before the Consultation on the Project "Interoceanic corredor Istmo de Tehuantepec"', 30 March. Available at: https://www.cndh.org.mx/documento/solicita-cndh-autoridades-federales-y-estatales-de-oaxaca-y-veracruz-otorgar-medidas (accessed 1 May 2020).

CNDH (2010), 'Catálogo de Localidades Indígenas'.

CONABIO (n.d.), 'Áreas de Importancia para la Conservación de las Aves (AICA)'. Available at: http://avesmx.conabio.gob.mx/AICA.html (accessed 1 May 2020).

CONABIO (2013), 'Estrategia para la Conservación y el Uso Sustentable de la Biodiversidad del estado de Veracruz'. Available at: http://repositorio.veracruz.gob.mx/medioambiente/wp-content/uploads/sites/9/2018/02/ECUSBE-VER-Estrategia-de-Conserv-y-Uso-Sust-de-la-Biodiversidad.pdf (accessed 1 May 2020).

CONABIO (2018), 'Estrategia para la Conservación y el Uso Sustentable de la Biodiversidad del estado de Oaxaca'. Available at: https://bioteca.biodiversidad.gob.mx/janium/Documentos/15091.pdf (accessed 1 May 2020).

CONEVAL (2018), 'Pobrezaestatal 2018'. Available at: https://www.coneval.org.mx/coordinacion/entidades/Paginas/inicioent.aspx (accessed 1 May 2020).

COPASA (2016), 'México confía a Copasa las obras del puerto de Veracruz', 5 June. Available at: http://www.copasagroup.com/es/colocacion-de-la-primera-piedra-en-edar-orense/ (accessed 1 May 2020).

COPASA (2019), 'Programa de Emisión de Pagarés COPASA 2019', 10 March. Available at: https://www.bmerf.es/docs/docsSubidos/MARF/

DIPagar%C3%A9sMARF/DBII_con_Anexos_-_MARF__versi%C3%B3n_
web__compressed__1_.pdf (accessed 1 May 2020).

Corredor Interoceánico del Istmo de Tehuantepec (2020), *Estatuto Orgánico del
Corredor Interoceánico del Istmo de Tehuantepec*. Available at: https://www.
gob.mx/ciit/documentos/estatuto-organico-del-corredor-interoceanico-del-
istmo-de-tehuantepec?idiom=es (accessed 1 May 2020).

El Universal (2020a), 'Oaxaca, entre los 10 estados con más feminicidios
durante enero de 2020', 4 March. Available at: https://oaxaca.eluniversal.
com.mx/seguridad/04-03-2020/oaxaca-entre-los-10-estados-con-mas-
feminicidios-durante-enero-de-2020 (accessed 1 May 2020).

El Universal (2020b), 'En Oaxaca se produce el 62% de la energía eólica
generada en el país', 6 January, by J.C. Zavala. Available at: https://oaxaca.
eluniversal.com.mx/estatal/06-01-2020/en-oaxaca-se-produce-el-62-de-la-
energia-eolica-generada-en-el-pais (accessed 1 May 2020).

ESCR-Net (n.d.), 'Captura Corporativa Definición y Características'.
Available at: https://www.escr-net.org/es/derechoshumanosyempresas/
capturacorporativa/caracteristicas (accessed 1 May 2020).

FIT (2019a), 'Contrato FIT GARMOP-CHM-N-09-AD-20', *CompraNet*.
Available at: https://compranet.hacienda.gob.mx/esop/guest/go/
opportunity/detail?opportunityId=1786749 (accessed 1 May 2020).

FIT (2019b), 'Fallo FIT-GARMOP-S-Z-18-2019-LP', CompraNet. Available
at: https://compranet.hacienda.gob.mx/esop/guest/go/opportunity/
detail?opportunityId=1772031 (accessed 1 May 2020).

FIT (2020), 'Fallo FIT-GARMOP-OP-Z-2019-LP', *CompraNet*. Available at:
https://sites.google.com/site/cnetuc/contrataciones (accessed 1 May 2020).

Gaceta Parlamentaria (Parliamentary Gazette) number 4372-VIII (2015),
'Iniciativa del ejecutivo federal, con proyecto de decreto por el cual se
expide la Ley Federal de Zonas Económicas Especiales y se adicionan
el artículo 9 de la Ley General de Bienes Nacionales'. Available at:
http://gaceta.diputados.gob.mx/PDF/63/2015/sep/20150929-VIII.pdf
(accessed 1 May 2020).

Government of Jalisco, *Secretaría de Gobernación* [Secretariat of Government]
(2008), 'Ley de proyectos de inversión y de prestación de servicios del estado
de Jalisco y sus municipios'. Available at: https://transparencia.info.jalisco.
gob.mx/sites/default/files/Ley%20de%20Proyectos%20de%20Inversion%20
y%20Prestacion%20de%20Servicios.pdf (accessed 1 May 2020).

INEGI (2019), 'Estadísticas a propósito del día internacional de la eliminación
de la violencia contra la mujer (25 de noviembre). Datos Nacionales',
21 November. Available at: https://www.inegi.org.mx/contenidos/
saladeprensa/aproposito/2019/Violencia2019_Nal.pdf (accessed 1 May 2020).

Lamberti, J., and T. Rothstein (2017), 'Empresas participantes en el proyecto
del Nuevo Aeropuerto de la Ciudad de México', *PODER*, 7 July. Available at:
https://www.colaboratorio.org/nuevo-aeropuerto-de-la-ciudad-de-mexico-
investigacion-corporativa (accessed 1 May 2020).

López Obrador, Andrés Manuel (2020), 'Rehabilitación del Corredor Interoceánico del Istmo y parques industriales impulsarán desarrollo en sur-sureste', *AMLO*, 7 June. Available at: https://lopezobrador.org.mx/2020/06/07/rehabilitacion-del-corredor-interoceanico-del-istmo-y-parques-industriales-impulsaran-desarrollo-en-sur-sureste-presidente (accessed 1 May 2020).

Martínez, F. (2019), 'Veracruz, primer lugar en feminicidios', *La Jornada*, 26 September. Available at: https://jornada.com.mx/2019/09/26/politica/016n1pol (accessed 1 May 2020).

Michelitsch, R., and R. Szwedzki (2017), 'Una década de alianzas público privadas en América Latina y el Caribe: ¿qué hemos aprendido?', October. Available at: https://blogs.worldbank.org/es/ppps/una-d-cada-de-alianzas-p-blico-privadas-en-am-rica-latina-y-el-caribe-qu-hemos-aprendido (accessed 1 May 2020).

Mujeres Del Istmo, las que con amor cuidan la tierra. Contra el machismo, la violencia y los desafíos que trae para las mujeres el Corredor Interoceánico (Women of the Isthmus, those who lovingly care for the land. Against machismo, violence and the challenges that the Interoceanic Corridor brings to women) (2019). Available at: https://istmoresiste.org.mx/serie-de-radio/ (accessed 1 May 2020).

Pérez Orozco, A. (2014), 'Subversión Feminista de la Economía. Aportes para un debate sobre el conflicto capital-vida', *Traficantes de Sueños*. Available at: https://www.traficantes.net/sites/default/files/pdfs/Subversi%C3%B3n%20feminista%20de%20la%20econom%C3%ADa_Traficantes%20de%20Sue%C3%B1os.pdf (accessed 1 May 2020).

PIAPPEM (n.d.), 'Experiencia mexicana en Asociaciones Público-Privadas para el desarrollo del Infraestructura y la provisión de servicios públicos'. Available at: https://piappem.org/file.php?id=295.

PODER (2019), 'Saltillo: El origen de la privatización de aguas mexicanas', *Rindecuentas*, 6 June. Available at: https://www.rindecuentas.org/reportajes/2019/06/06/saltillo-el-origen-de-la-privatizacion-de-aguas-mexicanas (accessed 1 May 2020).

PODER (2020), 'Tren Maya "como anillo al dedo" para las extractivas', 3 June. Available at: https://www.facebook.com/214825975198976/posts/3548377661843774 (accessed 1 May 2020).

RAN (2019), 'Estadística Agraria con perspectiva de género'. Available at: http://www.ran.gob.mx/ran/indic_gen/nucag-certynocert-resultados-2019.pdf (accessed 1 May 2020).

SCT (n.d.), 'Ferrocarril del Istmo de Tehuantepec, S.A de C.V', *FIT*. Available at: https://www.ferroistmo.com.mx (accessed 1 May 2020).

SEF (n.d.), 'Construcciones y Maquinaria SEF, S.A de C.V'. Available at: http://www.sefcym.com/index.php/nosotros (accessed 1 May 2020).

SEGOB (1981), 'Decreto por el que se aprueba el Programa Nacional de Desarrollo de las Franjas Fronterizas y Zonas Libres', *Diario Oficial de la*

Federación [Official Journal of the Federation], 12 November. Available at: http://dof.gob.mx/nota_detalle.php?codigo=4696464&fecha=12/11/1981 (accessed 1 May 2020).

SEGOB (2019a), 'Decreto por el que se abrogan los diversos de Declaratorias de las Zonas Económicas Especiales', *Diario Oficial de la Federación* [Official Journal of the Federation], 19 November. Available at: https://www.dof.gob. mx/nota_detalle.php?codigo=5579365&fecha=19/11/2019 (accessed 1 May 2020).

SEGOB (2019b), 'Decreto por el que se crea el organismo público descentralizado, con personalidad jurídica y patrimonio propio, no sectorizado, denominado Corredor Interoceánico del Ismto de Tehuantepec', *Diario Oficial de la Federación* [Official Journal of the Federation], 14 June. Available at: https://dof.gob.mx/nota_detalle.php?codigo=5562774&fec ha=14/06/2019 (accessed 1 May 2020).

SEMARNAT (n.d.), 'Ecorregiones terrestres de México', *Atlas Digital Geográfico.* Available at: http://gisviewer.semarnat.gob.mx/aplicaciones/Atlas2015/ biod_ETN1.html (accessed 1 May 2020).

SENER (2015), 'Plan Quinquenal de Expansión del Sistema de Transporte y Almacenamiento Nacional Integrado de Gas Natural, 2015–2019'. Available at: https://www.gob.mx/cenagas/acciones-y-programas/plan-quinquenal- de-expansion-del-sistema-de-transporte-y-almacenamiento-nacional- integrado-de-gas-natural-2015-2019 (accessed 1 May 2020).

SHCP (2019), 'Programa para el Desarrollo del Istmo de Tehuantepec', *Conferencia Binacional de Infraestructura.* Available at: https://www.gob. mx/programaistmo/articulos/programa-para-el-desarrollo-del-istmo-de- tehuantepec (accessed 1 May 2020).

SHCP and BANOBRAS (n.d.), 'Diseño, construcción, operación y mantenimiento de la Infraestructura de transporte del gasoducto Jáltipan, de Veracruz a Salina Cruz', *Proyectos México.* Available at: https://www. proyectosmexico.gob.mx/proyecto_inversion/037-gasoducto-jaltipan-salina- cruz (accessed 1 May 2020).

SinEmbargo, D. B. (2020), 'Peña dio a Cusaem, la compañía de seguridad de priistas del Edomex, al menos 3,389 millones en 5 años', 4 February. Available at: https://www.sinembargo.mx/04-02-2020/3724020 (accessed 1 May 2020).

World Bank (2017), 'PPPs Vital to Improve Infrastructure Quality in Latin America', 4 May. Available at: https://www.worldbank.org/en/news/press- release/2017/05/04/ppps-vital-to-improve-infrastructure-quality-in-latin- america (accessed 1 May 2020).

6

PPPs in publicly funded health insurance schemes: The case of PMJAY in India, or how women bear the brunt while the private sector expands

Sulakshana Nandi

Introduction

In India, access to health services is marked by extreme inequities resulting from factors like socio-economic and political status, geography and gender (Balarajan, Selvaraj and Subramanian, 2011). This is reflected in higher mortality rates, a larger disease burden and higher malnutrition among socio-economically vulnerable groups such as scheduled tribes (STs), scheduled castes (SCs),[1] rural populations and the urban poor. Within these groups, women are especially vulnerable. As India's liberalised economy 'progresses' on its development paradigm, women are disproportionately affected by increasing violence, dispossession and resource capture, environmental degradation, migration, informalisation of labour[2] and dominance of conservative right-wing politics. These processes, coupled with inadequate social welfare, decreasing provisions of public services and increasing privatisation, put women from historically oppressed castes, weaker socio-economic sections and indigenous communities particularly at risk.

While gender-based health inequities are a nationwide phenomenon, the situation is especially dire in some states. This study examines inequalities in access to health services with reference to the state of Chhattisgarh. Located in the south-eastern part of central India (see Map 6.1), Chhattisgarh is the tenth largest state and the seventeenth most populous[3] (RGI and Census Commissioner, 2011). Around 41 per cent of its geographical area is covered by forests (Forest Survey of India, 2017). The population is mostly rural, with only 22 per cent of households living in urban areas. Nearly 86 per cent of households are defined as poor. Of the total population, 31 per cent belong to the ST category and 13 per cent to SC (RGI and Census Commissioner, 2011).

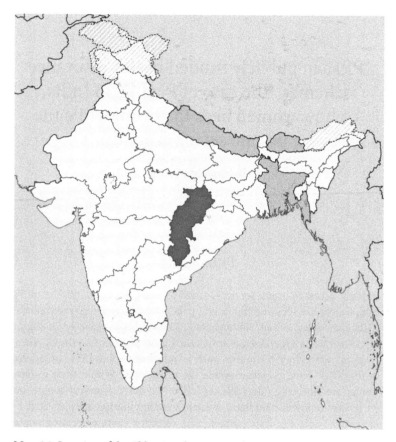

Map 6.1 Location of the Chhattisgarh state in India.

Source: https://commons.wikimedia.org/wiki/File:Chhattisgarh_in_India.svg.

Historically, indigenous communities have had poor access to public health programmes and services, with serious implications for the health of women in these communities. Although Chhattisgarh has seen a significant improvement in health indicators since 2000, it is still one of the lowest-performing states in India, with mortality rates higher than the national average (RGI, 2020). The launch of the National Rural Health Mission (NRHM) in 2005 led to some improvements in the public health system. However, the current right-wing government's 'flagship' programme, the Pradhan Mantri Jan Arogya Yojana (PMJAY) which is considered India's largest private-public partnership (PPP), threatens to reverse most of the previous advances.

How PMJAY became India's largest PPP

The backdrop

The structural adjustment programmes (SAPs) of the 1990s led to a gradual withdrawal of government from the social sector, damaging India's public health system (Rao, 2009). A new coalition government, the United Progressive Alliance (UPA), which came to power in 2004, was compelled to act to reverse the situation. In 2005, the UPA government launched the NRHM to provide much-needed financing to the government health system (NHSRC, 2012). With the introduction of the National Urban Health Mission (NUHM) in 2013, both rural and urban programmes were integrated under a common National Health Mission (NHM). Though the NRHM kept the door open for PPPs, the focus was on improving the public health system. It expanded the public health infrastructure; improved provision of primary healthcare services and hospital care, especially for maternal health; increased human resources for health; and expanded community participation for health governance and accountability (NHSRC, 2012). Despite implementation gaps and quality issues, these schemes led to visible improvements in health and health service indicators (Mukhopadhyay and Sinha, 2019).

The election of the right wing-led National Democratic Alliance (NDA) in 2014, however, dealt a blow to these advances by reducing funding for health and other social programmes. In 2015–16, health spending as a proportion of GDP was lower than what it had been in the early 1990s, at the time of the SAPs (Mukhopadhyay and Sinha, 2019). Since then, the NHM has witnessed a steady decline in budgetary allocation in real terms.

Publicly funded health insurance: The post-liberalisation landscape

Alongside the NRHM, many states introduced publicly funded health insurance (PFHI) schemes to protect the poor from catastrophic health expenditure (PHFI, 2011).[4] In 1999, the central government had opened up the health insurance sector to private players as part of its liberalisation policies, leading to an influx of private insurers (PHFI, 2011). The Rashtriya Swasthya Bima Yojana (RSBY) or National Health Insurance Scheme, launched by the labour ministry in 2007, was the first national-level scheme aimed at providing insurance cover for Below Poverty Line (BPL) households requiring hospital care. This was also the first time that the government contracted private sector hospitals on a large scale. Subsequently, many states expanded the coverage and scope of the RSBY. Chhattisgarh was among the first to implement the RSBY in 2009. In 2012, it expanded the scheme to all families (including the non-poor) in the state through the Mukhyamantri Swasthya Bima Yojana (MSBY) or Chief Minister's Health Insurance Scheme.

In 2018, the NDA government expanded the RSBY in the form of Ayushman Bharat-Pradhan Mantri Jan Arogya Yojana (AB-PMJAY), increasing the population coverage and the insurance coverage per household to Rs 500,000 (7,296 US dollars) annually from Rs 30,000 (440 USD) earlier (Chatterjee, 2018).

PFHI schemes, such as the PMJAY, are governed by contractual agreements between the public and private sectors. They are located within a regulatory framework and involve commercial interests. They are, therefore, categorised as PPPs (Khetrapal, Acharya and Mills, 2019). Private and public hospitals are empanelled through a contract to provide services at fixed rates. The hospitals are required to treat patients who have availed the scheme without charging them, while the government reimburses empanelled hospitals against payment claims submitted, either through an insurance company or a trust set up for the purpose.

During the UPA era, the RSBY was just one among many government health programmes, with the NHM receiving more prominence. The PMJAY, on the other hand, has been promoted as the main and only health programme of the NDA government. It has been advertised as the 'world's largest government-funded healthcare programme', disregarding not only larger universal schemes in other countries, but also the NHM. The political clout behind the PMJAY is evident in its association with the Prime Minister Narendra Modi, with the media referring to it as 'Modicare'. The PMJAY has also been promoted as a strategy to 'help India progressively achieve Universal Health Coverage (UHC) and Sustainable Development Goals (SDG)'.[5]

Methodology

Conceptual framework

This chapter integrates the conceptual framework on PPPs put forth by Development Alternatives with Women for a New Era (DAWN) (Rodríguez Enríquez, 2019) with a framework developed by the author to assess inequity in access to PFHI programmes for UHC. It is particularly interested in how PFHI schemes as PPPs, and particularly the PMJAY, affect women's access to healthcare (Nandi and Schneider, 2020a).

DAWN's PPP framework takes into account the context and main actors; the regulatory and legal frameworks; the characteristics, governance mechanisms, transparency, accountability, and gender and human rights analysis of individual PPPs as well as any resistance to them. The framework developed by the author for assessing the pathways of inequity in access to PFHI schemes is used to analyse the impact of an individual scheme on gender and human rights. This is done by linking the design, objectives and implementation of the scheme; the impact on service provision, utilisation and health system functions; the affordability, availability and acceptability of the scheme; and its health outcomes. Equity concerns, in this case regarding gender, are explicitly explored in the elements of the framework, and the whole analysis is embedded within the larger socio-economic and political context.

Data collection and analysis

The chapter is informed by a review of secondary data sources and participant observation by the author who is an activist for the Jan Swasthya Abhiyan (JSA) or People's Health Movement, India, and a member of the Public Health Resource Network (PHRN). The sources of secondary data include publications on PFHI schemes in India and Chhattisgarh, research by the author as part of her PhD dissertation and along with her collaborators, programme evaluation reports, media reports, websites, and campaign and advocacy documents.

Emergence of PFHI schemes in India

India's mixed healthcare system consists of a complex network of public health facilities and programmes which aim to provide universal preventive and curative health services at low or no cost. There is also a large for-profit private health sector which is heterogeneous, concentrated in urban centres, and provides healthcare on a 'fee-for-service' basis (Mackintosh et al., 2016). With healthcare costs on the rise, the proportion of households reporting catastrophic health expenditure in India increased from 15 per cent in 2004 to 18 per cent in 2014 (NHSRC, n.d.). Currently, out-of-pocket (OOP) payments by households alone account for 60.6 per cent of the total healthcare expenditure (NHSRC, 2018).

Those who designed the RSBY were critical and sceptical of the public provision of health services and had greater faith in the 'effectiveness of market-based healthcare provision' (Virk and Atun, 2015: 815). These preferences were rooted in neoliberal thinking and influenced by considerations such as individual choice, human capital development, and efficiency, competition, and productivity, rather than 'needs' and/or 'rights' (Virk and Atun, 2015). PFHI schemes were pitched as a 'business model' that would be profitable for all parties involved. Their very design prioritised profit maximisation over people's health.

The stated purpose of the PMJAY is to act 'as a steward' and 'align the growth of [the] private sector with public health goals'. The framers of the scheme expressed hope that 'with greater demand', the private sector would expand into 'the unserved areas of Tier 2 and Tier 3 cities'.[6,7] This opened up other avenues for the expansion of PPPs.

Main actors behind PFHI schemes

The government think tank NITI Aayog is a key actor in formulating the PMJAY and driving policy making on PPPs in India. It has launched a plethora of PPP initiatives that are considered 'complementary' to the PMJAY. This includes a plan to provide land and viability gap funding to the private sector to set up and operate hospitals in Tier 2 and Tier 3 cities, and a proposal to privatise district hospitals. Especially the second initiative, if implemented, would be disastrous for women, ST and SC communities, and rural populations.[8]

The role of corporate entities in promoting, implementing and developing PFHI schemes was evident from the beginning.[9] With the PMJAY, there has been visible participation from not only the private health sector (hospital owners and doctors' associations), but also international agencies (World Bank, GIZ), United Nations agencies (WHO, ILO), and philanthropic foundations (Bill & Melinda Gates Foundation) and their think tanks. Insurance companies and Third Party Administrators (TPAs) have a stake in the continuation of PFHI schemes. In addition, organisations working on digital health as well as software companies have also expressed interest.[10]

Private hospitals, especially corporate ones, and doctors' associations, such as the Indian Medical Association (IMA), have always acted as pressure groups, demanding that the government increase the rates for procedures under PFHI schemes, provide more subsidies and reduce regulation. Under the PMJAY, the involvement of the corporate health sector has been institutionalised. A private organisation, the Healthcare Federation of India (NATHEALTH), has been recognised as a formal partner of the National Health Authority (NHA), which is the implementing agency for the PMJAY, and doctors from the corporate sector are included on its governing board. Consultancy agencies, such as PwC,[11] echo demands to make PFHI schemes more profitable for the private sector. Amid the jostle of these players, there is no formal role for civil society in the functioning and regulation of these schemes.

Regulatory and legal framework of PFHI schemes

India's for-profit private health sector is largely unregulated and known for unethical practices (Gadre and Shukla, 2016; Mackintosh et al., 2016; Sengupta et al., 2017). This is especially true of corporate hospitals. The national Clinical Establishments Act (CEA), passed in 2010 after negotiations with the private sector, failed to include critical aspects such as patients' rights, regulation and display of treatment rates.[12] Chhattisgarh's own Act incorporates patients' rights but suffers from inadequate implementation (Nandi, Joshi and Dubey, 2016). The RSBY and the PMJAY were introduced against this backdrop of a largely unregulated healthcare sector dominated by powerful for-profit private players, which influenced the regulation of these schemes. A distinction needs to be made between the 'for-profit' and 'not-for-profit' private hospitals, as the latter usually operate in public interest.

The government has on occasion de-empanelled hospitals under PFHI schemes due to lapses or wrongdoings. However, doctors' lobbies (from both public and private sectors) have often united against such government actions. There have been instances where the governing body (trust) set up to implement and monitor PFHI scheme comprised owners of corporate hospitals who are themselves the recipients of a large proportion of the claims.

With the NHA as PMJAY's implementation agency, the Ministry of Health has been bypassed in this PPP. In August 2018, prior to the launch of the PMJAY, the government had attempted to outsource the functions of the NHA to a consultancy management agency.[13] Even though that move was quashed, an autonomous body like the NHA that bypasses the health ministry, in a context where the for-profit private sector already dominates and colludes with public administrators and health personnel, does not bode well for regulation and oversight.

During the RSBY implementation, Chhattisgarh had created a State Nodal Agency (SNA) under the Department of Health and Family Welfare (DoHFW) for the implementation and monitoring of PFHI schemes. While the governance of these schemes lies with the department, many officials who are responsible for fixing treatment rates and monitoring hospitals are themselves involved in private practice and own private hospitals, creating potential conflicts of interest.

Design and implementation of PFHI schemes

Most PFHI schemes cover a specific number of procedures and treatments, consisting mostly of hospitalisation and a few out-patient services. While the coverage of only hospitalisation services under these schemes and exclusion of out-patient services have been criticised by some, others have noted the potential risks of including out-patient care (Nandi and Schneider, 2020a).

These schemes are implemented either through an autonomous organisation (trust) set up by the state government to empanel hospitals and pay claims, or by hiring an insurance company and paying them premiums to handle the payments. Chhattisgarh has been implementing PFHI schemes through the insurance company system, but in 2020 it switched to direct payment of claims. The oversight of the scheme rests with the SNA at the state level and the NHA at the national level.

Transparency and accountability measures

Chhattisgarh runs a helpline to report grievances. However, an analysis of the helpline records shows that, perhaps due to the fear of retribution, few people complained against private hospitals (Nandi and Schneider, 2020b).

Data (even anonymised) on PFHI schemes is not available for public scrutiny, even though there is much emphasis on digitalisation. The author sought and received such data in Chhattisgarh but it is not otherwise available in public domain. The problem of transparency has worsened under the PMJAY. Data on the number of cases under the scheme is primarily made available to the public through Twitter updates. State factsheets uploaded onto the NHA website provide data for only a few broad indicators and are not updated regularly. Scheme data is made available to select researchers (for instance, the World Bank and the GIZ) and certain journalists. This means publications and studies using PMJAY data are produced by this very select group that is motivated by self-interest in advancing the scheme. Research on the PMJAY published by the NHA is often authored by people employed by these organisations, especially the World Bank, but this affiliation often remains unstated. The reports usually carry a disclaimer stating 'PMJAY data used in the analysis should not be utilised/quoted without prior permission of NHA,[14] which further restricts their use in public discourse.

In rural areas, even patients and their families are unable to easily access their own data, which is available only with the 'computer person' at a far-off health centre that has a computer. Paradoxically, the government's proposed digital health registry and digital health ID will allow commercial entities to sell medical data, thus making patients vulnerable to breaches of data privacy even as they remain unable to access their own information.

The increasing collusion between for-profit private hospitals and public administrators under PFHI schemes undermines any attempts at accountability. While dual practice by government doctors has always existed, PFHI schemes provide added monetary incentives – the ability to file insurance claims and extract illegal payments – to refer patients to their own private hospitals or those of their acquaintances.

Implications of PFHI schemes for women's access to health services

Exclusions in enrolment

State- and national-level studies on PFHI schemes have reported lower enrolment figures in remote rural areas and poorer districts among socio-economically vulnerable groups and indigenous communities in female-headed households and in the poor economic quintiles (Ranjan et al., 2018; Rao et al., 2014). Caste, indigenous status and gender have emerged as key determinants of inequity in enrolment and utilisation of health services (Health Inc, 2014; Rao et al., 2014; Thakur, 2015). With women already facing extreme hardships both within and outside their families in accessing healthcare, having to enrol in a PFHI scheme in order to access its benefits presents an additional barrier (RamPrakash and Lingam, 2018).

Most PFHI schemes are targeted at the poor, who are identified using government survey data. However, many poor people struggle to prove their eligibility (Sen and Gupta, 2017). Chhattisgarh has had a universal PFHI scheme since 2012 and one of the highest enrolment rates in the country. Currently, around 90 per cent of families and close to 75 per cent of individuals in the state are covered under MSBY and PMJAY. However, studies that focus on more vulnerable groups, such as Particularly Vulnerable Tribal Groups (PVTGs) and the urban poor, have found much lower enrolment rates (PHRN, 2017; SHRC CG, WHO India and Government of Chhattisgarh, 2020).

The RSBY entitled five family members, selected by the 'head of the family', to be enrolled on one card, creating room for possible gender-based and other forms of discrimination (RamPrakash and Lingam, 2018). Although the PMJAY removed the five-person limit, enrolment numbers in Chhattisgarh still show a gender gap. According to a 2019 study, the proportion of women enrolled in PFHI schemes in the state is marginally less (66 per cent) than the proportion of men (69 per cent) (SHRC CG, 2020). Individual women had 9 per cent less chance of enrolling in the scheme than men, and members of women-headed households had a 13 per cent less chance of being enrolled compared to those in households headed by men (SHRC CG, 2020).

Are women able to utilise PFHI schemes for hospitalisation?

Women have both a greater likelihood and higher rates of hospitalisation than men in some states (RamPrakash and Lingam, 2018; Ranjan et al., 2018), including Chhattisgarh (Nandi, Schneider and Dixit, 2017). However, whether hospitalised women are able to utilise PFHI schemes is a different story. Even with a universal PFHI scheme, more than a third of women who were hospitalised in Chhattisgarh were unenrolled (SHRC CG, 2020). When enrolled, women were often unable to utilise the scheme due to the non-availability of health facilities or refusal by hospitals under one pretext or another (Nandi et al., 2016; Nandi, Schneider and Garg, 2018). Ramabai, who belonged to a SC community in Sarguja district, was unable to avail of the family's PFHI enrolment when she was admitted to the intensive care unit of a private hospital after a possible miscarriage. The family was forced to cough up Rs 20,000 (260 USD) daily, excluding the cost of medicines. As the family struggled to arrange the necessary funds, they were informed by an acquaintance that 'he had seen her body wrapped up and kept on the floor somewhere'. Ramabai died. Her family found her body when they forced themselves into the ICU. The hospital forced them to deposit a further Rs 100,000 (1,333 USD) before releasing her body. They paid Rs 350,000 (4,666 USD) in hospital expenses.[15]

Availability of hospital care for women

Studies reveal that public, and not private, hospitals cater to more vulnerable groups under PFHI schemes (Prinja et al., 2013; Ranjan et al., 2018). This is also true of Chhattisgarh where women, indigenous communities and the poor have benefitted from the public health system regardless of PFHI enrolment (Nandi et al., 2016; Nandi, Schneider and Dixit, 2017).

Public hospitals in the state are distributed relatively uniformly compared with private hospitals which are concentrated in a few cities (non-tribal areas) (Nandi, Schneider and Garg, 2018). This inequitable distribution of private health facilities and utilisation of PFHI schemes is visible across states (CEHAT, 2017; Garg, 2018).

What are women being treated for under PFHI schemes?

PFHI schemes are utilised only for a small set of relatively profitable services, especially in the for-profit private sector (Dasgupta et al., 2013; Maurya and Ramesh, 2019). A PMJAY report analysing high- and very high-value claims (over Rs 30,000 or 400 USD), covering specialities such as cardiology, radiation oncology, cardio surgery, orthopaedics and neurosurgery, found that they were skewed against women. Of the total claims, 48 per cent were of women, but the proportion reduced to 38 per cent for high-value claims (Dong et al., 2019). However, women had a higher proportion of utilisation under oncology packages (Kaur, Jain and Bhatnagar, 2019).

In Chhattisgarh, the proportion of PMJAY claims is similar for men and women. Common claims included dental and ophthalmology services. For women, childbirth deliveries and conventional tubectomy (tubal ligation) constituted other highly utilised packages (SNA, 2019).

Experiences of women utilising the PFHI scheme

There is overwhelming evidence that, when utilising PFHI schemes, many women (1) incur high OOP costs due to illegal payments demanded by for-profit private hospitals, (2) face harassment and abuse when they are unable to pay, and (3) are subjected to unnecessary procedures and treatments.

(1) Women incur high OOP expenditure despite insurance coverage

Chhattisgarh has seen high OOP expenditure, especially in the for-profit private sector, since the inception of PFHI schemes (Nandi et al., 2016; Nandi, Schneider and Dixit, 2017). Despite an increase in the coverage amount, the same pattern continues under the PMJAY (Garg, Bebarta and Tripathi, 2020). Women incur higher OOP payments in the private sector regardless of whether or not they are insured. For enrolled women, the OOP expenditure was Rs 10,000 (133 USD) in the private sector compared to Rs 400 (5 USD) in the public sector (SHRC CG, 2020). In 2018–19, 93 per cent of complaints under the PMJAY were for money demanded by hospitals from patients (NHA, 2019). Such unethical practices saddle families with huge financial burden, forcing them to pay out of savings, take loans from family and friends, and sell or mortgage jewellery, land or other assets. Much of this burden is borne by women (Nandi et al., 2016; Nandi and Schneider, 2020b). As primary caregivers, women also bear the biggest brunt of health rights violations.

At a Right to Health convention organised by JSA Chhattisgarh, a participant belonging to the Gond tribe recounted how a Raipur private hospital refused to treat her husband under RSBY and made her pay Rs 240,000 (3,200 USD). When her husband was declared dead after ten days of hospitalisation, the hospital demanded an additional Rs 23,000 (306 USD) to release his body. She could only raise Rs 10,000. It is then that the hospital took her RSBY card and deducted the remaining Rs 13,000 and released his body. She would have to repay the money she had borrowed on her own (JSA Chhattisgarh, 2014).

(2) Women face harassment and abuse due to inability to pay

Women face abuse and humiliation from the staff and doctors at private hospitals when they are unable to pay the money illegally demanded of them. Hospitals do not allow patients to leave of their own free will, and instead, create circumstances that force patients' families to keep them at the hospital (Nandi and Schneider, 2020b). The following testimony illustrates how the private sector is prepared to go to any lengths to extract payment even when the PFHI scheme is used. Meena narrates:

> 'We told the doctor that we could not continue as we had run out of money and asked for the child to be discharged.' The senior doctor said: 'if your [economic] condition was not okay then why did you bring the child here? You should have taken him to Mekahara [government tertiary hospital] … You shouldn't have come here. You should have let him die.'[16]

(3) Women are subjected to unnecessary procedures and treatments

Since the first state PFHI schemes, women have been subjected to unnecessary procedures and treatments (Chatterjee, 2019; Nundy et al., 2013; Prasad and Raghavendra, 2012; RamPrakash and Lingam, 2018). Unnecessary hysterectomies and a rise in caesarean sections (C-sections) have been documented in private hospitals in many states, including Chhattisgarh. While for-profit private hospitals have always been performing unnecessary procedures/treatments, they are further incentivised to do so under PFHI schemes since the government pays for them.[17] This continues to be the trend under PMJAY too.

(3a) Unnecessary hysterectomies

National data shows that women with little or no formal education and from households with insurance coverage are more likely to undergo a hysterectomy (Prusty, Choithani and Dutt Gupta, 2018). In Chhattisgarh, cases of unnecessary hysterectomies emerged under the RSBY in 2012. Over a period of thirty months, nearly 7,000 cases of unnecessary hysterectomies were booked under the scheme, largely by for-profit private hospitals. Most of the women were between thirty and thirty-five years and belonged to a lower socio-economic strata. Similar incidents were also recorded in Bihar[18] and Andhra Pradesh.[19]

Many women were also (illegally) charged additional money for the operations. Two women testified that doctors in a private hospital in the city of Raipur in Chhattisgarh prescribed them a uterus removal procedure after they complained of stomach pain. One of the two women was also made to pay an extra Rs 20,000 (266 USD) in addition to Rs 30,000 (400 USD) she could avail with the RSBY card.[20] The women received neither compensation nor medical or other forms of support.

After these incidents emerged, the Chhattisgarh government placed restrictions on hysterectomies under the RSBY in the private sector. However, these guidelines were abandoned when the PMJAY was implemented in September 2018, leading to a fresh surge in hysterectomies in the state. An analysis of claims for hysterectomies under PMJAY between September 2018 and April 2019 shows that more than 75 per cent came from six states, led by Chhattisgarh (Kaur, Jain and Desai, 2019). More than 94 per cent of hysterectomy claims in the state came from the private sector (Kaur, Jain and Desai, 2019).

(3b) Caesarean sections

Chhattisgarh has also seen a high incidence of C-sections in the private sector under PFHI schemes. Claims data between September 2018 and 2019 shows that, under the PMJAY, 78 per cent of normal deliveries are performed by the public sector while 93 per cent of C-sections are performed by the private sector (SNA, 2019). Of the total deliveries under PMJAY, 29 per cent were C-sections, which is very high according to WHO's 2015 guidelines. For the private sector, this number was much higher at 63 per cent, propelled no doubt by monetary incentives provided by PFHI schemes.

Neglect of public health system and implications for women

Since the introduction of PFHI schemes, a larger proportion of claims have been made by the private sector. This trend continues under the PMJAY. In 2018–19, 62 per cent of the claims amount went to the private sector (NHA,

2019). This means that public funds, which could have been used to improve the public health system are, instead, channelled into the private sector which is concentrated in urban centres and mired in unethical practices.

As the private health sector captures a greater share of the market under the PMJAY, the scheme itself has seen significant increases in budgetary allocation. It was introduced as part of the Ayushman Bharat initiative which also includes a primary healthcare programme called Health and Wellness Centres (HWCs). The HWCs are a reorientation of the existing sub-centres and primary health centres that respond to community health needs by strengthening human resources and expanding the scope to cover non-communicable diseases (NCDs), mental health, etc., in addition to working on maternal and child health, and communicable diseases. In Chhattisgarh, functional HWCs have greatly increased the utilisation of public health services by women and the elderly, and enabled access to free medicines for NCDs (SHRC CG, WHO India and Government of Chhattisgarh, 2020). Yet, the national government, through higher budget allocations, has prioritised the PMJAY over HWCs and other government health programmes, including the NHM.

In 2019–20, the central government increased allocation to the PMJAY by 167 per cent to nearly Rs 40 billion (530 million USD) (JSA, 2019). In contrast, only Rs 16 billion (213 million USD) was allocated to HWCs, and that too was diverted from the NHM. In fact, allocation to the NHM had been steadily decreasing from 61 per cent in 2014–15 to 49 per cent in 2019–20.

In the 2020–1 Union Budget, allocation to the PMJAY was doubled (JSA, 2020). However, budget outlays for the NHM, which includes allocations to HWCs, Reproductive and Child Health (RCH), disease control programmes, immunisation and so on, were cut in real terms. Budget allocations for women-specific schemes across sectors (nutrition, health, etc.) shrunk, along with sharp reductions in capital outlays (meant for building hospitals, providing services and procuring equipment) (JSA, 2020).

Chhattisgarh's budgetary outlay for PFHI schemes increased forty times in eight years from Rs 200 million (2.7 million USD) in 2010–11 to Rs 8 billion (106 million USD) in 2018–19 (Garg, 2019). But this has been accompanied by a simultaneous reduction or stagnation in allocations for other health programmes. Though the NHM budget has been increasing in real terms in the state, the rate of increase is much lower than the PFHI budget (Nandi, 2019). The tribal sub-plan, which accounts for 39 per cent of the PFHI budget and is meant to benefit indigenous communities, is mainly utilised in non-tribal and urban centres which are dominated by private hospitals (Garg, 2019). This results in the transfer of resources away from more vulnerable communities and areas (Garg, 2019).

PMJAY and the Covid-19 pandemic

Since the first Covid-19 infection was reported in India on 29 January 2020, the figures multiplied rapidly, with over 117,000 average daily cases and more than 356,000 deaths as of 10 June 2021.[21] As the number of cases increased, so did the requirement for hospitalisation. Despite the quantum of resources directed towards the PMJAY and the for-profit private health sector, both failed to provide critical hospitalisation support during the ongoing pandemic. Initially private hospitals either shut operations or refused to admit Covid positive patients. Wherever the private sector treated such patients, they engaged in price-gouging and made people pay huge OOP bills.[22] While the government publicised free Covid testing and treatment under the PMJAY, private hospitals did not use these packages. According to news reports, only 2,132 claims were made under the PMJAY for Covid-19 treatment as of 20 May 2020.[23]

Overall claims under the PMJAY decreased drastically since the pandemic started, suggesting that private hospitals did not provide health services even to non-Covid patients. The average weekly claims during ten weeks of the national lockdown between March and June 2020 fell by over 51 per cent compared with twelve weeks before the lockdown, while claims in the early lockdown period declined by 76 per cent (Smith et al., 2020). This could partly be due to the inability of patients to travel for treatment due to the lockdown, but the major reason was that the private hospitals suspended their services or refused to admit patients under the PMJAY.

Data available on claims for Covid-19 hospitalisation under the universal PFHI scheme in Chhattisgarh shows that till 5 May 2021, there were 5,157 claims, which constitutes only 4 per cent of the total Covid-19 hospitalisations in the state (129,470) during that period (State Control and Command Centre, 2021). Of this, 77 per cent (3,978) claims were from the public sector and 23 per cent (1,179) from private hospitals, once again highlighting the failure of PFHI schemes to enable free hospitalisations, especially in the private sector.

Resistance of people's movements to PMJAY and other PPPs

The JSA, of which the author is a member, has been involved in the documentation of and research on implications of PFHI schemes for people, especially for the poor, women, and ST and SC communities. The JSA is the Indian regional circle of the global People's Health Movement (PHM). Its network partners include non-governmental organisations (NGOs) working on health, feminist organisations, people's science organisations, service delivery networks and trade unions.[24] Through evidence-based advocacy, direct street action and collaboration with other social movements, the JSA has put up strong resistance[25] against healthcare PPPs that have had negative implications for both people and government health systems.

The Chhattisgarh JSA unit has been involved in campaigns against privatisation of health services, PPPs and PFHI schemes (Nandi, 2018). Civil society organisations, including legal-aid, community-based and patients' rights groups and organisations, research institutes, and workers' unions under the Chhattisgarh JSA, have been actively monitoring the PMJAY and earlier schemes and providing documentary evidence and testimonials of violations (JSA Chhattisgarh, 2014, 2018). Community health workers (CHWs) from Chhattisgarh's state-wide CHW programme called Mitanin have been involved in monitoring and highlighting the issues women face in accessing health services, including those under PFHI schemes. CHWs have helped patients access the grievance redressal helpline and shared instances in which hospitals have been forced to return illegal OOP payments extorted from patients.

Following years of campaigning by the JSA and other groups, the ruling party that came to power in the 2018 elections in Chhattisgarh has developed new guidelines for PFHI schemes with a focus on public hospitals.[26] Under the revised universal healthcare scheme inaugurated in January 2020, a number of procedures related to primary and secondary care and those susceptible to provider-induced demand have been reserved for public hospitals. There is already a reversal of previous trends, with the public sector receiving a higher share of overall claims. However, while some ground has been reclaimed by the public sector in Chhattisgarh, the unethical practices of the for-profit private sector remain relatively unaffected.

Conclusion

As the largest PPP that the Indian government has ever promoted in healthcare, the PMJAY has prioritised the private sector over the public health system. This has diverted public resources away from the public health sector into the private sector. The under-resourcing of the public health system has proved to be a disaster for women's health and access to health services, especially those belonging to ST, SC, the poor and other vulnerable communities. Under the PMJAY, private interests have turned women's bodies into sites for profit making by subjecting them to unnecessary procedures and treatments. Through PFHI schemes, the government has prompted people to place their trust in the for-profit private sector, but has not put in place effective regulatory or grievance redressal mechanisms. The main objective of the scheme – preventing OOP expenditure – is far from realised. Instead, women face abuse and humiliation when resisting such payments.

The Covid-19 pandemic has further demonstrated that despite being prioritised in resource allocation, the PMJAY has failed to enable access to free healthcare when it was needed the most. The Indian government must recognise the failure of the PMJAY and abandon it. They must commit themselves to strengthening the public health system and making healthcare access more equitable. Instead of being promoted as a business or a commodity, healthcare must be reinstated as a right.

Notes

1   Recognising the discriminatory nature of the caste system in India, the Constitution of India classified disadvantaged social groups and communities into Scheduled Castes (SC) and Scheduled Tribes (ST) and made special provisions in order to undo socio-economic and political injustices towards them.
2   See 'Executive Summary: Report on the Status of Women in India'. Available at: https://wcd.nic.in/sites/default/files/Executive%20Summary_HLC_0.pdf.
3   The state has a population of just over 25.5 million.
4   Catastrophic health expenditure is an economic shock to families or individuals due to healthcare expenditure that is beyond their capacity to pay.
5   See 'Benefits of PMJAY'. Available at: https://pmjay.gov.in/benefits-of-pmjay.
6   About Pradhan Mantri Jan Arogya Yojana (PMJAY), see 'Why PM-JAY: A Background'. Available at: https://www.pmjay.gov.in/about-pmjay.
7   Tier 1 cities are the metropolitan cities, and Tier 2 and Tier 3 cities follow them in terms of lower population, levels of urban development, standards of living and other indicators.
8   See 'Central Government's Move to Privatise District Hospitals Spells Disaster for India's Poor', *Gaon Connection*. Available at: https://en.gaonconnection.com/central-governments-move-to-privatise-district-hospitals-spells-disaster-for-indias-poor.
9   The introduction of the Yeshasvini scheme in Karnataka (2002), for instance, is attributed to the founder of a corporate hospital chain (Venkat Raman and Björkman, 2008; Maurya and Mintrom, 2019).
10 See 'Ayushman Bharat Can Be a Success if Modi Govt Incentivises Digital Data for Private Players', *The Print*. Available at: https://theprint.in/opinion/

ayushman-bharat-can-be-a-success-if-modi-govt-incentivises-digital-data-for-private-players/353827.

11 See 'Panels to Review Ayushman Bharat Price Caps', *The Economic Times*. Available at: https://economictimes.indiatimes.com/news/politics-and-nation/panels-to-review-ayushman-bharat-price-caps/articleshow/69867242.cms.

12 See 'Patients Fleeced as Governments Dawdle', *The New Indian Express*. Available at: https://www.newindianexpress.com/thesundaystandard/2020/jan/26/patients-fleeced-as-governments-dawdle-2094601.html.

13 See 'Request for Qualification (RFQ) cum Request for Proposals (RFP) for Procurement of Project Management Consultant for ABNHPM'. Available at: https://pmjay.gov.in/node/169.

14 Considering that these selective reports are the only source of PMJAY data available in the public domain, and on the principle of public ownership of data sourced from public programmes, this paper uses and quotes these reports without any such 'permissions'. Reports are available at: https://pmjay.gov.in/resources/publication.

15 Case study developed from a complaint submitted by Ramabai's father-in-law to the health minister.

16 More details available in Nandi, 2019.

17 See 'The Uterus Snatchers of Andhra', *The Times of India*. Available at: https://timesofindia.indiatimes.com/india/The-uterus-snatchers-of-Andhra/articleshow/6239344.cms.

18 See '16,000 "Illegal" Hysterectomies Done in Bihar for Insurance Benefit', *Indian Express Archive*. Available at: http://archive.indianexpress.com/news/16000–illegal–hysterectomies-done-in-bihar-for-insurance-benefit/993625.

19 See 'Greedy Doctors Con 600 Tribal Women into Surgery', *Mumbai Mirror*. Available at: http://www.carped.org/attachments/article/30/Greedydoctors.pdf.

20 See 'Public Health, Private Tragedy', *The Hindu*. Available at: https://www.thehindu.com/opinion/op-ed/public-health-private-tragedy/article6633520.ece.

21 Johns Hopkins University Covid-19 Dashboard, June 2021. There are significant concerns about under-reporting.

22 See 'Statement on the Role of the Private Health Sector during the Covid-19 Pandemic', *Jan Swasthya Abhiyan*, People's Health Movement, India. Available at: http://phmindia.org/2020/04/28/statement-on-the-role-of-the-private-health-sector-during-the-covid-19-pandemic.

23 See 'Only 5,600 Health Insurance Claims – 3% of Total Covid Cases', *The Indian Express*. Available at: https://indianexpress.com/article/business/only-5600-health-insurance-claims-coronavirus-6438004.

24 For more details, see the website of the *Jan Swasthya Abhiyan*, People's Health Movement-India. Available at: http://phmindia.org/about-us.

25 See 'Saúde: Em Debate', 44 (1). Available at: http://revista.saudeemdebate. org.br/sed/issue/view/33/v.%2044%2C%20n.%20ESPECIAL%201.

26 See 'Chhattisgarh: A Single Healthcare Scheme to Raise Efficacy, Accountability', *The Indian Express.* Available at: https://indianexpress.com/ article/india/chhattisgarh-a-single-healthcare-scheme-to-raise-efficacy-accountability-6145898.

References

Balarajan, Y., S. Selvaraj and S. V. Subramanian (2011), 'India: Towards Universal Health Coverage: Health Care and Equity in India', *The Lancet*, 377 (9764): 505–15. Available at: 10.1016/S0140-6736(10)61894-6 (accessed 18 February 2020).

CEHAT (Centre for Enquiry into Health and Allied Themes) (2017), Suchitra Wagle and Nehal Shah, Government Funded Health Insurance Scheme in Maharashtra: Study of Rajiv Gandhi Jeevandayee Aarogya Yojana, Mumbai, Cehat. Available at: www.cehat.org/uploads/files/RGJAY%20Report.pdf.

Chatterjee, P. (2018), 'National Health Protection Scheme Revealed in India', *The Lancet*, 391 (10120): 523–4. Available at: 10.1016/S0140-6736(18)30241-1 (accessed 18 February 2020).

Chatterjee, P. (2019), 'Hysterectomies in Beed District Raise Questions for India', *The Lancet*, 394 (10194): 202. Available at: 10.1016/S0140-6736(19)31669-1 (accessed 18 February 2020).

Dasgupta, R., et al. (2013), 'What the Good Doctor Said: A Critical Examination of Design Issues of the RSBY through Provider Perspectives in Chhattisgarh, India', *Social Change*, 43 (2): 227–43. Available at: 10.1177/0049085713493043 (accessed 18 February 2020).

Dong, Di, et al. (2019), 'Raising the Bar: Analysis of PM-JAY High-Value Claims, PM-JAY Policy Brief 1'. Available at: https://www.pmjay.gov.in/sites/ default/files/2019-10/Policy%20Brief_Raising%20the%20Bar_High%20 Value%20Claims_10-10-19_WB.pdf (accessed 18 February 2020).

Forest Survey of India (2017), *India State of Forest Report, 2017*, Dehradun: Ministry of Environment & Forests. Available at: https://fsi.nic.in/isfr2017/ chattisgarh-isfr-2017.pdf (accessed 18 February 2020).

Gadre, Dr A., and Dr A. Shukla (2016), *Dissenting Diagnosis: Voices of Conscience from the Medical Profession*, Gurgaon: Random House.

Garg, S. (2018), 'Government Funded Health Insurance Schemes in India – Are They Able to Provide Services for the Scheduled Tribes Population?', in: *2nd National Conference on Health Technology Assessment*, Chandigarh: School of Public Health, PGI Chandigarh.

Garg, S. (2019), 'A Study of "Strategic Purchasing" as a Policy Option for Public Health System in India', PhD. Thesis. Mumbai: Tata Institute of Social Sciences.

Garg, S., K. K. Bebarta and N. Tripathi (2020), 'Performance of India's National Publicly Funded Health Insurance Scheme, Pradhan Mantri Jan Arogaya Yojana (PMJAY), in Improving Access and Financial Protection for Hospital Care: Findings from Household Surveys in Chhattisgarh State', *BMC Public Health*, 20 (1): 1–10. Available at: 10.1186/s12889-020-09107-4 (accessed 18 February 2020).

Garg, S., and S. Pande (2018), 'Learning to Sustain Change: Mitanin Community Health Workers Promote Public Accountability in India'. Available at: https://accountabilityresearch.org/publication/learning-to-sustain-change-mitanin-community-health-workers-promote-public-accountability-in-india/ (accessed 18 February 2020).

GIZ (2015), 'Health Insurance for India's Poor: Meeting the Challenge with Information Technology', Bonn and Eschborn. Available at: https://health.bmz.de/ghpc/case-studies/Health_Insurance_India_New/Health_insurance_for_India_s_poor_-_Long_version.pdf (accessed 18 February 2020).

Gupta, I., et al. (2017), 'Do Health Coverage Schemes Ensure Financial Protection from Hospitalization Expenses? Evidence from Eight Districts in India', *Journal of Social and Economic Development*, 19 (1): 83–93. Available at: 10.1007/s40847-017-0040-4 (accessed 18 February 2020).

Health Inc (2014), *Towards Equitable Coverage and More Inclusive Social Protection in Health*, Antwerp: ITG Press.

Jain, N. (2014), 'Rashtriya Swasthya Bima Yojana: A Step towards Universal Health Coverage in India', in: *India Infrastructure Report 2013/14: The Road to Universal Health Coverage*, New Delhi: Infrastructure Development Finance Company. Available at: http://www.idfc.com/pdf/report/2013-14/Chapter-10.pdf (accessed 18 February 2020).

JSA (2019), *Implications of the Interim Union Budget 2019–2020 for Health*, New Delhi: Jan Swasthya Abhiyan, 1–3.

JSA (2020), *Implications of the Union Budget 2020–21 for Health*, New Delhi: Jan Swasthya Abhiyan, 1–5. Available at: http://phmindia.org/wp-content/uploads/2020/02/Budget-2020-JSA-Analysis.pdf (accessed 18 February 2020).

JSA Chhattisgarh (2014), 'Report of Chhattisgarh JSA Convention', Raipur.

JSA Chhattisgarh (2018), 'Press Note on Chhattisgarh JSA Convention on Right to Health', Raipur. Available at: http://phmindia.org/wp-content/uploads/2018/04/JSA_chattisgarh_RTH.pdf (accessed 11 April 2019).

Kaur, S., N. Jain and S. Desai (2019), *Patterns of Utilization for Hysterectomy: An Analysis of EarlyTtrends from Ayushman Bharat Pradhan Mantri Jan Arogya Yojana (PM-JAY)*, New Delhi: National Health Authority.

Kaur, S., N. Jain and P. C. Bhatnagar (2019), *Early Trends from Utilization of Oncology Services: Insights from Ayushman Bharat Pradhan Mantri Jan Arogya Yojana (PM- JAY)*, New Delhi: Pradham Mantri Jan Arogya Yojana (PM-JAY).

Khetrapal, S., A. Acharya and A. Mills (2019), 'Assessment of the Public-Private-Partnerships Model of a National Health Insurance Scheme in India', *Social Science & Medicine*, 243: 112634. Available at: 10.1016/j. socscimed.2019.112634 (accessed 18 February 2020).

Mackintosh, M., et al. (2016), 'What Is the Private Sector? Understanding Private Provision in the Health Systems of Low-Income and Middle-Income', *The Lancet*, 388 (10044): 596–605. Available at: 10.1016/S0140-6736(16)00342-1 (accessed 18 February 2020).

Maurya, D., and M. Mintrom (2019), 'Policy Entrepreneurs as Catalysts of Broad System Change: The Case of Social Health Insurance Adoption in India', *Journal of Asian Public Policy*, 13 (1): 18–34. Available at: 10.1080/17516234.2019.1617955 (accessed 18 February 2020).

Maurya, D., and M. Ramesh (2019), 'Program Design, Implementation and Performance: The Case of Social Health Insurance in India', *Health Economics, Policy and Law*, 14 (4): 487–508. Available at: 10.1017/S1744133118000257 (accessed 18 February 2020).

Mukhopadhyay, I., and D. Sinha (2019), 'Painting a Picture of Ill-Health', in: Rohit Azad et al. (eds), *A Quantum Leap in the Wrong Direction?*, 155–79, New Delhi: Orient Black Swan.

Nandi, S. (2018), 'Struggle against Outsourcing of Diagnostic Services in Government Facilities: Strategies and Lessons from a Campaign Led by Jan Swasthya Abhiyan (People's Health Movement) in Chhattisgarh, India', *Journal of Social and Political Psychology*, 6 (2): 677–95. Available at: 10.5964/jspp.v6i2.923 (accessed 18 February 2020).

Nandi, S. (2019), 'Equity, Access and Utilisation in the State-funded Universal Insurance Scheme (RSBY/MSBY) in Chhattisgarh State, India: What Are the Implications for Universal Health Coverage?' (PhD. Thesis). Cape Town: School of Public Health, University of the Western Cape. Available at: http://etd.uwc.ac.za/xmlui/handle/11394/7393 (accessed 18 February 2020).

Nandi, S., and H. Schneider (2020a), 'Using an Equity-based Framework for Evaluating Publicly Funded Health Insurance Programmes as an Instrument of UHC in Chhattisgarh State, India', *Health Research Policy and Systems*, 18 (50): 1–14. Available at: 10.1186/s12961-020-00555-3 (accessed 18 February 2020).

Nandi, S., and H. Schneider (2020b), 'When State-funded Health Insurance Schemes Fail to Provide Financial Protection: An In-depth Exploration of the Experiences of Patients from Urban Slums of Chhattisgarh, India', *Global Public Health*, 15 (2): 220–35. Available at: 10.1080/17441692.2019.1651369 (accessed 18 February 2020).

Nandi, S., D. Joshi, and R. Dubey (2016), 'Unraveling the Clinical Establishment Act in Chhattisgarh: A Campaign and a Study', *BMJ Global Health*, 1 (S1): 40–1. Available at: https://gh.bmj.com/content/1/Suppl_1/A40 (accessed 18 February 2020).

Nandi, S., et al. (2016), 'Uncovering Coverage: Utilisation of the Universal Health Insurance Scheme, Chhattisgarh by Women in Slums of Raipur', *Indian Journal of Gender Studies*, 23 (1): 43–68. Available at: 10.1177/0971521515612863 (accessed 18 February 2020).

Nandi, S., H. Schneider and P. Dixit (2017), 'Hospital Utilization and Out of Pocket Expenditure in Public and Private Sectors under the Universal Government Health Insurance Scheme in Chhattisgarh State, India: Lessons for Universal Health Coverage', *PloS One*, 12 (11): e187904. Available at: 10.1371/journal.pone.0187904 (accessed 18 February 2020).

Nandi, S., H. Schneider and S. Garg (2018), 'Assessing Geographical Inequity in Availability of Hospital Services under the State-funded Universal Health Insurance Scheme in Chhattisgarh State, India, Using a Composite Vulnerability Index', *Global Health Action*, 11 (1). Available at: 10.1080/16549716.2018.1541220 (accessed 18 February 2020).

NHA (2019), 'Ayushman Bharat Pradhan Mantri Jan Arogya Yojana: Annual Report 2018–19', New Delhi.

NHSRC (2012), 'NRHM in the Eleventh Five Year Plan (2007–2012): Strengthening Public Health Systems', New Delhi. Available at: http://nhsrcindia.org/sites/default/files/NRHMin11thfiveyearplan.pdf (accessed 20 June 2018).

NHSRC (2018), 'National Health Accounts: Estimates for India FY 2015–16', New Delhi. Available at: https://main.mohfw.gov.in/sites/default/files/NHA_Estimates_Report_2015-16_0.pdf (accessed 18 February 2020).

NHSRC (n.d.), 'Household Healthcare Utilization & Expenditure in India: State Fact Sheets', New Delhi. Available at: http://nhsrcindia.org/sites/default/files/StateFactSheets_HealthcareUtilizationandExpenditureinIndia.pdf (accessed 18 February 2020).

NITI Aayog (2020), 'NITI Aayog Annual Report 2019–20', New Delhi. Available at: https://niti.gov.in/sites/default/files/2020-02/Annual_Report_2019-20.pdf (accessed 18 February 2020).

Nundy, M., et al. (2013), *The Rashtriya Swasthya Bima Yojana (RSBY) Experience in Chhattisgarh: What Does It Mean for Health for All ?*, New Delhi: Sama: Resource Group for Women and Health. Available at: https://www.researchgate.net/publication/304525632_The_Rashtriya_Swasthya_Bima_Yojana_RSBY_experience_in_Chhattisgarh_What_does_it_mean_for_Health_for_All (accessed 18 February 2020).

PHFI (2011), 'A Critical Assessment of the Existing Health Insurance Models in India', New Delhi. Available at: http://planningcommission.nic.in/reports/sereport/ser/ser_heal1305.pdf (accessed 18 February 2020).

PHRN (2017), 'Exploring Health Inequities amongst Particularly Vulnerable Tribal Groups: Case Studies of Baiga and Sabar in Chhattisgarh and Jharkhand States of India Report of a Study by Public Health Resource Network', Trivandrum.

Prasad, N. P., and P. Raghavendra (2012), 'Healthcare Models in the Era of Medical Neo-liberalism: A Study of Aarogyasri in Andhra Pradesh', *Economic & Political Weekly*, 47 (43): 118–26. Available at: https://www.epw.in/journal/2012/43/special-articles/healthcare-models-era-medical-neo-liberalism.html (accessed 18 February 2020).

Prinja, S., et al. (2013), 'Equity in Hospital Services Utilisation in India', *Economic & Political Weekly*, 48 (12): 52–8. Available at: https://www.epw.in/journal/2013/12/special-articles/equity-hospital-services-utilisation-india.html (accessed 18 February 2020).

Prinja, S., et al. (2017), 'Impact of Publicly Financed Health Insurance Schemes on Healthcare Utilization and Financial Risk Protection in India: A Systematic Review', *PloS One*, 12 (2): e0170996. Available at: 10.1371/journal.pone.0170996 (accessed 18 February 2020).

Prusty, R. K., C. Choithani and S. D. Gupta (2018), 'Predictors of Hysterectomy among Married Women 15–49 Years in India', *Reproductive Health*, 15 (3). Available at: 10.1186/s12978-017-0445-8 (accessed 18 February 2020).

RamPrakash, R., and L. Lingam (2018), 'Publicly Funded Health Insurance Schemes (PFHIS): A Systematic and Interpretive Review of Studies Does Gender Equity Matter?', *eSSH*. Available at: http://www.esocialsciences.org/eSSH_Journal/Repository/6N_PubliclyFundedHealthInsuranceSchemes_Rajalakshmi.pdf (accessed 12 July 2019).

Ranjan, A., et al. (2018), 'Effectiveness of Government Strategies for Financial Protection against Costs of Hospitalization Care in India', *BMC Public Health*, 18. Available at: 10.1186/s12889-018-5431-8 (accessed 18 February 2020).

Rao, M. (2009). '"Health for All" and Neoliberal Globalisation: An Indian Rope Trick', in: L. Panitch and C. Leys (eds), *Socialist Register 2010: Morbid Symptoms*, London: Merlin Press, 262–78. Available at: https://socialistregister.com/index.php/srv/article/view/6774 (accessed 20 June 2018).

Rao, M., et al. (2014), 'Changes in Addressing Inequalities in Access to Hospital Care in Andhra Pradesh and Maharashtra States of India: A Difference-in-differences Study Using Repeated Cross-sectional Surveys', *BMJ Open*, 4 (6): e004471. Available at: 10.1136/bmjopen-2013-004471 (accessed 18 February 2020).

RGI and Census Commissioner (2011), 'Census of India Website'. Available at: http://censusindia.gov.in/2011-Common/CensusData2011.html (accessed 29 May 2018).

RGI (2020), 'Sample Registration System (SRS) Bulletin', 53 (1). New Delhi: Government of India. Available at: https://censusindia.gov.in/vital_statistics/SRS_Bulletins/SRSBulletin_2018.pdf (accessed 18 February 2020).

Rodríguez Enríquez, C. (2019), *Corporate Accountability and Women's Human Rights: An Analytical Approach to Public-Private Partnerships (PPPs)*, Suva: Development Alternatives with Women for a New Era (DAWN). Available at: https://dawnnet.org/wp-content/uploads/2021/04/DAWN-Discussion-Paper-31_-PPPs-analytical-framework.pdf (accessed 18 February 2020).

Sen, K., and S. Gupta (2017), 'Masking Poverty and Entitlement: RSBY in Selected Districts of West Bengal', *Social Change*, 47 (3): 339–58. Available at: 10.1177/0049085717715557 (accessed 18 February 2020).

Sengupta, A., et al. (2017), 'The Rise of Private Medicine in South Asia', *BMJ*, 357: j1482. Available at: 10.1136/bmj.j1482 (accessed 18 February 2020).

Smith, O., et al. (2020), 'PM-JAY Policy Brief 8: PM-JAY under Lockdown: Evidence on Utilization Trends', New Delhi.

SNA (2019), *Data of PMJAY and MSBY Utilisation from September 2018 to October 2019*, Raipur: Department of Health and Family Welfare, Chhattisgarh.

State Health Resource Centre Chhattisgarh, World Health Organization India and Government of Chhattisgarh (SHRC CG, WHO India and Government of Chhattisgarh) (2020), 'Demand Side Assessment of Primary Healthcare in Chhattisgarh', Raipur.

State Health Resource Centre Chhattisgarh (SHRC CG) (2020), *Study on Pradhan Mantri Jan Arogaya Yojana (PMJAY) in Chhattisgarh State through Household Surveys*, Raipur: SHRC Chhattisgarh.

Thakur, H. (2015), 'Study of Awareness, Enrollment, and Utilization of Rashtriya Swasthya Bima Yojana (National Health Insurance Scheme) in Maharashtra, India', *Frontiers in Public Health*, (January): 282. Available at: 10.3389/fpubh.2015.00282 (accessed 18 February 2020).

Venkat Raman, A., and J. W. Björkman (2008), 'Public-Private Partnerships in India', in: A. Venkat Raman and J. W. Björkman (eds), *Public-Private Partnerships in Health Care in India: Lessons for Developing Countries*, 1, Abingdon-New York: Routledge.

Virk, A. K., and R. Atun (2015), 'Towards Universal Health Coverage in India: A Historical Examination of the Genesis of Rashtriya Swasthya Bima Yojana – The Health Insurance Scheme for Low-income Groups', *Public Health*, 129 (6): 810–17. Available at: 10.1016/j.puhe.2015.02.002 (accessed 18 February 2020).

7

PPPs in agro-energy and their impact on women's rights: The case of Addax Bioenergy Sierra Leone

Hussainatu J. Abdullah

Introduction

The near-total destruction of the country's ailing infrastructure during the 1991–2002 civil war prompted the government of Sierra Leone (GoSL) to make infrastructure restoration one of the pillars of its post-war development agenda. The aim was to move the country from post-war humanitarian assistance to socio-economic development and poverty reduction. To achieve this goal, the GoSL sought counsel from the World Bank's (WB) Public-Private Infrastructure Advisory Facility (PPIAF) in 2009 (World Bank, 2011). The PPIAF provided technical assistance to Sierra Leone's public enterprises by entering into long-term contractual arrangements with private sector service providers and developing minimum standards and regulations to govern private-public partnership (PPP) contracts (World Bank, 2011). These efforts resulted in the inclusion of PPPs as a financing mechanism for infrastructure development in the Agenda for Prosperity, Sierra Leone's third-generation poverty reduction strategy (PRS) in force during 2013–18 (GoSL, 2013).

When it comes to gender equality, the discourse on PPPs is dominated by two perspectives. The first, promoted by donor governments and international financial institutions (IFIs) such as the World Bank Group (WBG), advocates for PPPs as the instrument of choice for financing the United Nations' Sustainable Development Goals (SDGs) and makes the case for gender mainstreaming these projects. It is worth noting that Sierra Leone's PPP framework remains profoundly gender insensitive even though the WBG and its agencies have been instrumental in shaping these policies (Eurodad, 2018; WBG, 2019). The second viewpoint comes from social justice campaigners such as gender equality and women's rights activists, civil society organisations (CSOs) and trade unions. These groups argue that it is impossible to use the PPP framework, driven as it is by a profit-maximisation motive, to attain long-term social development, including gender equality (Eurodad, G&DN and FEMNET, 2019).

This chapter uses the PPP contract between GoSL and the private sector entity Addax Bioenergy Sierra Leone Limited (ABSL) as a case study to analyse how the project undermined women's rights and social development in its areas of operation. Broadly, the chapter is divided into two parts. The first part reviews the country's infrastructure sector, explores its legal and regulatory framework on PPPs, and traces the PPP landscape in the country with emphasis on the energy and agriculture sectors. The second part uses a social justice lens to examine the socio-economic impact of the ABSL PPP, its repercussions on labour and women's rights, and the resistance mounted against the project.

Overview of the infrastructure sector

Sierra Leone's civil conflict unleashed untold misery on its citizens and left the country's social, economic and physical infrastructure completely destroyed. About 75 per cent of privately operated vehicles were burnt or destroyed, several boats were sunk in the coastal areas, feeder roads were dug out, and bridges were damaged by the rebels (World Bank, 2001). Water facilities in rural and urban areas as well as fishing infrastructures were destroyed (IMF, 2005). Electricity generation declined drastically from a peak of 196 GW hours in 1984 to 25–30 GW hours in 2000 (GoSL, 2003). In the provincial headquarters of Bo and Kenema in the southern and eastern provinces, respectively, electricity generation nearly collapsed (GoSL, 2008).

Between 2006 and 2009, Sierra Leone was ranked among the bottom six countries on the African Infrastructure Development Index (AIDI)[1] (AfDB, 2011). Despite significant investments in the sector since 2009, the country's AIDI average of 7.4 for 2009–11 was half the continental average of 14.8 over the same period (AfDB, 2015). Between 2016 and 2018, it slipped further to land among the bottom ten countries on the index (AfDB, 2018). The country has one of the lowest rates of penetration and the highest costs of public utility services in the continent (AfDB, 2018). Its infrastructure deficit worsened due to a high rate of urbanisation (AfDB, 2018).

Following the end of the civil war in 2002, the GoSL prioritised its development goals to focus on 'conflict resolution; restoration of security; democracy and good governance [...] physical infrastructures that would lay the foundation for achieving sustainable growth and poverty reduction' (IMF, 2005: 57). In the infrastructure sector, the aim was to improve energy supply and the road and transport network and build information and communications technology (ICT) (IMF, 2008). To achieve these goals, the government resorted to private sector funding through the PPP modality for public infrastructure projects in the water, power, roads, ports, airports and telecommunications sectors (GoSL, 2013).

Institutional, legal and regulatory frameworks for PPPs

The process to create a legal platform for private investment in public infrastructure development started with the publication of PPP Regulations under the Public Procurement and Disposal Act (PPDA), 2005 in 2009. The PPDA outlined the GoSL's commitment to PPPs as a priority mechanism to address the infrastructure budget shortfall, and provided a pathway for the enactment of a law for PPP delivery (GoSL, n.d.-a). This agenda was further buoyed by the Private and Financial Sector Development (PFSD) project which sought to support the country's efforts to generate more foreign and local investments and build government capacity to engage in sustainable and beneficial PPPs (Solution Africa, 2019). Together, these culminated in the adoption of the PPP Policy and the enactment of the PPP Act. No. 11 2014 (Solution Africa, 2019). The Act set the standards for PPP procurement based on service delivery, risk transfer and good governance process (GoSL, n.d.-a). It also paved the way for the establishment of the Public Private Partnership Unit (PPPU).

The PPPU was funded by the African Development Bank (AfDB), the International Finance Corporation (IFC), the UK's Department for International Development (DfID) and the WB. The WB and IFC supported the GoSL in drafting the PPP Bill to ensure adherence to international best practices (DfID, 2014, 2018). Between 2013 and 2015, the GoSL, AfDB and United Nations Development Programme (UNDP) provided resources worth 2.14 million British pounds (GBP) to support the establishment of the PPPU (see Table 7.1).

Table 7.1 Donor Support for Sierra Leone's Public-Private Partnership Unit, 2013–15.

Item	Funder	Amount
Staff salaries and running costs	GoSL	490,000 GBP
International PPP advisor	UNDP	250,000 GBP
Financial and legal advisors and training	AfDB	200,000 GBP
Equipment, technical assistance, and studies	DfID	1,200,000 GBP
Total		2,140,000 GBP

Source: DfID Annual Review Summary Sheet 2014.

The PPP landscape

The PPPU works in the energy, agriculture, fisheries, transportation, health and education sectors. The current PPP landscape in Sierra Leone consists of four projects in the energy sector, and one each in the transportation and fisheries sectors (see Table 7.3 in Annex 1 for details). The ongoing PPPs in the energy sector include Bumbuna Phase II Hydro Power Project, Western Area Generation Project (or the Kissy HFO Project),[2] Solar Era, 25 MW Betmai Hydro, Addax Bioenergy Sierra Leone/Sunbird, Planet Core Solar and United Nations Office for Project Services (UNOPS) (see Annex 1 for more details on the last two PPPs).

Situating the emergence of ABSL within Sierra Leone's development agenda

ABSL straddles Sierra Leone's energy and agriculture sectors. According to one of its investors, the AfDB, the PPP project was fully aligned with the GoSL's social investment and development objective policy, as outlined in its second-generation PRS, the Agenda for Change 2008–12 (AfDB, 2009). It also shared the same goals as Sierra Leone's investment policy, being a large agricultural and industrial project that would:

1. Provide job opportunities at all skill levels;
2. Provide significant foreign direct investment (FDI);
3. Be export-oriented;

4. Make extensive use of local raw materials;
5. Ensure the development and transfer of a variety of skills and technologies;
6. Produce a surplus of electricity for commercial purposes; and
7. Make use of renewable energy resources (AfDB, 2009).

The AfDB also notes that the ABSL project was in line with the National Sustainable Agriculture Development Plan (NSADP) and the sector-wide Smallholder Commercialization Programme (SCP), aimed at achieving the objectives of the Agenda for Change (AfDB, 2009).

The energy sector

The immediate post-war energy sector was characterised by inadequate production capacity, a non-integrated transport system and a distribution system with only 35,000 connections (WBG, 2011). Against this backdrop, the PPIAF, called upon to assist in reviewing the options available on financing, ownership and operation of the power sector, recommended a combination of government facilitation with private resources and international community assistance as a gateway to increasing the rate of energy access in the country (WBG, 2011). The funding was used to review the performance of the National Power Authority (NPA) and the Bo-Kenema Power Service (BKPS). Subsequently, the 2005 NPA Act allowed private sector participation in the energy sector, repealing the NPA's monopoly over the generation, transmission and supply of electricity, and related matters (WBG, 2011). Finally, the passage of the 2011 Electricity Act unbundled the country's energy sector.

Almost ten years since the thirteen-year Electricity Sector Reform roadmap was set in motion, Sierra Leone's electricity situation has shown some improvement, but remains abysmal overall. The 16 per cent electricity access rate is among the lowest in the world, with roughly 90 per cent of the country's 172,000 users located in the urban parts of Freetown (World Bank, 2019). Only five of the sixteen district capitals are partially supported by a combination of small diesel units and mini-hydropower plants, and the electrification rate in rural areas is almost non-existent (World Bank, 2019). The GoSL, with support from development partners such as the WB, the Japan International Cooperation Agency (JICA), the DfID and several PPP arrangements, is leveraging various energy platforms such as hydroelectricity, thermal generation and solar power to achieve universal access to electricity.

The agriculture sector

Sierra Leone's agricultural agenda promotes foreign investment and a market-led approach for private sector development of commercial agriculture. The strategy is premised on the belief that the private sector drives the organisation of value chains that bring the market to smallholders and commercial farms, a concept known as Agriculture for Development, or A4D as per the WB's 2008 Report (Oakland Institute, 2011). This strategy was adopted in the NSADP which aims to 'increase the agriculture sector's contribution to the national economy by increasing productivity through commercialisation and private sector participation' (Oakland Institute, 2011: 11).

Critics note that 'the agribusiness framework will benefit only traders and retailers while transforming smallholders into out-growers' (Christian Aid, 2013: 12). ABSL is part of the GoSL's industrial-scale agriculture programme that CSOs describe as land grabbing. According to the 2015 National Land Policy (NLP), land grabbing refers to as 'an act of claiming ownership of a piece of land without following appropriate procedures recognized by statutory or customary law in Sierra Leone' (GoSL, 2015: xii).

A host of institutions were established to further the government's agenda for the commercialisation of agriculture. The focal point in this agenda is the Sierra Leone Investment and Export Promotion Agency (SLIEPA) instituted in 2007 to 'assist and inform investors and exporters' on conducting business in Sierra Leone (GoSL, 2015: 13). Established with direct assistance from the IFC and Foreign Investment Advisory Services (FIAS), the DfID and the International Trade Centre (ITC), the SLIEPA promotes large-scale agriculture projects in sugar and palm oil with incentives to attract investments into the country. The key points used by the agency to attract potential investors include:

1. Agricultural labour cost of 2–3 US dollars (USD) per day is at par with other African countries and lower than Asia or Latin America;
2. Labour regulation is relatively flexible, with productivity-based payments;
3. Leases on good agricultural land range from 5 to 20 USD per year (compared to 100+ USD in Brazil, 450+ USD in Indonesia and 3,000+ USD per hectare in Malaysia);
4. There are no charges for utilisation of water resources;
5. Electricity rates are high, but since palm oil producers are expected to generate their own power and sell to the grid, high rates are beneficial; and
6. Tax rates are very attractive, with zero per cent tax on corporate income and imported inputs for qualified investors. (GoSL, 2015)

Other WBG initiatives to promote land commercialisation and privatisation include SLIEPA's Agribusiness Investment Task Force (AITF), the Investment Climate Facility (ICF),[3] land registration in the Western Area where land is freehold[4] and the IFC's programme to Remove Administrative Barriers to Investments (RABI). In addition, investors in Sierra Leone are protected under accords with two WB-affiliated risk agencies that provide various types of insurance to protect their investments, including against political risks. Due to the pro-investment climate in the country, FDI increased from 8 million USD per year in the 2000–5 period to 81 million USD in 2007 (GoSL, 2015).

Women's land rights

Sierra Leone was bequeathed a dual land tenure system by the British colonial government at the time of independence because the country was ruled as two separate entities: the colony and the protectorate. The colony constitutes the capital city of Freetown and its environs, where land ownership is based on freehold, meaning land can be freely bought and sold. Land ownership in the rest of the country is based on leasehold. In this legal system, land is the 'property' only of the indigenous land-owning families, known as 'natives', with usufruct land rights. The 1927 Protectorate Land Act barred non-natives (including Krios, foreigners, foreign companies and even missionary churches) from leasing land in the provinces for more than fifty years and allowed extensions of only up to twenty-one years (Oakland Institute, 2011).

While women are the primary producers and farmers in the country, their access to land is hindered by customary law as well as legal barriers in Sierra Leone's Constitution (FAO, 2016). Under customary law, even women who are members of land-owning families are barred from filing lawsuits over land disputes in court in certain parts of the country, have little or no access to desirable land, are left out of transactions involving family land, have no rights of inheritance and succession related to land, and are inadequately represented in land-related decision-making at various levels (Conteh and Thompson, 2019). Women also cannot seek recourse within the formal legal system because it exempts customary law from non-discrimination provisions, and places restrictions on the application of customary law in civil matters (Conteh and Thompson, 2019).

Land reform advocates have demanded equity for women, marginalised groups and 'non-natives' in order to end the discriminatory practices inherent in the leasehold system. Land reform is also championed by international financial institutions such as the WBG in order to improve investor access to land (Oakland Institute, 2011). These efforts led to the enactment of the NLP and the incorporation of the Voluntary Guidelines on the Responsible Governance of Tenure of Land, Fisheries and Forest (VGGT) into the policy (Namati, 2015). In 2015, the NLP called for a constitutional amendment and repeal, modification or elimination of all prejudiced laws, policies, customs and practices against women (Conteh and Thompson, 2019). The yet-to-be-implemented policy has provisions to individualise land, end the distinction between 'native' and 'non-native' rights to land, strengthen women's access and control over land, create a binding framework for responsible large-scale investments in land, situate land management structures at the community level and bring certainty to land transactions with the introduction of a compulsory title registration system (Namati, 2015). In addition, the policy proposes eight strategies to promote women's rights to land and property.

Namati, a global network of grassroots legal advocates working on land and environmental justice in Sierra Leone, drafted two land bills in 2020 that promote women's land rights and participation. The first, the Model Customary Land Bill, aims to give legal effect to provisions in the 2015 NLP. Among other provisions, it limits large-scale land acquisitions to 5,000 hectares and mandates that decisions about family land receive the approval of at least 75 per cent of male and female family members above eighteen years of age. The terms on which the 5,000 hectares can be exceeded are detailed in the Model Land Commission Bill (see Annex 3). The objective of this Bill is to establish the National Land Commission and other land administration bodies in Sierra Leone in line with the 2015 NLP. One of its crucial provisions stipulates that women should constitute at least 40 per cent of the members of the Board, Land Commissioners, District-level Commissioners, the Chiefdom Land Committee and the Town/Village Area Land Committee (Namati, 2020b).

ABSL: A brief background

Although operational prior to the commencement of Sierra Leone's PPP programme, ABSL is classified as a PPP project since a private sector entity, in partnership with development financial institutions (DFIs), partnered with the GoSL to generate electricity (Bread for the World, 2016). ABSL became operational in 2011 after a three-year negotiation between the GoSL, local leaders in the project areas and ABSL officials. The company is a fully owned subsidiary of the Swiss-based Addax and Oryx Group Limited (AOG). The parent company was formed in 1987 as an oil, gas and bioethanol exploring and trading company, and is a key player in Africa's energy industry. It is incorporated in Malta, a European tax haven which offers a high level of anonymity. The financial reports of AOG are, therefore, unavailable in the public domain (Bread for the World, 2016).

ABSL was established in 2008 to create a sustainable investment model for biofuels in Africa (Business Wire, 2011). The project was to develop a greenfield integrated agricultural and renewable energy product to produce fuel ethanol and electricity (AfDB, 2009). It was expected to produce about 90,000 cubic metres of ethanol per annum for the European Union (EU) market and 32 MW of nominal electrical power for the ethanol refinery, of which 15 MW would be sold to Sierra Leone's national grid through a power purchase agreement (PPA) with the NPA (AfDB, 2009).

The project is located in the chiefdoms of Makari Gbaniti and Bombali Sheboro in the Bombali District and the Malal Mara Chiefdom in the Tonkolili District, in the Northern Province of Sierra Leone (AfDB, 2009). The project area is surrounded, in the west and south, by the Rokel River, from which the project would draw water for irrigation (ActionAid, 2013). It was estimated that the project would utilise 2 per cent of the Rokel River water (Swedwatch, 2017). Even though lands were leased in 2010, cane cultivation started much earlier, and ethanol and electricity production commenced in 2014 (Bread for the World, 2016). ABSL leased a total of 57,000 hectares of land, more than the net needs of the project (AfDB, 2009). However, the lease included a relinquishment clause allowing ABSL to return unused land with a five-year grace period within which land had to be either developed or given up. Farmers were free to continue their operations on the land that was given up (AfDB, 2009).

The project used 14,300 hectares of land, constituting 10,000 hectares of irrigated sugarcane estates, land for project infrastructure, including an ethanol factory, a power plant, resettlement areas, roads, irrigation infrastructure and supporting infrastructure such as a power line connecting the power plant to the national grid (AfDB, 2009). In addition, approximately 2,000 hectares were developed as part of the Farmer Development Programme (FDP) that works in conjunction with the Food and Agriculture Organization (FAO) to secure the per capita food baseline in the project area (AfDB, 2009). A further 1,800 hectares were used as ecological corridors and buffer areas to protect existing pockets of biodiversity (AfDB, 2009). The land for the irrigation pivots was chosen based on the criteria of agricultural sustainability, proximity to the factory and water sources, and avoidance of villages, forests and food-producing areas, with the aim of minimising economic and physical displacement (AfDB, 2009).

The land lease was for fifty years, with the possibility of a further 21-year renewal. Fifty per cent of the 12 USD per hectare annual rental fee would go to the landowners, 20 per cent to the chiefdoms, another 20 per cent to the district councils and 10 per cent to the national government (Oakland Institute, 2011). ABSL's employment figures vary depending on the source. The Memorandum of Understanding (MoU) states that 3,000 people would be employed in the first phase of production between 2010 and 2013, and another 1,000 people would be added in the second phase between 2013 and 2015 (Oakland Institute, 2011). The ABSL website, however, acknowledges no more than 2,000 'direct jobs', without defining the term. ABSL's Environmental, Social and Health Impact Assessment (ESHIA) puts the employment figure at 2,200 permanent and 2,500 seasonal workers, locally recruited.

While the project was being formalised, the then opposition party, Sierra Leone People's Party (SLPP), which is currently in power, expressed concern that the production of bioenergy would consume land that could otherwise be used for food production, thus endangering food security. However, the then ruling party, All People's Congress (APC), and its ally in parliament, the People's Movement for Democratic Change (PMDC) party, supported the MoU and the Sierra Leone parliament ratified it on 10 November 2010 (Oakland Institute, 2011). A stabilisation clause in the MoU exempted ABSL 'from any law that comes into effect or is amended, modified, repealed, withdrawn or replaced, that has a material adverse effect on Addax (or its contractors or shareholders)' (Christian Aid, 2013: 13). This locked future governments and generations into the terms of this MoU, and presumably the actual lease, until 2060 (Oakland Institute, 2011). Clause 7(i) mandated that 'All disputes shall be referred to and finally resolved by arbitration in London before three arbitrators under the Rules of Arbitration of the International Chamber of Commerce from time to time' (Oakland Institute, 2011: 14). This clause made it impossible for landowners who could not afford foreign travel to seek justice (SiLNoRF and BfA, 2014).

While ABSL was granted tax exemptions that would allow it to save 135 million USD on its tax bill over the next ten years (SiLNoRF and BfA, 2014), the GoSL levied a 15 per cent goods and services tax (GST) in January 2010 to increase the domestic revenue base. The use of tax incentives to attract FDI has been widely criticised, including by the International Monetary Fund (IMF). In addition to general exemptions for all companies, ABSL enjoyed extra concessions from the government (see Table 7.2).

AOG mobilised two African development financial institutions and six European development financial institutions (EDFIs) to fund ABSL. The Netherlands Development Finance Company (FMO) and the Emerging Africa Infrastructure Fund (EAIF) were the co-lead arrangers for 142 million euros provided by the DFIs (Cordiant, 2011). The German Investment

Table 7.2 Tax Incentives for Agribusinesses and ABSL.

Standard rate for all companies	Incentives for all agribusinesses	Special deal for ABSL
Corporate income tax	10-year exemption	Special deal: 13-year exemption up to 31 December 2022
3% import duty on raw materials/agricultural inputs	Exemption	Same
0% import duty on plant/ machinery equipment for 5 years	Same	Same
15% withholding tax on interest	Same	Special deal: 5%
Withholding tax on dividends: 50% exemption	Same	Same
Profit from leasing property: Tax deductible allowance of 20%	Same	Special deal: Lease rents are allowable reduction not subject to withholding tax
Other		Special deal: Other bona fide business payments and expenses are deductible against tax and not subject to withholding tax

Source: Christian Aid (2013), 'Who is Benefitting?' Available at: https://www.christianaid.org.uk/sites/default/files/2017-08/who-is-benefitting-sierra-leone-report-july-2013.pdf (accessed 16 February 2020).

Corporation (Deutsche Investitions-und Entwicklungsesellschaft or DEG), the Belgian Investment Company for Developing Countries (BIO), the EAIF, FMO, the AfDB, the South African Industrial Development Corporation (IDC) and the Canadian Cordiant-managed ICF Debt Pool also invested in the project. FMO and Sweden-based DFI Swedfund joined AOG as equity partners (Cordiant, 2011) (see Annex 2 for more details). The total investment was stated variously as 257 million euros, 267 million euros, 400 million euros and 455 million euros (Bread for the World, 2016) (see Table 7.4 in Annex 2).

ABSL adopted a slew of environmental and social standards and safeguards, including the South African Industrial Development Corporation's Code of Ethics, the AfDB's Integrated Safeguard System, the Equator Principles, the Guiding Principles on Business and Human Rights and several in-house standards of the DFIs (Bread for the World, 2016). In 2009, all sixteen EDFIs adopted the Principles of Responsible Finance which is based on the United Nations Declaration of Human Rights, the International Labour Organization (ILO) Core Conventions, and the International Finance Corporation Performance Standards (IFC-PS), which became the reference standards for all other standards and safeguards (Bread for the World, 2016). All DFIs, except the IDC and AfDB, adopted the IFC-PS which was conditional to the contractual relations of all the other DFIs with ABSL (Bread for the World, 2016). The association with the DFIs played a role in ABSL receiving the first African Certification by the Roundtable for Sustainable Biomaterials (RSB) (Swedwatch, 2017). The RSB certification allowed ABSL to meet the EU's requirement that all biofuels that count towards its renewable targets should have a certificate of sustainability verification. It also eased the entry of ABSL's biofuels into EU markets when production started in 2014 (ActionAid, 2013). Moreover, the company became the first operation in Sierra Leone to be registered as a Clean Development Mechanism project of the UN Framework Convention on Climate Change (ActionAid, 2013).

Local and international non-governmental organisations (NGOs) contradicted ABSL's glowing portrayal of itself as an environmentally sustainable project that would create a win-win situation for all stakeholders, ensure food security and protect livelihoods. The NGOs pointed out that its operations failed to adhere to the RSB criteria by negatively impacting food security; violating the principle of free, prior and informed consent (FPIC); and carrying out involuntary resettlement of project residents (SiLNoRF and BfA, 2013b). They also noted that the project disregarded the land rights of local communities and threatened their livelihoods (ActionAid, 2013). Citing this flouting of criteria and an audit process that was weak and inadequate to assess biofuel projects, they demanded the withdrawal of ABSL's RSB certification (SiLNoRF and BfA, 2013b). ABSL, however, ignored these criticisms (FAO, 2014).

Impact of ABSL PPP on women's rights and gender equality

Unlike other parts of the country, the Northern Province, where ABSL operates, is known for its strict adherence to the customary practice of denying women both access to and ownership of land (Sesay, 2015). ABSL followed this discriminatory practice by failing to establish a quota guaranteeing female employment in the company:

> Several women said they wished for more opportunities to work with ABSL, and company decision makers would like to employ them because they are more reliable and conscientious machine operators. However,

they also reported that employing women had often caused problems with husbands and speculated that many women were likely barred by their husbands from seeking jobs with ABSL.

(SEI, 2015)

As of May 2015, only 6 per cent of ABSL's employees were women (SiLNoRF and BfA, 2016). The company's reluctance to rock the boat could be partly attributed to the DFIs' failure to include the promotion of women's rights as a value to be abided by. This despite the fact that AfDB, one of the DFIs, requires all projects funded by its member countries to reserve at least 30 per cent of their jobs for women. Surprisingly, the AfDB did not advocate for this quota in the case of ABSL.

The outcome of ABSL's gender-based discriminatory practices included displacement, loss of access to fertile land used for food production, and food insecurity. Although women typically do not own land, even their access to farmland diminished with the presence of ABSL. As most farmlands are under long leases, female farmers lost their livelihoods as leased areas overlapped with their fields. The company's presence also made female farmers' access to farmlands difficult due to the stiff competition for land to grow sugarcane which, unlike jatropha (a non-food crop for ethanol), cannot be grown on marginal lands (SiLNoRF and BfA, 2016). Furthermore, ABSL's activities such as land clearance and the damming of rivers worsened the water quality, and the chemicals used by the company contaminated the water during the rainy season (SEI, 2015). Fish stock in the Rokel river decreased and fishing in the streams stopped due to levelling and drainage of the land. As a result, women had to travel to either Makeni or Freetown to buy fish (SiLNoRF and BfA, 2016). The time spent on these chores reduced the scope for women to participate in productive activities, increased physical fatigue, and left them with little time for leisure and relaxation.

Female farmers struggled to support their families, including paying for their children's education (SiLNoRF and BfA, 2016). Some women were displaced from their agricultural land because they changed from bush fallowing farming (which has a long fallow period and can only be done if there is a large tract of land available) to cultivation or intensive farming with a short fallow period (SiLNoRF and BfA, 2016). Changing cultivation has low productivity in terms of output per hectare (Arifin and Hudoyo, 1998). The cost of production, labour, fertilisers and farm tools increased as well (SiLNoRF and BfA, 2016). As one female farmer noted, 'Addax has not made our lives better since they occupy [*sic*] our farmlands' (SiLNoRF and BfA, 2016: 48).

In response to the shortage of farmlands and the high cost of living, some female farmers took to charcoal burning as a survival strategy. According to one female farmer, 'These days, I have no access to farmland because Addax took over our family land. I can't pay my children's school fees except if I engage in charcoal burning, which is still inadequate to address my family's needs' (SiLNoRF and BfA, 2016). Charcoal burning is not only detrimental to the environment because of the greenhouse gases (GHGs) emitted, but also causes deforestation and biodiversity loss as well as respiratory health problems. The women also stated that the company's activities have resulted in a scarcity of firewood, forcing them to spend long hours gathering fuelwood. Others were pleased that the company allowed them to collect the stumps from the fields it had cleared (SEI, 2015).

ABSL's appropriation of large swathes of fertile land (bolilands) and the inadequacies of its social programmes intensified food insecurity in its operational area. Rice yields in the project location fell to 170 kilogram per hectare (kg/ha) compared to 250 kg/ha outside the project area (SiLNoRF and BfA, 2016). Food (vegetable and fruits) that was earlier freely available around the bushes and fields became scarce and had to be bought. This made the diets of children less diverse (SiLNoRF and BfA, 2016). Food insecurity in the area was characterised by reduced food intake by adults (up to five days a week), absence of buffer stock of pulses that could last throughout the year, rationing of food portions for children because of falling supplies and consumption of fewer varieties of food (Yengoh and Armah, 2015). One female farmer summarised it thus:

> I was farming rice with other tuber crops. When the produce was too much to be kept for ourselves, we sent some to our brothers and sisters in the city. I processed gari [a local flour produced from grated cassava] to send the children to school [...] I am suffering now, always hungry. My children have been sent out of school because I cannot pay their fees.
> (Yengoh and Armah, 9521)

Social programmes such as the Village Vegetable Garden (VVG) have not improved the situation of women in the area. The programme was introduced in 2013 to contribute to the diversification of food. In contrast to the FDP, which focused on rice production and favoured male farmers (SiLNoRF and BfA, 2016), women, a majority of whom are vegetable growers, were the intended beneficiaries of the VVG. However, despite a fifty-year land lease, ABSL offered only a year's free enrolment to participants and encouraged them to register as Farmer-Based Organizations (FBO) at the end of the programme (SiLNoRF and BfA, 2016). Groups registered as FBOs could access government aid to build and cultivate their plots, but many participants reported that the programme was badly organised, and they received wrong, rotten or pest-infested seeds. Participants with fields that were close to the river complained of flooding, others of non-profitability and the subsequent loss of lands they used for planting (SiLNoRF and BfA, 2016). A few participants, however, benefitted from the VVG and were able to sell some of their produce in the market. Overall, women who are part of the programme reported 117 grievances compared with 16 positive remarks.

Resistance against ABSL

In June 2013, over 2,000 local staff at the Addax Estates at Mabilefu and Rokel in the Malal Mara Chiefdom in the Tonkolili District protested against poor working conditions in the company. Their grievances included 'disrespect and violation of the human rights of local staff; disregard for Sierra Leone's labour laws; interference in staff union activities; failure to deliver on promises; falsification of information; and dispensation of expired drugs through the company doctor' (Politico SL, 2013). The workers demanded the resignation of General Manager John Moult and refused to 'enter into any negotiations until we receive irrevocable confirmation of his departure' (Politico SL, 2013). They also wanted the 'number of expatriates to be cut down considerably [...] to minimise cost' (Politico SL, 2013).

Masethele, a small village in the Malal Mara Chiefdom, objected to its entire 2,796-acre land space being leased out to ABSL by the chiefdom council. They were dissatisfied with both the lease agreement and the lack of consultations prior to its finalisation (Sierra Express Media, 2013). ABSL paid a fixed rent of 3.60 USD per acre and, in a bid to make the lease more palatable to the communities, introduced 'acknowledgement agreements' directly with representatives of land-owning families (Sierra Express Media, 2013). Under these agreements, an additional 1.40 USD per acre was paid to landowners who acknowledged the fifty-year lease agreement signed with the chiefdom councils (Sierra Express Media, 2013). The Mashele community steadfastly refused to accept its allotted share of the rent paid by ABSL to the chiefdom council. As one female resident stated, 'The council should have asked us if we wanted to lease our entire village to Addax, but they didn't, and we don't want to give all our land to Addax' (Sierra Express Media, 2013).

ABSL's insistence on its right to the entire village under the lease agreement and the community's resolve to hold on to their land led to a gridlock which lasted over two years (Sierra Express Media, 2013). In late 2012, Namati, with support from Sierra Leone Network on the Right to

Food (SiLNoRF), started representing the community in negotiations with ABSL to reach an agreement acceptable to both parties (Sierra Express Media, 2013). In the end, it was agreed that the company's leasehold title would cover 626 acres instead of the entire village land, and it would pay rent and other proceeds only for the land under sugarcane cultivation. An agreement to this effect, signed on 8 March 2012, was the first time the company accepted an area smaller than originally leased lands (Sierra Express Media, 2013). The opposition of the Woreh Yeamah and Woreh Wanda communities to ABSL's use of their lands was resolved in 2013 (SiLNoRF and BfA, 2014).

Socio-economic impact of ABSL in northern Sierra Leone

Contrary to its aim of becoming a model for sustainable large-scale agriculture investment in Africa, the ABSL project has been marked by the casualisation of labour, failure of social programmes and the violation of FPIC. Its national workforce was dominated by casual workers who were daily wage earners and had no social entitlements such as annual leave, sick leave and redundancy benefits. As of March 2015, only 3.4 per cent of the 3,850-strong workforce were permanent staff with fixed monthly salaries; 38.2 per cent were permanent staff with salaries rated daily, subject to the number of working days in a month; and the remaining 58 per cent were temporary workers employed on fixed-term contracts ranging from three to six months a year (SiLNoRF and BfA, 2016).

The project violated FPIC rights of landowners who claimed they were duped by both ABSL and the local authorities who enticed them to hand over their lands with promises that were later not honoured. The rent was not negotiated but imposed by the government and ABSL. The landowners noted that they had originally agreed to rent out degraded and marginal lands to the project, not their entire villages, including residential areas, roads and forests. The land grab that followed prompted them to demand a renegotiation of the lease (SiLNoRF and BfA, 2013b).

Annual monitoring reports for 2011–15 by the SiLNoRF, Bread for All (BfA) and other critics of large-scale land investments in Sierra Leone, demonstrate that ABSL's presence in the project area had both beneficial *and* adverse impacts. On the positive side, ABSL was open to dialogue with stakeholders, paid the land lease and acknowledgement fees, provided a treatment and prevention centre for Ebola, increased household incomes, made infrastructure improvements, provided skills training for a significant number of workers and fulfilled its employment obligations. The FDP, which was among the company's multiple social programmes, encouraged farmers to grow more rice, while the VVG improved the livelihoods of some women and provided food security. Liaison committees and a formal grievance mechanism set up by ABSL paid heed to the concerns of the communities. In addition, a multi-stakeholder forum (MSF) administered by the University of Makeni provided a platform for discussing concerns among various stakeholders and civil society groups and monitored project development (Swedwatch, 2017).

However, its adverse impacts outweighed the positive ones. Poor employment opportunities, the failure of the FDP and the inadequate compensation paid to land leasers strengthened the criticism against ABSL (Approdev, 2013). As mentioned before, the RSB certification for ABSL's biofuel project was deemed improper because it was awarded without a thorough audit. Besides, the RSB's definition of sustainability was inadequate, focusing only on GHGs and ignoring the other two pillars of sustainability – social equity and long-term economic profitability for all stakeholders (SiLNoRF and BfA, 2013a). Critics have noted that the certification should not have been awarded to a company that was evolving rapidly and had not started production. Finally, the company violated the RSB's criteria of food security, FPIC and voluntary resettlement. Over the long term, the project increased poverty, out-migration of young people, alcoholism and domestic violence in its operational areas (SiLNoRF and BfA, 2013a).

The production and provision of electricity was a key selling point used by ABSL to convince national and local governments and community residents to accept its proposal of building an ethanol factory in Sierra Leone. Critics who challenged the entire project and the electricity provision in particular were decried as anti-development agents (SiLNoRF and BfA, 2013b). Although the company started electricity supply in November 2014, SiLNoRF and BfA observed that:

> In reality, the production of electricity lasted a few weeks. It is still not public knowledge as to the exact timing, and how much electricity was produced and supplied to the national grid.
>
> (SiLNoRF and BfA, 2013b: 22)

Electricity generation, which was halted in 2015 due to the Ebola virus disease (EVD) outbreak, resumed under Sunbird Bioenergy Mabilafu Project (SBMP), the new owner of ABSL. As before, there was no disclosure on the amount of electricity produced and sold to the national grid (SiLNORF and BfA, 2020). SBMP's contract was cancelled in 2018 with a change of government. The GoSL revoked the contract because of the exorbitant cost of electricity, which it stated was unsustainable, especially since cheaper power was available from other providers (SiLNORF and BfA, 2020). The cancellation of the contract resulted in delayed payment of employees' salaries and land lease payments to chiefdoms by the company, showing how dependent SBMP was on government patronage (SiLNORF and BfA, 2020).

Downsizing ABSL, transition to Sunbird Bioenergy and sale to Browns Investment Plc

ABSL scaled down its activities on 1 July 2015, five years after signing the fifty-year land lease. The DFIs exited the project in December 2015 and the new owner, Sunbird Bioenergy Africa Limited (Sunbird Bioenergy Group), came on board in September 2016. ABSL claimed that project goals were not met because of low sugarcane yields and ethanol production, and theft and sabotage by local communities (Bread for the World, 2016). Undisclosed cost overruns of about 150 million euros, a 27 per cent decline in ethanol prices in the EU, and the outbreak of Ebola also contributed to ABSL's demise (Bread for the World, 2016; Swedwatch, 2017).

While AOG repaid the debt financing to the DFI lenders who supported the project, Swedfund and FMO sold their ABSL shares back to the parent company (Swedwatch, 2017). Since the DFIs did not conduct human rights due diligence before exiting the ABSL project, dialogue with local communities deteriorated and holding the company accountable became harder (Swedwatch, 2017). Local employees lost their jobs. More than 1,000 permanent workers were placed on leave with only 45 per cent of their monthly salaries paid, and over 2,000 short-term (casual) employees were made redundant (SiLNoRF and BfA, 2016). ABSL's social programmes, including the FDP and the VVG, were first scaled down and later closed (SiLNoRF and BfA, 2016). The consequent loss of income and the end of mitigation measures resulted in increased food insecurity, greater school dropout rates, and societal problems such as gender-based violence, alcoholism and child abandonment (Swedwatch, 2017).

The closure of ABSL was finalised on 30 September 2016, with the transfer of 75.1 per cent stake to a group of investors led by Sunbird Bioenergy while AOG held the remaining 24.9 per cent (Sunbird Energy, 2016). Sunbird Bioenergy describes itself as 'an energy company with a portfolio of sustainable biofuel projects in sub-Saharan Africa, that takes a comprehensive approach to biofuel projects, which includes fair agricultural land leases, sustainable farming and feedstock production, world-class biorefineries as well as inclusive community development and improved livelihoods' (Sunbird Energy, 2016). However, this glowing picture was debunked by critics who brought to light the company's questionable financial and ownership structure. The business director of its parent company NoCOO Limited, Richard Antony Bennett, is also a non-executive director of China New Energy Limited (CNEL) 'with whom Sunbird cooperates closely'. The group of companies under CNEL was in an insolvent situation and traded as a non-going concern, as per a December 2015 financial report. The group had net liabilities worth 803,000 euros by the end of that year. Since its May 2011 IPO, CNEL's share price dropped from 10 GBP to 1 GBP on 8 July 2016 (Bread of the World, 2016).

Critics have questioned how a high-profile project like ABSL, which saw participation from several DFIs, could fail. They have also asked why the GoSL allowed the sale of ABSL to a company with a dubious financial history and without the financial wherewithal to re-operationalise the project (Bread of the World, 2016). Regrettably, the concerns of social critics were ignored, and in 2019 Sunbird Bioenergy Mabilafu Project sold the company to a group of Sri Lankan business tycoons in collaboration with Browns Investments Plc (Bread of the World, 2016). Like Sunbird Bioenergy, Browns Investments has a shifty financial history. Its acquisition of 66.67 per cent of Grey Reach Investments gave it ownership of just over 50 per cent of Sunbird Bioenergy Sierra Leone (Browns bought 66.67 per cent of Grey Reach and owns 75.1 per cent of Sunbird Bioenergy Sierra Leone) (Bread of the World, 2016). Browns Investments' 50 per cent acquisition cost 30 million USD, putting the company's total equity value at 60 million USD, a 60 per cent decline from its 2011 equity value of 150 million USD (Bread of the World, 2016). In financial terms, the loss translates to about 90 million USD of equity (Bread of the World, 2016). Given the poor financial outcomes of this high investment project, SiLNORF and BfA have argued 'that these large-scale monocultures in the hands of big companies are in no way "sustainable" development' (Bread of the World, 2016).

Conclusion

The application of a social justice perspective in the analysis of PPPs in Sierra Leone contradicts the narrative touted by the IFIs and the government that such funding instruments can advance social development. ABSL failed to provide the sustained electricity that it promised despite robust financial investment from eight DFIs, including two African DFIs/development banks, and tax incentives from the GoSL. Instead of attaining a better life, with food security and decent work with good working conditions and wages, the inhabitants in ABSL's operational areas were left more impoverished than before the company's arrival. ABSL continued the culture of discrimination against women by refusing to implement a gender quota to advance female employment in its operations.

Going forward, the operationalisation of the provisions of the NLP and the two model bills formulated by Namati[5] will hopefully enhance women's rights in all sectors of Sierra Leone's rural economy. The robust provisions of the bills, including the provisions to promote responsible investment and the curtailment of land acquisitions to 5,000 hectares at the initial phase of investment, can reverse the ongoing land grabs occurring across rural Sierra Leone and protect the rights of land-owning families, including women.

Notes

1   AIDI ranks countries based on energy, telecommunications, road, social infrastructure and access to sanitation.
2   Includes the capital city Freetown and the entire peninsula.
3   ICF is a WBG entity which receives funding and expertise from the IFC. It is a public-private partnership backed by several powerful sponsors, including Anglo American, Coca Cola, Shell Foundation, SAB Miller, Unilever and Standard Bank.
4   Absolute and permanent tenure in which land can be bought and sold freely.
5   See Sections 3.2 and 3.5 above.

References

ActionAid (2013), 'Broken Promises: The Impacts of Addax Bioenergy in Sierra Leone on Hunger and Livelihoods'. Available at: https://actionaid.org/sites/default/files/broken_promises_final.pdf (accessed 16 February 2020).
AfDB (2009), 'Executive Summary of the Environmental and Social and Health Impact Assessment' (of the Addax Bioenergy Project in Sierra Leone). Available at: https://www.afdb.org/fileadmin/uploads/afdb/Documents/Environmental-and-Social-Assessments/Addax%20Bioenergy%20-%20ESHIA%20summary%20-%20Final%20EN.pdf (accessed 16 February 2020).
AfDB (2011), 'Infrastructure and Growth in Sierra Leone'. Available at: https://www.afdb.org/fileadmin/uploads/afdb/Documents/Project-and-Operations/

Infrastructure%20and%20Growth%20in%20Sierra%20Leone.pdf (accessed 16 February 2020).

AfDB (2013), 'Sierra Leone: Country Strategy Paper 2013–2017'. Available at: https://www.afdb.org/sites/default/files/documents/projects-and-operations/2013-2017_-_sierra_leone_country_strategy_paper_01.pdf (accessed 16 February 2020).

AfDB (2015), 'Level 1: Development in Sierra Leone'. Available at: https://www.afdb.org/fileadmin/uploads/afdb/Documents/Development_Effectiveness_Review_In_Sierra_Leone/CDER_Sierra_Leone__En__Level_1.pdf (accessed 16 February 2020).

AfDB (2018), 'The African Infrastructure Development Index 2018'. Available at: https://www.afdb.org/fileadmin/uploads/afdb/Documents/Publications/Economic_Brief_-_The_Africa_Infrastructure_Development_Index.pdf (accessed 16 February 2020).

Afrik 21 (2019), 'Sierra Leone: IFC Finances 50 MW Solar Project', by J. M. Takouleu. Available at: https://www.afrik21.africa/en/sierra-leone-ifc-finances-50-mw-solar-project (accessed 16 February 2020).

Approdev (2013), 'Policy Brief: The Role of European Development Finance Institution in Land Grabs, May 2013'. Available at: https://actalliance.eu/wp-content/uploads/2016/04/aprodev_policy_brief_dfi_and_landgrabs_final_may2013.pdf (accessed 16 February 2020).

Arifin, B., and A. Hudoyo (1998), 'An Economic Analysis of Shifting Cultivation and Bush-Fallow in Lower Sumatra', Southeast Asia Policy Research Working Paper, No, 1. Available at: http://old.worldagroforestry.org/sea/Publications/files/workingpaper/WP0019-04.pdf (accessed 16 February 2020).

Awoko Newspaper (2017), 'Sierra Leone News: Land Rights Policy Contributes to Poverty Reduction'. Available at: https://awokonewspaper.sl/sierra-leone-news-land-rights-policy-contributes-to-poverty-reduction/ (accessed 16 February 2020).

Bread for the World (2016), 'The Weakest Should Not Bear the Risk'. Available at: https://www.brot-fuer-die-welt.de/fileadmin/mediapool/2_Downloads/Fachinformationen/Analyse/Analyse_64_en-The_Weakest_Should_not_Bear_the_Risk.pdf (accessed 16 February 2020).

Business Wire (2011), 'Addax Bioenergy Signs Loan Agreement for €258 Million Renewable Energy Project in Sierra Leone', 17 June. Available at: https://www.businesswire.com/news/home/20110617005346/en/Addax-Bioenergy-Signs-Loan-Agreement-%E2%82%AC258-Million (accessed 16 February 2020).

Christian Aid (2013), 'Who Is Benefitting?' Available at: https://www.christianaid.org.uk/sites/default/files/2017-08/who-is-benefitting-sierra-leone-report-july-2013.pdf (accessed 16 February 2020).

Conteh, S., and E. Thompson (2019), 'Toward a Customary Land Bill in Sierra Leone: A Review of Law and Policy', Namati, Freetown, Sierra Leone.

Cordiant (2011), 'Development Finance Institutions Announce Financial Close of Pioneering Addax Bioenergy Project in Sierra Leone'. Available at: http://intranet.cordiantcap.com/press_release/development-finance-institutions-announce-financial-close-of-pioneering-addax-bioenergy-project-in-sierra-leone (accessed 16 February 2020).

DfID (2014), 'Annual Review-Summary-Sheet'. Available at: https://devtracker.dfid.gov.uk/projects/GB-1-203819/documents (accessed 16 February 2020).

DfID (2018), 'Business Case and Intervention Summary'. Available at: https://devtracker.dfid.gov.uk/projects/GB-1-203819/documents (accessed 16 February 2020).

Eurodad (2018), 'History REPPPeated: How Public-Private Partnerships Are Failing', by M. J. Romero and J. Ravenscroft. Available at: https://eurodad.org/files/pdf/1546956-history-repppeated-how-public-private-partnerships-are-failing-.pdf (accessed 16 February 2020).

Eurodad, G&DN and FEMNET (2019), 'Can Public-Private Partnerships Deliver Gender Equality?', by M. J. Romero. Available at: https://d3n8a8pro7vhmx.cloudfront.net/eurodad/pages/443/attachments/original/1590686869/Can_public-private_partnerships_deliver_gender_equality_.pdf?1590686869 (accessed 16 February 2020).

FAO (2014), 'Responsible Agricultural Investments in Developing Countries: How to Make Principles and Guidelines Effective', by K. Havnevik. Available at: https://www.government.se/49b727/contentassets/45137cb380734c2fbf97717673cef39c/responsible-agricultural-investments-in-developing-countries (accessed 16 February 2020).

FAO (2016), 'Securing Land Tenure Rights for Farmers in Sierra Leone'. Available at: http://www.fao.org/in-action/securing-land-tenure-rights-sierra-leone/en (accessed 16 February 2020).

FAO (2018), 'National Gender Profile of Agriculture and Rural Livelihoods: Sierra Leone'. Available at: http://www.fao.org/3/I9554EN/i9554en.pdf (accessed 16 February 2020).

GIZ (2018), 'Diagnostic Study of the TVET Sector in Sierra Leone'. Available at: https://www.giz.de/en/downloads/giz2018-de-Diagnostic%20Study%20of%20the%20TVET%20Sector%20in%20Sierra%20Leone.pdf (accessed 16 February 2020).

GoSL (2003), 'Sierra Leone Vision 2025: "Sweet-Salone"'. Available at: https://unipsil.unmissions.org/sites/default/files/vision_2025.pdf (accessed 16 February 2020).

GoSL (2008), 'An Agenda for Change: Second Poverty Strategy Reduction (PRSP 11) 2008–2012'. Available at: https://unipsil.unmissions.org/sites/default/files/agenda_for_change_0.pdf (accessed 16 February 2020).

GoSL (2013), 'The Agenda for Prosperity: Road to Middle Income Status – Sierra Leone's Third Generation Poverty Reduction Strategy Paper 2013–2018'. Available at: http://www.sierra-leone.org/Agenda%204%20Prosperity.pdf (accessed 16 February 2020).

GoSL (2015), 'Final National Land Policy of Sierra Leone'. Available at: http://extwprlegs1.fao.org/docs/pdf/sie155203.pdf (accessed 16 February 2020).

GoSL (n.d.-a), 'Legal Framework'. Available at: https://ppp.gov.sl/legal-framework (accessed 16 February 2020).

GoSL (n.d.-b), 'The Public Private Partnership Unit (PPPU)'. Available at: https://ppp.gov.sl/ (accessed 16 February 2020).

GoSL (n.d.-c), 'Public Private Partnership Unit Brochure'. Available at: https://ppp.gov.sl/wp-content/uploads/2019/12/PPP_BROCHURE.pdf (accessed 16 February 2020).

IMF (2005), 'Sierra Leone: Poverty Reduction Strategy Paper – Progress Report'. Available at: https://www.imf.org/external/pubs/ft/scr/2005/cr05191.pdf (accessed 16 February 2020).

IMF (2008), 'Sierra Leone: Poverty Reduction Strategy Paper – Progress Report'. Available at: https://www.imf.org/external/pubs/ft/scr/2008/cr08250.pdf (accessed 16 February 2020).

Namati (2015), 'Namati Welcomes Sierra Leone's Progressive New National Land Policy'. Available at: https://namati.org/news-stories/namati-welcomes-sierra-leones-progressive-new-national-land-policy (accessed 16 February 2020).

Namati (2020a), *Summary Model Customary Land Bill*, Namati, Freetown.

Namati (2020b), *Model Land Commission Bill*, Namati, Freetown.

Namati (2020c), *Customary Land Rights Legal Review Report*, Namati, Freetown.

Oakland Institute (2011), 'Understanding Land Investment Deals in Africa: Country Report: Sierra Leone'. Available at: https://www.oaklandinstitute.org/sites/oaklandinstitute.org/files/OI_SierraLeone_Land_Investment_report_0.pdf (accessed 16 February 2020).

Politico SL (2013), 'Addax Bio-energy under Fire in Sierra Leone', by M. J. Bundu, 13 June. Available at: https://www.politicosl.com/node/1319 (accessed 16 February 2020).

SEI (2015), 'Agriculture Investment and Rural Transformation: A Case Study of the Makeni Bioenergy Project in Sierra Leone'. Available at: https://mediamanager.sei.org/documents/Publications/Climate/SEI-PR-2015-09-Makeni-Project.pdf (accessed 16 February 2020).

Sesay, B. J. (2015), *Effects of Addax Bioenergy Investment on Female Farmers' Rights to Land and Their Livelihoods in Bombali District, Sierra Leone*, Lund University. Available at: http://lup.lub.lu.se/luur/download?func=downloadFile&recordOId=5470857&fileOId=5470859 (accessed 16 February 2020).

Sierra Express Media (2013), 'Masethele Village in Important Land Renegotiation with Addax Bioenergy Sierra Leone Limited', 13 March. Available at: https://sierraexpressmedia.com/?p=53981 (accessed 16 February 2020).

SiLNoRF and BfA (2012), 'Monitoring Report August 2012'. Available at: https://sites.google.com/site/silnorf/news-1/monitoring-report-july-2012 (accessed 16 February 2020).

SiLNoRF and BfA (2013a), 'Analysis of RSB Certificate March 2013'. Available at: https://sites.google.com/site/silnorf/news-1/analysis-of-rsb-certificate-march-2013 (accessed 16 February 2020).

SiLNoRF and BfA (2013b), 'RSB Complaint September 2013'. Available at: https://sites.google.com/site/silnorf/news-1/rsb-complaint-september-2013 (accessed 16 February 2020).

SiLNoRF and BfA (2014), 'Monitoring 2014'. Available at: https://sites.google.com/site/silnorf/news-1/monitoring-report-2014 (accessed 16 February 2020).

SiLNoRF and BfA (2016), 'Final Monitoring Report on the Scale Down of Addax Bioenergy in Makeni, Sierra Leone (July 2014–June 2016)'. Available at: https://brotfueralle.ch/content/uploads/2019/03/2016-Monitoring-report-Silnorf.pdf (accessed 16 February 2020).

Solution Africa (2019), 'Private and Financial Sector Development Project'. Available at: http://www.southsouthworld.org/component/k2/46-solution/2400/private-and-financial-sector-development-project (accessed 16 February 2020).

Sunbird Energy (2016), 'AOG Transfers Ownership of Pioneering Bioethanol and Green Electricity Operation in Sierra Leone'. Available at: https://www.sunbirdbioenergy.com/2016/09/30/aog-transfers-ownership-of-pioneering-bioethanol-and-green-electricity-operation-in-sierra-leone-to-sunbird-bioenergy (accessed 16 February 2020).

Swedwatch (2017), 'No Business, No Rights'. Available at: https://swedwatch.org/wp-content/uploads/2017/11/86_Sierra-Leone_171108.pdf (accessed 16 February 2020).

UNOPS (n.d.), 'Access to Energy: Giving Sierra Leone the Power to Change Lives'. Available at: https://www.unops.org/news-and-stories/stories/access-to-energy-giving-sierra-leone-the-power-to-change (accessed 16 February 2020).

WBG (2011), 'PPIAF Assistance in Sierra Leone'. Available at: http://documents.worldbank.org/curated/en/188111468167372625/pdf/758740PPIAF0As00Box374359B00PUBLIC0.pdf (accessed 16 February 2020).

WBG (2016), 'Project Information Document (PID): Appraisal Stage: Western Area Power Generation Project'. Available at: http://documents.worldbank.org/curated/en/223741467993762150/pdf/AB7825-PID-P153805-Initial-Appraisal-Box396261B-PUBLIC-Disclosed-5-25-2016.pdf (accessed 16 February 2020).

WBG (2019), 'Gender Equality & PPPs'. Available at: https://ppp.worldbank.org/public-private-partnership/ppp-sector/gender-impacts-ppps/impacts-ppps-gender-inclusion (accessed 16 February 2020).

World Bank (2001), 'Sierra Leone: Joint Staff Assessment of the Interim Poverty Reduction Strategy Paper'. Available at: http://documents.worldbank.org/

curated/en/275861468759854663/pdf/multi0page.pdf (accessed 16 February 2020).

World Bank (2019), 'World Bank Helps Sierra Leone Improve Operational Performance of the Energy Sector'. Available at: https://www.worldbank.org/en/news/press-release/2019/05/17/world-bank-helps-sierra-leone-improve-operational-performance-of-the-energy-sector (accessed 16 February 2020).

World Bank (2020), 'PPP Unit (Sierra Leone)'. Available at: https://library.pppknowledgelab.org/documents/3924?ref_site=kl (accessed 16 February 2020).

Yengoh, G. T., and F. A. Armah (2015), 'Effects of Large-Scale Acquisition on Food Insecurity in Sierra Leone', *Sustainability*, 7 (7): 9505–39. Available at: https://doi.org/10.3390/su7079505 (accessed 16 February 2020).

Appendix

Annex 1: Ongoing PPPs in Sierra Leone's Energy Sector

Planet Core Solar

IFC is supporting Planet Core Solar through a 40 million USD funding to generate 50 MW of electricity within one or two years. A 25 MW power plant will be built in Makarie Gbanti, Bombali District, 195 kilometres from the capital city Freetown. The remaining 25 MW will be produced by several mini-hydro plants in Kambia, Port Loko, Kamkewi, Kono, Mile 91, Moyamba, Pujehun, Bo, Kailahun and Bonthe. The energy will be sold by Electricity Distribution and Supply Company (EDSA) for onward distribution to customers (Afrik 21, 2019).

United Nations Office for Project Services (UNOPS)

The Rural Renewable Energy Project is funded by the UK's DfID and implemented by the UNOPS. The project represents a drive for clean energy access, together with the sustainable growth of the country's energy capacity. The 345-million-GBP project is expected in several phases over a period of four years. The first phase, which was successfully completed in July 2017, involved the installation of solar power in community centres. The second phase extended access to electricity to houses, schools and businesses in fifty rural villages by installing distribution networks in each village. This will create fifty independent mini grids. In addition, the project has been opened to private sector companies which were invited to tender their services to run power supply networks in each village through a competitive selection process. It is projected that private sector involvement will generate 5.7 million GBP (approximately 7.5 million USD) worth of co-investments in the final phase, developing larger mini grids in an additional forty villages. At the time of writing, the project was slated to be completed by the end of 2020 (UNOPS, n.d.).

Table 7.3 Current PPP Projects in Sierra Leone.

Project	Brief description	Status
Bumbuna Phase II Hydro Power Project	Joule Africa, an internationally renowned developer, demonstrated interest in the Bumbuna II hydro-electric project that will provide an additional 146 MW. Joule has completed feasibility studies and subsequently conducted value engineering work that enhances affordability of the project. The power purchase agreement (PPA) and implementation agreement (IA) have been negotiated and signed. The Bumbuna Phase II power project will complement the existing 50 MW Bumbuna Phase I project and it is a strategic action to achieve the sector's sustainable energy strategy for all.	The PPA and another project document approved by cabinet and subsequently ratified by Parliament.
Kissy HFO-Power Project (128 MW)	GoSL, through EDSA, partnered with TCQ of UAE and Globeleq of UK to conclude a 20-year build-operate-transfer (BOT) independent power purchase (IPP) arrangement that will deliver 128 MW in three phases. Phase I will generate 57 MW and 39 MW each for Phases II and III. This project reached commercial close in 2016 and has attracted many big global financiers including the World Bank Group member IFC, AfDB, Frontier Markets Fund Manager (FMFM) and Globeleq. The project will be located at Kissy Dock Yard and negotiations are in progress to reach financial close.	The PPA and other project documents approved by the cabinet and subsequently ratified by the House of Parliament.

Project	Brief description	Status
Solar ERA	GoSL, through EDSA, has an IPP agreement with Solar Era for development of a solar power generation project of 25 MW, with a first phase of 5 MW that is to be constructed in Bo District. The PPA and IA have been negotiated and signed and the developer is working on obtaining financing to start construction.	Financial close. Developers are sourcing finance for the project.
25 MW Betmai Hydro	Sewa Energy Resources, a company incorporated in Sierra Leone, conducted a feasibility study (undertaken by CEMMATS Group SI Ltd.) on a run-off-river close to Magbogba village in the Saunda Futowusu Chiefdom, Tonkolili District. The PPA is completed and is awaiting concurrence from the Attorney General and MoFED.	PPA and implementation agreement approved through executive clearance and subsequently ratified by Parliament.
Fish Harbour and Industrial Processing	Sierra Leone is concluding several work streams to ascertain EU certification for the export of marine products. This project will enhance the marine industry by developing a docking facility and processing platform for the local market and exporting purposes.	Concept note developed and the unit, in collaboration with the Ministry of Fisheries, is sourcing funding for the feasibility.
Transshipment Container Part (TIDFORE Project)	The PPPU partnered with the Ministry of Transport and Aviation in the development of a transshipment container port on a 25-year build-own-operate-transfer (BOOT) PPP arrangement. Sky Rock Management Limited and National Port Development formed an SPV concessionaire and contracted TIDFORE on an engineering, procurement and construction (EPC) contract basis to construct the new part in accordance with the specified design. The financing is provided by ICBC Bank of China.	Concession agreement and other project documents were approved by the cabinet and subsequently ratified by Parliament.

Source: Handbook for PPPs in Sierra Leone. Compiled by author from various sources.

Annex 2: ABSL's DFI Partners

The Netherlands Finance Company (FMO)

FMO is the Dutch development bank. It supports developing and emerging markets by investing in ambitious entrepreneurs. FMO believes a strong private sector leads to economic and social development, empowering people to employ their skills and improve their quality of life. FMO focusses on four sectors that have high development impact: financial institutions, energy, housing and agribusiness. With an investment portfolio of 5 billion euros, FMO is one of the largest European bilateral private sector development banks.

Emerging Africa Infrastructure Fund (EAIF)

EAIF is a PPP able to provide long-term USD- or euro-denominated debt or mezzanine finance on commercial terms to finance the construction and development of private infrastructure in sub-Saharan Africa. EAIF provides loans to projects across a wide range of sectors including telecom, transport, water and power, among others. The fund is advised by Frontier Markets Fund Manager (FMFM), a division of Standard Bank. FMFM also advises GuarantCo, a guarantee fund which credit enhances local currency debt issuance by private municipal and parastatal entities for infrastructure projects in lower-income countries around the world.

African Development Bank (AfDB)

The AfDB Group's mission is to help reduce poverty, improve living conditions of African people and mobilise resources for the continent's economic and social development. With this objective in mind, the institution aims at assisting African countries, individually and collectively, in their efforts to attain sustainable economic growth. To this end, the Bank seeks to stimulate and mobilise internal and external resources to promote investments as well as provide its regional member countries with technical and financial assistance.

BIO

BIO is a development finance institution (DFI) established in 2001 in the framework of the Belgian Development Cooperation to support private sector growth in developing and emerging countries. BIO finances the financial sector, enterprises and private infrastructure projects. Endowed with a capital of 465 million euros, BIO provides tailored long-term financial products (equity, quasi-equity, debt and guarantees) and finances technical assistance programmes and feasibility studies. BIO also encourages its business partners to implement environmental, social and governance standards. BIO operates as an additional partner to the traditional financial institutions and looks for projects with a balance between return on investment and development impact. BIO is a member of EDFI.

Infrastructure Crisis Facility Debt Pool (ICF-DP)

ICF Debt Pool addresses the continuing restricted availability of financing for emerging market infrastructure caused by the retraction of major commercial institutions from emerging markets as they continue to refocus their lending activities on their home markets. The ICF-DP is a 500 million-euro fund of loans supported by the German government and funded by KfW Entwicklungsbank under a guarantee from the German government. The ICF-DP was launched in October 2009 and is managed by Cordiant Capital Inc, an emerging market fund manager that is a signatory to the UN Principles for Responsible Investment.

Swedfund International AB

Swedfund International AB offers risk capital and know-how for investments in Africa, Asia, Latin America and Eastern Europe (non-EU members). Swedfund's vision is to contribute to the development of viable businesses, thereby stimulating sustainable economic development in its investment countries. Swedfund specialises in the field of complex investment environments with a high level of country risk. With a broad spectrum of financial solutions, combined with knowledge and experience, Swedfund enables its partners to invest more successfully.

Industrial Development Corporation (IDC) of South Africa Limited

The IDC is a self-financing South African national development finance institution. Its primary objectives are to contribute to the generation of balanced, sustainable economic growth in Africa and the economic empowerment of the South African population. It promotes economic prosperity through the building of competitive industries and enterprises based on sound business principles. The IDC's mission is to be a primary driving force of commercially sustainable industrial development and innovation for the benefit of South Africa and the rest of the African continent.

Table 7.4 DFI Co-financing of Addax Bioethanol Sierra Leone.

DFI	Debt as per 16 June 2011* 55.6 per cent (million euro)	Additional finance as per 31 December 2015 ** (million euro)	Equity= 44.4 per cent*** (million euro)	Cash (million euro)
AfDB	25			
DEG	20			
PIDG: ICF-DP	21	27,70 USD		
PIDG-EAIF	20	31.31 USD		
IDC	22			
FMO	25****			
BIO	10			
DFI 2011 debt, total	147,23			
Swedfund			10	
FMO			25	
Addax Bioenergy			72.1	19.76
Total various quotes	258/267/400/455	493	107.1	19.76

Source: (* (Cordiant, 2011), *** (PIDG, Data 2), *** as informed by AfDB in letter dated 20 June 2016, available with Bread for the World, **** shown in different documents as both loan and equity.)

Annex 3: Terms on Which Land Exceeding 5,000 Hectares May Be Acquired in Sierra Leone

1. The investor should have used up all, or substantially all, of the initial land acquired for its business.
2. The investor should not be in breach of the lease agreement with the communities or in breach of any of its licence conditions from the Environment Protection Agency, the National Minerals Agency or any other government regulator.
3. The investor shall draft and submit a business case for additional land, setting out the following:

   - The reason/s for and the amount of additional land required;
   - The available funds to be invested in the additional land;

- The likely impact of the additional acquisition on land supply within the community or communities hosting the investment;
- Timeframe for the utilisation of the additional land;
- Likely impact of the additional acquisition on the sources of water across the communities; and
- Alternative methods of achieving its business aims without additional acquisition of land.

4. The investor should provide evidence of initial discussions with communities on the additional acquisition and 'in principle' consent from the community.
5. The investor should have been supporting a robust out-grower scheme within its area of operation.
6. The investor should undertake additional environmental, social and health impact assessment with respect to the additional acquisition.

Part Four

Impact of PPPs on human rights: Building resistances at local level

A feminist human rights approach to Ghana's public market PPPs: The case of the dome market

Gertrude Dzifa Torvikey and Sylvia Ohene Marfo

Introduction

Located in West Africa, Ghana has a population of about 30 million, of whom 51 per cent are women (Ghana Statistical Service, 2016). Over the past three decades, the country has made impressive progress on developing a democratic and multiparty political system. However, two major parties continue to dominate the political landscape. In addition, Ghana's democratic advancement has not benefitted both men and women equally, as women continue to struggle to obtain the same socio-economic rights as men. Socio-cultural norms restrict the participation of women in public spaces and ensure that their political engagement remains lower than that of men.

In 2018, Ghana's gross domestic product (GDP) grew 6.3 per cent to 65,556 billion US dollars (USD), while gross national income (GNI) per capita stood at 4,650 USD. This put Ghana in the lower-middle-income category, meaning that the country could no longer access certain types of loans available only to poorer countries. Consequently, it now has to borrow at higher interest rates and compete with other borrowers in order to access loans on favourable terms. Ghana's economic performance is also a Janus-headed one, as jobless growth, high unemployment and increasing gender-based inequality keep pace with a rising GDP (Aryeetey and Baah-Boateng, 2016). The labour market is highly gender-segregated and segmented, with 64.7 per cent women economically active compared with 71.4 per cent men (Ghana Statistical Service, 2016).

Over the years, the country's development agenda has incorporated the private sector into service delivery and infrastructure projects. The shift from a statist development to private sector inclusion predates the structural adjustment programme (SAP) and the economic recovery programmes that started in the 1980s. The privatisation of state-owned enterprises (SOEs) began in earnest after the overthrow of the Kwame Nkrumah regime in 1966. The SOEs had been established as part of a national project that undertook a policy of increased industrialisation, import substitution and self-determination during the early years (1957–66) of Ghana's independence from Britain. From the late 1960s onwards, the country moved towards state partnerships with multinational organisations and international finance institutions (IFIs), especially in the agricultural sector (Graham, 1993).

Against this backdrop, the SAP conditionalities increased the private sector's involvement in development. Ghana was the first African country to accept the market- and public sector-driven reform policies inspired by the World Bank (WB), International Monetary Fund (IMF) and other donor institutions (Awortwi, 2011). From the 1980s, the country embarked on a vigorous privatisation of state entities in line with the loan conditionalities of the Bretton Woods Institutions (BWIs). Appiah-Kubi (2001) notes that between 1987 and 1999, 14 per cent of Ghana's GDP came from privatisation. By 2005, over 335 SOEs in the agriculture and manufacturing sectors had been privatised (Bank of Ghana, 2005), and Ghana was praised as a SAP success story. Public-private partnerships (PPPs) were a key component of the state's systematic de-investment and the corresponding institutionalisation of private sector participation in development.

This chapter focuses on the construction of lockable shops and open sheds at the Dome Market in the Great Accra Region via a PPP, and the resistance of women traders to these projects. Based on qualitative research and a review of relevant documents, the study aims to highlight the ramifications of market PPPs for gender equality and the socio-economic rights of women. Broadly, the chapter can be divided into two parts. The first half explores the historical backdrop as well as the current trends and patterns of PPPs in the country. The second half begins by looking at the situation of women traders in Ghana's markets before examining this in the context of the PPP for the redevelopment of the Dome Market.

Methodology

The study is based on both primary and secondary data. The primary data consists mainly of twenty-six qualitative interviews conducted with the staff of relevant institutions in the Ga East Municipal Assembly, the Dome Zonal Council and the Dome Market leadership as well as with the women and tenants displaced by the market PPP. Non-participant observation and transect walks in the market were used to gather information that could not be gleaned from formal interviews. One focus group discussion (FGD) was organised with seven female traders in the market. Secondary data sources included document reviews, particularly the PPP policy and contracts signed between the Municipal Assembly and the contractors.

Privatisation of public space: The latest phase of PPPs

PPPs in Africa in general, and in Ghana in particular, should be seen in light of the transmission of global standards and regulatory regimes to national levels. Since the beginning of the new millennium, the United Nations (UN) agencies, international financial institutions (IFIs), governments, continental bodies, continental development banks, international consulting firms and corporate forums, among others, have endorsed PPPs as a development instrument and an alternative to traditional development financing. From their perspective, the PPP model is distinct from privatisation but framed within the same equity-*versus*-efficiency logic and other arguments used to back privatisation. The UN's Sustainable Development Goal (SDG) 17, which is about 'partnerships for the goals', illustrates the global institutional consensus on PPPs as a development instrument and financing regime, making it a global policy. PPPs found a prominent place in the UN's post-2015 agenda report – which was authored by the WB and gave birth to the SDGs – giving them even greater legitimacy.

While some PPP projects predate regulatory regimes, the similarities in the frameworks adopted by many African countries are hard to overlook. In most countries, PPPs are hosted at the ministries of finance with the creation of PPP units, demonstrating the fiscal-mindedness of the model. The laws and policies are almost uniform, and emerged within the same decade. This is evident from Tanzania's Public-Private Partnership Act No. 18 of 2010 and its 2014 amendment; Sierra Leone's Public-Private Partnership Act, 2010; Kenya's Public-Private Partnership Act No. 15 of 2013 and Uganda's Public-Private Partnership Act, 2014. A crucial part of these laws is the emphasis on solicited and unsolicited bids for PPPs, which runs counter to transparency and accountability principles. These are also top-down regulatory regimes with crucial implications for local-level institutions.

The PPP trajectory: Context, trends and patterns

Ghana's PPP trajectory developed in tandem with the global push for these instruments of funding and the call for legal frameworks to regulate them. The arguments for including PPPs in Ghana's development agenda were similar to those associated with privatisation in the 1980s, namely financial crises and an increasing sovereign debt. Ghana's debt-to-GDP ratio rose consistently from 2011, climbing to 60 per cent by 2018, and projected to reach 62 per cent in 2020. The trend was similar to the 1980–90 period which witnessed the privatisation of SOEs. During this time, the private sector was an active participant in the management and delivery of public services such as sanitation, water, energy and telecommunications (Osei-Kyei and Chan, 2015), but the state remained the sole provider of physical infrastructure aided by international donors and national budget funds. That left a funding gap of 0.4 billion USD per year (World Bank, 2011). Ghana's status as a lower-middle-income country meant it could only access high-interest loans. This, together with the funding crunch prompted by the 2007–8 global financial crisis, led Ghana to fall back on PPPs, as global pension funds looked for safe havens to invest in.

Table 8.1 PPPs with Financial Closure in Ghana, 1999–2019.

Project name	Sector	Financial closure year	Investment amount (million USD)
Electricity Company of Ghana Distribution and Retail Business Concession	Electricity	2019	580.00
Tema LNG Import Terminal	Ports	2017	550.00
Tema Port Expansion	Ports	2016	1,500.00
Amandi Energy Power Plant	Electricity	2016	552.00
Bridge Power	Electricity	2016	953.00
Kpone Independent Power Project	Electricity	2014	900.00
African Coast to Europe Submarine Communications Cable Phase 1	ICT	2012	700.00
Sunon-Asogli Gas-Fired Power Plant	Electricity	2007	590.00
West African Gas Pipeline Company Limited	Natural gas	2005	590.00
Takoradi 2 and 3	Electricity	1999	550.00

Source: World Bank (2011), 'Ghana's Infrastructure: A Continental Perspective', Policy Research Working Paper 5600. Washington DC: World Bank; MoFEP (2019), 'The Annual Public Debt Report for the 2018 Financial Year'. Available at: http://www.mofep.gov.gh (accessed 26 January 2020).

A national PPP policy was under discussion in 2004 and guidelines to that effect were launched in 2011 (MoFEP, 2011). Thereafter, a PPP Bill was proposed in 2013 and introduced in December 2020. The Public Private Partnership Act, 2020 replaced the national policy on PPPs. While this legislative framework was being formulated, twenty-six PPP projects in the energy, port infrastructure and telecommunications fields attained financial closure between 1990 and 2019 (see Table 8.1).

Between 2017 and 2018, thirty-two PPP contracts were signed in other sectors such as social and health, transportation, industry, water and waste management, of which more than half (52.3 per cent) were in the social and health sectors (MoFEP, 2019).

Most social sector PPPs are market projects, pointing to a trend of such partnerships entering women's economic spaces. The intersection between the formality of PPPs and the informality of the community markets – which provides economic survival and asset accumulation opportunities to Ghanaian women – has important implications for gender equality and human rights. Private finance in the informal sector raises questions about *who* owns and controls *what* in the PPP model.

Currently, the Public Investment Division (PID), under the Ministry of Finance and Economic Planning (MoFEP), is responsible for developing the legal, institutional and regulatory framework for PPP programmes in the country. The PID works in collaboration with the PPP Approval Committee which provides technical expertise to support relevant ministries, departments and agencies in the development and management of prospective transactions. The PID also has a Project and Financial Analysis (PFA) unit and the PPP Advisory Unit (PAU) which perform gatekeeping functions (see Table 8.2).

There are several PPP models operating in the country, with build-operate-transfer (BOT) being the most favoured. The lack of expertise, however, is seen as a challenge to their successful implementation (Osei-Kyei, Chan and Dansoh, 2017).

PPPs have been an integral part of the economic and political conditionalities that characterised development aid in the global South since the 1980s. Aid conditionalities have impacted governance, human rights and democracy in the recipient countries. The period since the 1980s has seen aid ideologies shift from market fundamentalism to inclusive neoliberalism (Mawuko-Yevugah, 2014), and from direct to indirect conditionalities. The new development aid architecture has exacerbated existing power inequalities by reproducing the politics of inclusion and exclusion as well as by co-opting and incorporating selected actors into the state and global

Table 8.2 Institutions, Actors and Mandates in Ghana's PPP Framework.

Key mandate	Actors
Spearheading, developing regulatory framework, coordination and provision of advisory services, budgeting and risk management for all PPP projects	MoFEP and its appropriate units – Public Investment Division (PID), Project and Financial Analysis Unit (PFA), PPP Advisory Unit (PAU), Debt Management Division (DMD) and the Budget Division.
Planning infrastructure	National Development Planning Commission through its National Infrastructure Plan (NIP)
Approval authorities	PPP Approval Committee Cabinet General Assembly of the Metropolitan, Municipal, and District Assemblies (MMDAs) Parliament
Regulatory authorities	Public Procurement Authority, Public Utilities Regulatory Commission, Water Resources Commission, Ghana Railway Development Authority, etc.
Facilitating roles	Ministry of Trade and Industry
Contracting authorities	MMDAs Ministries, Departments, and Agencies (MDAs)
Legal and judicial issues	Attorney General's Department and the Legal Division of the MoFEP

Source: MoFEP (2011), 'National Policy on Public Private Partnerships (PPP)'. Available at: http://www.mofep.gov.gh (accessed 26 January 2020).

institutional frameworks. This structure, in turn, has been transmitted from the central to local governments and citizens (Crawford, 2008). Ghana's local governance structures illustrate these disjunctures.

Local governance in Ghana

Although decentralisation was meant to increase citizen participation in Ghana's development trajectory, the state continues to appoint district/municipal chief executives instead of making the position an elected one. This top-down approach means the voices of citizens are not reflected in the design and implementation of projects undertaken by local governments. It also weakens the local governance bodies, using them to rubber-stamp donor packages and development projects.

The SAPs changed the nature of the state's role in development. While, in the pre-SAP period, the Ghanaian state funded 50 per cent of all local government activities, the post-SAP period saw a major shift in the relationship between the state and local governments. By 1985, the state had reduced its financial assistance to the local assemblies but expanded their role, leaving them scrambling to increase revenue (Crook, 2017). With fewer funds and more responsibilities,[1] the assemblies became extremely dependent on taxes from residents and began to use the markets as key sites for revenue mobilisation.

The Ministries, Departments and Agencies (MDAs) and Metropolitan, Municipal and District Assemblies (MMDAs) are contracting authorities for PPPs at the local level. The District Assembly Common Fund (DACF) has been operational for over two decades and remains the primary source of financing for infrastructure development. The districts operate on tight budgets due to delays in the release of the DACF, inadequate allocations and the politicised nature of the disbursement, all of which affect their operations. The common fund is capped at 1.2 million Ghanaian Cedi (GHS) (240,000 USD at current rates) for the entire year. This makes internal revenue mobilisation crucial for generating resources. Property taxes, although a key component of the MMDAs' revenues, do not provide sufficient funds. In the past, the MMDAs' borrowing was limited to 5,000 USD per year, which was woefully inadequate given their tasks and responsibilities. While the Public Financial Management Act 921 of 2016 allowed the MMDAs to borrow from internal sources, there were administrative bottlenecks as the MoFEP was charged with approving loan applications beyond a certain threshold. Until recently, the MMDAs could utilise the DACF for developmental projects. In 2018, however, the central government proposed the retention of 80 per cent of the funds for its flagship School Feeding, Planting for Food and Jobs and Nation Builders Corps (NaBCO) programme, leaving the assemblies with only the remaining 20 per cent for development. Local-level PPPs thus became a means for the assemblies to show their governance strength (Seidu, 2018).

Local authorities rely overwhelmingly on resources from the informal sector which accounts for 80 per cent of Ghana's economy. Especially in the big cities, local markets have become essential arenas for tax extraction. Two types of taxes are collected in the markets – flat daily tolls paid by both mobile/ambulatory and stationary traders, and Business Operating Permits (BOPs) paid annually by traders in the big shops and stores. BOP rates are further differentiated by the size of the trading unit and the type of goods in it. Despite the centrality of markets as a source of revenue, the central government does not build them directly and the local assemblies do not have adequate resources. Historically, women and communities themselves created and set up markets. With the state taking an interest in them more recently for the sake of political expediency, PPPs have become an important vehicle for market development. Nine out of eighteen PPPs listed at the national level in 2019 were market projects. Many well-known markets in major cities – such as Kejetia, Kotokuraba, Shea nut, Aboabo, Afiakobi, Kojokrom and Old Tamale – have already been built or completed as PPPs (Seidu, 2018). BOT is the preferred model as the local assemblies only have to provide the land and it is the financiers' responsibility to raise capital.

Women, markets and the Ghanian state

Market trading in Ghana, and most parts of West Africa, is the domain of women. Markets enable women to achieve economic autonomy and assert themselves, socially and culturally, as citizens (Darkwah, 2007b). Market trading is both an accumulative and a survival strategy for many women in the country (Clark, 1994). This is a consequence of colonial-era policies which favoured male education over that of women. Men who used to trade left for school, and women, especially those who were not literate, began to replace them in market trading, converting the markets into female spaces (Aidoo, 1985). In recent times, especially after the SAP-induced retrenchment and high unemployment levels, women and men of different educational backgrounds have found the market to be a secure space for economic survival.

Historically, traders and the state – both the colonial and postcolonial state – have shared an ambivalent relationship with temporary alliances and fallouts. The state is the landowner, extracting rent through the allocation of market stalls and space, and levying tolls, taxes, license fees and BOP fees. In return, the state is required to secure the working environment for traders through sanitation, electricity and security provisions. However, the socio-economic interests of traders are almost always at odds with the state's quest to control this space.

National-level economic transformations have a bearing on the local markets as traders adopt strategies to take advantage of government policies or protect their interests during periods of economic expansion and contraction (Clark, 2010b, 2004). Whereas agricultural goods were the main trading items in the past, the SAPs opened up avenues for women to trade in consumer goods in the 1980s. Their trading centres shifted from rural-urban and urban-rural to sub-regional and international destinations (Darkwah, 2007a, 2002). The SAP policies facilitated imports of consumer goods, and the more prosperous traders travelled from Ghana to global manufacturing and trade centres in Asia and Europe to buy goods. However, the SAPs also eroded the gains that the women made, as currency devaluation affected profits.

Historically, the state has used scapegoating techniques to control the economic activities of market traders. Markets were the main targets of state repression during the economic crisis of the 1980s. They were sites of the worst forms of brutality, where women were stripped naked and flogged (Britwum, 2013; Clark, 2010a; Robertson, 1983). More generally, market women are often accused of economic sabotage in times of macroeconomic crises and blamed for causing shortages of goods and price hikes. The demolition of the country's then premier Makola No One market in 1979 is illustrative of this. Soldiers, acting on behalf of the government, used bulldozers to raze the foremost centre of women's economic activity during the military regime of the Armed Forces Revolutionary Council (AFRC). The demolition was meant to punish the women for their 'wickedness' and 'economic sabotage'. Other markets were also destroyed by the military regime in the Ashanti, the Eastern and the Western regions. Manuh (1993) attributes the state's resentment towards the economic activities of market women to patriarchal ideologies regarding the 'proper' role of women in society, inherited from the colonial era.

Furthermore, traders are consistently harassed by city authorities for allegedly making cities unclean. They are often violently evicted and relocated against their will in the name of city beautification and formalisation of the informal trading sectors (Spire and Choplin, 2018). Given this history of the state's engagement with the markets, the use of PPPs to 'develop' and 'modernize' these spaces can only be treated with scepticism.

Markets are social, economic and political spaces since local, national and global policies have a bearing on activities conducted here. They are sites for contestation of central and local government policies (Assimeng, 1990). The contentions revolve around urban planning, price controls, trade regulations and the control of the sector in general. They also become sites for political activism (Awuah, 1997; Clark, 2010b) when traders resist and defend their collective and individual interests and socio-economic rights.

Market traders have their own unique leadership structure. Depending on their size, commodity associations are the smallest unit of organisation in any market. These associations are constituted of traders who sell similar items and mobilise themselves as groups around products/commodities such as yams, maize, vegetables, fruit and used clothing (Britwum and Akorsu, 2017). Each commodity association has a leader known as the 'item queen' who is either elected or nominated. The associations act as trade regulators, negotiate with other commodity traders, settle disputes, provide credit and financial assistance to their members, and support their general welfare. Each market has a 'queen' who oversees all activities by coordinating with item leaders. This leadership structure, with queens in the traditional chieftaincy role, shows the social embeddedness of the market space. Although the market is hierarchical in its class and ethnic dimensions, the leadership structure revolves around cooperation and collectivistic ideologies. According to Awo (2010), market leaders negotiate their interests by leveraging their networks. Hendriks (2017) posits that the power wielded by associations, through a structure that combines partisanship and non-partisanship, makes it imperative to involve them in the development planning of the markets.

In January 2013, the Ga East Municipal Assembly used the DACF and the 2011 District Development Fund, totalling 101,538 GHS (17,478 USD at the current exchange rate),[2] to build seventy-two sheds in the market for traders. The women had user rights to trade in the sheds as long as they wished but these finally belonged to the assembly. This arrangement did not give women the autonomy they enjoyed when they built their own sheds. Market spaces are umbilical cords that link generations of women in a family. Sheds can be privately owned, heritable and traded as occupational gifts to a child (Clark, 1994; Seidu, 2018). Once the assembly involved itself in shed building, the ownership of the market began to change.

The Dome Market redevelopment PPP

The Dome Market, located in the Dome Zonal Council of the Ga East Municipal Assembly, is arguably the biggest market in the zonal area and essential for revenue generation. The market emerged along a railway line as women took advantage of the transport hub to trade. Once rail transport stopped, following the collapse of the Achimota Bridge, traders mobilised to start the market at its current location. The Municipal Assembly purchased the land but the structures were built, owned and controlled by individual traders. By the end of 2019, there were about 3,000 traders in the market. Thereafter, the assembly decided to rebuild the market using the BOT PPP model, introducing lockable shops and open sheds/stalls as part of a modernisation drive.

PPP model 1: Construction of lockable stores

The first batch of agreements to build lockable shops was signed in 2014 between the assembly and seven Ghanaian private contractors selected arbitrarily. Some contractors made bids while the assembly handpicked others. In one 2016 agreement, the contractor indicated a project cost of 2.5 million GHS (431,034 USD)[3] but later had to work with the assembly's technocrats to ensure that the project was profitable. It was unclear how the value for money variables was determined. In all, 209 units of lockable shops of different sizes – the dimensions ranged between 3 metres by 1.8 metres and 4.2 metres by 3.6 metres – were built by the contractors and completed in 2018.

As per the agreement, the lockable shops would belong to the contractor for the first twenty years, after which they would become the property of the assembly. In addition, contractors have to 'donate' one unit of each store to the assembly which, in turn, would use them as microfinance, sanitation and information centre offices. In reality, contractors added the price of the 'donated' units to the leasing prices, shifting the cost burden to the traders. All the PPP shops had electricity, and about 85 per cent had sanitation amenities such as toilets and washbasins, but despite the existence of a water tank in the market, many shops did not have running water. The occupants of the PPP stores had to pay for the water they used in their shops.

PPP model 2: Construction of open market sheds/stalls

In addition to lockable shops, the BOT agreement also covered the construction of 1,700 open sheds/stalls for the market. The plan included one assembly administration block to be used as a health post, police post, sanitation office, credit facility office, day-care centre, etc. The first 100 sheds under this plan were completed in 2018. Approximately 2,300 traders were already registered as users of the space when the new PPP project was being planned. These traders, who had each paid a 30-GHS (5.17 USD) registration fee to the assembly, were to be considered for the allocation of units once the sheds/stalls were built. However, with only 1,700 sheds planned under the PPP, the project would end up displacing 600 traders.

Under the agreement, the assembly would rent the shed on behalf of the financiers and use the revenue to pay them. For each shed that was built and allocated, the assembly would charge individual traders 9,000 GHS (1,552 USD) for ten years, comprising a 2-GHS (0.35 USD) daily rate.

Dome Market PPP: Who benefits?

Debates about the importance of PPPs must consider whether or not they benefit end users. The pitfalls of the Dome Market lockable shops and open sheds/stalls are instructive in this regard.

Insufficient consultation with traders

The Dome Market leadership – including the item queens and the market queen – was part of consultations undertaken before the start of the project. The leaders were promised that existing traders would be prioritised in the allocation of shops upon completion of the project. The leaders requested that the design of the shops take into account the items sold in the market as well as the financial capacity of the women traders so that the shops remain usable and affordable. To this end, they asked for smaller and preferably open sheds/stalls. Later, it became clear that the participation of the market leadership was only an 'add them and stir' affair as their views were not incorporated in the project design. The assembly and the contractors built closed lockable shops that were inappropriate for the items sold.

The women displaced by the lockable shops PPP complained that the allocation process was not transparent. In December 2018, a fire destroyed a number of container stores[4] owned by a group of forty women. This was the third such fire in that part of the market since December 2013. The site of these fires, a busy main road in front of the Dome Market, led the women to suspect that they were the handiwork of arsonists and the assembly was using this tactic to pressurise them. The assembly had tried to evict these women several times in the past to make way for the construction of PPP shops. Each time, the women refused. All traders in that part of the market lost their wares in the 2018 fire. It is worth noting that women in Ghana's market typically work in precarious conditions and outbreaks of fire are frequent.[5] Following this incident, the Member of Parliament (MP) for the area convinced the aggrieved women to vacate the space and promised to prioritise them in the allocation of shops/stalls. Finally, only one of the forty displaced traders obtained a shop at the modernised site. The women blamed this on information asymmetry, the high cost of leasing and unfavourable terms of payment.

Akos, thirty-two, and a graduate of tertiary education, who lost three shops in the fire, complained about the process and cost of obtaining a new shop: 'I do not know if the allocation of the PPP shops is politicised or [if] some elements in the political and municipal assembly structures have hijacked it for their interests. Things are not clear, and we are confused.'

The fragmentation of market leadership

The market PPP also changed the process of shop ownership and further polarised an already politicised space. In the past, the market queens decided on space allocation and integration of traders into the market. They were contracted to collect market tolls on behalf of the assembly, which they did efficiently. An assembly official confirmed that revenue collection in the market was smoother when the market leadership was in charge. However, the politicisation and fragmentation of the 'market front' took the contract away from the market leadership. In its place, a committee of twenty-one people comprising politicians, party foot soldiers, traditional authorities and others was tasked with collecting tolls. This process was abandoned only after a dip in the revenue collected.

The Municipal Chief Executive (MCE) of the assembly, who, until her appointment in 2017, was a trader in the market, refused to recognise the existing leadership and, instead, appointed another market queen. In a rerun of party and state-centred politics, the market leadership became partisan as the MCE belonged to the then ruling party and the derecognised market queen was reportedly a member of the opposition party at the time.

The politicisation of the market increased the vulnerability of traders. Although divided, some women directed their energies at challenging the assembly's unilateral imposition of a new market queen while others resisted the PPP project. In July 2017, the women threatened to stage a naked protest against the politically motivated imposition of a new market queen. The resistance to the PPP, however, was complicated by two parallel leaderships – one derecognised and the other deemed illegitimate.

Many women blamed the PPP for fragmenting the 'women's front' in the market and weakening their mobilisation strategies. Under the PPP contracts, contractors and middlemen became key players in determining shop ownership. It was the prerogative of the contractors to rent shops for the first twenty years. During this time, the contractor leased them to whoever could afford the rent, a process over which the assembly and the market leadership had no control. As a result, the new occupants of the shops were often 'foreign' to the space, did not identify with the market leadership and comply with its governance regime. The leadership was thus weakened and unable to organise due to internal divisions.

The lease process, cost and payment system

Many traders found themselves excluded from the market due to the high cost of shops/stalls constructed under the PPP. These costs were not disclosed in the contract. Instead, the contractors/financiers determined the price only after the construction was completed. The rented shops were also non-transferable, which means that, once leased, they could not be sublet.

Besides high costs, the payment system itself was not sensitive to the financial abilities of women. Rents worth 40,000 GHS (10,000 USD) for shops on the top floor, and 65,000 GHS (13,000 USD) for ground floor shops, were to be paid in cash. These amounts were well above the means of the average trader whose annual turnover did not typically exceed 15,000 GHS (3,000 USD). This arrangement was not only the result of poor planning but also an exclusionary tactic aimed at bringing more affluent traders into the market. The assembly preferred traders who could pay the fixed BOP annually, thereby making revenue collection and planning more manageable, compared with the daily toll payments made by smaller traders.

With a ten-year lease period that did not guarantee the security of tenure and was priced beyond the reach of most traders, the PPP sheds/stalls generated far more protests and resistance than the lockable shops. The women challenged the requirement to pay the entire lease amount of GHS 9,000 (1,551 USD) upfront. They also rejected the MP's offer to subsidise each trader with 1,500 GHS (259 USD) to bring the cost down to 7,500 GHS (1,293 USD), considering it to be a trap.

Male control of women's economic space

Market PPPs represent the elite male capture of local government for individual benefit, and male control over women's economic spaces. The contractors were men who, technically and legally, owned specific parts of the market for a fixed number of years stated in the agreements. It is safe to assume that, in a few years, these men would predominantly own and control the markets, restricting the economic, social and political rights of women.

Transparency and accountability

The assembly may have intended to use PPPs to modernise the market by decongesting it and improving the general working environment for traders, but its decisions were taken unilaterally. Decisions on project design, costs, location, selection of financiers, prices of leases and procedures for allocation of shops/stalls were taken by the assembly without taking into account the views of the market leaders and traders. This information was also not publicly disclosed. The market leadership's suggestions, especially with regard to the design of shops, were ignored.

This affected the economic rights of the women whose very livelihoods were altered by the project. The exclusion of the women from redevelopment planning also led to massive displacement and inappropriate designs in other markets (Asante, 2020).

The state must return: Women resist the Dome Market PPP

Despite fragmentations in the 'women's front', the PPP sheds triggered a number of protests. Concerns about the lockable shops that had already been completed by then, and the consequent dispossession of traders, culminated into a bigger protest when the open sheds were under construction. Women traders used various strategies to record their disapproval. They confronted the assembly officials and sought an audience with the Speaker of the Parliament, who was earlier an MP on the ticket of the ruling New Patriotic Party (NPP), to register their complaint about the PPP and its costs. When this attempt was unsuccessful, they petitioned the Head Office of the NPP in Accra. Thereafter, the case travelled from the party head office to the President who referred it to the Ministry of Special Development Initiatives.

The women also used the impending December 2020 general election as a bargaining chip, as the constituency in which the market is located had voted for the ruling party in the past elections. The NPP had increased its share of votes in the constituency from 60 per cent in 2008, to 61.93 per cent in 2012 and 62.52 per cent in 2016. Having realised that the stakes were high in the upcoming general election, the women threatened to abstain from voting or vote against the ruling party at the presidential and parliamentary levels. This elicited a commitment from the Ministry of Special Development Initiatives to investigate the cost of the sheds.

Eventually, the women's protests succeeded in putting an end to the shed PPP project and forced the state to take over the redevelopment of the market. The 100 sheds completed under the PPP were allocated, and the state took over the construction of 500 sheds as part of its agreement with the traders. The new sheds were smaller, as previously suggested by the women. The new design also recognised the fact that the items sold in the market – such as vegetables, perishable food crops, fruit and fish – could not be sold in lockable shops. Acknowledging the women's inputs, the municipal engineer said, 'The agitation of the women has helped in redesigning the new PPP sheds. It has also informed the new phase which the government will fund and which will be free of charge to the traders.'

Impact of the Dome Market PPP on gender and human rights

The exclusion of traders from market redevelopment plans and implementation has been a frequent occurrence in the country, especially in recent years (Okoye, 2020). Such exclusions violate human rights-based approaches to development such as participation, accountability, non-discrimination, equality, empowerment and legality. Feminist critiques of PPPs have highlighted the pitfalls of the model and the ways in which women's interests are forsaken in market-driven development paradigms. Written in the language of neoliberal development, PPPs ostensibly support women's empowerment (Prügl and True, 2014) but, in reality, do not take into consideration heterogeneity among women.

In the case of the Dome Market PPP, information available about the project was vague. Many women did not know the contractors or how to contact them. The information process was hijacked by middlemen, further complicating the traders' quest to lease shops. Some middlemen rented the lockable shops in their own names and sublet them at exorbitant prices for shorter periods. In one ground floor shop that we visited, a young man explained that he had, with the help of his mother, leased it at 50,000 GHS (8,621 USD) for six years. The going price for it, according to the assembly, was 65,000 GHS (13,000 USD) for twenty years. The young man did not know the contractor. In other cases, the middlemen added their commissions to the total cost of the shops. Many shops were sublet in violation of the assembly bylaws stipulated in the allocation letters. This means the assembly did not know the actual occupants although they paid the BOP fee. This was either an act of collusion or negligence on the part of the assembly. Many shops also remained vacant due to high rents. The market modernisation process thus had little accountability and no safeguards. Mechanisms for resolving the issues the women raised or the gross economic injustices committed against them were weak or non-existent.

As mentioned earlier, most of the current users of the PPP shops had not been selling in the market previously. Wealthy female traders from significant markets, such as Makola, used this opportunity to rent more shops as an accumulation strategy. The project thus created new spatial, economic and social differentiations among traders. PPP shop owners had more space and sold items in a supermarket-like fashion, while other traders sold in the more decrepit areas of the market. These conditions seemingly justified the modernisation drive. In reality, it was not the small traders of Dome Market, but rather wealthier traders from other markets as well as middlemen and financiers who benefitted from the PPP project.

Despite the many pitfalls of the market PPP, the project design included previously absent sanitation facilities which benefitted traders in those shops. The shed PPP that was withdrawn after the women's protests included a medical facility and a day-care centre. These facilities are to be provided in the new structures being developed by the government. However, traders fear that government participation could threaten the livelihoods of those who do not support the ruling dispensation. When the sheds are completed, traders will have to pay an allocation fee which will be determined by the assembly. Moreover, since the number of sheds is not enough to cater to all the traders, the allocation will be done on a first-come-first-served basis, raising concerns about politicisation. Thus, while the shed PPP has been abandoned, the possibility of politicised allocation – a burning issue in other markets of Ghana as well[6] – continues to worry women traders in the Dome Market.

Given the historical relationship between the state and the traders, the women's call to the state to intervene in the market is an ambivalent move, though not a surprising one. The 'return of the state' has implications for the traders' economic survival. With the state taking over the construction of the new stalls, the women stand indirectly dispossessed, since the market which is now being modernised was originally built by them. Traditionally, the women owned the structures, no matter how small. Now, however, they will become tenants of the state.

The women who were displaced by the PPP shops complained about livelihood insecurity as the assembly did not resettle them. Some pointed out that they could have sold their goods in front of other shops in the earlier market setup, but are unable to do so now since they do not share the same cordiality with the new owners. Reiterating the information asymmetry, the traders argued that, had they known about the prices of the shops earlier, they would have secured a few through a collective funds model and then divided the shops into smaller units among themselves. Instead, some of the displaced traders were forced to become hawkers in the market while others stopped trading entirely. Those who still had spaces were constantly harassed by the assembly's task force for squatting and threatened with eviction. Others had to squeeze their wares into tiny spaces or sell items that fit the vulnerable situation in which they now find themselves.

In prioritising profit, the market PPPs put principles of non-discrimination and equality on the back burner. The cost of the PPP shops excluded poorer traders structurally. But while the project disempowered the women, it did not silence them completely. They mobilised, protested and brought the state back into the development of the market.

Conclusion

Ghana's privatisation trajectory has entered a new phase in which PPPs are increasingly being used for infrastructure financing and development. This is happening against the backdrop of the Ghana Beyond Aid agenda, the country's attainment of lower-middle-income status and the subsequent drying up of donor funds. In this context, PPPs have proven useful. Nevertheless, they are not without consequences and criticisms. The existence of a law on PPP financing does not necessarily solve the many complexities that entangle equity and efficiency, or private sector logic with public sector requirements. In Africa, the negative consequences of PPPs have been blamed on (the lack of) expertise, as though that could solve the ideological complexities that characterise the financing model and explain the power inequalities between the global North and South, and between men and women. In fact, the tyranny of expertise is one of the reasons why the private sector is allowed to drive the process. Besides, PPPs should be seen as global-level politics transmitted to the local level. Resource constraints at the local level make PPPs the first alternative for development.

The markets, from which women derive their economic autonomy, are attracting PPPs in the name of modernisation. However, as seen in the Dome Market case, the PPP project failed to improve the economic status of the traders. Instead, traders were dispossessed with no resettlement options. The processes leading to the implementation of the PPP were opaque, as the assembly and the project financiers had no accountability to the women in the market. The project deepened the already fragmented governance structures in the market. Notwithstanding these odds, the women put up a fierce resistance, using all the weapons at their disposal to bring the government back into market development. Their protests were a pushback against efficiency-driven economic development and its profit-maximisation logic, and their demand that the state fulfil its social contract was a call for justice in an era of elite capture of government and the state's de-investment in public infrastructure development.

However, we must not lose sight of the election cycle in Ghana and the *politricks* of unsustainable election promises. The women are aware of this possibility as they race against time, with 500 sheds and other facilities, including day-care centres, a police station, a medical clinic, etc., at varying stages of completion. Commodity leaders and associations are at the forefront of this hectic struggle, mobilising their members and ready to mount further protests in the event of politicisation of stall allocations.

Notes

1 The Local Government Law of 1988 and the Local Government Act (Act 462) of 1993 came into force to devolve power, functions and responsibility at the local level.
2 1 GHS=USD 0.60994 in 2011 (average).
3 1 USD=GHS 5.8 (June 2020).
4 Container stores, built from repurposed shipping containers, can be installed as movable shops or on cemented floors. They are common in Ghana's economy both in local markets and along streets.
5 Market fire outbreaks are some of the most common reminders of congestion, unplanned nature and unsanitary conditions of the market.
6 'Ho Traders Unhappy about Allocation of Market Stalls', *GhanaWeb*. Available at: https://www.ghanaweb.com/GhanaHomePage/NewsArchive/Ho-traders-unhappy-about-allocation-of-market-stalls-989944.

References

Aidoo, A. (1985), 'Women in the History and Culture of Ghana', *Research Review*, 1 (1): 14–51.

Appiah-Kubi, K. (2001), 'State-owned Enterprises and Privatization in Ghana', *The Journal of Modern African Studies*, 39 (2): 197–229. Available at: https://www.jstor.org/stable/3557262 (accessed 20 January 2020).

Aryeetey, E., and W. Baah-Boateng (2016), 'Understanding Ghana's Growth Success Story and Job Creation Challenges', UNU-WIDER Working Paper 2015/140, Helsinki: United Nations University World Institute for Development Economics Research. Available at: www.wider.unu.edu/publication/understanding-ghana%E2%80%99s-growth-successstory-and-job-creation-challenges (accessed 8 October 2018).

Asante, L. A. (2020), 'Urban Governance in Ghana: The Participation of Traders in the Redevelopment of Kotokuraba Market in Cape Coast', *African Geographical Review*. Available at: 10.1080/19376812.2020.1726193 (accessed 20 January 2020).

Assimeng, M. (1990), 'Women in Ghana: Their Integration in Socio-economic Development', *Research Review*, 6 (1): 57–68.

Awo, M. A. (2010), *Marketing and Market Queens: A Case of Tomato Farmers in the Upper East Region of Ghana*, Gedruckt mit Genehmigung der Philosophischen Fakultät der Rheinischen Friedrich-Wilhelms-Universität, Bonn.

Awortwi, N. (2011), 'An Unbreakable Path? A Comparative Study of Decentralization and Local Government Development Trajectories in Ghana and Uganda', *International Review of Administrative Sciences*, 77 (2): 347–77.

Available at: https://journals.sagepub.com/doi/10.1177/0020852311399844 (accessed 20 January 2020).

Awuah, E. (1997), 'Mobilizing for Change: A Case Study of Market Trader Activism in Ghana', *Canadian Journal of African Studies*, 31 (3): 401–23. Available at: https://www.jstor.org/stable/486193 (accessed 20 January 2020).

Bank of Ghana (2005), *Ghana's Privatization Programme: Lessons and Way Forward*, BoG Policy Briefing Paper, Accra: Bank of Ghana.

Britwum, A. O. (2013), 'Market Queens and the Blame Game in Ghanaian Tomato Marketing', in: Christoph Scherrer and Debdulal Saha (eds), *The Food Crisis: Implications for Labor*, Munich: Rainer Hampp Verlag.

Britwum, A. O., and A. D. Akorsu (2017), 'Market Women's Associations in Ghana', in: Balghis Badri and Aili Mari Tripp (eds), *Women's Activism in Africa*, 48–60, London: Zed Books.

Clark, G. (1994), *Onions Are My Husband: Survival and Accumulation by West African Market Women*, Chicago, IL-London: University of Chicago Press.

Clark, G. (2004), 'Managing Transitions and Continuities in Ghanaian Trading Contexts', *African Economic History*, 32: 65–88. Available at: https://www.jstor.org/stable/3601618 (accessed 20 January 2020).

Clark, G. (2010a), *African Market Women: Seven Life Stories from Ghana*, Bloomington, IN: Indiana University Press.

Clark, G. (2010b), 'Gender Fictions and Gender Tensions Involving "Traditional" Asante Market Women', *African Studies Quarterly*, 11 (2–3): 43–66. Available at: https://asq.africa.ufl.edu/clark_spring10/ (accessed 20 January 2020).

Crawford, G. (2008), 'Poverty and the Politics of (De)centralisation in Ghana', in: G. Crawford and C. Hartmann (eds), *Decentralisation in Africa: A Pathway out of Poverty and Conflict?*, 107–44, Amsterdam: Amsterdam University Press.

Crook, Richard C. (2017), 'Democratic Decentralisation, Clientelism and Local Taxation in Ghana', *IDS Bulletin*, 48 (2): 15–30. Available at: https://bulletin.ids.ac.uk/index.php/idsbo/article/view/2857/ONLINE%20ARTICLE (accessed 20 January 2020).

Darkwah, A. K. (2002), 'Trading Goes Global: Ghanaian Market Women in an Era of Globalization', *Asian Women*, 15: 31–49.

Darkwah, A. K. (2007a), 'Work as Duty and as Joy: Understanding the Role of Work in the Lives of Ghanaian Female Traders of Global Consumer Goods', in: Sharon Harley (ed), *Women's Labor in the Global Economy: Speaking in Multiple Voices*, 206–20, New Brunswick, NJ-London: Rutgers University Press.

Darkwah, A. K. (2007b), 'Making Hay while the Sun Shines: Ghanaian Female Traders and Their Insertion into the Global Economy', in: Nandini Gunewardena and Ann Kingsolver (eds), *The Gender of Globalization: Women Navigating Cultural and Economic Marginalities*, 61–84, Santa Fe, NM: School for Advanced Research Press.

Ghana Statistical Service (2016), *2015 Labour Force Survey*, Accra: Ghana Statistical Service.

Graham, Y. (1993), 'Law, State and the Internationalization of Agricultural Capital in Ghana: A Comparison of Colonial Export Production and Post-colonial Production for the Home Market', PhD. Thesis, University of Warwick.

Government of Ghana – The Public Private Partnership Act 2020 (Act 1039).

Hendriks, T. D. (2017), 'Collaboration and Competition: Market Queens, Trade Unions and Collective Action of Informal Workers in Ghana's Makola Market', *Interface: A Journal for and about Social Movements*, 9 (2): 162–87. Available at: http://www.interfacejournal.net/wordpress/wp-content/uploads/2017/12/Interface-9-2-Hendriks.pdf (accessed 20 January 2020).

Lynch, G., and G. Crawford (2012), 'Democratization in Africa 1990–2010: An Assessment', in: G. Crawford and G. Lynch (eds), *Democratization in Africa: Challenges and Prospects*, 1–36, Abingdon-New York: Routledge.

Manuh, Takyiwaa (1993), 'Women, State and Society under PNDC Rule in Ghana', in: Emmanuel Gyimah-Boadi (ed), *Ghana under PNDC Rule*, 176–95, Dakar: CODESRIA Books.

Mawuko-Yevugah, L. (2014). *Reinventing Development Aid Reform and Technologies of Governance in Ghana*, Abingdon: Routledge.

MoFEP (2011), 'National Policy on Public Private Partnerships (PPP)'. Available at: http://www.mofep.gov.gh (accessed 26 January 2020).

MoFEP (2019), 'The Annual Public Debt Report for the 2018 Financial Year'. Available at: http://www.mofep.gov.gh (accessed 26 January 2020).

Okoye, V. (2020), *Street Vendor Exclusion in 'Modern' Market Planning: A Case Study from Kumasi, Ghana*, WIEGO Resource Document No. 15 Manchester, UK: WIEGO.

Osei-Kyei, R., A. P. C. Chan, and A. Dansoh (2017), 'Public-Private Partnership in Ghana', in: Ali Farazmand (eds), *Global Encyclopaedia of Public Administration, Public Policy, and Governance*, Cham: Springer.

Osei-Kyei, R., and A. P. C. Chan (2015), 'Review of Studies on the Critical Success Factors for Public-Private Partnership (PPP) Projects from 1990 to 2013,' *International Journal of Project Management*, 33 (6): 1335–46.

Prügl, E., and J. True (2014), 'Equality Means Business? Governing Gender through Transnational Public-Private Partnerships', *Review of International Political Economy*, 21 (6): 1137–69. Available at: https://www.tandfonline.com/doi/abs/10.1080/09692290.2013.849277 (accessed 20 January 2020).

Robertson, C. (1983), 'The Death of Makola and Other Tragedies,' *Canadian Journal of African Studies*, 17 (3): 469–95. Available at: https://www.tandfonline.com/doi/abs/10.1080/00083968.1983.10804032 (accessed 20 January 2020).

Seidu, A. (2018), *Public-Private Partnerships in Ghana: Interrogating the Efficacy of a Politically Convenient Practice*, Friedrich Ebert Stiftung, Accra, Ghana.

Spire, A., and A. Choplin (2018), 'Street Vendors Facing Urban Beautification in Accra (Ghana): Eviction, Relocation and Formalization,' *Articulo: Journal of Urban Research*, 17–18. Available at: http://journals.openedition.org/articulo/3443 DOI: 10.4000/articulo.3443 (accessed 20 January 2020).

Tsikata, D. (1989), 'Women's Political Organizations, 1951–1987', in: E. Hansen and K. A. Ninsin (eds), *The State, Development and Politics in Ghana*, 73–94, London: CODESRIA.

World Bank (2011), *Ghana's Infrastructure: A Continental Perspective*, Policy Research Working Paper 5600. Washington DC: World Bank. See also, PPP Knowledge Lab, Ghana PPP Framework. Available at: https://pppknowledgelab.org/countries/ghana (accessed 20 January 2020).

9

PPPs in the Parirenyatwa Group of Hospitals in Zimbabwe: Institutional precarities and piecemeal solutions

Nyasha Masuka

Introduction

In Zimbabwe, public-private partnerships (PPPs) were introduced in the health sector to bridge the funding gap created by the reduction in public health expenditure in the aftermath of the structural adjustment programmes (SAPs) adopted by the government at the behest of the World Bank (WB) and International Monetary Fund (IMF) in the mid-1990s. However, the PPPs that are currently operational in public hospitals across the country have not been consistently guided by *any* regulatory framework. When such a framework did exist, the implementation processes did not abide by them, nor did they take into account human rights and/or gender equality. Besides, most PPPs in sector are based on Memoranda of Understanding (MoUs) that are unenforceable, not guided by adequate legal advice, and do not require the participation of the people and communities most affected by these partnerships.

This has created barriers to accessing healthcare services and worsened health outcome indicators, particularly for women. For instance, while there is a policy exempting pregnant and lactating women from paying user fees when accessing health services, there is no legislation for its enforcement. This has led to cases where women have been either denied such care or detained in maternity wards after failing to pay for the services used. Prohibitive costs also prevent women from accessing care in the private wings of public hospitals or procuring medicines from private pharmacies in public hospitals.

Methodology

For this chapter, I conducted desk reviews of available literature on health sector PPPs in Zimbabwe and other low-income countries (LICs) in sub-Saharan Africa, using keywords such as PPP, gender equality, Zimbabwe, health sector, LICs and sub-Saharan Africa. The reviewed material included public health and gender equality legislations in Zimbabwe, legislations governing PPPs in general and the health sector in particular, and media articles on announcements and opinions about PPPs in the health sector by actors who either support or have been aggrieved by them.

I also used participatory methods in the form of key informant interviews (KIIs) with chief executive officers (CEOs), clinical directors, clinicians, professional health associations, healthcare professionals working in public hospitals and civil society organisations (CSOs). For fear of victimisation, informants consented to interviews on the condition of anonymity.

To strengthen the analysis of how health-related PPPs are formulated and implemented in Zimbabwe and how they have impacted gender equality and human rights, I also drew on my professional experience of working in public health. My experience is relevant to the chapter given the paucity of literature on the subject. This is also why this chapter draws heavily on publications by the Regional Network for Equity in Health in East and Southern Africa (EQUINET) and the Training and Research Support Centre (TARSC) to gain insights on the Zimbabwean health system and its transformation over time in relation to health service organisation and the private health sector.

Overview of Zimbabwe's health sector

After its independence from Britain in 1980 following ninety years of colonial rule, Zimbabwe adopted and implemented the primary healthcare (PHC) approach identified as key to the attainment of the goal of Health for All at the Alma-Ata Declaration of 1978 (Ray and Masuki, 2017). This approach entailed the decentralisation of health services to administrative wards using the PHC principle of Equity in Health (Nyazema, 2010). According to an EQUINET Discussion Paper, three waves of socio-economic developments – high public health expenditure in 1980–90, liberalisation and privatisation in 1990–2000 and economic downturn from 2000 to the present – have shaped Zimbabwe's health sector (Munyuki and Jasi, 2009).

To date, the Government of Zimbabwe (GoZ) constructed 1,091 health facilities and institutions, bringing the total number of such facilities to

1,779.[1] The country made impressive progress on health indicators in the first decade after independence, with life expectancy increasing to sixty years, immunisation coverage reaching over 80 per cent of the target population and infant mortality rate (IMR) falling to 46 per 1,000 live births by 1989 (Lennock, 1994). By 2000, immunisation and antenatal coverage (ANC) had reached 89 per cent, and infant mortality had been reduced by 80 per cent between 1980 and 1998 (Munyuki and Jasi, 2009). Between 1980 and 1987, Zimbabwe increased health expenditure by 80 per cent or 2.3 per cent of the gross domestic product (GDP), almost three times higher than the sub-Saharan Africa average of 0.8 per cent of GDP (Tren and Bate, 2005).

However, there were growing inequities in health service provision from the mid-1990s onwards due to the implementation of the SAPs that resulted in economic liberalisation, privatisation and a reduction in public expenditure. The National Health Strategy (NHS) of 1997–2007 aimed at creating opportunities for the private sector, scaling up decentralisation and outsourcing services. Post 2000, the health sector deteriorated due to foreign currency shortages, inadequate export performance, reduced capital inflows, withdrawal of multilateral financing institutions and the scaling down of bilateral creditors.

Total health expenditure fell from a peak of 10.8 per cent of GDP in 1998 to 7 per cent in 2005. The decline in public health spending was accompanied by a corresponding increase in private expenditure in the sector. At 53 per cent, out-of-pocket (OOP) expenditure by households constituted the largest component of private health spending in 2001. Per capita public health expenditure had decreased to 8.55 US dollars (USD) by 2000, against 23.60 USD recommended by the 1997 Commission of Review for Health. By 2008, per capita health expenditure had hit rock bottom at 0.19 USD.

Moreover, since 2000, there has been a massive brain drain in the healthcare sector, which began losing 20 per cent of medical personnel per month. Between 2004 and 2008, up to 75 per cent of personnel exited the sector.

The health system nearly collapsed in 2008 amid the health worker crisis and a nationwide cholera outbreak. After a marginal economic recovery and renewed investment in health services in 2009–12, growth declined again during 2013–17, with 72 per cent of the population living below the national poverty line and 21 per cent on less than 1.90 USD a day (World Bank, 2016). The share of private entities in the financing of health expenditure fell from 53.7 per cent in 2015 to 32.8 per cent in 2017 and 29.2 per cent in 2018.[2] Household expenditure on health fell because a third of all the income groups – non-poor, poor and very poor – were unable to afford healthcare.[3] Total health expenditure declined 9.6 per cent between 2015 and 2017, and increased 27.3 per cent between 2017 and 2018. However, the increase in expenditure did not meet the government's financing deficit during this period, which stood at 1,138.09 million USD in 2015, decreased to 877.4 million USD in 2017, and increased to 952.8 million USD in 2018, constituting 78.6 per cent, 67 per cent and 57.2 per cent of the total financing, respectively.[4]

These developments had a deleterious effect on previously robust health indicators in Zimbabwe. Norman Nyazema (2010) argues that the adoption of neoliberal policies did not take into account gender equality and had a disastrous effect on women's access to comprehensive and quality health services. He demonstrates the link between the reduction in public health spending and the increase in maternal morbidity and mortality, and notes that Zimbabwe's Constitution, at the time, did not recognise the right to health.[5]

The Maternal Mortality Ratio (MMR) reached an all-time high of 960 deaths per 100,000 live births in 2010, and remained high at 651 deaths per 100,000 live births in 2015, according to data from the Zimbabwe Health and Demographic Survey (ZDHS). The under-five child mortality rate was at sixty-nine deaths per 1,000 live births, with 27 per cent of children under five years of age showing stunted growth.[6] Overall life expectancy declined from sixty years in 1990 to forty-three years by 2010 (Nyazema, 2010).

The socio-economic crises and succession battles within the ruling party resulted in the ouster of Zimbabwe's first President Robert Mugabe in a military *coup* in November 2017 (BBC News, 2017). The new government that came to power in 2018, headed by President Emmerson Mnangagwa, adopted the Vision 2030 agenda, seeking to transform the country into an upper-middle-income (UMI) society. The Transitional Stabilisation Programme (TSP) was implemented from October 2018 to December 2020 to achieve macro and fiscal stabilisation and lay the foundation for triple 'S' – strong, sustainable and shared – growth. However, austerity measures adopted in the 2019 Annual Plan/Budget eroded salaries even as the cost of living increased more than five fold.

The government's health budget for 2019 was 650 million USD. At 52.13 USD purchasing power parity (ppp) per capita, or 7 per cent of the national budget, it was a far cry from the 86 USD ppp recommended by the World Health Organization (WHO), or 15 per cent of the national budget recommended by the Abuja Declaration. The budget was revised to 1.2 billion Zimbabwean dollars (ZWD) (120 million USD or 7.50 ZWD ppp per capita at official exchange rates) in August 2019 after the devaluation of the ZWD in February 2019.[7] This effectively reduced the health budget by 81.5 per cent in real USD terms. Seventy-five per cent of the 1.2 billion ZWD was directed towards payment of salaries, leaving only 300 million ZWD (30 million USD) for operational service delivery.[8] This increased the reliance on funding from Health Development Partners (HDPs), mainly for the implementation of vertical disease control programmes. Since then, domestic funding for health has been on an increasing trend (for salaries) while external funding has been on a downward trajectory. Between 2014 and 2019, budget allocations by the government increased from 287 million USD to 755 million USD, whereas external funding during the same period fell from 389 million USD to 368 million USD.[9] However, the value of government contributions in USD ppp terms is much less because of real economic inflation against the background of an officially controlled exchange rate which gives USD and ZWD a parity of 1:1. External funding has also been highly dependent on specific partners, namely, the Global Fund and the United States Government Partners.[10]

The Joint Ventures Partnerships Act adopted by the Mugabe government in 2016 was aimed at guiding and encouraging PPPs in every sector in order to plug the public funding gap. Thereafter, the Mnangagwa regime introduced the 'Zimbabwe is Open for Business' mantra to stimulate investments in private for-profit ventures in the country. Many so-called mega deals[11] made media headlines since the implementation of the TSP, but the public is yet to see the results, let alone the benefits, of these investments. As the country lagged behind on Universal Health Coverage (UHC) and PHC, the government also attempted to engage foreign investors to form PPPs with central public hospitals for delivery of super-specialised care. In the aftermath, the MMR decreased from 651 per 100,000 live births in 2015 to 462 per 100,000 live births in 2019, with skilled birth attendance and institutional delivery ranging from 82 per cent in rural areas to 94 per cent in urban areas. However, under-five child mortality increased to seventy-three per 1,000 live births in 2019, ranging from fifty-one deaths per 1,000 for the richest people, to ninety-one per 1,000 for the poorest (UNICEF, 2019).

In 2018, the Ministry of Health and Child Care (MoHCC) suspended all PPPs in the sector in order to review their performance and develop a cost-effective and transparent framework for such projects (Daily News, 2018). The decision came after pushback from the chairperson of the Parliamentary Portfolio Committee on Health who argued that the poor were facing financial barriers to accessing care at a central hospital that had numerous unevaluated PPPs. Nurses at the same hospital downed tools in solidarity with patients, including pregnant women who were unable to access care.

As far back as 1980, Zimbabwe had adopted the Planning for Equity in Health policy to deal with inequities in health status and healthcare. Over the next decade, successive health ministries held that the private sector had a distortionary effect on the allocation of health resources (Munyunki and

Jasi, 2009). The thinking changed with the NHS 1997–2007 which sought to engage both the public and private sectors in health service provision. This strategy transformed the role of the MoHCC into one of 'supporting, promoting and advocating for the provision of quality health services and care to all citizens', and outlined four main areas of reform:

1. Decentralisation aimed at creating an enabling administrative, managerial and operational environment for all stakeholders in the health sector, to ensure that both public and private investments in health are linked to the achievement of national health objectives;
2. Management strengthening and development of managerial and institutional capacity;
3. Subcontracting non-core services and involving the private sector in service provision at all levels; and
4. Enacting the Medical Services Act, 1998 to regulate the operations of stakeholders in the health sector.

By 2009, Zimbabwe had not made any concrete commitments with regard to the health sector. EQUINET attributes this lack of commitment to the predominance of for-profit private players and international investors in the sector. This is evident from the fact that there are as many registered private health facilities in the country as government facilities (see Table 9.1).

EQUINET points out four types of capital investments in the health sector during liberalisation. These include:

1. Mergers and acquisitions;
2. Foreign direct investment (FDI);
3. Incentives to the private sector such as training subsidies and tax incentives;
4. Contracting out (outsourcing).

Table 9.1 Registered Health Facilities by Ownership in Zimbabwe in 2020.

Ownership	Number of registered health facilities
GoZ	1,217
Private	1,218
Mission hospitals	112
Total	2,547

Source: Health Professions Authority website (www.hpa.co.zw).

Whyle and Olivier (2016), in the journal *Health Policy and Planning*, reveal eight distinct public-private engagement (PPE) models in the southern African context (see Table 9.2).

The case study highlighted in this chapter fits two of the above-mentioned models:

1. Contracting out (outsourcing); and
2. Dual practice regulations

Table 9.2 Public-Private Engagement Typology.

Public-private partnerships	Highly collaborative Risk sharing Long term Contractual Shared decision-making
Social marketing	Uses private sector marketing and communication tools Increased uptake of public goods Usually involves subsidisation
Sector-wide approach	Non-contractual Shared decision-making Centred around national sectoral strategies Pooled funding
Public-private mix	Non-contractual Collaborative Vertical disease focus Involves actors from all sectors
Vouchers	Demand-side financing Defined benefits Target groups
Contracting out	Contractual Short term No shared decision-making 'Buying services'
Dual practice Regulations	Regulatory control of dual practice Between state and public sector physicians
Financial support	Public financing of private sector Grants or public insurance Non-contractual

Source: Whyle, E. B., and J. Olivier (2016), 'Models of Public-Private Engagement for Health Services Delivery and Financing in Southern Africa: A Systematic Review', *Health Policy and Planning*, 31(10): 1515–1529. Available at: https://academic.oup.com/heapol/article/31/10/1515/2567069 (accessed 11 February 2020).

Munyuki and Jasi (2009) describe various modes of 'contracting out' agreements in Zimbabwe, many of which are covered by our case study. The authors also group the eight forms of PPEs described by Whyle and Olivier (2016) into contracts for the provision of non-clinical services and clinical services (see Table 9.3). The case study described in this chapter includes contracts for both types of services.

Table 9.3 Modes of Contracting Out to Private for-Profit Providers in Zimbabwe in 2009.

Type of contract	Functions of contract	Current national status of contracting
Non-clinical services	Catering	Principle generally accepted at national level. No evidence of contracting out services at central, provincial and district hospitals. Catering services still publicly provided.
	Cleaning	Still publicly provided at all facilities. (Moves to start at Parirenyatwa hospitals in 1995 were shelved). All cleaning functions are owned and provided by the government.
	Security	Publicly provided at all facilities.
	Maintenance (land and building)	Publicly provided by Ministry of Public Works that owns the buildings. Government employed groundsmen to do general maintenance through MPC.
	Maintenance (equipment)	Hospital equipment maintained by public facilities themselves through the hospital equipment department that exists at all facilities. Internal contracting exists in the form of MPC doing maintenance for certain plant equipment. For some equipment, out-servicing of technical staff from specialised private providers is done, but on a 'as per need' basis. Government purchases equipment from the private sector but largely retains the maintenance of the equipment. Only mortuary maintenance is contracted out at central hospitals.
	Laundry	Central, provincial and district hospitals increasingly outsourcing laundry with private for-profit launderers. Internal contracting with some central hospitals providing laundry services for district hospitals.
	Billing	Patient billing done by public facilities. Some public facilities using private debt collectors to collect outstanding patient fees.

Clinical services	Hospitalised care	Mission hospitals, although privately owned, act as agents for the government and provide comprehensive care packages in districts, which could otherwise be government provided. Local authorities are required by government to provide care and receive grants from the central government.
	Ambulatory care and related services	Both private and public sectors provide ambulatory services. Private for-profit providers are, however, not contracted for ambulatory services. There is a large number of private for-profit emergency facilities offering day care as well as in-patient services. Private physicians offer a variety of services to self-referred day patients at their private rooms and clinics. They can also bring their patients to the casualty and emergency wards of public facilities. Local government facilities offer ambulatory services from which they collect fees, not on behalf of the central government. Public facilities also provide ambulatory services at their casualty, out-patient and emergency wings.
	Public health	All public health functions are provided by the government. There are, however, some private for-profit sectors (such as mines and agricultural facilities) that provide public health in their environments as a requirement of their industrial activities monitoring. They are not under contract to do so, as this is a regulatory requirement

Source: Munyuki, E., and S. Jasi (2009), 'Capital Flows in the Health Care Sector in Zimbabwe: Trends and Implications for the Health System', EQUINET Discussion Paper Series 79. Rhodes University, Training and Research Support Centre, SEATINI, York University, EQUINET: Harare.

Gender equality and PPPs: A case study of the Parirenyatwa Group of Hospitals

The Parirenyatwa Group of Hospitals (PGH) is a central public teaching hospital that was established during the colonial era to cater to white settlers. Post independence, it was open to all citizens. The hospital is run under the Parirenyatwa Hospitals Act (Acts 16/1975, 39/1981; R.G.Ns 1135/1975, 899/1978, 6/2000, 22/2001) promulgated in 1975 to establish the Parirenyatwa Hospitals Board of Governors (PHBG) to manage the hospitals and provide for their functions, including care and treatment of the sick, medical education and research (see Annex 1).

PPP case 1: Laundry PPP at PGH

Ideally, the PPPs at the Parirenyatwa hospitals should have involved the PHBG, the MoHCC, health professionals working at the hospitals, the Zimbabwe Investment Authority, other government ministries, parliamentarians, patient groups and civil society representatives as the main actors. Instead, according to key informants in the management, the first contract at the PGH came about as a reaction to a crisis by the CEO and hospital management in 2008. The hospitals' laundry equipment had become old and dysfunctional and they could not afford to send linen to be laundered by private service providers. This posed a serious threat to the provision of critical surgical services for the biggest specialist quaternary teaching hospital in Zimbabwe. The management approached three laundry companies to form a PPP for laundry services at the hospitals. The conditions stipulated that the private company would refurbish the hospitals' laundry equipment, bring their own equipment and accept all the hospitals' laundry business.

The laundry companies refused the partnership on the grounds that they would essentially be subsidising the government while also running the risk of late or non-payment for services in a hyper-inflationary environment. Thereafter, another private laundry company that the management had not considered earlier approached the hospital, seeking to conduct a feasibility study. Post the study, the company agreed to enter into a PPP with the hospital for laundry services. The draft agreement was authorised by the Joint Venture Unit in the Office of the President and Cabinet (OPC) and is operational to date.

According to Whyle and Olivier's (2016) typology, the laundry PPP would be classified as a contracting out arrangement, a short-term contract with no shared decision-making in which the hospital would be 'buying services' from the contractor. This arrangement essentially guarantees the private partner business without competition and can, therefore, be monopolistic. It can also result in poor-quality services and saddle the hospital with huge legal costs if it tries to terminate the contract. In the present case, however, informants expressed satisfaction with the quality of services rendered.

PPP case 2: PPP to admit private patients into PGH

The second PPP is an agreement between the board of governors and doctors employed by the PGH to admit private patients into the hospital, and can be classified under dual practice regulation. The hospitals' private wing, called the D-Floor, offers healthcare services exclusively to those who are adequately insured or can afford private healthcare, while the poor use the public wing.[12] Clinical specialists who work at the hospitals are allowed to admit private patients to the D-Floor where they are charged private rates *while being admitted to a public hospital*. Patients pay 'hotel fees'[13] and are billed for all medical and surgical consumables and drugs used for treatment during the period of admission.

This PPP arose in response to the socio-economic meltdown that culminated in the collapse of the Zimbabwean economy in 2008, and is provided for by the Medical Services Act, 1998. The Act, operationalised in 2001, acknowledges the importance of the private health sector and grants incentives to private for-profit healthcare providers, such as allowing them access to public hospitals for treating private patients (Munyuki and Jasi, 2009). The government had started failing to pay doctors reasonable salaries as far back as 1989, prompting them to go on strike almost every year since then (Mail & Guardian, 2017). Responding to this predicament, and with an eye on continuing the provision of specialist clinical services at the Parirenyatwa hospitals, the PHBG allowed specialists to admit private patients into the D-Floor to supplement their paltry salaries. Under the PPP, admission rights are reserved for specialists who have provided care to a certain number of patients in the public wing of the hospital over a specified period of time. In addition, the specialists must accept public patients on their operating list without discrimination.

Mudyarabikwa and Madhina (2000) note that the informal arrangement of accessing private practice facilities in exchange for providing free services to public patients is open to abuse. While the system of granting admission rights is relatively transparent and objective, there are no concrete measures to counter the moral hazard of specialists limiting care for poor patients in the public side of the hospital and shunting them to the private wing. During the study conducted for the EQUINET Discussion Paper, the MoHCC had directed institutions to stop admission of private patients, particularly in maternity wards of public hospitals, as practitioners were unwilling to attend to public patients after admitting private ones. Informants in the management pointed out instances where nurses in the public wings of the hospitals directed patients awaiting surgical and medical procedures to the private rooms of specialists who were supposed to care for them in the public wing. Patients experienced prompt service on the D-Floor, but there is no evidence that they received better quality care or had better health outcomes (Patouillard et al., 2007). Many patients – predominantly poor and disadvantaged women – who could not afford private care either developed medical complications due to delays in getting appropriate care, or ended up asking to be discharged and sought care in one of the nearby mission hospitals where services are both available and cheaper (Malmborg et al., 2006). This disproportionate impact on women can be attributed to the lack of attention paid to gender equality in the arrangement between the doctors and the hospital board; the PPP does not account for the fact that women are the worst affected by the deterioration in the country's socio-economic situation (Percival et al., 2014).

The PPP does not just discount the human rights of women patients but also of the (mostly) female nurses who work on the D-Floor. Informants indicated that, under the Medical Services Act, only physicians, surgeons, anaesthetists and operating theatre nurses are paid privately at market rates by patients or medical insurance. Ward nurses who attend to patients postoperatively are on a government salary and do not receive any extra payment. While some doctors pay ward nurses informally, others use punitive measures if nurses do not provide appropriate care to the patients. These discriminatory and ad-hoc practices have led to conflicts and resistance to this PPP.

To address these issues, a new PPP aimed at providing surgical operating suites and diagnostic equipment at the Parirenyatwa hospitals is under formulation. In 2018, the office of the Permanent Secretary for Health directed all central government hospitals to issue tenders for PPPs to establish super-specialist centres of excellence for clinical services. This came after a media announcement to this effect by the then Minister of Health and Child Care, himself a former central hospital CEO who presided over some PPPs whose effectiveness was never evaluated. The tenders published by PGH invited private investors to partner with the hospital by investing in the refurbishment of the D-Floor and surgical operating suites, and acquiring modern high-tech diagnostic equipment and/or technology. The hospital would reciprocate by sharing the private wing with the private investors and allowing them to provide super-specialist clinical services that the hospital itself is unable to offer.

People living in Zimbabwe currently travel to India, China and Singapore to obtain super-specialist services. In 2018 alone, medical tourism by a small fraction of the population was worth an estimated 400 million USD, equivalent to the annual budget of the MoHCC for 2019.[14] The new PPP for Parirenyatwa hospitals aims to capture this market of patients who travel overseas for treatment.

Dual practice PPEs, according to Whyle and Olivier (2016), are contractual, long-term, highly collaborative and involve risk sharing and shared decision-making. The PGH PPP, however, came as a directive from the MoHCC, without consultations with health professionals working at the hospital, the public and lawmakers.

In June 2019, the Zimbabwe College of Public Health Physicians (ZCPHP) submitted a policy paper to the MoHCC reviewing the directives that guide

PPPs at public hospitals. The paper noted possible blindspots such as hospital care being prioritised over primary healthcare, and risks such as profiteering by private companies at the expense of the poor, conflicts of interest and changes in the political climate. To this end, the ZCPHP recommended PPPs in the area of primary healthcare, technical teams to examine contracts before the MoHCC's commitment, transparency in PPP formulation processes, clear implementation and monitoring strategies, agreements timed with political cycles (not more than five years), separation of power and function in the formulation of PPPs and semi-autonomy for sub-national bodies to explore PPPs with support from the head office and the college.[15]

According to informants, there were eight bidders for PGH's super-specialist clinical services PPP – five international and three local investors. Of the three investors who were shortlisted – one international and two local – only two managed to conduct feasibility studies. The management is yet to complete adjudicating on the proposals developed by them. The partnership is envisaged as a build-operate-transfer (BOT) model. After refurbishing the D-Floor, the investor would operate it as a private super-specialist unit till the time they recover their initial capital and make enough profit. Thereafter, the D-Floor would be handed back to the hospital.

According to the WB, such an arrangement could leave the state and taxpayers with huge legacy debt. Moreover, the private investor could take over the rest of the hospital to fulfil contractual obligations in the event of failure of the government and patients to pay for super-specialist services.[16] This is especially concerning given that Zimbabwe has demonstrated, over the past three decades, that it has little or no capacity to fund health service provisions adequately.[17]

Another key issue for the hospital management is to ensure that poor and vulnerable people, who need care but are unable to pay for it, can also access services. On this, the management's solution is to offer private investors tax rebates and holidays based on the number of non-paying patients they have cared for, and provide them with duty-free certificates for the equipment and drugs they bring into the country.

PPP case 3: Renal dialysis PPP at PGH

PGH's third PPP is with a private company that provides renal dialysis services. It started in 2009 when the hospital's renal dialysis equipment broke down and there was no funding for a replacement. The private company, the sole agent in Zimbabwe for an international manufacturer of renal dialysis equipment, offered to supply and service new renal dialysis equipment for 'free'. In return, the hospital would have to buy a certain quantity of consumables every year exclusively from the company and perform a certain number of dialysis sessions. Like the laundry partnership, this PPE would also come under a contracting out arrangement. The risks include the supplier's monopoly over the provision of renal dialysis bundles and the condition of a minimum number of consumables that must be bought by the hospital. In contrast to Whyle and Olivier's (2016) description of contracting out arrangements as short-term, the renal dialysis contract has been renewed three times since 2009, without ever going to a new investor.

Key informants in the management said the hospital had entered into the agreement without stakeholder consultations and considerations of how it would impact women's health and rights. Patients were paying out of pocket for renal dialysis at the Parirenyatwa hospitals until 2018, when the MoHCC started providing ringfenced funding. Currently, there is no policy which mainstreams gender equality with regard to financial access to renal dialysis services at the hospital. A total of 181 Chronic Renal Disease (CRD) patients undergo dialysis at the Parirenyatwa hospitals, and receive three sessions a week each. A total of 7,476 dialysis sessions were provided in 2019.[18] Attesting to the lack of attention to gender equality, the dialysis records do not disaggregate numbers according to gender.

PPP case 4: Mbuya Nehanda maternity hospital PPP at PGH

The maternity hospital at PGH has public and private wings. The 'hotel facilities' are available only to patients in the private wing, but everyone receives care in the same operation theatres and is operated on by the same doctors. The PPP, which combines public and private areas of the hospital and can thus be classified under dual practice regulation, exacerbates inequalities between women, in that, poorer women in the public wing often have to bring their own medical and surgical sundries such as gloves and pads while women in the private wing are provided with these items because they can afford to pay for them. Informants highlighted a case where a woman died in labour in the public wing because the few nurses and doctors available were busy with emergencies in the private ward. According to PGH's Health Information Department, only 10.4 per cent of its 8,008 deliveries in 2019 involved private patients,[19] demonstrating that few women can afford the services of the private maternity wing.

PPP case 5: Pharmacy PPP at PGH

The fifth PPP at the Parirenyatwa hospital, formalised in 2014, is with a private pharmacy that operates in a building outside the main hospital building, but within the hospital grounds. Unable to adequately stock the public pharmacy, which needs provisions worth 20 million USD per year, the management decided that patients who could not get the required drugs from the hospital would benefit from a private pharmacy within hospital grounds. Here, they could buy the same drugs without incurring the cost of travelling to other pharmacies in town. The private pharmacy pays rent equivalent to 1,000 USD a month to the hospital, which itself does not buy any drugs or consumables from the pharmacy. As such, this contract does not come under any of the classifications described by Whyle and Olivier (2016).

There is no evidence that a private pharmacy within hospital grounds has improved the availability of drugs. If anything, the lack of stakeholder consultations and the failure to pay attention to gender equality and human rights mean patients have no choice but to buy even more expensive drugs at this pharmacy, especially if they are from rural areas and unfamiliar with the capital Harare, or have come to the hospital at night (Mugwagwa et al., 2017; Prata et al., 2005).

Gender and human rights impact of the Parirenyatwa PPPs

Gender inequalities in healthcare access can be attributed to (1) the underfunding of the sector, (2) the overreliance on funding from global health initiatives, (3) government directives to health institutions to form PPPs to alleviate funding gaps and (4) the failure to enforce regulatory and legal frameworks that mainstream gender equality in donor-funded projects and PPPs.

The Constitution of Zimbabwe, amended and approved in 2013, recognises the rights of men and women to equal opportunities in the political, economic, cultural and social spheres, and guarantees the right to equal pay. It declares void (under Section 4.28) all customs, traditions and cultural practices that infringe on women's rights. It also calls for the state to ensure gender balance and fair representation of disadvantaged groups and promote the participation of women in all spheres of society. However, this is not reflected in the health sector where all health ministers have been men and only two out of eight permanent secretaries of health are women. Of the seven members of PHBG, only two are women. The Public Health Act does not mention gender equality in the composition of hospital board appointments or secondment to various ministry positions. It also leaves considerations of private investments in the public sector and joint venture partnerships to the discretion of the accounting officer (Permanent Secretary for Health), without making any references to gender equality. The absence of women in positions of power means they do not have a voice in the formulation of PPP policies in the health sector in general, and at the Parirenyatwa hospitals in particular.

The second National Gender Policy of 2013–17 sought to achieve a 'gender-just society' and 'eradicate gender discrimination and inequalities in all spheres of life and development'. However, it did not specifically mention gender equality in health policies and PPPs. Key informants agreed that the PPP agreements at PGH did not take into account gender equality parameters; it was simply assumed that women would benefit from them. This approach did not consider the fact that women were particularly disadvantaged in terms of education, employment opportunities and income and, therefore, had little access to private services in the hospital. As mentioned earlier, most specialists with admission rights on the D-Floor are male and the (mostly) female nurses manning the D-Floor wards do not benefit from the PPP. Informants in the management and staff indicated incidents where they have detained women patients after childbirth because of failure to pay their bills. This contravenes the Zimbabwe Reproductive, Maternal, Newborn, Child, Adolescent Health and Nutrition Quality Improvement Guidelines of 2018.

The NHS 2016–20 emphasises, under Goal 5, its aim to '[a]chieve gender equality and empower all women and girls', and brings to the fore the need to address specific challenges that affect women and girls who tend to be disproportionately affected by poverty, diseases, violence and other social ills. The subject of PPPs is alluded to in Goal 3 which calls for an improvement in 'the enabling environment for service delivery' through multisectoral partnerships. The NHS 2016–20 also notes that 'the private for-profit sector presents opportunities for widening access to quality services beyond the middle-class, but a key challenge is the absence of a defined public-private partnership framework within which to cooperate'. The strategic thrust is thus on developing a PPP policy. Besides these declarations in the NHS, none of the PGH PPPs were guided by a framework that mainstreamed gender equality and human rights.

Zimbabwe is a signatory to several regional and international protocols, treaties, conventions and other instruments aimed at protecting and promoting gender equality, including the Convention on the Elimination of all Forms of Discrimination against Women (CEDAW), the Southern Africa Development Community Gender and Development Protocol (including its Addendum on Prevention and Eradication of Violence Against Women and Children), the Beijing Platform for Action, the Protocol to the African Charter on Human and People's Rights on the Rights of Women, 2005 (also known as the Maputo Protocol) and the Universal Declaration of Human Rights. But there is no evidence that the principles of these protocols were considered in the formulation of the health sector PPPs. Key informants from the management and staff at Parirenyatwa were unaware that Zimbabwe was a signatory to these treaties.

Transparency and accountability

In 2000, a study by Kumaranayake et al., found several weaknesses in Zimbabwe's healthcare regulatory system. The focus is on individual inputs, the study noted, rather than health system organisations. The system aims to control entry and quality rather than explicitly checking quantity, price or distribution. It also fails to address market-level problems such as anti-competitive practices and the lack of patient rights, and does not regulate private insurers. The Medical Services Act, for instance, allows the health minister to set user fees payable at public hospitals. However, it does not address issues of equity with regard to the payment of user fees, thus exposing vulnerable sections of the population to financial barriers to healthcare.

Informants in the management knew about the Zimbabwe Joint Ventures Partnerships Act of 2016 and the Zimbabwe Investment and Development Agency Bill of 2019 which were introduced to regulate PPPs. They acknowledged that they were supposed to review all PPPs and align them to this new legal framework. However, this was proving to be difficult because the existing contracts were formulated without a guiding framework. In any case, the new framework is silent on gender participation and gender mainstreaming in joint ventures and partnerships.

The PGH PPPs were innovative responses to government underfunding. However, the process was spearheaded by the management, did not allow for the participation of women, healthcare professionals or citizens, and did not consider human rights. This is similar to findings by the Zimbabwe Coalition on Debt and Development (ZIMCODD) with regard to another central hospital in Zimbabwe.[20] Sixty-seven per cent of people interviewed by ZIMCODD were unaware that there was a PPP at the hospital and did not know how it worked. This lack of transparency is at the root of the community's mistrust and suspicion of these projects. An audit of PPPs ordered by the Permanent Secretary for Health in 2016, following the ZIMCODD report, revealed that hospital revenues witnessed a major decline after the PPPs were operationalised, and that the fees paid for services accrued only to private partners and did not benefit the hospital or community (Newsday, 2019).

Key informants at Parirenyatwa also bemoaned the lack of transparency and accountability in the formulation of PPPs, and indicated that the issue came as a directive from the ministry and even led to the resignation of the clinical director who did not agree with the approach. Clinicians working at the hospital were asked to make their submissions on PPPs without any consultations or inputs on whether the policy decision was suitable for the hospital. Informants among health professionals working at the Parirenyatwa hospitals only knew that a tender was published for PPPs in 2018. They did not know how much money was being paid to the laundry service provider, the cost of renal dialysis bundles that the hospital was buying, what the private pharmacy was paying as rent to the hospital or what the income was being used for. We managed to learn what was going on with the newly proposed PPP after interviewing key informants in the management.

Acts of resistance

PPPs for pharmacy services were implemented at two other central hospitals that cater to the lower income quintiles of the population in the high-density suburbs of Harare, and at a central hospital in the second largest city Bulawayo in the southern part of the country. These PPPs, as well as the ones at the Parirenyatwa hospitals, faced fierce resistance from both health workers and the general public due to the lack of transparency and accountability in their formulation and implementation.[21] Demonstrations were held until three private pharmacies at other central hospitals were closed, leaving only the ones at the Parirenyatwa hospitals still in operation.

Key informants in the management acknowledged that there was serious resistance to the PPPs on the D-Floor, to the renal dialysis PPP, initially, and to the private pharmacy PPP. Key informants among staff working at the Parirenyatwa hospitals confirmed that doctors and nurses who did not benefit from the D-Floor partnership were not happy with the arrangement. In 2019, the Senior Hospital Doctors Association filed, before the clerk of parliament, a petition against the directive asking central hospitals to engage in PPPs, arguing that these partnerships prevent the poor from accessing healthcare and have become opportunities for corruption (New Zimbabwe, 2019). Seventy-two per cent of respondents in the ZIMCODD study indicated that the central hospital with PPPs discriminated against the poor who could not afford to pay the exorbitant charges and had to forego treatments, often resulting in death.

The fact that resistance to PPPs at central hospitals resulted in an audit whose results were published indicates that there is still institutional integrity that serves public interest. However, the lack of action taken following these damning findings also demonstrates the inherent weaknesses in existing regulatory frameworks. The lack of enforcement of regulatory frameworks is largely attributable to deep-rooted corruption that has dogged Zimbabwe since independence (Mwatwara and Mujere, 2015).

It is worth noting that the chief proponent of PPPs in the health sector in recent times was the then Minister of Health and Child Care (2018–20) who was also the former CEO of the Chitungwiza Central Hospital, the site of the damning 2016 audit report. The minister was fired from government on 7 July 2020 after being implicated in a corruption scandal involving the procurement of testing materials for Covid-19 without a competitive tender process (The Guardian, 2020). In July 2020, the Acting Minister of Health and Child Care wrote a directive suspending all PPPs in public hospitals, pointing to a realisation that the PPPs were not formulated in a transparent manner (Press Reader, 2020).

Conclusion and recommendations

Massive public funding was injected into Zimbabwe's health sector during the first decade after independence in 1980, with marked improvements in health coverage and outcome indicators. The main goal for the government during this period was to provide comprehensive, integrated, continuous and quality health services in an equitable manner through decentralisation of services, thus meeting the needs of vulnerable groups. However, the implementation of the SAPs resulted in liberalisation and privatisation of the health sector with no consideration for gender equality and human rights, creating barriers to healthcare access and worsening health outcome indicators, particularly for women. In the aftermath, health PPPs were formulated without adequate consultations, transparency and accountability, prompting resistance from healthcare professionals, legislators and citizens. Resistance to PPPs and acts of corruption associated with them resulted in the dismissal of the previous Minister of Health and Child Care and the cancellation of all PPPs in public hospitals by the Acting Minister.

Based on this analysis, and with an eye on invigorating the public health system in Zimbabwe, this paper recommends the following:

1. Develop a compulsory National Health Insurance Scheme funded through the progressive taxation of citizens and corporations that can also be supported by health development partners;
2. Prioritise the coverage of essential health services for vulnerable populations, especially women, children and the needy, through this scheme; and

3. Adapt health sector PPPs to the Joint Ventures Partnerships Act and the Zimbabwe Investment and Development Agency Act by involving all actors and taking into account gender equality and human rights. Enforce legal frameworks in a transparent manner, moving from public-private partnerships (PPPs) to what could be termed public-private-professionals-people partnerships (PPPPPs).

Notes

1   MoHCC District Health Information System version 2.30.
2   Zimbabwe National Health Accounts Survey Report 2017/20.
3   Zimbabwe PICES report 2018 (launched but unpublished).
4   Zimbabwe National Health Accounts 2017/18 (validated and launched but unpublished).
5   It was adopted in the 2013 Constitution.
6   Zimbabwe National Statistics Agency and ICF International. Zimbabwe demographic and health survey 2015: Final report. Rockville, MD: Zimbabwe National Statistics Agency (ZIMSTAT) and ICF International; 2016. Available at: www.dhsprogram.com.
7   ZWD traded at 1 USD to 18.77 ZWD by January 2020 from 1 USD to 2.50 ZWD in February 2019.
8   Zimbabwe Ministry of Health and Child Care presentation at the Health Financing Symposium, 13–14 February 2020.
9   Clinton Health Access Initiative, Zimbabwe Ministry of Health and Child Care Round 4 Resource Mapping Report, 2019. Available at: www.clintonhealthaccess.org.
10 Clinton Health Access Initiative, Zimbabwe Ministry of Health and Child Care Round 4 Resource Mapping Report, 2019. Available at: www.clintonhealthaccess.org.
11 Mega deals are transactions that involve huge sums of foreign direct investment and are supposed to give the impression that they will solve Zimbabwe's economic woes.
12 This feature is peculiar to PGH because the hospital was built to serve the well-to-do during the colonial era; the practice continued after independence.
13 These are fees that allow patients to be allocated to the wing in the hospital with better quality infrastructure.
14 As per the Minister of Finance and Economic Development's 2019 budget statement.
15 Nyasha Masuki, 'PPP Model Overview'. Available at: https://drive.google.com/drive/folders/1oTp45kJNHdw2gJqAfFrRUBFHbVKy01vo?usp=sharing.
16 World Bank Group Public-Private-Partnerships Legal Resource Center 2016. Available at: www.worldbank.org.

17 Zimbabwe National Health Accounts Survey 2013, 2015. Available at: www.who.int.
18 Parirenyatwa Renal Dialysis Register 2019. Available at: apps.mohcc.gov.zw.
19 MoHCC DHIS 2 Parirenyatwa Hospital 2019. Available at: apps. mohcc.gov.zw.
20 Available at http://zimcodd.org/wp-content/uploads/2020/02/Research-findings-report-on-social-and-economic-impacts-of-public-private-partnership-agreements-to-the-realisation-of-the-right-to-health-The-case-of-Chitungwiza-Central-Hospital.pdf.
21 Daily News (2018), 'Gvt Suspends Hospitals' Private Partnerships', 29 January. Available at: https://dailynews.co.zw/articles-2018-01-29-gvt-suspends-hospitals-private-partnerships.

References

BBC News (2017), 'Zimbabwe Crisis: Army Takes over, Says Mugabe Is Safe', 15 November. Available at: https://www.bbc.com/news/world-africa-41992351.

Daily News (2018), 'Gvt Suspends Hospitals' Private Partnerships', 29 January. Available at: https://dailynews.co.zw/articles-2018-01-29-gvt-suspends-hospitals-private-partnerships (accessed 11 February 2020).

Kumaranayake, L., S. Lake, P. Mujinja, C. Hongoro, and R. Mpembeni (2000), 'How Do Countries Regulate the Health Sector? Evidence from Tanzania and Zimbabwe', *Health Policy and Planning*, 15 (4): 357–67. Available at: https://www.researchgate.net/publication/12205082_How_Do_Countries_Regulate_the_Health_Sector_Evidence_from_Tanzania_and_Zimbabwe (accessed 11 February 2020).

Lennock, J. (1994), *Paying for Health: Poverty and Structural Adjustment in Zimbabwe*, UK and Ireland: Oxfam.

Mail & Guardian (2017), 'How to Fund a Failing Health System', by A. Kotze, 6 April. Available at: https://mg.co.za/article/2017-04-06-00-how-to-fund-a-failing-health-system (accessed 11 February 2020).

Malmborg, R., G. Mann, R. Thomson, and S. B. Squire (2006), 'Can Public-Private Collaboration Promote Tuberculosis Case Detection among the Poor and Vulnerable?', *Bulletin of the World Health Organization*, 84 (9): 752–8. Available at: https://www.scielosp.org/pdf/bwho/2006.v84n9/752-758 (accessed 11 February 2020).

Masuka, N. (2019), 'PPP Model Overview'. Available at: https://drive.google.com/drive/folders/1oTp45kJNHdw2gJqAfFrRUBFHbVKy01vo?usp=sharing.

Mudyarabikwa, O., and D. Madhina (2000), 'An Assessment of Incentive Setting for Participation of Private For-Profit Health Care Providers in Zimbabwe', Small Applied Research 15. Partnership for Health Reform Project, Abt Associates Inc.: Bethesda MD. Available at: www.shopsplusproject.org/resource-center/assessment-incentive-participation-private-profit-health-care-providers (accessed 11 February 2020).

Mugwagwa, J. T., J. K. Chinyadza, and G. Banda (2017), 'Private Sector Participation in Health Care in Zimbabwe: What's the Value-Added?', *Journal of Healthcare Communications*, 2 (2). Available at: https://healthcare-communications.imedpub.com/private-sector-participation-in-health-carein-zimbabwe-whats-the-valueadded.pdf (accessed 11 February 2020).

Munyuki, E., and S. Jasi (2009), 'Capital Flows in the Health Care Sector in Zimbabwe: Trends and Implications for the Health System', EQUINET Discussion Paper Series 79. Rhodes University, Training and Research Support Centre, SEATINI, York University, EQUINET: Harare.

Mwatwara, W., and J. Mujere (2015), 'Corruption and the Comrades: Mugabe and the "Fight" against Corruption in Zimbabwe, 1980–2013', in: Sabelo J. Ndlovu-Gatsheni (ed.), *Mugabeism? History, Politics, and Power in Zimbabwe*, 181–99, Basingstoke-New York: Palgrave Macmillan. Available at: https://link.springer.com/chapter/10.1057%2F9781137543462_11 (accessed 11 February 2020).

New Zimbabwe (2019), 'Zim Doctors Blast Govt Hospital Privitisation Bid', by P. Mandivengerei, 8 December. Available at: https://www.newzimbabwe.com/zim-doctors-blast-govt-hospital-privatisation-bid (accessed 11 February 2020).

Newsday (2019), 'Health Minister Sees Red over Audit Report', by P. Mbanje, 7 December. Available at: https://www.newsday.co.zw/2019/12/health-minister-sees-red-over-audit-report (accessed 11 February 2020).

Nyazema, N. Z. (2010), 'The Zimbabwe Crisis and the Provision of Social Services: Health and Education', *Journal of Developing Societies*, 26 (2): 233–61. Available at: https://journals.sagepub.com/doi/abs/10.1177/0169796X1002600204 (accessed 11 February 2020).

Patouillard, E., C. A. Goodman, K. G. Hanson, and A. J. Mills (2007), 'Can Working with the Private for-Profit Sector Improve Utilization of Quality Health Services by the Poor? A Systematic Review of the Literature', *International Journal of Equity in Health*, 6 (17). Available at: https://equityhealthj.biomedcentral.com/track/pdf/10.1186/1475-9276-6-17 (accessed 11 February 2020).

Percival, V., E. Richards, T. MacLean, and S. Theobald (2014), 'Health Systems and Gender in Post-Conflict Contexts: Building Back Better?', *Conflict and Health*, 8 (19). Available at: https://conflictandhealth.biomedcentral.com/track/pdf/10.1186/1752-1505-8-19 (accessed 11 February 2020).

Prata, N., D. Montagu, and E. Jeffreys (2005), 'Private Sector, Human Resources and Health Franchising in Africa', *Bulletin of the World Health Organization*, 83 (4): 274–9. Available at: https://www.researchgate.net/publication/7870343_Private_sector_human_resources_and_health_franchising_in_Africa (accessed 11 February 2020).

Press Reader (2020), 'Govt Suspends Private Pharmacies, Labs, Canteens at Hospitals', by Nqbani Ndlovu, 24 July. Available at https://www.pressreader.com/zimbabwe/newsday-zimbabwe/20200724/281694027100061 (accessed 3 September 2022).

Ray, S., and N. Masuki (2017), 'Facilitators and Barriers to Effective Primary Health Care in Zimbabwe', *African Journal of Primary Health Care & Family Medicine*, 9 (1). Available at: www.scielo.org.za/pdf/phcfm/v9n1/67.pdf (accessed 11 February 2020).

The Guardian (2020), 'Zimbabwe Health Minister Facing Coronavirus Corruption Charge Sacked', by Nyasha Chingono, 9 July. Available at: https://www.theguardian.com/global-development/2020/jul/09/zimbabwe-health-minister-facing-coronavirus-corruption-charge-sacked (accessed 3 September 2022).

Tren, R., and Dr R. Bate (2005), 'Despotism and Disease: A Report into the Health Situation of Zimbabwe and Its Probable Impact on the Region's Health', Africa Fighting Malaria and American Enterprise Institute: Washington, DC. Available at: https://reliefweb.int/report/zimbabwe/despotism-and-disease-report-health-situation-zimbabwe-and-its-probable-impact (accessed 11 February 2020).

UNICEF (2019), 'Zimbabwe Multiple Indicator Cluster Survey Report 2019'. Available at: www.unicef.org. Zimbabwe reports (accessed 11 February 2020).

Whyle, E. B., and J. Olivier (2016), 'Models of Public-Private Engagement for Health Services Delivery and Financing in Southern Africa: A Systematic Review', *Health Policy and Planning*, 31 (10): 1515–29. Available at: https://academic.oup.com/heapol/article/31/10/1515/2567069 (accessed 11 February 2020).

World Bank (2016), 'Zimbabwe: Country Profile'. Available at: http://databank.worldbank.org/data/Views/Reports/ReportWidgetCustom.aspx?Report_Name=CountryProfile&Id=b450fd57&tbar=y&dd=y&inf=n&zm=n&country=ZWE (accessed 24 September 2017).

Appendix

Annex 1: The establishment and constitution of the PHBG

The Parirenyatwa Hospital Act says 'there is hereby established a board, to be known as the Parirenyatwa Hospitals Board of Governors, which shall be a body corporate and shall in its corporate name be capable of suing and being sued and, subject to this Act, of performing all such acts as bodies corporate may by law perform'.

The PHBG reports to the Health Services Board, the employer of all public health workers in Zimbabwe, and the chairman of the Board also reports to the Minister of Health and Child Care. The composition of the Board is as follows:

(1) Subject to section 6 of the Act, the Board shall consist of fourteen members, of whom –

    (a) one shall be a person who is not practising medicine for gain appointed as chairman by the Minister; and

    (b) one shall be the Medical Superintendent ex officio;

    (c) and five shall be appointed by the Minister, of whom –

        (i) four shall be persons who are not medical practitioners; and

        (ii) one shall be an officer of the ministry responsible for health; and

    (d) two shall be appointed by the Minister, of whom –

        (i) one shall be selected from a panel of three persons who are staff members of the Faculty of Medicine whose names have been submitted by the Council of the University of Zimbabwe; and

        (ii) one shall be selected from a panel of three persons who are not staff members of the Faculty of Medicine whose names have been submitted by the Council of the University of Zimbabwe; and

    (e) two shall be members of the clinical teaching staff appointed by the Minister from a panel of four persons, all of whom shall be full-time staff members of the Faculty of Medicine at the University of Zimbabwe, elected by the clinical teaching staff in the manner fixed in terms of subsection (3); and

    (f) one shall be a medical practitioner appointed by the Minister from a panel of three persons whose names have been submitted by the governing body of the Zimbabwe Medical Association; and

    (g) one shall be an honorary consultant appointed by the Minister from a panel of two persons whose names have been submitted by the honorary consultants; and

    (h) one shall be a nurse appointed by the Minister from a panel of three persons whose names have been submitted by the governing body of the Zimbabwe Nurses Association.

(2) The Deputy Medical Superintendent shall ex officio be an alternate member to the Medical Superintendent and shall act as a member when the Medical Superintendent is unable for any reason to attend a meeting of the Board.

(3) The panel of persons referred to in paragraph 2 of subsection (1) shall be elected –

(a) in the case of the first election held in terms of this Act, in accordance with such procedure as the Minister may fix;

(b) in the case of any subsequent election, in accordance with such procedure as the Board may from time to time fix.

10

Unhealthy partnerships: PPPs in Fiji's Lautoka and Ba hospitals

Lice Cokanasiga

Introduction

In recent decades, major infrastructure projects such as ports, roads and public services, including healthcare, have been financed through public-private partnerships (PPPs). Under PPP contracts, private companies build and operate public services and infrastructure while much of the financial risk is borne by the concerned public body. Since the 1990s, Bretton Woods institutions (BWIs), such as the World Bank (WB) and the International Monetary Fund (IMF), have pushed states to implement fiscal reforms that support the use of PPPs to channel investment finance into development projects, thereby locking in state debt. According to these institutions, PPPs help develop and upgrade infrastructure and improve the effectiveness of public services while enhancing the capacity of human resources as and when the business environment is right.

No wonder then that PPPs have emerged at the top of the development financing options exercised by governments and multilateral development banks (MDBs) in the global effort to achieve the United Nations' Sustainable Development Goals (SDGs). Especially in the last two decades, the utilisation of private financing has skyrocketed as governments in the least developed, developing or developed countries turn to such instruments to execute their development projects.

In 2018, the government of Fiji proposed that the Lautoka Hospital and the newly built Ba Sub-regional Hospital be transformed from public to PPP-provided services under a concession agreement. The upgraded hospitals would provide health services for 337,041 people in the country's western division (Fiji Government Media Centre, 2018) that is home to a quarter of Fiji's population. While the Ba Hospital would be redeveloped, the Lautoka Hospital would be extended with an additional wing of 305 beds.

This chapter examines the implications of undertaking PPPs in Fiji's health sector by exploring the Ba and Lautoka Hospital project as a case study. It attempts to bring together the relevant evidence to study the gender and human rights consequences of PPPs as well as the crucial elements for strengthening a feminist approach to PPPs. The chapter is divided into three main sections. While the first section briefly outlines the methodology of this research, the second section explores Fiji's socio-economic landscape and the ways in which PPPs fit into the country's economic strategy, especially with regard to its health sector. Section 3 examines Fiji's first health sector PPP, the Ba and Lautoka hospitals project, and identifies the main actors involved. The final section explores the gender and human rights implications as well as transparency and accountability concerns of this PPP, and highlights the resistance mounted by the Fiji Nursing Association (FNA) with support from the global trade union federation Public Services International (PSI).

Methodology

This research was carried out following feedback on an initial outline presented at an inter-regional meeting of PPP case study writers, leaders and resource persons from Development Alternatives With Women for a New Era (DAWN) in Dakar, Senegal. The chapter draws on a desk review of relevant literature on financing development via PPPs as well as health narratives in Fiji that question the relevance of such financing and examine gender-responsive budgeting. Furthermore, interviews were conducted with the relevant stakeholders of the project, including the FNA, and PSI which supported the FNA in its campaign against the PPP mode of operating the Lautoka and Ba hospitals. The main limitation of the study is that the author did not have access to the relevant PPP contracts which are not publicly accessible. Going forward, there is scope for gathering further information and conducting in-depth analysis specifically on how gender inequalities, pay gaps and discriminations play out in PPP contracts.

PPPs in Fiji's health sector

The economic landscape

Prior to the global Covid-19 pandemic, international travel was growing rapidly in Fiji, turning its tourism sector into a key driver of economic development. The revenue generated from tourism stood at 1.2 billion

US dollars (USD) in 2010 and rose to a further 1.8 billion USD in 2016. As a source of foreign exchange, tourism earnings outshone the next seven major contributors combined, including remittances, mineral water, sugar, gold, fish, garments and timber receipts ((Wainiqolo and Shivanjali, 2018)). The economic upturn in the tourism sector also impacted sectors such as agriculture, transport, wholesale and retail trading, accommodation and food services, the arts, entertainment and recreation, and taxes.

A brief overview of the health sector

Health is recognised as a fundamental human right in Fiji's Constitution. However, large sections of the country's total population of 884,887[1] – men constitute 50.7 per cent of the population while women make up 49.3 per cent – continue to suffer from non-communicable diseases (NCDs) such as diabetes and hypertension because of lifestyle changes, poor diet, smoking, changing patterns of physical activity and continuing malnutrition problems, particularly among school children and women. The double burden of NCDs and infectious diseases impacts the health of individuals and the population as a whole, and has the potential to affect broader socio-economic development.

As of 2019, there were 804 doctors attending to the population while 196 medical worker positions lay vacant (Boyle, 2019). The most recent doctor-to-patient ratio is 1:800 (Talei, 2019).[2] At the time of writing this chapter (in June 2020), the pandemic had placed enormous stress on the already heavily burdened public health system which was stretched to emergency overdrive due to the large numbers of patients seeking medical attention for the deadly virus. In an effort to stop its spread, Fiji's Ministry of Health (MoH) set up fever clinics, directing public hospitals to serve as isolation facilities. Patients seeking medical attention for other conditions were advised to go to community healthcare facilities (Department of Information, 2020).

Health sector financing

Health services in Fiji are provided mainly through the MoH. Clinical, preventative and rehabilitative healthcare services fall under the responsibility of the Ministry of Health and Medical Services (MoHMS). Clinical care services are available at hospitals and some health centres while preventative healthcare services are provided through preventative care programmes, health centres and nursing stations. Healthcare services are implemented through a decentralised health system that administers integrated care at primary, secondary and tertiary levels. However, the administration and management of human resources, finance, drugs and medical supplies are centralised. The government is the largest source of funding for health service provisions.

The health sector is mainly supported by taxation revenue[3] accumulated through indirect taxes such as value added tax (62.8 per cent) and customs tax (33 per cent) as well as direct taxes which include income tax (26.4 per cent).[4] The primary source of income tax is the formal employment sector. The funding thus available has proven to be insufficient to cover the current per capita health expenditure (which includes spending by both public and private sources) of 188.41 USD.[5] This figure is among the lowest among Pacific Island countries. The underfunded healthcare system is barely able to cope with an increasingly disease-burdened population.

A study by Negin et al. (2013) reveals that, in 2010, the Fiji government financed 61 per cent of the country's total health expenditure while 9 per cent came from external funding. The Australian government alone accounted for 60 per cent of the total external funds, with the Global Fund and World Health Organization (WHO) being the next largest sources. It is worth noting that Fiji is much less dependent on external funding compared to the other Pacific Island countries (2013).[6]

In 2018, the Fijian government increased the allocation to the health ministry by over 77 million Fijian dollars (FJD) (USD 36.9 million), taking the overall health sector budget to 387.7 million FJD (Lacanivalu, 2018). However, underfunding remains a perennial challenge. Besides, the migration of skilled healthcare workers exacerbates an already chronic shortage of human resources in the sector. A 2008 study by Joel Negin quantifying the contribution of Australia and New Zealand to the Pacific Islands' healthcare worker brain drain pegged the annual (training) cost to the Fiji government of twenty-three doctors who resigned in 1999 at 7 million USD. The hiring of expatriate doctors to replace them cost an additional 1.4 million USD per year.[7] Typically, skilled healthcare workers migrate to care facilities overseas in search of better work conditions, training opportunities and salaries, as well as due to Fiji's history of *coups d'état*.

Alongside the shortage of doctors, Fiji's healthcare system is also understaffed when it comes to nurses. According to Filomena Talawadua (2020),[8] the shortage has reached critical levels, with the current ratio of nurses-to-patients varying between 1:15,000, 1:12,000 and 1:7,000. Such a wide gap makes effective community and public healthcare impossible (2020). Against the backdrop of an underfunded health sector with a depleted workforce, PPPs are presented as a pragmatic and income-generating solution.

Promotion of PPPs

Private sector financing and involvement in the provision of essential public services is not new. PPPs, in particular, have been promoted as the solution to plug the financing shortfall that hinders governments from realising the SDGs. However, there is also a keen political interest in deploying PPPs to leverage private finance in all sectors of the economy, including health. In Pacific Island countries, MDBs enter into partnerships with developed countries, such as Australia, that are traditional donors in the region, providing budgetary support on health and education.[9]

The first PPP proposal in Fiji's health sector came in 2007 from India's Apollo Group. The group had planned to establish a new multi-million dollar (USD) Apollo Pacific Hospital in Lautoka with state-of-the-art features that would reduce outgoing overseas medical tourism. It would also offer other special medical, surgical and treatment services at affordable costs and reduced insurance premiums.[10] The plan (see Table 10.1) was approved by Fiji's interim cabinet in the same year (Waradi, 2007). However, there have been no developments since then.

More than a decade later, as Fiji was preparing for elections in 2018, quiet negotiations ensued between the government and the International Finance Corporation (IFC)[11] to transform two public hospitals in the western region of Fiji into a PPP. Since then, some information has emerged on the key players

Table 10.1 Apollo Group's Proposed 44 million USD Hospital PPP in Fiji, 2007.

First phase of project	70 million FJD (44.5 million USD) a) State-of-the-art medical hospital with core services of primary, secondary and tertiary healthcare; b) Initial capacity of 176 beds would rise to 200–250 beds with 50 per cent occupancy rate in the first year which will continue to rise over the next 8 years. <u>Training Institute</u> For local and overseas students and doctors in specialised skills, nursing and allied healthcare. <u>Employment</u> Providing necessary exposure that will enhance careers of doctors, nurses and paramedics.

Source: Pacific Island Report (2007), 'India's Apollo Group Plans $44 Million Hospital in Fiji', 27 September. Available at: http://www.pireport.org/articles/2007/09/27/india%C3%A2%C2%80%C2%99s-apollo-group-plans-44-million-hospital-fiji (accessed 26 May 2020).

central to this decision-making and the process of selection of partners for this PPP venture. The broader question of whether the PPP model is a suitable investment option for Fiji's health sector remains unaddressed.

Fiji's first health sector PPP

Role of donors

PPPs are expensive exercises. In order for a contract to work, actors must have prior experience of undertaking similar projects. With an eye on achieving SDG 3 which promotes good health and well-being, the Fijian government sought assistance from the IFC to invite expressions of interest from internationally certified hospital operators to redevelop the Lautoka and Ba hospitals. In general, the IFC's role is to promote economic development by investing in for-profit and commercial projects. To this end, it is no stranger to investing in private healthcare companies. As with other MDBs, the IFC is guided by, and partners with, the governments of Australia and New Zealand for the implementation of projects in the Pacific Islands.

For the Ba and Lautoka hospitals PPP, the IFC provided transaction advisory services to the Fiji government, which included technical, financial, environmental, legal and social due diligence to design a structure that balances the interests of both private investors and the government. However, it did not specify how the transaction structure would ensure that the private sector generates revenue from this operation, thus creating the possibility of imposition of fees for services or compromising quality for profit (IFC, 2019).

Australia, through the Australian Trade and Investment Commission (Austrade),[12] successfully negotiated for an Australian private medical company to implement the PPP for both hospitals. One of Austrade's major functions includes developing international markets for Australian companies and strengthening the country's tourism industry.[13]

After the IFC and the Austrade, the Pacific Private Sector Development Initiative (PSDI) is the third major actor in this PPP. The PSDI is a regional technical assistance programme launched in partnership with the governments of Australia and New Zealand, and the Asian Development Bank (ADB). Its goal is to reduce the cost of doing business in the Pacific and enable the private sector to formalise and grow, thus purportedly creating jobs, increasing tax revenue and lifting people out of poverty. One of the major modes of implementation of this strategy is to reform state-owned enterprises (SOEs) and pursue PPPs.[14] PSDI's role in the Lautoka and Ba hospitals PPP was to support the preparation and design of the contract.

Role of the private sector

Aspen medical: From conflict country operation to PPPs

In 2018, the Fiji government announced that it would partner with the Australian company Aspen Medical for redeveloping and upgrading the Lautoka and Ba hospitals. Under the twenty-three-year contract, which would take the form of a PPP, Aspen Medical would develop, finance, upgrade, operationalise and maintain Fiji's second largest hospital in Lautoka as well as the new Ba Sub-regional Hospital (see Table 10.2).

Aspen Medical's first operation in the Pacific began in 2004 in the Solomon Islands, where it provided medical and dental care and environmental services to the Regional Assistance Mission to the Solomon Islands (RAMSI) personnel and other Australian government employees during a period of ethnic violence. The RAMSI was being led by Australia which labelled the South Pacific as an 'arc of instability'. In so doing, Australia was trying to bolster its image by emphasising its stance on the 'war on terror' and showing the world that it could be trusted to maintain order in a geographical area purportedly under its sphere of influence.[15]

Table 10.2 Aspen Medical's Obligations in the Lautoka and Ba Hospitals PPP.

Location	Obligations
Ba Sub-regional Hospital	Upgrading newly-built hospital with 70 beds;
	Absorbing all services from the existing Ba Mission Hospital;
	The new hospital is ready but currently not in use.
Lautoka Hospital	Undertaking initial assessments and infrastructure repairs, ensuring effective service delivery at the hospital until further renovations can be completed;
	Renovating the building to include 305 beds in compliance with Australian health facility standards;
	Installing new ICT system to feature patient management administration, enhancing communication facilities, financial management and building management;
	Providing a 100-bed student accommodation;
	Achieving international standards accreditation for the services provided for both hospitals.

Source: Aspen Medical (2019), 'Aspen Medical Signs Contract to Manage Two Hospitals over the Next Two Decades as Part of Fiji's Public-Private Partnership'. Available at: https://www.aspenmedical. com/news/news/aspen-medical-signs-contract-manage-two-hospitals-over-next-two-decades-part-fiji%E2%80%99s-public (accessed 26 May 2020).

The success of Aspen's bid in the Ba and Lautoka PPP can be attributed primarily to Austrade. According to its website, Austrade has 'the power to open doors, unlock opportunities and help Australia's businesses expand their exports'.[16] At an Australian Parliamentary Inquiry into the country's trade relationship with the Pacific Islands, Austrade's Acting General Manager stated:

> We've been helping their [Aspen's] export aspirations since day one when the company first started delivering services in the Solomon Islands in the early 2000s. In 2018, the government of Fiji announced Aspen Medical would be its key partner in delivering healthcare in reforming Fiji's healthcare system. Austrade has stood side by side with Aspen Medical throughout its two decades in the Pacific, in a number of Pacific countries now. Importantly, Aspen Medical has helped to accredit hospitals in the Pacific and to bring them up to international standards. The work is commercial but the effect is universal.[17]

Legal advice from Ashurst LLP

Ashurst LLP promotes itself as a 'leading multinational law firm and a trusted adviser to corporations, financial institutions, and governments worldwide'.[18] According to its website, its role includes providing advice on markets for hospitality, defence, health, energy, roads and ports, to name a few. It advises public sector clients, sponsors, contractors, equity investors and debt financiers on a range of PPP projects.

Ashurst LLP played a lead advisory role in getting the Fiji National Provident Fund (FNPF) to invest in the country's first health sector PPP. It is also increasing its presence in Fiji by advising the FNPF on the acquisition of 20 per cent of the total ordinary shares issued by Energy Fiji Limited.[19] In this way, Ashurst LLP has become an active player in the privatisation and financialisation of public services in Fiji.

Role of the Fijian state

Fiji National Provident Fund

Formed in 1966 under the Fiji National Provident Fund Act, the FNPF is the largest financial institution in Fiji, and the only superannuation fund in the country mandated by law to collect compulsory contributions from employees and employers towards retirement savings of workers.

In 2011, a reform of the FNPF was carried out by the Promontory Group Consultants and Actuaries of Singapore, hired by the Fijian government to advise on pension reform. This consultation led to the Fiji National Provident Fund Transition Decree 2011 (Decree No. 51) and the Fiji National Provident Fund Decree 2011 (Decree No. 52). A class action lawsuit was filed in the high court against these two decrees. The petitioner, a pensioner who had the support of several civil society groups, challenged the decrees as a breach of contract on the part of FNPF since they reduced pensions by 8.7 per cent which was not enough to sustain the livelihoods of pensioners at the time and in the future. The lawsuit was, however, dismissed because decrees cannot be challenged in a Fijian court of law (Singh, 2013).

These decrees, in turn, cleared the path for utilising FNPF funds to finance PPP projects. Under the advice of Ashurst LLP Australia, the FNPF invested in the Lautoka and Ba hospitals PPP with Aspen Medical. By using the only pension fund in the country to finance infrastructure projects, the government essentially treated it like a bank that it could withdraw from in order to sustain investments and acquisition of shares. FNPF members were not made aware of the uses to which their pension funds were being put, and the implications of this PPP investment for them.

Fiji government

In 2019, on the IFC's advice, the current government repealed the Fiji Islands Public Private Partnerships Act 2006 on grounds that it restricted private investments. Currently, all PPP investments are guided by the new PPP policy[20] prepared and supported by the PSDI.

The Lautoka and Ba hospitals PPP project was first proposed in parliament in March 2018, with Fiji's Attorney General announcing that the country was looking to provide a high-quality medical facility that could house high-tech equipment provided by India. In 2014, Indian Prime Minister Narendra Modi, during his visit to Fiji, had proposed turning the country into a medical hub for the region because of its strategic location. Fiji's Prime Minister Josaia Voreqe 'Frank' Bainimarama held further bilateral discussions on the project in 2018 (Radio New Zealand, 2018). Throughout this time, the government maintained that the project is not an instance of privatisation. It argued that the PPP would advance Fiji's medical tourism, improve doctor training and lower costs for Fijians who were travelling overseas for health services (see Table 10.3). The parliamentary opposition has consistently challenged this position (Pratibha, 2018).

Echoing the Fijian government's assertion that both Lautoka and Ba hospitals are to remain public hospitals, open to all Fijians, IFC's Pacific

Table 10.3 Fiji Government's Case for the Lautoka and Ba Hospitals PPP.

Case	Reasons
Medical tourism	Tourism is Fiji's major revenue earner. The government is positioning Fiji as a possible destination for patients from Australia and New Zealand who are insured and on the waiting list for elective surgery.
Training for doctors	Fiji's healthcare personnel lack exposure, specialised training and access to various procedures. The new health PPP can potentially change this for the better.
Expanding into new forms of tourism	Fiji was to host an international seminar but, because the western division did not offer a number of emergency services if the need arose, the seminar was moved to another country. With an internationally certified hospital, such seminars could be held in Fiji.
No additional cost to Fijians	There will be no additional costs to those accessing public health services. The government is also trying to ensure that Fijians who had traditionally opted to go overseas for their medical check-ups, get checked locally. This would mean that the money is spent in Fiji.

Source: Tabulated from an article in the *Fiji Sun*, 'Public Private Partnership not Privatisation', published on 13 March 2018. Available at: https://fijisun.com.fj/2018/03/13/public-private-partnership-not-privatisation-says-acting-pm (accessed 26 May 2020).

manager Thomas Jacobs stated that the hospitals will also benefit Fiji's neighbouring countries whose citizens currently have to travel to Australia or Singapore for medical treatment. He added that these new facilities would mean improved tertiary treatment, maternity care and treatment for NCDs such as heart problems or diabetes for the people living in Lautoka and Ba and, more broadly, the western division of Fiji (Jacobs, 2018).

However, according to Michael Whaites who is part of PSI in Australia, arrangements such as the one proposed in Fiji conflate privatisation with economic development. According to him, the best way to provide health is through government-provided and government-run health services (Whaites, 2018).

Key concerns

As a twenty-three-year contract, Fiji's first PPP will involve multi-decade requirements on operation and maintenance. More worryingly, staffing will be managed by Aspen Medical and the FNPF. Historically, this work has been performed by public sector employees.

One of the main critics of the transition from public health to PPPs is the Fiji Nursing Association (FNA) which has challenged the model's potential negative impact on working conditions. With Aspen Medical in charge of staffing at the two hospitals, public health workers find themselves in limbo. Even though the Attorney General has promised that no jobs will be lost during the transition, workers will still need to reapply for their jobs under the new arrangement. This means nurses do not know if they will retain their jobs once Aspen takes over and, if they do, what their remuneration and working conditions would be.

From the FNA's perspective, the Fijian government did not adequately clarify the meaning and impacts of PPPs to healthcare workers and the Fijian public. The quiet way in which the PPP was finalised meant it received little public attention. In 2018, the FNA was alerted by the PSI about the government's plans for the Lautoka and Ba hospitals. Thereafter, FNA representatives questioned the government on why it was recommending the privatisation of the two hospitals through a PPP.[21] Over time, the dispute between the FNA and the government gave way to more pressing issues such as a global pandemic and domestic politics. Nonetheless, the FNA still stands firm in its objective of protecting health workers and community healthcare in the country.

The reasons offered by the Fiji government for undertaking the PPP were simplistic and, therefore, cause for concern. PPP concession agreements are usually complex, negotiated and renegotiated at multiple levels, often resulting in changes in the terms and conditions, without scrutiny or the scope for redress. This often hinders public finance and the communities that host and/or are supposed to benefit from the specific projects. There are also administrative and management costs to be taken into account. For example, since the Ba Hospital is already constructed but not in operation, a negotiation or renegotiation on the building's suitability for medical operations could be protracted. Would this add to the costs already outlined in the contract? In the event of a change, who would pay for the additional material needed for the new facility? Will the expensive facilities at the new Ba Sub-regional Hospital ensure better medical care and services compared to the existing Ba Mission Hospital?

Hosting international forums is a revenue source for the Fiji government, and demonstrates the extent to which the government is focused on accommodating the international community rather than local people. The installation of the latest and specialised facilities in the PPP hospitals raises questions about whether the Fijian people can still afford these services. Most people who live along the west coast of Fiji are hotel, airline and airport workers and sugarcane farmers who are unlikely to be able to afford expensive healthcare. It is unclear whether the government will subsidise treatment costs in such cases.

Instead of seeking expensive private financing, the Fijian government could support the MoH by upgrading, renovating and building the Lautoka and Ba hospitals' state-of-the-art information and communication technology (ICT) systems. For preventative and curative healthcare, budgetary support is, in any case, available from external sources. In addition, the MoH is already in the business of training healthcare workers.

The provision to establish international hospitals in Fiji is also a point of worry. In his maiden speech in parliament, Fiji's Minister of Health Ifereimi Waqainabete had said that this partnership would come at no cost to the taxpayer and, instead, 'leverage local investment from the FNPF and foreign investment from the private sector to construct and equip facilities' (Waqainabete, 2018). But as the FNA secretary general Filomena Talawadua (2020) asserts, international hospitals need to be financed externally, and not through pension funds of citizens and workers of Fiji. The FNPF is the only pension fund in Fiji and taxpayer savings are currently financing the PPP.

FNA resistance: Is the PPP a healthy investment for Fiji?

This situation calls for a robust awareness campaign to explain to the public in general, and the health worker community in particular, what a PPP is and what it means for the public health sector. This must include addressing questions like: what will PPPs mean for community healthcare? Do they amount to privatisation of health services? Will health services remain affordable under a PPP regime? Is there a specific market that this regime is targeting?

The FNPF, in particular, should hold consultations with its membership on its investment aspirations, with the aim of clarifying the following: is it necessary to use membership funds to finance such a risky and expensive health sector exercise? Why is the FNPF using membership funds to invest in something that has never been tried before in Fiji, given that there are many examples of failures of this type of contract in other countries? Does this mean that active workers, both now and in the future, will have to contribute more to the retirement system if the project fails to yield the desired investment returns or turns out to be a failure? The Lautoka Hospital is the main referral hospital in the western division (2020). All emergency cases, from maternity to surgery, are transferred to it. Under the PPP model, will these and other health services be offered free of charge to the public by the hospital? At what point will patients have to begin to pay for Aspen Medical's services? Where is the justification or assessment that proves the community requested a transition from the current public hospitals to the new arrangement?

At the time of writing this paper, the feasibility study of the Lautoka and Ba hospital PPP was still unavailable. The lack of information on this project, right from the start, makes it difficult for relevant stakeholders in the healthcare system to participate effectively in the PPP process. An interview conducted with the former Fiji nursing director revealed that the feasibility study was not made available to them at the time (Lutua, 2020). The association has asked for the study to be made available.

Existing constraints, however, should not mean that the public should simply accept the imposition of this new arrangement. Till the feasibility study is made available, the Fijian public can do the following:

1. Examine PPP modalities in general as well as the contracts of failed PPPs in Australia and in other countries;
2. Bring the key actors of the health system, including doctors, nurses and administrators, in conversation with civil society and the public at large;
3. Examine the implications of a PPP contract of twenty/fifty years, including what it would involve, the different decades of development it would undergo and, more importantly, the accountability process it must undergo;
4. Provide policy space for current and future governments to change or terminate the contract should the delivery of health services fail or not match the quality and/or standards agreed upon.

Trade unions in Fiji have actively taken up this work. In the lead-up to the 2018 national elections, they circulated petitions and fact sheets among communities which would be affected by the PPP. The unions are driven by the hope that their communities would stand with them to say that healthcare is a human right and should not be up for sale.

Resilience of nurses and their safety nets

Public health nurses are trained to adapt to their environment, which is perennially short of resources and staff. They are tasked with ensuring the comfort of their patients, some of whom can, under medication, behave in a way that is offensive to nurses (Talawadua, 2020). To ensure that patients get the best care, nurses are trained to act within guidelines as well as think outside the box. To deal with the complexities of the work environment, public health nurses use the social safety nets available to them to solve the challenges that they face every day. For example, nurses can access counselling services in cases of high stress. This enables them to provide quality care to patients. Talawadua worries that the same safety nets will not be available in a privatised context (Talawadua, 2020). Besides, private healthcare nurses face the dilemma of treating a patient as well as making sure that the hospital's profit target is met. This can force healthcare workers to ignore their professional training values and practices.

PSI support to FNA

At the 2018 WB annual meeting in Bali, the FNA's National Council Executive member Isimeli Tatukivei questioned the effectiveness of health PPPs and expressed concern at the Fiji government's proposal to privatise two hospitals (PSI, 2018). Contrary to what nurses were told by the government, Tatukivei insisted that the PPPs are a form of privatisation.

An interview with Kate Lappin (2020)[22] of the PSI revealed that even the IMF has criticised the way in which the IFC handles PPPs on small island developing states. In fact, the IMF rarely recommends PPPs for small states because of the difficulty in attracting private sector investments (IMF, 2018). One particular concern with PPPs is that they may be used to bypass spending controls, move public investment off budget and take debt off the government balance sheet even though the state still bears most of the risks involved and faces potentially heavy fiscal costs (IMF, 2004). In contrast, PPPs offer private investors a protected and guaranteed income, PSI argues.

Lack of transparency and consultations

Presently, the PPP contract for the Lautoka and Ba hospitals is not available to the public, and neither is there any public or legal opinion that can shed light on the nature of the contract. PPPs are complex arrangements and the role of transaction costs, risks and types of relationships are important issues to consider. Thus far, the media has only mentioned that the contract with Aspen Medical is expected to last twenty-three years, and the project will need an overall investment of 80 million FJD (37.5 million USD).

One of the most pressing concerns is the role of the key actors who support this PPP. Donor partners such as Australia and the IFC are aware of the unique economic vulnerabilities of small island states. Yet, there are no clarifications on who bears the ultimate risk and repays the debt if the PPP should fail. Australia's support to the PSDI facility fits into the country's overall goal of economic integration through free trade agreements in the Pacific Islands. As part of the 'aid for trade' strategic goal, Australia is looking for economic opportunities in the Pacific region and it does so by advancing Australian interests and investments in the region.

The IFC itself is a strong advocate of PPPs. When approached by a government to facilitate or assist in a project, the organisation targets public sector policy reform so as to ensure that their investments do not face any obstacles or structural bottlenecks. It was the IFC which advised the Fijian government to revise the Fiji Islands Public Private Partnerships Act 2006, leading to the repeal and replacement of the Act with the Public Private Partnership Policy 2019.

While doctors and nurses of the Lautoka and Ba hospitals were consulted about the partnership before inviting expressions of interest,[23] the outcome of this consultation is not publicly available. There is no media coverage or mention of whether the people of Lautoka and Ba had been consulted. FNPF members, which include both the working population and pensioners, should be made aware of how their pension fund is being invested and spent on their behalf. They need to know what a PPP is, what it will cost the public and how it will benefit them, the nature of the contract in question and past experiences of PPP projects in other countries.

There is no publicly available data on how this PPP will impact women's access to healthcare and hospital facilities. A report by the MoH reviewing the National Health Accounts from 2011 to 2015 shows that female patients accounted for 60 per cent of in-patient expenditure (40.7 million FJD or 18.86 million USD). Yet, there is no clarity on how the quality of healthcare available to women will change in the two hospitals under the PPP.

Conclusion: Are PPPs a panacea for Fiji's ailing health sector?

If the information gaps in the Lautoka and Ba hospitals PPP are anything to go by, the promotion of such partnerships in developing countries should be examined carefully. Fiji's economy is vulnerable to external shocks, as has been observed during the downturn caused by the Covid-19 pandemic. The IMF's concern about PPPs on small island developing states (IMF, 2004; 2018) should be heeded by the government of Fiji as a red flag. Equally, the intention and motivations underlying the actions of Ashurst LLP, the IFC, Austrade and the PSDI should be scrutinised. These actors act as conduits for private sector companies, allowing them to establish themselves locally by pushing for public sector reforms that work in private interest. Ashurst LLP's advice to the FNPF to invest in a risky business model that jeopardises the people's savings should be called into question in this light.

The FNA's determination to protect not only the basic rights of its members, but also the basic health rights of the communities, should be the starting point for mobilising public awareness and attention. The continuous challenge posed by the association to the privatisation of the Lautoka hospital should motivate the Fijian public. Public support is especially crucial at the time when trade unions have no right to assembly (currently illegal) and find their freedom of expression subject to heavy scrutiny by the state. The FNA's call for a new feasibility study for the PPP should be supported and recommended to the government. The PPP contract should also be made available for public scrutiny.

By its own admission, one of the main reasons the government is pushing for this PPP is to strengthen Fiji's medical tourism. However, worldwide, the experience with medical tourism has been that it diverts resources away from the local population by prioritising overseas patients, and places further constraints on health resources, supplies and personnel in general, and public health resources in particular (Greer, 2014). Despite health being recognised as a fundamental human right in Fiji's Constitution, most people do not have health insurance and can only afford to visit public hospitals. Fiji's public health sector must, therefore, approach health as a human right and prioritise Fijians instead of seeing it as a niche service or a market for medical tourism.

The questions that the public should now ask include:

1. When can nationwide consultations on this PPP venture, with all concerned healthcare service stakeholders, be held?
2. When can consultations be held with communities in the western division such as faith-based organisations, heads of provinces, women and gender organisations, the disability society and farming communities?
3. When will the public be informed about the objectives of the PPP contract?
4. When will the government disclose the full details and structure of the PPP contract, including how it will deliver health services and who will bear the risks?
5. When will a strict and independent monitoring and evaluation process be established? What is the mechanism for redress in case things do not proceed as planned?
6. What impact will the PPP have on populations in Lautoka and Ba, including its gender-based impact? How will the transition of the hospitals impact these communities, especially those who use the Lautoka Hospital as the main referral hospital?

7. Who will pay for the financing? How will the FNPF benefit from this investment and why is the PPP using pension funds, which is public money, to invest in this project without consulting its members? Who advises the FNPF on investments? Are the advisors working for the people or the for-profit enterprises?

These are potential guidelines for consultations on current and future PPPs. It is critical that the government, from this point on, proceeds with caution, or even better, steps back and reviews the process in order to ensure that all nurses, doctors and communities are involved, and that the Fijian public is fully informed about the PPP. The government should also ensure that the financing obtained from pension funds is used for PPPs if and only if the public supports it. Overall, the PPP process should be transparent, accountable and formulated through adequate consultations so that the people who are most affected by it are heard and not just left to listen to a parliamentary debate that excludes them from the discussion.

Notes

1 See 'Fiji Bureau of Statistics Releases 2017 Census Results', The Fijian Government. Available at: https://www.fiji.gov.fj/Media-Centre/News/Fiji-Bureau-of-Statistics-Releases-2017-Census-Res.
2 According to the World Health Organization, OECD member countries have 3.4 practising physicians, on an average, for every 1,000 patients.
3 Please refer to Annex 1: Literature Review.
4 Parliament of the Republic of Fiji (2018), 'Budget 2018–2019 Taxation and Other Government Revenue. Budget Briefings 2018'. Available at: http://www.parliament.gov.fj/wp-content/uploads/2018/07/Government-Revenue-2018-19-FINAL.pdf.
5 World Bank (2017), 'Current Health Expenditure Per Capita (Current US$)'. Available at: https://data.worldbank.org/indicator/SH.XPD.CHEX.PC.CD.
6 According to WHO, in OECD countries the average ratio is 3:4 per 1000 patients.
7 WHO (2004), 'The Migration of Skilled Health Personnel in the Pacific Region: A Summary Report', World Health Organization for the Western Pacific, Manila, Philippines. Available at: https://iris.wpro.who.int/bitstream/handle/10665.1/5501/9290611758_eng.pdf.
8 Annex 2 includes the questionnaire for the interview with Filomena Talawadua.

9   Annex 1 complements this overview.
10 Pacific Islands Report (2007), 'India's Apollo Group Plans $44 Million Hospital in Fiji', 27 September. Available at: http://www.pireport.org/ articles/2007/09/27/india%C3%A2%C2%80%C2%99s-apollo-group-plans-44-million-hospital-fiji.
11 IFC is the private sector arm of the World Bank. It has projects in Fiji, Kiribati, Papua New Guinea, Samoa, Solomon Islands, Timor-Leste, Tonga and Vanuatu. Available at: https://www.ifc.org/wps/wcm/connect/848fad73-4f99-4097-b473-adb8e3ddf5d6/IFC+Advisory+Services+Repo rt+1990-2010.pdf?MOD=AJPERES&CVID=j1ax3GB.
12 See Austrade: 'About Us'. Available at: https://www.austrade.gov.au/About/ about#:~:text=The%20Australian%20Trade%20and%20Investment%20 Commission%20%E2%80%93%20Austrade,the%20world%20and%20 the%20world%20to%20Australian%20businesses.
13 See Austrade: 'About Us'. Available at: https://www.austrade.gov.au/About/ about#:~:text=The%20Australian%20Trade%20and%20Investment%20 Commission%20%E2%80%93%20Austrade,the%20world%20and%20 the%20world%20to%20Australian%20businesses.
14 See the Pacific Private Sector Development Initiative website. Available at: http://www.adbpsdi.org/who-we-are/about-psdi.
15 Aspen Medical (2020), 'Over a Decade Providing Healthcare Support to AFP and ADF Personnel in Solomon Islands'. Available at: https://www. aspenmedical.com/content/over-decade-providing-healthcare-support-afp-and-adf-personnel-solomon-islands.
16 See the Australian Trade and Investment Commission. Available at: https:// www.austrade.gov.au/about/about.
17 See Parliament of Australia. Available at: https://parlinfo.aph.gov.au/ parlInfo/search/display/display.w3p;db=COMMITTEES;id=committees% 2Fcommjnt%2Faa838082-3df7-4934-9253-400129d4dc47%2F0001;query =Id%3A%22committees%2Fcommjnt
</br>%2Faa838082-3df7-4934-9253-400129d4dc47%2F0000%22.
18 See Ashurst website. Available at: www.ashurst.com.
19 Ashurst LLP (2019), 'Ashurst Advises the Fiji National Provident Fund on its Acquisition of 20 per cent of the Total Issued Ordinary Shares in Energy Fiji Ltd', 27 December. Available at: https://www.ashurst.com/en/news-and-insights/news-deals-and-awards/ashurst-advises-the-fnpf-on-acquisition-of-20-per-cent-of-shares-in-energy-fiji.
20 Section 2.2 Ministry of Economy Public Private Partnership Policy, 2019.
21 Isimeli Tatukivei was speaking at the meeting on PPPs organised by PSI at the World Bank and IMF Annual Meeting on 12–14 October 2018.
22 Annex 3 includes the questionnaire for the interview with Kate Lappin.
23 Pratibha, J. (2018), 'Public-Private Partnership Not Privatisation, Says Acting MP', *Fiji Sun,* 13 March. Available at: https://fijisun.com. fj/2018/03/13/public-private-partnership-not-privatisation-says-acting-pm.

References

Ashurst LLP (2019), 'Ashurst Advises the Fiji National Provident Fund on Its Acquisition of 20% of the Total Issued Ordinary Shares in Energy Fiji Ltd', 27 December. Available at: https://www.ashurst.com/en/news-and-insights/news-deals-and-awards/ashurst-advises-the-fnpf-on-acquisition-of-20-per-cent-of-shares-in-energy-fiji (accessed 26 May 2020).

ADB (2008), 'Public Private Partnerships. Pacific Private Sector Policy Brief', April. Available at: https://www.adb.org/publications/public-private-partnerships (accessed 26 May 2020).

ADB (2017), 'ADB Helps PNG Expand Port Moresby International Airport Using PPP', News Release, 2 February. Available at: https://www.adb.org/news/adb-helps-png-expand-port-moresby-international-airport-using-ppp (accessed 26 May 2020).

Aspen Medical (2019), 'Aspen Medical Signs Contract to Manage Two Hospitals over the Next Two Decades as Part of Fiji's Public-Private Partnership'. Available at: https://www.aspenmedical.com/news/news/aspen-medical-signs-contract-manage-two-hospitals-over-next-two-decades-part-fiji%E2%80%99s-public (accessed 26 May 2020).

Aspen Medical (2020), 'Over a Decade Providing Healthcare Support to AFP and ADF Personnel in Solomon Islands'. Available at: https://www.aspenmedical.com/content/over-decade-providing-healthcare-support-afp-and-adf-personnel-solomon-islands (accessed 26 May 2020).

Boyle, M. (2019), 'Brain Drain in the Health Sector Curbed Says Dr. Waqainabete', *FBC News*, 13 February. Available at: https://www.fbcnews.com.fj/news/health/brain-drain-in-the-health-sector-curbed-says-dr-waqainabete (accessed 26 May 2020).

Department of Information (2020), 'COVID-19: Labasa Hospital to be an Isolation Facility', *Fiji Sun*, 5 April. Available at: https://fijisun.com.fj/2020/04/05/covid-19-labasa-hospital-to-be-an-isolation-facility (accessed 26 May 2020).

Deo, R. (2018), 'Fiji "Missed Opportunity" to Promote Gender Equality in Budget', interviewed by S. Rench for *Public Finance Focus*, 3 July. Available at: https://www.publicfinancefocus.org/news/2018/07/fiji-missed-opportunity-promote-gender-equality-budget1 (accessed 26 May 2020).

Eurodad (2018), 'History RePPPeated. How Public-Private Partnerships Are Failing'. Available at: https://eurodad.org/files/pdf/1546956-history-repppeated-how-public-private-partnerships-are-failing-.pdf (accessed 26 May 2020).

Fiji Government Media Centre (2018), 'Fiji Bureau of Statistics Release 2017 Census Results', 10 January. Available at: https://www.fiji.gov.fj/Media-Centre/News/Fiji-Bureau-of-Statistics-Releases-2017-Census-Res (accessed 26 May 2020).

Fiji Ministry of Economy (2019), 'Public Private Partnership 2019'. Available at: https://www.fijichamber.com/uploads/content/42631983307521566777429_ Public_Private_Partnership_Policy.pdf (accessed 26 May 2020).

Fiji Women's Rights Movement (2019), 'National Budget 2019–2020 Analysis'. Available at: http://www.fwrm.org.fj/images/national_budget_analysis.pdf (accessed 26 May 2020).

Greer, S. L. (2014), 'The Globalization of Health Care: Legal and Ethical Issues', *Journal of Health Politics, Policy and Law*, 39 (6): 1289–94 DOI: org/10.1215/03616878-2829664 (accessed 26 May 2020).

IFC (2019), 'Public-Private Partnership Stories. Fiji: Lautoka and Ba Hospitals'. Available at: https://www.ifc.org/wps/wcm/connect/ fbec1baa-08ce-45cf-9d3c-a6d1854a4ea6/Fiji-Health-PPP-Story. pdf?MOD=AJPERES&CVID=mSDV5kh (accessed 26 May 2020).

IMF (2004), 'Public-Private Partnerships', prepared by the Fiscal Affairs Department (in consultation with other departments, the World Bank and the Inter-American Development Bank), 12 March. Available at: https:// www.imf.org/external/np/fad/2004/pifp/eng/031204.pdf (accessed 26 May 2020).

IMF (2018), '2017 Staff Guidance Note on the Fund's Engagement with Small Island Developing States'. Available at: https://www.imf.org/en/Publications/ Policy-Papers/Issues/2018/01/26/pp121117-2017-staff-guidance-note-on- the-funds-engagement-with-small-developing-states (accessed 26 May 2020).

Irava, W., and R. Prasad (2012), 'A Case Study on the Public and Private Mix of Health Services in Fiji', Suva: Centre for Health Information Policy and Systems Research, Fiji National University. Available at: https://www.fnu. ac.fj/collegeofmedicine/images/chipsr/publications/CHIPSR_case_study_ public_private_mix.pdf (accessed 26 May 2020).

Jacobs, T. (2018), 'Questions over Hospital Upgrade Motives in Fiji', interviewed by J. Meyer for *Dateline Pacific*, 15 May. Available at: https://www.rnz.co.nz/ international/programmes/datelinepacific/audio/2018644994/questions- over-hospital-upgrade-motives-in-fiji (accessed 26 May 2020).

Kumar, A. (2018), 'Three Amputations a Day: Fiji Diabetes Death Rate Worst in the World', 30 May. Available at: https://www.stuff.co.nz/world/south- pacific/104333879/three-amputations-a-day-fiji-diabetes-death-rate-worst- in-the-world (accessed 26 May 2020).

Lappin, K. (2020), Interview via skype, May (see Annex 3 for questionnaire).

Lowy Institute (2016), 'Australia's Foreign Aid'. Available at: https://www. lowyinstitute.org/issues/australian-foreign-aid (accessed 26 May 2020).

Lucanivalu, L. (2018), 'Increase in Health Ministry Budget Has Been Progressive: Akbar', *Fiji Sun*, 10 March. Available at: https://fijisun.com. fj/2018/03/10/increase-in-health-ministry-budget-has-been-progressive- akbar (accessed 26 May 2020).

Lutua, K. (2020). Personal Interview.

Lyons, K. (2020), 'Australia Slashes Pacific Aid Funding for Health as Region Battles Medical Crises', 18 February, *Guardian Australia*. Available at: https://www.theguardian.com/world/2020/feb/18/australia-slashes-pacific-aid-funding-for-health-as-region-battles-medical-crises (accessed 26 May 2020).

McCaig, E. (2019), 'We Do a Lot of Cutting: The Rise of Diabetic Amputations in the Pacific', interviewed by T. Aualiitia for *ABC Pacific Mornings*, 11 July. Available at: https://www.abc.net.au/radio-australia/programs/pacificmornings/diabetic-amputations/11298552 (accessed 26 May 2020).

MoHMS and WHO (2018), 'Ministry and WHO Clarify Report on Fiji's Diabetes Rate', *Fiji Sun*, 19 June. Available at: https://fijisun.com.fj/2018/06/19/ministry-and-who-clarify-report-on-fijis-diabetes-rate (accessed 26 May 2020).

Morgan, J. (2015), 'Country in Focus: Turning the Tide of Diabetes in Fiji', *The Lancet Diabetes & Endocrinology*, 3 (1): 15–16. Available at: https://doi.org/10.1016/S2213-8587(14)70240-2 (accessed 26 May 2020).

Negin, J., W. Irava, D. Leon, C. Malau, and C. Morgan (2013), 'Sustainable Health Financing in the Pacific: Tracking Dependency and Transparency', 9 January. Available at: http://devpolicy.org/what-constitutes-donor-dependence-20130109/?print=print (accessed 26 May 2020).

Negin, J. (2008), 'Australia and New Zealand's Contribution to Pacific Island Health Worker Brain Drain', *Australian and New Zealand Journal of Public Health*, 32 (6): 507–11. Available at: https://doi.org/10.1111/j.1753-6405.2008.00300.x (accessed 26 May 2020).

Nicholas, I. (2015), 'PNG PM Officially Opens Expanded Jackson International Airport', 7 January. Available at: http://www.pireport.org/articles/2015/07/01/png-pm-officially-opens-expanded-jackson-international-airport (accessed 26 May 2020).

Pacific Island Report (2007), 'India's Apollo Group Plans $44 Million Hospital in Fiji', 27 September. Available at: http://www.pireport.org/articles/2007/09/27/india%C3%A2%C2%80%C2%99s-apollo-group-plans-44-million-hospital-fiji (accessed 26 May 2020).

Pacific Islands Forum Secretariat (2017), 'National Economies and Commitments to Benefit from Gender Responsive Budgeting'. Available at: https://www.forumsec.org/2017/06/14/national-economies-and-commitments-to-benefit-from-gender-responsive-budgeting (accessed 26 May 2020).

Parliament of the Republic of Fiji (2018), 'Budget 2018–2019 Taxation and Other Government Revenue. Budget Briefings 2018'. Available at: http://www.parliament.gov.fj/wp-content/uploads/2018/07/Government-Revenue-2018-19-FINAL.pdf (accessed 26 May 2020).

Parry, Jane (2010), 'Pacific Islanders Pay Heavy Price for Abandoning Traditional Diet', *Bulletin of the World Health Organization*, 88 (7): 484.

Post Courier (2018), 'Medical Board Puts Aspen Medical Services on Notice', 26 January. Available at: https://postcourier.com.pg/medical-board-puts-aspen-medical-services-on-notice (accessed 26 May 2020).

Pratibha, J. (2018), 'Public-Private Partnership Not Privatisation Says Acting PM', *Fiji Sun*, 13 March. Available at: https://fijisun.com.fj/2018/03/13/public-private-partnership-not-privatisation-says-acting-pm (accessed 26 May 2020).

PSI (2018), 'Fiji Nurse Questions Privatisation at World Bank's Annual Meeting in Bali'. Available at: http://www.world-psi.org/fr/node/11649 (accessed 26 May 2020).

Radio New Zealand (2017), 'Indian Hospital Group Features at Fiji Health Forum', *Radio New Zealand*, 21 April. Available at: https://www.rnz.co.nz/international/pacific-news/329198/indian-hospital-group-features-at-fiji-health-forum (accessed 26 May 2020).

Singh, R. (2013), 'Fiji National Provident Fund', Powerpoint presentation at the PSI/FES Forum on Pensions and Social Security, Singapore. Available at: https://www.world-psi.org/sites/default/files/documents/research/fiji_national_provident_fund_-_rajeshwar_singh.pdf (accessed 26 May 2020).

SIBC Online (2019). 'Engineering Procurement for Tina Hydro Power Project Signed', 1 October. Available at: http://www.sibconline.com.sb/engineering-procurement-for-tina-hydro-power-project-signed (accessed 26 May 2020).

Talawadua, F. (2020). Interview. 27 May (see Annex 2 for questionnaire).

Talei, F. (2019), 'Fiji Health Minister: Two Doctors Committed Suicide Because of Work Stress', Fiji Sun, 14 February. Available at: https://fijisun.com.fj/2019/02/14/two-doctors-commited-suicide-work-stress/ (accessed 26 May 2020).

Tatukivei, I. T. (2018), 'Fiji Nurse Questions Privatisation at World Bank's Annual Meeting in Bali', 15 October. Available at: http://www.world-psi.org/fr/node/11649 (accessed 26 May 2020).

Wainiqolo, I., and S. Shivanjali (2018), 'Modelling Fiji's Tourism Arrivals', Economics Group Working Paper, Reservice Bank of Fiji. Available at: https://www.rbf.gov.fj/modelling-fijis-tourism-arrivals/ (accessed 26 May 2020).

Waqainabete, Ifereimi (2018), 'Move Concerns FNA', maiden speech in Parliament, reported by V. Kumar of *The Fiji Times*, 13 December. Available at: https://www.fijitimes.com/move-concerns-fna (accessed 26 May 2020).

Waradi, T. (2007), 'India's Apollo Group Plans $44 Million Hospital in Fiji', interviewed by *The Fiji Times*, 26 September. Available at: http://www.pireport.org/articles/2007/09/27/india%C3%A2%C2%80%C2%99s-apollo-group-plans-44-million-hospital-fiji (accessed 26 May 2020).

Whaites, M. (2018), 'Questions over Hospital Upgrade Motives in Fiji', interviewed by J. Meyer. *Radio New Zealand*, 15 May. Available at: https://www.rnz.co.nz/international/programmes/datelinepacific/

audio/2018644994/questions-over-hospital-upgrade-motives-in-fiji (accessed 26 May 2020).

WHO (2004), 'The Migration of Skilled Health Personnel in the Pacific Region: A Summary Report', *World Health Organization for the Western Pacific, Manila, Philippines.* Available at: https://iris.wpro.who.int/bitstream/handle/10665.1/5501/9290611758_eng.pdf (accessed 26 May 2020).

World Bank (2017), 'Current Health Expenditure Per Capita (current US$)'. Available at: https://data.worldbank.org/indicator/SH.XPD.CHEX.PC.CD?end=2017&start=2017&view=bar&year=2017 (accessed 26 May 2020).

Appendix

Annex 1: Literature Review

Since 2004, there has been a great increase in the amount of money invested in PPPs in the developing world. In 2015, the UN Conference on Financing for Development featured PPPs significantly in the Addis Ababa Action Agenda, strongly endorsing these instruments as a 'means of implementation of the 2030 Agenda for Sustainable Development' (Eurodad, 2018).

According to the WB's Overview in 2012, PPPs were being used in 134 developing countries and contributed about 15–20 per cent of the total infrastructure investment (World Bank, 2017). Governments are increasingly pivoting towards the use of PPPs to provide basic public services for their citizen in sectors such as power, water, transportation, education and health. PPPs are being promoted as instruments to finance development projects.

The definition of a PPP varies. The WB defines PPPs as 'long-term contracts between a private party and a government agency, for providing a public asset or service, in which the private party bears significant risk and management responsibility' (World Bank, 2017). The Asian Development Bank (ADB) defines PPPs as 'agreements between the public and private sectors for the provision of assets and/or services such as power, water, transportation, education and health' (ADB, 2008).

Financing development

Private financing of public services has increased greatly over the past twenty-five years, in both the global North and South, as a means of keeping debt levels down. In 2015, UN member countries adopted the SDGs, a universal framework of seventeen global goals to be achieved by the year 2030. SDG 3, in particular, seeks to ensure good health and well-being for all. PPPs are at the top of the development agendas of governments, and MDBs are often presented as crucial in the fight to achieve the SDGs.

Enter public-private partnerships

PPPs have been touted as the panacea for the financing shortfall that prevents countries from achieving the SDGs in economic infrastructure such as roads, airports and ports. They have also been identified as critical to accessing services such as health, education, water and electricity in the global North and South (Eurodad, 2018).

As a key indicator of sustainable development and a fundamental human right, governments are faced with the challenge of improving health standards in their countries. Poor health threatens the rights of children to education, limits economic opportunities for both men and women, and increases poverty both within communities and countries around the world. In addition to being a cause of poverty, health is impacted by poverty and is strongly connected to other aspects of sustainable development, including availability of water and sanitation, gender equality, climate change, and peace and stability (SDG Compass, n.d.).

PPPs in the Pacific and Fiji and their role in infrastructure projects

Large-scale infrastructure projects are delivered through PPPs. As part of the scaling-up of investments in the Pacific, MDBs such as the World Bank Group (WBG) and the ADB are also major partners in infrastructure projects. This section will look at two examples of bankable projects funded by the ADB and the WBG in financing development which coordinates public and private capital.

In the Solomon Islands, a contract was recently signed between Tina Hydropower Limited (THL) and the Hyundai Engineering Company Limited (HEC) for building a hydro dam (SIBC Online, 2019). The major partners include the WB, the Australian Department of Foreign Affairs and Trade (DFAT), the International Finance Corporation (IFC), the Green Climate Fund (GCF), the Economic Development Corporation Fund (EDCF) of the Government of Korea, the ADB, the International Renewable Energy Agency (IRENA) and the European Investment Bank. The commercial partners to this project are Korea Water Corporation (K-water), HEC and the Solomon Power Company. The project has been touted as the first national PPP development project for the Solomon Islands that will increase the employment rate.

In Papua New Guinea, the PPP Act 2014 is in operation as of January 2018 (Post Courier, 2018). In November 2018, the country hosted the Asia-Pacific Economic Cooperation (APEC) meeting. To prepare itself to welcome participants at the APEC meeting, the government of Papua New Guinea, through the National Airport Corporation (NAC), signed a contract with the ADB to provide transaction advisory services through a PPP. The ADB supported the NAC in improving the infrastructure at the Jackson International Airport by extending the main runway and building a new international passenger terminal to meet the projected growth in air services up to the year 2040 (ADB, 2017).

In this PPP, the ADB was supported by the PSDI facility established in 2008 to provide technical assistance, research and knowledge products on key infrastructure issues for Pacific Island countries. Other development partners in the facility include Australia Aid, New Zealand's Ministry of Foreign Affairs (MFAT), the WB, European Union and the Japan International Corporation Agency.

Under the PPP arrangement, the Jackson International Airport in Port Moresby was renovated and expanded to become a world-class terminal facility that can process two million passengers a year (Nicholas, 2015). Prior to the renovation, the airport was processing 800,000 passengers per year even though the terminal building was built for a maximum of 300 passengers (Nicholas, 2015). The Australian and New Zealand Bank (ANZ Bank) funded the project.

PPPs and health in the Pacific and Fiji

Changes in lifestyle, including the decline of traditional dietary customs and nutrition, the decrease in physical activity and the steady integration into the global cash economy have had a substantial and sobering effect on the prevalence of non-communicable diseases (NCDs) in the Pacific region. The prevalence of diabetes in adults in the Pacific region is among the highest in the world (Parry, 2010), with 16 per cent of the population diagnosed with some form of the disease (McCaig, 2019). Fiji is no exception (Morgan, 2015).

In 2017, Fiji's Ministry of Health and Medical Services and the WHO clarified that cardiovascular-related deaths exceeded those related to diabetes in Fiji (MoHMS and WHO, 2018). In 2019, media reports on the ongoing concerns about diabetes highlighted the fact that amputations relating to diabetes accounted for 40 per cent of hospital operations in the country (McCaig, 2019).

The disease is responsible for 188 out of 100,000 deaths in the country and, according to the MoHMS, approximately 33 per cent of Fijians are diabetic. This means that Fiji has already exceeded the WHO's 2030 prediction of an 8 per cent prevalence of diabetes in the country. There are three amputations a day according to the Diabetes Fiji project manager Viliame Qio (Kumar, 2018).

Not only is death from diabetes the highest in Fiji among the Pacific countries, the disease is also the top cause of disability in the country. Sedentary lifestyles, poor eating habits, food security issues and climate change are the main factors behind the diabetes crisis.

According to a study by Negin et al. (2013), data gathered from Samoa, Tonga, Vanuatu and the Federated States of Micronesia showed that the health expenditure in these countries were dependent in large part on external financing. Vanuatu, for instance, received 16.5 per cent of total health expenditure support from external donors, Samoa received 21.4 per cent and Tonga 39.2 per cent (2013). The reliance of Tonga on external financing is four times greater than that of Fiji (2013). Samoa and Tonga's major partners, including Australia, New Zealand and the World Bank, all contribute similar amounts (2013). The Federated States of Micronesia's total health expenditure is funded, almost entirely, by government grants from the United States. Public financing accounts for approximately 10 per cent of health expenditure, proving that the country is almost entirely dependent on external funding (2013). The 2013 study also acknowledged that, because of the lack of data on Pacific Island countries, it is unable to fully capture the situation on the ground (2013).

In February 2020, a Senate Inquiry in Australia revealed that the country's funding support for health programmes across the Pacific region had been slashed over the past five years. In the Cook Islands, health funding was reduced by 75 per cent, in Fiji by 22 per cent, in the Solomon Islands by 13 per cent and in Samoa, which has been devastated by a measles outbreak, by 36 per cent (Lyons, 2020). This was part of an overall cut in aid to the Pacific (see Table 10.4).

Australia's former Treasurer Joey Hockey said in 2014 that savings worth 3.7 billion Australian dollars (AUD) in the foreign aid programme over the following four years would offset new commitments in defence and national security for the country (Lowy Institute, 2016) even in times of an epidemic.

Gender-responsive budget

At a regional training workshop hosted by the Pacific Islands Forum Secretariat (PIFS) in 2017, aimed at improving the understanding of the financial benefits and impacts of spending on men and women, and planning gender-responsive budgets, Pacific decision-makers were urged to maintain their commitments on gender equality with increased and better-targeted funding. Currently, in the Pacific region, targeted government spending on women is very low – around 1 per cent of national budgets (Pacific Islands Forum Secretariat, 2017).

Table 10.4 Australia Health and Overall Aid Spending Cuts in the Pacific Islands.

Country	Health budget cut (%)	Overall aid spending cut over 5 years (%)
Cook Islands	75	26
Fiji	22	5
Samoa	13	14
Solomon Islands	13	Steady
Tonga	Not available	10
Tuvalu	Not available	17
North Pacific	Not available	42
Nauru	Not available	Steady
Vanuatu	Not available	41

Source: Lyons, K. (2020), 'Australia Slashes Pacific Aid Funding for Health as Region Battles Medical Crises', 18 February, *Guardian Australia*. Available at: https://www.theguardian.com/world/2020/feb/18/australia-slashes-pacific-aid-funding-for-health-as-region-battles-medical-crises (accessed 26 May 2020).

In Fiji's 2019–20 budget, the allocation for the Ministry of Women, Children and Poverty Alleviation fell by 4 per cent (Fiji Women's Rights Movement, 2019). This ministry may not be a policy-line agency, but it does provide community-based development services mainly to Fijian women. Perhaps, a more in-depth look at how gender mainstreaming is reflected throughout all ministries will be more effective for such areas as health, tourism, national planning and education, to name a few. In response to the 2018 budget announcement, activist Roshika Deo (2018) said that although the budget, at first glance, appeared to be inclusive, it did not address inequalities. For a national budget to be gender responsive, it needs to identify ways in which public spending and revenue impacts men and women differently, and attempt to achieve gender equality. She added that while *all* public sectors would gain from a gender analysis, education, health, agriculture, social welfare and disability sectors would particularly benefit from analyses of their gender *impact* (2018).

Information on gender mainstreaming is crucial in informing the different health needs of men and women in order to help with budgetary allocation of the MoHMS and the Ministry of Women, Children and Poverty Alleviation in Fiji. The question then is: how did the government determine the need to change the Lautoka and Ba hospitals from public hospitals to full-scale PPP hospitals without strengthening the existing types of partnerships that exist? One such partnership is with the Sahyadri Hospital Services, a chain of private hospitals in India. Under the arrangement, Sahyadri Hospitals would provide specialised tertiary healthcare previously unavailable in Fiji at a subsidised cost in order to reduce the need to seek treatment overseas. At the same time, they would build local capacity by training Fiji's health workers (Irava and Prasad, 2012).

Annex 2: Questionnaire for the Interview with Filomena Talawadua

1. Can you tell us a little about the Lautoka and Ba hospitals?

    - Do you have enough nurses at the two hospitals to address health issues and treat them adequately?

2. When did you first hear about the transition of the two hospitals from public entities to a PPP?

3. According to a *Fiji Sun* report, the Attorney General stated that the government had 'reached out' to the doctors and nurses at the two hospitals about the transition, and their response was overwhelming. Are you aware of this consultation? How were they consulted?

    - Over the telephone?
    - Over a week-long workshop?
    - By email?
    - Was the FNA consulted?

4. We understand that PSI had supported the FNA regarding the PPP of the Lautoka and Ba hospitals. What was the FNA's understanding of PPPs prior to the engagement with PSI?

5. How did the engagement with PSI assist the FNA's campaign against this PPP?

6. Was a feasibility study done to assess the need for a PPP?

    - Were healthcare workers consulted?

7. As a long serving public servant/nurse, can you tell us your experiences of public and private healthcare?

8. In your view, will the PPP project benefit:

    - Nurses?
    - The Fijian public?

9. What are the main reasons for the transition of the Lautoka and Ba hospitals from a publicly funded structure to a PPP-financed project?

Annex 3: Questionnaire for the Interview with Kate Lappin, PSI

1. Can you describe PSI's work with PPPs and private financing in the healthcare sector in Australia and other regions of the world?
2. Why was PSI concerned about the proposed PPP at the Lautoka and Ba hospitals?

   - How did PSI engage with the topic? What was the reaction of the FNA when it was first made aware of the PPP?
   - When did you first hear about the PPP?

3. We have come across examples of hospitals that also transitioned to PPPs and subsequently returned to public administration in Australia. What lessons are there for Fiji to consider?
4. Is there promotion on:

   - Medical tourism?
   - Proper healthcare for international meetings?
   - Upskilling workers?
     - Are these typical reasons or even a good basis for Fiji to venture into PPPs? Are there any reasons you know of and think we should be aware of before going down the PPP path?

5. The contract for the two hospitals was signed between the Fiji government and Aspen Medical in January 2019. Other than these two parties, others have not signed the contract (according to the interview with Filomena Talawadua of FNA).

   - What challenge will this hold for the public?
   - How can the public keep all parties accountable for service delivery?

6. What is the PSI's experience with other PPPs in the Pacific or in the health sector?
7. Has the PSI worked with other Pacific Island countries on PPPs?

   - What lessons are there for other Pacific Island countries in this regard?

8. This project requires 80 million FJD of private financing to work. Given the many PPP projects that failed, this is a very ambitious, but very shaky, ground to start a PPP in Fiji's health sector …
9. Fiji's promotion of medical tourism is understandable because tourism is the major foreign-exchange earner. But with a global pandemic raging, there are no tourists now …

10. Do you think PPPs for the health sector can work? If so, how do you think it can?
11. Public health sector *versus* value for money, efficiency and effectiveness ...
12. What have been the general experiences of PPPs?

Conclusion

Corporate capture of development in times of exacerbated crises: Implications for democratic governance, rights and global inequality

Corina Rodríguez Enríquez and Masaya Llavaneras Blanco

The case studies presented in this book highlight how public-private partnerships (PPPs) of various types and across sectors work in practice, shedding light on their many similarities and some differences. By taking a broad look at the diverse characteristics and consequences of PPPs in the global South, they offer lessons on the implications of these projects for governance, access to services, social inequalities and rights enforcement.

This final chapter uses a Southern and intersectional feminist approach to trace common concerns and points of divergence that emerge from the case studies discussed thus far in the book. It offers critiques of the PPP model based on these case studies and puts forth some ideas for a social and political agenda for regulation of such partnerships. Finally, it argues for reclaiming the central role of the state in public provisions and rights guarantees in a way that is commensurate with feminist mobilising on these issues.

Expanding global capitalism, promoting corporate capture

The predominance of multinational corporations is a defining feature in the expansion of global capitalism. The private sector has emerged as a key catalyst and actor in development initiatives, with implications for power relations between state and corporate interests at the national and global levels.

As the case studies demonstrate, international financial institutions (IFIs), particularly the World Bank (WB), actively promote the PPP model through their technical support teams, training processes, and loan and grant conditionalities. That leaves states to play rather ambiguous roles. While the official discourse presents governments as neutral regulators, in practice, they often act as promoters and even protectors and subsidisers of the PPP model. This takes place in three ways. Firstly, on the advice of the IFIs, states design regulatory frameworks that favour private investment. The same set of policy prescriptions limit transparency and accountability, and favour opaque implementation processes. Secondly, governments provide public funds that benefit PPPs, often before the projects are implemented, without any corresponding benefit accruing to the public. These public investments essentially act as indirect public subsidies to the private sector. Finally, PPP contracts peg states as the guarantor of last resort, particularly in the face of contingent liabilities. States frequently shoulder not only the costs, but also the risks of these projects.

In addition to promoting the PPP model, IFIs and other global institutions also provide technical guidance that informs the terms of contracts. Such guidance ensured that the agreement between the government of Sierra Leone and the Addax company, for example, was especially generous to the latter, allowing it to lease land for fifty years, offering tax benefits and exempting it from any national legislation that could materially impact the company, its suppliers and shareholders. The PPP agreements signed by governments in Peru and Mexico were similarly detrimental to the public interest. In Peru, the procedural opacity created by successive amendments to the PPP contract for the Alberto Barton Hospital and its primary healthcare centre benefitted private companies. In Mexico, the state indirectly subsidised the PPPs in the Isthmus of Tehuantepec Corridor by allowing private companies to use existing public infrastructure such as the Isthmus railway operated by the state-owned majority holding company and a gas pipeline administered by the national gas company.

One of the most serious implications of PPPs is their impact on power relations between individuals and the state, between states (at different levels), and between states and the private sector. A recurring point that emerges from these case studies is how PPPs alter governance dynamics at the local level (see the chapter on Ghana), at the provincial, state or regional levels (see the chapters on Chhattisgarh in India and Tehuantepec in Mexico), as well as in the national and global arenas.

Sovereignty in policy making is constantly contested and negotiated in PPP mediations that take place at different levels of government, such as national, regional and local, and involve various institutions, including ministries of finance, health, public works and transport. Where intellectual elites and national epistemological communities are aligned with the IFIs and other international cooperation organisations, policy-making processes are influenced by prescriptions that emphasise fiscal retrenchment, privatisation and efficient resource management.

Corporate capture is evident in all the case studies, regardless of the varying national histories of states. Notorious in this regard is the case of Ethiopia where public enterprises were an exceptional feature of the developmental state in the era of socialism, giving the state a dominant role in the management of development. Nevertheless, the pro-private investment narrative made significant headway in the country through an economic liberalisation programme that began with the privatisation of flagship state-owned enterprises (SOEs) and continues today with a new generation of PPP projects.

Wielding the 'good PPP' narrative

As noted in the introduction to the book, the consolidation of the PPP paradigm rests on the deliberate construction of a narrative that attributes inefficiency, unaccountability and corruption to the state, and exonerates the private sector from the same characteristics.

Again, the Ethiopian case study presents an astute analysis of how such a narrative is constructed and disseminated in local and international media. It demonstrates how PPPs were uncritically presented as a real opportunity for the Ethiopian economy, and the shift from the centrality of SOEs to economic liberalisation and privatisation was treated as inexorable. The WB, while recognising the achievements of the country's historical development model, harped on 'its inevitable limit as a prudent economic strategy'. PPPs were thus imposed as destiny, reminiscent of Margaret Thatcher's imposition of financial deregulation and austerity in the 1980s under the guise of 'there is no alternative'.

This narrative was not born with PPPs, nor are they a recent development. PPPs are part of a long-standing privatisation process which instrumentalises a state in need of financing to suggest that a turn to the private sector is the only viable solution. The case of Peru falls squarely within this trajectory. The drive that started in the 1990s with the privatisation of public companies and the deregulation of markets is now being continued in the South American country with the promotion of PPPs.

Developments in Senegal also reflect this renewed emphasis on attracting private investments. Structural adjustment programmes (SAPs) since 1985 forced the country to open up its economy to international competition as a way of accelerating growth. These programmes, in turn, clearly established the link between the push for private financing and a high public debt burden, which radically reduced the space for public policy implementation. SAPs introduced in the 1980s also spelled a decline in the public provision of essential goods and services, such as health, in Kenya. This precedent will certainly be taken up by PPPs in Kenya, whose business model includes fee-paying service provisions. While many publicly owned and operated services also charge user fees, including in the health sector, the difference is that, unlike private initiatives that are led by profit making, public sector entities are not guided by full-cost-recovery principles.

It is noteworthy that the insistence that global South countries rely on private finance comes from the same actors that have systematically failed to fulfil their commitment to allocate resources towards the development of these countries. Data suggests that governments across the global North have historically fallen short of their commitment to allocate 0.7 per cent of their gross national income (GNI) towards Official Development Assistance (ODA) meant to promote economic development and welfare in developing nations.[1]

Yet, the strength of the narrative extolling the virtues of PPPs in financing infrastructure works and the provision of public services is such that other forms of financing do not appear in public discussion. This is evident in Fiji where PPPs to build and/or develop hospitals were approved without any consultation with civil society even though the model had previously never been implemented in the country's healthcare sector. Moreover, the discussion on PPPs in the sector was framed in terms of attracting businesses and capital, rather than improving local public health service provisions.

Geopolitics of PPPs

The implementation of the PPP model has important geopolitical implications linked to market expansion and control over certain regions with recent colonial histories. Against this backdrop, the preceding chapters studied power relations that reproduce colonial patterns in the postcolonial era, permeate from the global to the local, and facilitate the concentration of economic and political power in the hands of the corporate elite.

The Fijian case study, for instance, sheds light on Australia's neocolonial influence in the Pacific region. Using the framework of its development policy led by the Australian Trade and Investment Commission (Austrade), the country is pushing for Australian private investment in the region. By its own admission, one of Austrade's functions includes developing international markets for Australian companies. It stands to reason that in promoting the PPP agreement between its private domestic company Aspen Medical and the Fiji National Provident Fund (FNPF), Australia was not so much ushering in development and access to rights in the region as expanding the market for its own private sector to invest in.

Territorial sovereignty conflicts also arise within states in disputes between national governments and local and community authorities. In Mexico, infrastructure development in the Isthmus of Tehuantepec did not seek consent from peasant and indigenous communities living in the region, leading them to question the very territorial sovereignty that the Mexican state exercised in its negotiations with the national and international (mostly Spanish) private sector. These communities also did not recognise the validity of the assemblies convened by the government to settle the resultant dispute. It should be noted that this territorial dispute extends beyond the Mexican nation-state. As a region with the potential to connect the Atlantic and Pacific oceans, the territory affected by the Interoceanic Corridor of the Isthmus of Tehuantepec lies at the heart of a historical geopolitical concern.

Obfuscating transparency, brandishing gender equality

The lack of transparency and accountability in PPP implementation, reflected in all the case studies, is exacerbated by the implicit contradiction between public and corporate interests. Shareholder interest irremediably precedes all other interests in corporate decision-making. Against this backdrop, opacity is fuelled by the public messaging that frames PPPs as complex, technocratic deals that must be drafted by experts and can be understood only by them. In this way, political agreements that must take into account all stakeholders, including the people affected, are turned into unintelligible documents. This logic expands the gap between civil society and the decision-making processes that affect people's living conditions.

The WB's technical missions feed this deliberately constructed opacity, resulting in contracts that often do not go through the requisite stakeholder participation processes or community consultations, and are not made public or accessible. This situation fails to consider the needs of people who will be affected most by the design of a PPP project, precludes their participation at all stages of decision-making and hinders citizen monitoring of the project implementation process.

In the Mexico case study, for instance, environmental authorisation procedures were reduced to mere 'formalities' to facilitate private investment. Such procedures require time for information circulation, elaboration, consultation and advocacy. They also require space for deliberation and dialogue between citizens and institutions. None of these processes were forthcoming in the Tehuantepec Corridor PPP project. What was presented as administrative agility were in fact undemocratic practices with severe negative impacts on indigenous and peasant communities and territories.

PPPs often reflect the cooptation of gender justice issues that currently prevails in global governance institutions. This involves the championing of gender equality by the most unlikely actors in rather instrumental ways. The earlier 'add women and stir' strategy now manifests as an 'add gender equality and stir' approach, pushing for the cosmetic inclusion of gender equality goals in PPP contracts and policies. At first glance, Senegal's incorporation of gender equality and human rights among the parameters used to adjudicate public funds looks like a positive change. However, closer examination reveals that the weights assigned to them were inconsequential to the future of any project. In this case, even though gender mainstreaming was adopted as a necessary criterion, it had little impact on the policy-making process.

Detrimental impact of PPPs on social rights

The negative impact of PPPs on material living conditions and the realisation of fundamental rights are evident in all the case studies. The highway built in Senegal via the PPP displaced people from the project area, leading to social and economic hardships. Re-establishing neighbourhood ties, a crucial factor in women's survival strategies, was difficult and many social support networks were lost. The displacement also produced additional costs for the state in the form of resources that needed to be allocated to populations whose socio-economic vulnerabilities were exacerbated by the project. Amidst the higher investment costs, the supposed benefits of the PPP were not realised. On the contrary, the toll highway generated new costs for the general population.

In addition to the explicit costs, the Senegalese case also highlights the hidden socio-economic costs generated by PPP projects. The toll highway led to an increase in traffic accidents due to poor lighting. The project's labour practices reproduced gender-based discrimination by rewarding those who worked night shifts, disadvantaging pregnant women who are prohibited under Senegalese law from undertaking such jobs.

In the same vein, Sierra Leone's energy sector PPP saw Addax Bioenergy Sierra Leone (ABSL) fail to generate enough electricity to meet project goals, pay inadequate compensation to displaced residents and systematically violate social and environmental standards. Again, it is not only the direct economic costs of the PPP that are relevant, but also the socio-economic costs of its omissions.

These costs are often disproportionately borne by women. The ABSL PPP was reluctant to hire women in sufficient numbers and refused to adopt an employment gender quota that is part of IFIs' recommendations to make these projects more 'gender-sensitive'. Furthermore, most of those displaced were women who lost access to fertile land and clean water, and were plunged into food insecurity.

Most of the health sector case studies provide similar evidence of the detrimental and disproportionate impact of PPPs on women. The chapters on Peru and Zimbabwe demonstrate how PPPs reduced access to, increased costs of, and lowered the quality of maternity and reproductive health services. In India's Chhattisgarh and Zimbabwe, the implementation of PPPs increased the out-of-pocket expenses women had to incur to access health services. These schemes also deepened inequality, as evidenced by the physical segmentation in the provision of health services in the Parirenyatwa Group of Hospitals in Zimbabwe.

The disastrous effects of the model were particularly evident in Chhattisgarh where caste, indigenous status and gender produced significant gaps in access to and quality of health services as well as in health outcomes. Women belonging to indigenous communities and historically oppressed castes were subjected to unnecessary surgeries without their informed consent, often leading to tragic health outcomes, including preventable deaths.

The evidence presented in these chapters is, therefore, a far cry from the narrative that frames PPPs as an efficient and transparent model that positively impacts people's lives.

Social resistance

Diverse social resistance movements have emerged in the face of the pro-PPP narrative promoted by pro-business groups, some governments and international organisations. In some cases, resistance is based on historical struggles over land, and cultural and labour rights. In others, resistance is a response to the desperation produced by the privatisation of everyday life. Organising against PPPs takes many forms, including structured mobilisation, advocacy and spontaneous actions. Some resistance movements have been successful in delaying or even reversing these projects while others have faced roadblocks. However, they all emphasise that it is possible to confront corporate narratives that present PPPs as the only valid option.

In Fiji, Zimbabwe and Peru, nurses' and doctors' unions emerged as key players in the resistance against PPPs in the health sector. In some cases, they succeeded in partially reversing privatisation processes. In others, they were instrumental in denouncing poor working conditions and the decline in access to public services. Trade union resistance is particularly important when PPP projects impact social provisions such as health and education. These are sectors with feminised employment, where women's working conditions are threatened by the very logic that drives and promotes PPPs.

Trade union organising has the potential to produce positive outcomes in other sectors as well. Collective organising could have helped advance demands for women's quotas at ABSL. In Ghana's Dome Market, women vendors mobilised to neutralise and reverse the privatisation drive that threatened their livelihoods. They combined institutional and informal channels of resistance, turning to representatives in the legislature, the national office of the ruling party and even the President who, in turn, directed them to the Ministry of Special Development Initiatives. At the same time, women carried out sustained protests in the physical space of the market. Resistance in physical spaces is crucial as it keeps political mobilisation rooted in everyday life. It sheds light on the material implications of policies presented as abstract and technical fixes, and calls attention to issues of livelihoods and survival. It can also mobilise collectivities and spur the formation of broader coalitions.

The case studies presented in this book illustrate the various forms of violence against women reproduced by the PPP model. Institutional and labour violence, dispossession, and in some cases, physical violence and death are part of the everyday lived experiences of women, especially those who are racialised and poor. This explains why women are often at the heart of these resistances. In Mexico, indigenous and Afro-Mestizo women led diverse resistance movements, determined to confront what they regard as 'death projects'. They persisted in their efforts towards building autonomy through community surveillance tactics, community radio, community generation of electricity, strengthening of community assemblies and planting of food they deem healthy. Their resistance was not only an act of denunciation, but also an attempt to generate alternative ways of resolving social provision and reproduction. Even as they opposed the current corporate logic, they pointed to other possible ways of building the economy and conducting politics.

Reclaiming the state for public provision and guarantee of human rights

The responsibility of the state as the guarantor of rights is inescapable. This is particularly relevant in enforcing the rights and meeting the needs of women and girls, and poor and racialised groups who face greater structural constraints. As the case studies demonstrate, civil society, and women in particular, demand this responsibility from the state. Fully aware of the violence that can be meted out by state forces and the collusion between corporate and national interests, this demand does not idealise the state, but holds it accountable. With corporations only answerable to their shareholders, it is the responsibility of the state to ensure that the provision of social protections and the guarantee of the rights of people are not held hostage to profit-making motives.

In most case studies, states decline to fulfil their regulatory role, and instead, advance corporate interests, effectively functioning as partners of the private sector. In India, the state, as a key promoter of PPPs, especially through the privatisation of health insurance, shifted the cost of accessing health services on to individuals while maintaining a public system whose funding is constantly strained. Needless to say, the impact of the state's rollback from public provisions was felt disproportionately by the poor and the marginalised. In Zimbabwe, public hospitals gave free rein to private managers who turned service users into 'clientele' and even divided the physical space for PPP and public health service provision. The cases of Kenya and Ethiopia reflect the consequences of the state using the expansion of services for historically excluded populations as an excuse to retreat from its public provider role and create new business opportunities for private capital (domestic or foreign).

The case of Ghana's Dome Market is particularly relevant in this regard. Women market vendors, whose relationship with the state has historically been conflicted, demanded the return of state intervention in the functioning of the market. Although hierarchical, the traditional governance structure allowed women access to selling spaces and accorded them leadership roles in internal decision-making processes. The transition to privatised management under the PPP overthrew these structures, displaced women leaders and put the livelihoods of women vendors and their families at risk. Taking advantage of elections in Ghana, women vendors negotiated with the national government to mobilise on their behalf at the local level. The specific developments in the Dome Market necessitated bringing the state back as a regulator even though women vendors were aware that this was not a permanent solution to the problem of market governance. Vendors could interact with and make themselves heard by the state, whereas the private sector, which was not accountable to them, simply ignored their demands and displaced them. In the Dome Market, as in the other cases, resistance was about creating and recreating democratic spheres.

The democratic management of public policy is part of the challenge of recovering democracies and resisting the authoritarian and illiberal regimes that are currently making a resurgence globally. Against this backdrop, it is essential to shift the narrative away from consumers and capitalist consumption to focus on the rights and well-being of citizens,[2] denizens and the people. The case studies, as well as the ongoing pandemic, demonstrate the profound conflict between democratic rights, livelihoods and survival on the one hand, and capitalist profit-maximisation motives on the other. In India, private sector hospitals, which are incentivised by the PMJAY health insurance programme, either refused to treat Covid-19 patients or made them pay large out-of-pocket bills once admitted. Even so, the figures for respiratory care (indicative of Covid-19 infections) provided through PMJAY in 2020 were lower than those observed in the previous year, even as cases surged, pointing to the structural failure of the PPP model in the face of a crisis.

A feminist review of PPPs from the global South

As we come to the end of this edited volume, we ask ourselves what does a feminist perspective from the global South bring to a critical review of the PPP model? Many of the critical observations made in the book, based on the evidence provided by the case studies, coincide with others made in the past as well as contemporaneous research on the subject. Through this book, we have attempted to make three fundamental contributions from the feminist perspective.

Firstly, the chapters in this book take a systemic view that allows us to understand not only how the PPP model operates in a global economy underwritten by corporate capture of development strategies, but also how it is mounted on a structure of overlapping inequalities that are, in turn, deepened and reproduced by the model. In this sense, an intersectional feminist lens underscores the implications that PPPs have on the ground realities of women, racialised and indigenous groups, peasants, informal workers and local communities.

Secondly, the analysis is rooted in lived experiences. A feminist lens allows us to bring the everyday realities of patients and hospital workers, displaced communities, users with limited access to services and street vendors, among others, to the table. The case studies demonstrate that while PPPs are presented as a technocratic fix that streamline and optimise policy processes, in reality, their implementation has had negative consequences for people. These projects have reduced access to food, water, energy, health services and decent work; disturbed livelihoods; and worsened living conditions. Amidst claims that PPPs are technical agreements incomprehensible to most people, they have affected everyday life in obvious ways.

Thirdly, a transformative vocation is at the core of the Southern feminist approach presented here. Our analysis disputes the narrative that pegs PPPs as the only solution to the state's difficulties in providing social services and guaranteeing rights. We, therefore, propose a series of recommendations aligned with regulating PPPs and holding corporations and governments accountable in order to prevent and repair the abuses and inequalities that they reproduce. This book also urges feminists, especially Southern intersectional feminists, to be vigilant of the constant threat of cooptation and instrumentalisation of our agendas. 'Add gender and stir' is not an acceptable way forward, and we cannot be satisfied by such mainstreaming efforts. They might be welcome, but they are not enough.

In line with what has already been suggested by analysis, activism and advocacy, we emphasise the need to:

1. Continue producing evidence on the true costs and concrete impacts of PPPs and other forms of corporate capture, thereby disputing conventional technocratic narratives and identifying alternatives;
2. Promote regulatory frameworks that consolidate mechanisms for citizen and denizen participation, and call for transparency and monitoring of agreements and contracts, implementation processes and management of PPPs;
3. Demand that autonomous social, gender and environmental impact studies of PPP projects be made mandatory;
4. Demand consolidation of information systems that allow citizen and denizen monitoring, evaluation and control of the impacts (economic, social, gendered and environmental) of development projects;
5. Promote genuine participatory mechanisms that respect and amplify the voices of the various stakeholders involved in the projects in order to ensure democratic decision-making;
6. Guarantee regulatory frameworks for PPPs that protect peoples' interests, especially of the communities and territories directly affected by development interventions; and

Explore alternatives beyond PPPs that may replace them once the contracts expire. A future of public provision is preferred and possible.[3]

Beyond this, it is necessary to question the austerity narrative that sustains the promotion of PPPs, and simultaneously strengthen a counter-narrative that takes into account the need to recover the state and public provision as fundamental elements in development. We say this with full awareness of how states and economic and political elites in the global South have historically functioned as guarantors of sectoral interests and minority privileges, and colluded with corporate interests. We also say this with awareness of the colonial logics that have historically dispossessed indigenous groups in the name of the nation-state.

The transformative potential of a feminist perspective rests precisely on making these exploitative and extractive logics and practices visible. The aim is to build awareness and social resistance as well as take concrete actions to transform institutions. Recognising that the ability to enforce rights rests with the state, feminist activism emphasises the need to recreate a state at the service of people and not corporate interests.

For this to happen, the state must be contested and inhabited. The participation of feminists in public management, and particularly in decision-making positions, is a necessary condition for this perspective to permeate. This presence is necessary at the national and sub-national levels where decisions on PPP projects are made, and in global governance where this paradigm is promoted and reproduced, with political interest disguised as technical knowledge. Simultaneously, social movements (including feminist movements) need to be present in decision-making spaces, holding governments accountable at every level and visibilising issues that are ignored or forgotten.

The potential for transforming the relationship between the public and private sectors involves a central dispute over power and resources. In this, the gender justice agenda intersects with the fiscal and tax justice agenda. The struggle to dismantle the mechanisms that allow tax evasion and permanent one-sided flow of resources from countries in the global South to the North must be strengthened. These outflows are, in large part, responsible for the persistent fiscal constraints faced by countries in the South. Such fiscal hardships, in turn, make room for narratives that promote state and private sector partnerships as the only viable solution. At the same time, it is necessary to address the central problem of countries' indebtedness, its repercussions on loan conditionalities and the pressure it puts on the use of public funds. Furthermore, the reform of the international financial architecture – that plays a central role in promoting PPP agreements – is crucial to dismantling the corporate capture of the global economy and laying the foundations of transformative horizons. Bringing a feminist lens to fiscal policy and global governance is the key to shifting development finance away from corporate capture and deploying it in public interest.

Notes

1 Data on net ODA can be found here: https://data.oecd.org/oda/net-oda.htm.
2 When we use the word 'citizens', we are not referring to the exclusionary logic whereby subjects are bearers of rights only in relation to a nation-state that recognises them as political subjects. Rather, we refer to citizenship from a radical standpoint that recognises the political subjectivities of all subjects as social beings, notwithstanding their migratory status, nationality or place of birth.
3 For concrete examples on the pushback to privatisation and PPPs, especially through remunicipalisation see: https://www.municipalservicesproject. org. On global activism on returning to public provision, see: https:// futureispublic.org/global-manifesto/.

Further reading

Books

Adams, B. and Martens, J. *Fit for Whose Purpose? Private Funding and Corporate Influence in the United Nations.* New York: Global Policy Forum, 2015.

Alarco Tosoni, G. and Salazar, C. *Riesgos Público-Privados: fallas regulatorias en las Asociaciones Público-Privadas y recomendaciones de política para la región desde el caso peruano.* Lima: Latindadd, 2019.

Alexander, N. *Infrastructure Investment and Public Private Partnerships.* Washington DC: Heinrich-Böll-Stiftung, 2016.

Alexander, N. *The Hijacking of Global Financial Governance?* Washington DC: Heinrich-Böll-Stiftung, 2018.

Berhe, M. G. *Laying the Past to Rest: The EPRDF Ethiopian State-Building.* London: Hurst & Company, 2020.

Clark, G. *African Market Women: Seven Life Stories from Ghana.* Bloomington: Indiana University Press, 2010.

Clark, G. *Onions Are My Husband: Survival and Accumulation by West Africa Market Women.* Chicago: University of Chicago Press, 1994.

Eurodad. *History Repeated. The Failures of PPPs.* Brussels: Eurodad, 2018.

Eurodad, FEMNET, G&DN. *Can Public-Private Partnerships Deliver Gender Equality?* Brussels: Eurodad, 2019.

Epstein, G. A. *Financialisation and the World Economy.* Cheltenham, UK: Edward Elgar Publishing, 2006.

EsSalud. *Hacia La Modrnización De La Seguridad Social En El Perú. Libro Blanco 2.* Lima: Social Health Insurance, 2019.

Gadre, A. and Shukla, A. *Dissenting Diagnosis: Voices of Conscience from the Medical Profession.* Gurgaon: Random House, 2016.

Garg, S. 'Government Funded Health Insurance Schemes in India – Are They Able to Provide Services for the Scheduled Tribes Population?', in: *2nd National Conference on Health Technology Assessment.* Chandigarh: School of Public Health, PGI Chandigarh, 2018.

Health Inc. *Towards Equitable Coverage and More Inclusive Social Protection in Health.* Antwerp: ITG Press, 2014.

IEG-WB. World Bank *Group Support to Public-Private Partnerships: Lessons from Experience in Client Countries.* Washington DC: World Bank, 2012.

Lennock, J. *Paying for Health: Poverty and Structural Adjustment in Zimbabwe.* United Kingdom: Oxfam, 1994.

Mawuko-Yevugah, L. *Reinventing Development Aid Reform and Technologies of Governance in Ghana.* Abingdon: Routledge, 2014.

Oqubay, A. *Made in Africa: Industrial Policy in Ethiopia*. Oxford: Oxford University Press, 2015.

People's Working Group on Multistakeholderism. *The Great Takeover: Mapping of Multistakeholderism in Global Governance*. Amsterdam: The Transnational Institute, 2021.

Pessino, C. 'Tratamiento de pasivos contingentes', Presentación en el Seminario.' *Espacio Fiscal y Proyectos de Inversión. El Rol de las APP*. Lima: Banco Interamericano de Desarrollo, 2016.

Political Constitution of Peru. *Eleventh Official Edition*. Lima: Ministry of Justice and Human Rights, 2016.

Rahmato, D. *The Peasant and the State: Studies in Agrarian Change in Ethiopia 1950s–2000s*. Addis Ababa: Addis Ababa University Press, 2008.

Sawaré, A. *L'encadrement Des Partenariats Public-Privé Par La Régulation Et Les Unités De PPP en Afrique: Le Cas De L'Union Économique et Monétaire Ouest Africaine*. Paris: Édilivre, 2019.

Zeleke, E. C. *Ethiopia in Theory: Revolution and Knowledge Production 1964–2016*. Leiden: Brill, 2019.

Chapter in edited books

Britwum, A. O. 'Market Queens and the Blame Game in Ghanaian Tomato Marketing', in *The Food Crisis: Implications for Labor* edited by C. Scherrer and D. Saha 53–71. Munich: Rainer Hampp Verlag, 2013.

Britwum, A. O. and Akorsu, A. D. 'Market Women's Associations in Ghana', in *Women's Activism in Africa* edited by B. Badri and A. Mari Tripp 48–60. London: Zed Books, 2017.

Crawford, G. 'Poverty and the Politics of (De)centralisation in Ghana', in *Decentralisation in Africa: A Pathway Out of Poverty and Conflict?* edited by G. Crawford and C. Hartmann 107–44. Amsterdam: Amsterdam University Press, 2008.

Crawford, G. and Lynch, G. 'Democratization in Africa 1990–2010: An Assessment', in *Democratization in Africa: Challenges and Prospects* 1–36. Abingdon: Routledge, 2012.

Darkwah, A. K. 'Work as Duty and as Joy: Understanding the Role of Work in the Lives of Ghanaian Female Traders of Global Consumer Goods', in *Women's Labor in the Global Economy: Speaking in Multiple Voices* edited by S. Harley 206–20. New Brunswick: Rutgers University Press, 2007.

Darkwah, A. K. 'Making Hay while the Sun Shines: Ghanaian Female Traders and Their Insertion into the Global Economy', in *The Gender of Globalization: Women Navigating Cultural and Economic Marginalities* edited by N. Gunewardena and A. Kingsolver 61–84. Sante Fe: School for Advanced Research Press, 2007.

Hauge, J. and Chang, H. 'The Concept of a Development State', in *The Oxford Handbook of the Ethiopian Economy* edited by F. Cheru, C. Cramer and A. Oqubay 824–41. Oxford: Oxford University Press, 2019.

Manuh, T. 'Women, State and Society under PNDC Rule in Ghana', in *Ghana Under PNDC Rule* edited by Gyimah-Boadi, Emmanuel 176–95. Dakar: CODESRIA, 1993.

Mwatwara, W. and Mujere, J. 'Corruption and the Comrades: Mugabe and the "Fight" against Corruption in Zimbabwe, 1980–2013', in *Mugabeism? History, Politics and Power in Zimbabwe* edited by S. J. Ndlovu-Gatsheni 181–99. New York: Palgrave Macmillan, 2015.

Mukhopadhyay, I. and Sinha, D. 'Painting a Picture of Ill-Health', in *A Quantum Leap in the Wrong Direction?* edited by R. Azad, S. Chakraborty, S. Ramani and D. Sinha 155–79. New Delhi: Orient Black Swan, 2019.

Osei-Kyei, R., Chan, A. P. C. and Dansoh, A. 'Public-Private Partnership in Ghana', in *Global Encyclopaedia of Public Administration* edited by A. Farazmand. Cham: Springer, 2017.

Parsitau, D. S. 'The Impact of Structural Adjustment Programmes (SAPs) on Women's Health in Kenya', in *Governing Systems in Africa* edited by M. Sama and V. Nguyen 191–200. Dakar: CODESRIA, 2008.

Rao, M. 'Health for All and Neoliberal Globalisation: An Indian Rope Trick', in *Socialist Register 2010: Morbid Symptoms* edited by L. Panitch and C. Leys 262–78. London: Merlin Press, 2009.

Tsikata, D. 'Women's Political Organizations, 1951–1987', in *The State, Development and Politics in Ghana* edited by E. Hansen and K. A. Ninsin 73–94. London: CODESRIA, 1989.

Venkat Raman, A. and Björkman, J.W. 'Public-Private Partnerships in India', in *Public-Private Partnerships in Health Care in India: Lessons for Developing Countries* edited by A. Venkat Raman and J. W. Björkmn 53–105. Abingdon-New York: Routledge, 2008.

Journal articles

Aidoo, A. 'Women in the History and Culture of Ghana'. *Research Review* 1, no. 1 (1985): 14–51.

Appiah-Kubi, K. 'State-owned Enterprises and Privatization in Ghana'. *The Journal of Modern African Studies* 39, no. 2 (2001): 197–229. https://www.jstor.org/stable/3557262

Asante, L. A. 'Urban Governance in Ghana: The Participation of Traders in the Redevelopment of Kotokuraba Market in Cape Coast'. *African Geographical Review* DOI: 10.1080/19376812.2020.1726193

Ashine, Y. 'When Theory Misses History'. *African Review of Books* 14, no. 1 (2018): 10–12. https://www.researchgate.net/publication/335570979_vol14_n1_yonas_ashine_when_theory_misses_history/link/5d6e288f92851c853888a0d7/download

Assimeng, M. 'Women in Ghana: Their Integration in Socio-economic Development'. *Research Review* 6, no. 1 (1990): 57–68.

Awortwi, N. 'An Unbreakable Path? A Comparative Study of Decentralization and Local Government Development Trajectories in Ghana and Uganda'. *International Review of Administrative Sciences* 77, no. 2 (2011): 347–77. https://journals.sagepub.com/doi/10.1177/0020852311399844

Awuah, E. 'Mobilizing for Change: A Case Study of Market Trader Activism in Ghana'. *Canadian Journal of African Studies* 31, no. 3 (1997): 401–23. https://www.jstor.org/stable/486193

Balarajan, Y., S. Selvaraj and S. V. Subramanian. 'India: Towards Universal Health Coverage: Health Care and Equity in India'. *The Lancet* 377, no. 9764 (2011): 505–15 DOI: 10.1016/S0140-6736(10)61894-6

Bravo, S. 'Asociaciones Público Privadas En El Sector Salud'. *Revista de Derecho Administrativo-RDA* 13, no. 472 (2013): 123–41. http://revistas.pucp.edu.pe/index.php/derechoadministrativo/article/view/13472

Campagnac, E. and Deffontaines, G. 'Une Analyse Socio-Économique Critique Des PPP'. *Revue D'Économie Industrielle* 140, no. 1 (2012): 45–79. https://journals.openedition.org/rei/5474

Chatterjee, P. 'National Health Protection Scheme Revealed in India'. *The Lancet* 391, no. 10120 (2018): 523–4 DOI: 10.1016/S0140-6736(18)30241-1

Chuman, J. and Okungu, V. 'Viewing the Kenyan Health System through an Equity Lens: Implications for Universal Coverage'. *International Journal of Equity in Health* 10, no. 22 (2011) DOI: https://doi.org/10.1186/1475-9276-10-22

Clark, G. 'Gender Fictions and Gender Tensions Involving "Traditional" Asante Market Women'. *African Studies Quarterly* 11, no. 2–3 (2010): 43–66. https://asq.africa.ufl.edu/clark_spring10/

Clark, G. 'Managing Transitions and Continuities in Ghanaian Trading Contexts'. *African Economic History*, no. 32 (2004): 65–88. https://www.jstor.org/stable/3601618

Crook, R. C. 'Democratic Decentralisation, Clientelism and Local Taxation in Ghana'. *IDS Bulletin* 48, no. 2 (2017): 15–30. https://bulletin.ids.ac.uk/index.php/idsbo/article/view/2857/ONLINE%20ARTICLE

Darkwah, A. K. 'Trading Goes Global: Ghanaian Market Women in an Era of Globalization'. *Asian Women* 15 (2002): 31–50. https://www.nawi.africa/trading-goes-global-ghanaian-market-women-in-an-era-of-globalization/

Dasgupta, R., Nandi, S., Kanungo, K., Nundy, M., Murugan, G. and Neog, R. 'What the Good Doctor Said: A Critical Examination of Design Issues of the RSBY through Provider Perspectives in Chhattisgarh, India'. *Social Change* 43, no. 2 (2013): 227–43 DOI: 10.1177/0049085713493043

Diagne, A. 'Politiques Commerciales, Intégration Régionale et Distribution Des Revenus Au Sénéga'. *Mondes En Dévelopment* 3, no. 135 (2006): 101–29. https://www.cairn.info/revue-mondes-en-developpement-2006-3-page-101.htm

Garg, S., Bebarta, K. K. and Tripathi, N. 'Performance of India's National Publicly Funded Health Insurance Scheme, Pradhan Mantri Jan Arogaya Yojana (PMJAY), in Improving Access and Financial Protection for Hospital Care: Findings from Household Surveys in Chhattisgarh State'. *BMC Public Health* 20, no. 1 (2020): 1–10 DOI: 10.1186/s12889-020-09107-4

Genre, V. 'Les Nouveaux Visages du Financement du Développement en Afrique Subsaharienne: Risques et Opportunités'. *Techniques Financières et Développement* 123, no. 2 (2016): 15–25.

Greer, S. L. 'The Globalization of Health Care: Legal and Ethical Issues'. *Journal of Health Politics, Policy and Law* 39, no. 6: 1289–94 DOI: 10.1215/03616878-2829664

Gupta, I., Chowdhury, S., Trivedi, M. and Prinja, S. 'Do Health Coverage Schemes Ensure Financial Protection from Hospitalization Expenses? Evidence from Eight Districts in India'. *Journal of Social and Economic Development* 19, no. 1 (2017): 18–93 DOI: 10.1007/s40847-017-0040-4

Hall, D., Lobina, E. and Terhorst, P. 'Re-municipalisation in the Early Twenty-First Century: Water in France and Energy in Germany'. *International Review of Applied Economics* 27, no. 2 (2013): 193–214 DOI: 10.1080/02692171.2012.754844

Hendricks, T. D. 'Collaboration and Competition: Market Queens, Trade Unions and Collective Action of Informal Workers in Ghana's Makola Market'. *Interface: A Journal for and about Social Movements* 9, no. 2 (2017): 162–87. http://www.interfacejournal.net/wordpress/wp-content/uploads/2017/12/Interface-9-2-Hendriks.pdf

Khetrapal, S., Acharya, A. and Mills, A. 'Assessment of the Public-Private-Partnerships Model of a National Health Insurance Scheme in India'. *Social Science and Medicine* 243, no. 112634 (2019) DOI: 10.1016/j.socscimed.2019.112634

Kumaranayake, L., Lake, S., Mujinja, P., Hongoro, C. and Mpembeni, R. 'How Do Countries Regulate the Health Sector? Evidence from Tanzania and Zimbabwe'. *Health Policy and Planning* 15, no. 4 (2000): 357–67. https://www.researchgate.net/publication/12205082_How_Do_Countries_Regulate_the_Health_Sector_Evidence_from_Tanzania_and_Zimbabwe

Mackintosh, M., Channon, A., Karan, A., Selvaraj, S., Cavagnero, E. and Zhao, H. 'What Is the Private Sector? Understanding Private Provision in the Health Systems of Low-Income and Middle-Income'. *The Lancet* 288, no. 10044 (2016): 596–605 DOI: 10.1016/S0140-6736(16)00342-1

Malmborg, R., Mann, G., Thomson, R. and Squire, S. B. 'Can Public-Private Collaboration Promote Tuberculosis Case Detection among the Poor and Vulnerable?'. *Bulletin of the World Health Organization* 84, no. 9 (2006): 752–8. https://www.scielosp.org/pdf/bwho/2006.v84n9/752-758

Maurya, D. and Mintrom, M. 'Policy Entrepreneurs as Catalysts of Broad System Change: The Case of Social Health Insurance Adoption in India'. *Journal of Asian Public Policy* 13, no. 1 (2019): 18–34 DOI: 10.1080/17516234.2019.1617955

Maurya, D. and Ramesh, M. 'Program Design, Implementation and Performance: The Case of Social Health Insurance in India'. *Health Economics Policy and Law* 14, no. 4 (2019): 487–508 DOI: 10.1017/S1744133118000257

Mkandawire, T. 'Thinking about Development States in Africa'. *Cambridge Journal of Economics*, 25, no. 3. (2001): 289–314.

Morgan, J. 'Country in Focus: Turning the Tide of Diabetes in Fiji'. *The Lancet Diabetes & Endocrinology* 3, no. 1: 15–16. https://doi.org/10.1016/S2213-8587(14)70240-2

Mugwagwa, J. T., Chinyadza, J. K. and Banda, G. 'Private Sector Participation in Health Care in Zimbabwe: What's the Value-Added?'. *Journal of Healthcare Communications* 2, no. 2 (2017): 1–10. https://healthcare-communications.imedpub.com/private-sector-participation-in-health-carein-zimbabwe-whats-the-valueadded.pdf

Mwabu, G. 'Healthcare Reform in Kenya: A Review of the Process'. *Health Policy* 32, no. 1 (1995): 245–55.

Nandi, S. 'Struggle against Outsourcing of Diagnostic Services in Government Facilities: Strategies and Lessons from a Campaign Led by Jan Swasthya Abhiyan (People's Health Movement) in Chhattisgarh, India'. *Journal of Social and Political Psychology* 6, no. 2 (2018): 677–95 DOI: 10.5964/jspp.v6i2.923

Nandi, S., Dasgupta, R., Garg, S. and Sinha, D. 'Uncovering Coverage: Utilisation of the Universal Health Insurance Scheme, Chhattisgarh by Women in Slums of Raipur'. *Indian Journal of Gender Studies* 23, no. 1 (2016): 43–68 DOI: 10.1177/0971521515612863

Nandi, S., Joshi, D. and Dubey, R. 'Unraveling the Clinical Establishment Act in Chhattisgarh: A Campaign and a Study'. *BMJ Global Health* 1, no. S1 (2016): 40–1. https://gh.bmj.com/content/1/Suppl_1/A40

Nandi, S. and Schneider, H. 'Using an Equity-based Framework for Evaluating Publicly Funded Health Insurance Programmes as an Instrument of UHC in Chhattisgarh State, India'. *Health Research Policy and Systems* 18, no. 50 (2020a): 1–14 DOI: 10.1186/s12961-020-00555-3

Nandi, S. and Schneider, H. 'When State-funded Health Insurance Schemes Fail to Provide Financial Protection: An In-depth Exploration of the Experiences of Patients from Urban Slums of Chhattisgarh, India'. *Global Public Health* 15, no. 2 (2020b): 220–35 DOI: 10.1080/17441692.2019.1651369

Nandi, S., Schneider, H. and Dixit, P. 'Hospital Utilization and Out of Pocket Expenditure in Public and Private Sectors under the Universal Government Health Insurance Scheme in Chhattisgarh State, India: Lessons for Universal Health Coverage'. *PloS One* 12, no. 11 (2017): e187904 DOI: 10.1371/journal.pone.0187904

Nandi, S., Schneider, H. and Garg, S. 'Assessing Geographical Inequity in Availability of Hospital Services under the State-funded Universal Health Insurance Scheme in Chhattisgarh State, India, Using a Composite Vulnerability Index'. *Global Health Action* 11, no. 1 (2018) DOI: 10.1080/16549716.2018.1541220

Negin, J. 'Australia and New Zealand's Contribution to Pacific Island Health Worker Brain Drain'. *Australian and New Zealand Journal of Public Health* 32, no. 6 (2008): 507–11. https://doi.org/10.1111/j.1753-6405.2008.00300.x

Nyazema, N. Z. 'The Zimbabwe Crisis and the Provision of Social Services: Health and Education'. *Journal of Developing Societies* 26, no. 2 (2010): 233–61. https://journals.sagepub.com/doi/abs/10.1177/016979 6X1002600204

Osei-Kyei, R. and Chan, A. P. C. 'Review of Studies on the Critical Success Factors for Public-Private Partnership (PPP) Projects from 1990 to 2013'. *International Journal of Project Management* 33, no. 6 (2015): 1335–46.

Parry, J. 'Pacific Islanders Pay Heavy Price for Abandoning Traditional Diet'. *Bulletin of the World Health Organization* 88, no. 7 (2010): 484.

Patouillard, E., Goodman, C. A., Hanson, K. G. and Mills, A. J. 'Can Working with the Private for-Profit Sector Improve Utilization of Quality Health Services by the Poor? A Systematic Review of the Literature'. *International Journal of Equity in Health* 6, no. 17 (2007). https://equityhealthj. biomedcentral.com/track/pdf/10.1186/1475-9276-6-17

Percival, V., Richards, E., MacLean, T. and Theobald, S. 'Health Systems and Gender in Post-Conflict Contexts: Building Back Better?'. *Conflict and Health* 8, no. 19 (2014). https://conflictandhealth.biomedcentral.com/track/ pdf/10.1186/1752-1505-8-19

Pingeot, L. 'In Whose Interest? The UN's Strategic Rapprochement with Business in the Sustainable Development Agenda'. *Globalizations* 13, no. 2 (2016): 188–202 DOI: 10.1080/14747731.2015.1085211

Prasad, N. P. and Raghavendra, P. 'Healthcare Models in the Era of Medical Neo-liberalism: A Study of Aarogyasri in Andhra Pradesh'. *Economic & Political Weekly* 47, no. 43 (2012): 118–26. https://www.epw.in/ journal/2012/43/special-articles/healthcare-models-era-medical-neo-liberalism.html

Prata, N., Montagu, D. and Jeffreys, E. 'Private Sector, Human Resources and Health Franchising in Africa'. *Bulletin of the World Health Organisation* 83, no. 4 (2005): 274–9. https://www.researchgate.net/ publication/7870343_Private_sector_human_resources_and_health_ franchising_in_Africa

Prinja, S., Chauhan, A. S., Karan, A., Kaur, G. and Kumar, R. 'Impact of Publicly Financed Health Insurance Schemes on Healthcare Utilization and Financial Risk Protection in India: A Systematic Review'. *PloS One* 12, no. 2 (2017): e0170996 DOI: 10.1371/journal.pone.0170996

Prinja, S., Kumar, M. I., Pinto, A., Jan, S. and Kumar, R. 'Equity in Hospital Services Utilisation in India'. *Economic and Political Weekly* 48, no. 12 (2013): 52–8. https://www.epw.in/journal/2013/12/special-articles/equity-hospital-services-utilisation-india.html

Prügl, E. and True, J. 'Equality Means Business? Governing Gender through Transnational Public-Private Partnerships'. *Review of International Political Economy* 21, no. 6 (2014): 1137–69. https://www.tandfonline.com/doi/abs/1 0.1080/09692290.2013.849277

Prusty, R. K., Choithani, C. and Gupta, S. D. 'Predictors of Hysterectomy among Married Women 15–49 Years in India'. *Reproductive Health* 15, no. 3 (5 January 2018) DOI: 10.1186/s12978-017-0445-8

Ranjan, A., Dixit, P., Mukhopadhyay, I. and Thiagarajan, S. 'Effectiveness of Government Strategies for Financial Protection against Costs of Hospitalization Care in India'. *BMC Public Health* 18, no. 501 (2018) DOI: 10.1186/s12889-018-5431-8

Rao, M., Katyal, A., Singh, P. V., Samarth, A., Bergkvist, S., Kancharla, M., Wagstaff, A., Netuveli, G. and Renton, A. 'Changes in Addressing Inequalities in Access to Hospital Care in Andhra Pradesh and Maharashtra States of India: A Difference-in-differences Study Using Repeated Cross-sectional Surveys'. *BMJ Open* 4, no. 6: e004471 DOI: 10.1136/ bmjopen-2013-004471

Ray, S. and Masuki, N. 'Facilitators and Barriers to Effective Primary Health Care in Zimbabwe'. *African Journal of Primary Health Care & Family Medicine* 9, no. 1 (2017). www.scielo.org.za/pdf/phcfm/v9n1/67.pdf

Robertson, C. 'The Death of Makola and Other Tragedies'. *Canadian Journal of African Studies* 17, no. 3 (1983): 469–95. https://www.tandfonline.com/doi/ abs/10.1080/00083968.1983.10804032

Salari, P., Di Giorgio, L., Illinca, S. and Chuma, J. 'The Catastrophic and Impoverishing Effects of Out-Of-Pocket Healthcare Payments in Kenya'. *BMJ Global Health* 4, no. 6. (2019): 1–13. https://gh.bmj.com/content/ bmjgh/4/6/e001809.full.pdf

Sen, K. and Gupta, S. 'Masking Poverty and Entitlement: RSBY in Selected Districts of West Bengal'. *Social Change* 47, no. 3: 339–58 DOI: 10.1177/0049085717715557

Sengupta, M., Mukhopadhyaya, I., Weerasinghe, M. C. and Karki, A. 'The Rise of Private Medicine in South Asia'. *BMJ* 2017; 357: j1482 DOI: https://doi. org/10.1136/bmj.j1482 (Published 11 April 2017).

Spire, A. and Choplin, A. 'Street Vendors Facing Urban Beautification in Accra (Ghana): Eviction, Relocation and Formalization'. *Articulo: Journal of Urban Research*, no. 17–18 (2018). http://journals.openedition.org/articulo/3443

Thakur, H. 'Study of Awareness, Enrollment, and Utilization of Rashtriya Swasthya Bima Yojana (National Health Insurance Scheme) in Maharashtra, India'. *Frontiers in Public Health* January (2015): 282 DOI: 10.3389/ fpubh.2015.00282

Virk, A. K. and Atun, R. 'Towards Universal Health Coverage in India: A Historical Examination of the Genesis of Rashtriya Swasthya Bima Yojana – The Health Insurance Scheme for Low-income Groups'. *Public Health* 129, no. 6 (2015): 810–17 DOI: 10.1016/j.puhe.2015.02.002

Whyle, E. B. and Olivier, J. 'Models of Public-Private Engagement for Health Services Delivery and Financing in Southern Africa: A Systematic Review'. *Health Policy and Planning* 31, no. 10 (2016): 1515–29. https://academic.oup.com/heapol/article/31/10/1515/2567069

Yengoh, G. T. and Armah, F. A. 'Effects of Large-Scale Acquisition on Food Insecurity in Sierra Leone'. *Sustainability* 7, no. 7 (2015): 9505–39. https://doi.org/10.3390/su7079505

Laws

1. Law No. 26790. 'Law of Modernization of the Social Security in Health'. *Official Gazette El Peruano*, 1997: 15 May.
2. Law No. 26842. 'General Health Law'. *Official Gazette El Peruano*, 1977: 15 July.
3. Law No. 27056. 'Law for the Creation of the Social Health Insurance (ESSALUD)'. *Official Gazette El Peruanao*, 1999: 29 January.
4. Law No. 28424. 'Temporary Tax on Net Assets'. *Official Gazette El Peruano*, 2004: 21 December.
5. Law No. 29344. 'Framework Law for Universal Health Insurance'. *Official Gazette El Peruano*, 2009: 9 April.

Legislative and supreme decrees

1. Legislative Decree No. 1012. 'Framework Law on Public-Private Partnerships for the Generation of Productive Employment and Establishes Regulations for Expediting the Process of Promoting Private Investment'. *Official Gazette El Peruano*, 2008: 13 May.
2. Legislative Decree No. 1224. 'Framework for the Promotion of Private Investment through Public-Private Partnerships and Projects in Assets'. *Official Gazette El Peruano*, 2015: 25 September.
3. Legislative Decree No. 1362. 'Regulates the Promotion of Private Investment through Public-Private Partnerships and Projects in Assets'. *Official Gazette El Peruano*. 2018: 21 July.
4. Supreme Decree No. 025-2007-TR. 'It Establishes Provisions Related to Social Security in Health and Social Health Insurance'. *Official Gazette El Peruano*, 2007: 20 December.
5. Supreme Decree No. 146-2008-EF. 'Regulations of the D.L. 1012 That Approves the PPP Framework Law'. *Official Gazette El Peruano*, 2008: 8 December.
6. Supreme Decree No. 144-2009-EF. 'They Modify Art.9 of the D.S. No. 146-2008-EF (Regulations of DL 1012)'. *Official Gazette El Peruano*, 2009: 24 June.

7. Supreme Decree No. 410-2015-EF. 'They Approve Regulations of the Legislative Decree No. 1224 Framework Law for the Promotion of Private Investment through Public-Private Partnerships and Projects in Assets'. *Official Gazette El Peruano*, 2018: 30 October.

PhD thesis

Garg, S. 'A Study of "Strategic Purchasing" as a Policy Option for Public Health System in India', PhD. Thesis. Mumbai: Tata Institute of Social Sciences, 2019. https://shodhganga.inflibnet.ac.in/handle/10603/259965

Graham, Y. 'Law, State and the Internationalization of Agricultural Capital in Ghana: A Comparison of Colonial Export Production and Post-colonial Production for the Home Market', PhD. Thesis. Coventry: University of Warwick, 1993. http://wrap.warwick.ac.uk/2310/1/WRAP_THESIS_Graham_1993.pdf

Nandi, S. 'Equity, Access and Utilisation in the State-funded Universal Insurance Scheme (RSBY/MSBY) in Chhattisgarh State, India: What Are the Implications for Universal Health Coverage?', PhD. Thesis. Cape Town: School of Public Health, University of the Western Cape, 2019. http://etd.uwc.ac.za/xmlui/handle/11394/7393

Video

Ayah, R. and Ndii, D. 'An Insider's Take on Kenya's Public Health System'. Accessed 18 February 2020. https://www.youtube.com/watch?v=BZK3IU0kyqs

Website content

Abiye, Y. 'Saudi Energy Firm Awarded First Solar Project under PPP'. *The Reporter Ethiopia*. Accessed 20 February 2020. https://www.thereporterethiopia.com/article/saudi-energy-firm-awarded-first-solar-project-under-ppp

ActionAid. 'Broken Promises: The Impacts of Addax Bioenergy in Sierra Leone on Hunger and Livelihoods'. Accessed 16 February 2020. https://actionaid.org/sites/default/files/broken_promises_final.pdf

ActionAid. 'Who Cares for the Future: Finance Gender Responsive Public Services! Full Report'. Accessed 18 February 2020. https://actionaid.org/sites/default/files/publications/final%20who%20cares%20report.pdf

ADB. 'ADB Helps PNG Expand Port Moresby International Airport Using PPP'. Accessed 26 May 2020. https://www.adb.org/news/adb-helps-png-expand-port-moresby-international-airport-using-ppp

ADB. 'Public Private Partnerships. Pacific Private Sector Policy Brief'. Accessed 26 May 2020. https://www.adb.org/publications/public-private-partnerships

AfDB. 'Executive Summary of the Environmental and Social and Health Impact Assessment'. Accessed 16 February 2020. https://www.afdb.org/fileadmin/uploads/afdb/Documents/Environmental-and-Social-Assessments/Addax%20Bioenergy%20-%20ESHIA%20summary%20-%20Final%20EN.pdf

AfDB. 'Infrastructure and Growth in Sierra Leone'. Accessed 16 February 2020. https://www.afdb.org/fileadmin/uploads/afdb/Documents/Project-and-Operations/Infrastructure%20and%20Growth%20in%20Sierra%20Leone.pdf

AfDB. 'Level 1: Development in Sierra Leone'. Accessed 16 February 2020. https://www.afdb.org/fileadmin/uploads/afdb/Documents/Development_Effectiveness_Review_In_Sierra_Leone/CDER_Sierra_Leone__En__Level_1.pdf

AfDB. 'Sierra Leone: Country Strategy Paper 2013–2017'. Accessed 16 February 2020. https://www.afdb.org/sites/default/files/documents/projects-and-operations/2013-2017_-_sierra_leone_country_strategy_paper_01.pdf

AfDB. 'The African Infrastructure Development Index 2018'. Accessed 16 February 2020. https://www.afdb.org/fileadmin/uploads/afdb/Documents/Publications/Economic_Brief_-_The_Africa_Infrastructure_Development_Index.pdf

Africa Check. 'As Help from Cuba Arrives, Is There Only One Kenyan Doctor for Every 16,000 People?' Accessed 18 February 2020. https://africacheck.org/reports/as-help-from-cuba-arrives-is-there-only-one-kenyan-doctor-for-every-16000-people

AFDZEE. 'Anexo 4.1 Análisis de mercado y demanda potencial, ZEE de Coatzacoalcos'. 2018.

AFDZEE. 'Dictamen de la Zona Económica Especial de Coatzacoalcos'. 2018.

AFDZEE. 'Dictamen de la Zona Económica Especial de Salina Cruz'. 2018.

AFDZEE. 'Presentación del Programa para el Desarrollo del Istmo de Tehuantepec'. Accessed 1 May 2020. https://www.gob.mx/zee/es/articulos/presentacion-del-programa-para-el-desarrollo-del-istmo-de-tehuantepec?idiom=es

Agencia de Noticias. 'Pueblos de Oaxaca Exigen Frenar Obra De Remodelación del Ferrocarril'. *Istmo Press*. Accessed 1 May 2020. http://www.istmopress.com.mx/istmo/pueblos-de-oaxaca-exigen-frenar-obra-de-remodelacion-del-ferrocarril

Alarco Tosoni, G. '¿Negocio Público Privado? Ventajas y Desventajas de Las Asociaciones Públicas Privadas (APP) en América Latina'. Accessed 21 September 2020. http://www.latindadd.org/wp-content/uploads/2018/08/

NEGOCIO-PUBLICO-PRIVADO-VENTAJAS-Y-DESVENTAJAS-DE-LAS-
APP-EN-AMERICA-LATINA.pdf

Alarco Tosoni, G. 'Corrupción, neoliberalismo y asociaciones público privadas',
Otra Mirada. Accessed 21 September 2020. http://www.otramirada.pe/
corrupci%C3%B3n-neoliberalismo-y-asociaciones-p%C3%BAblico-
privadas

Ali, A. A. 'Full English Transcript of Ethiopian Prime Minister Abiy Ahmed
Ali's Inaugural Address'. Accessed 18 February 2020. https://www.opride.
com/2018/04/03/englishpartial-transcript-of-ethiopian-prime-ministerabiy-
ahmeds-inaugural-address

ANSD (Agence Nationale de la Statisque et de la Démographie). 'Deuxiè
Enquête De Suivi De La Pauvreté au Sénégal'.

ANSD (Agence Nationale de la Statisque et de la Démographie). 'Enquête
Nationale Sur L'Emploi Au Sénégal Deuxième Trimestre'.

ANSD (Agence Nationale de la Statisque et de la Démographie). 'Enquête
Sénégalaise Auprè Des Ménages'.

ANSD (Agence Nationale de la Statisque et de la Démographie). 'Rapport
Global Du Recensement Général Des Entreprises'.

ANSD (Agence nationale de la statistique et de la démographie). 'Violeces
basées sur le genre et pouvoir d'action des femmes'. Publication réalisée dans
ce cadre du partenariat entre ONU FEMMES et l'ANSD pour la mise en
oeuvre due Projet (Publication produced in partnership with UN Women
and ANSD as part of the project 'Support on Gender Statistics'). Accessed
15 February 2020. https://www.ansd.sn/ressources/publications/Rapport-
VBG_ANSD-2019.pdf

Approdev. 'Policy Brief: The Role of European Development Finance Institution
in Land Grabs, May 2013'. Accessed 16 February 2020. https://actalliance.
eu/wp-content/uploads/2016/04/aprodev_policy_brief_dfi_and_landgrabs_
final_may2013.pdf

Arifin, B. and Hudoyo, A. 'An Economic Analysis of Shifting Cultivation and
Bush-Fallow in Lower Sumatra: Southeast Asia Policy Research Working
Paper No. 1'. Accessed 16 February 2020. http://old.worldagroforestry.org/
sea/Publications/files/workingpaper/WP0019-04.pdf

Aryeetey, E. and Baah-Boateng, W. 'Understanding Ghana's Growth Success
Story and Job Creation Challenges: UNU-WIDER Working Paper 2015/140'.
Accessed 8 October 2018. www.wider.unu.edu/publication/understandinggh
ana%E2%80%99sgrowthsuccessstory-and-job-creation-challenges

Ashurt LLP. 'Ashurst Advises the Fiji National Provident Fund on Its
Acquisition of 20% of the Total Issued Ordinary Shares in Energy Fiji Ltd'.
Accessed 26 May 2020. https://www.ashurst.com/en/news-and-insights/
news-deals-and-awards/ashurst-advises-the-fnpf-on-acquisition-of-20-per-
cent-of-shares-in-energy-fiji

Aspen Medical. 'Aspen Medical Signs Contract to Manage Two Hospitals
over the Next Two Decades as Part of Fiji's Public-Private Partnership'.

Accessed 26 May 2020. https://www.aspenmedical.com/news/news/aspen-medical-signs-contract-manage-two-hospitals-over-next-two-decades-part-fiji%E2%80%99s-public

Aspen Medical. 'Over a Decade Providing Healthcare Support to AFP and ADF Personnel in Solomon Islands'. Accessed 26 May 2020. https://www.aspenmedical.com/content/over-decade-providing-healthcare-support-afp-and-adf-personnel-solomon-islands

Astatike, D. 'Public-Private Partnership in Store for Addis Rail Line'. *Capital Ethiopia*. Accessed 20 February 2020. https://www.capitalethiopia.com/featured/public-private-partnership-in-store-for-addis-rail-line

Awo, M. A. 'Marketing and Market Queens: A Case of Tomato Farmers in the Upper East Region of Ghana'. Accessed 20 January 2020. https://bonndoc.ulb.uni-bonn.de/xmlui/bitstream/handle/20.500.11811/4261/2335.pdf?sequence=1&isAllowed=y

Awoko Newspaper. 'Sierra Leone News: Land Rights Policy Contributes to Poverty Reduction'. Accessed 16 February 2020. https://awokonewspaper.sl/sierra-leone-news-land-rights-policy-contributes-to-poverty-reduction/

Baca, E. 'Las asociaciones público-privadas en el Perú: ¿Beneficio público o negocio privado?'. Accessed 21 September 2020. http://propuestaciudadana.org.pe/wp-content/uploads/2017/09/Estudio-APP.pdf

Bank of Ghana. 'Ghana's Privatization Programme: Lessons and Way Forward: BoG Policy Briefing Paper'. Accessed 20 January 2020. https://www.bog.gov.gh/wp-content/uploads/2019/07/privatization-policy-brief.pdf

Barigaba, J. 'Civil Society Seeks Reforms to Tem Trade Suits Losess'. Accessed 18 February 2020. https://www.theeastafrican.co.ke/news/ea/Civil-society-seeks-reforms-to-stem-trade-suits-losses/4552908-5376918-p4x360z/index.html

BBC News. 'Zimbabwe Crisis: Army Takes Over, Says Mugabe Is Safe'. Accessed 11 February 2020. https://www.bbc.com/news/world-africa–41992351

Bebbington, A., Schurra, M. and Bielich, C. 'Mapeo de Movimientos Sociales en el Perú Actual'. Accessed 21 September 2020. https://hummedia.manchester.ac.uk/schools/seed/socialmovements/publications/reports/Bebbingtonetal_InformeMapeodeMovimientosSocialesPeru.pdf

Benavente, P., Escaffi, J., Távara, J. and Segura, J. 'Las Alianzas Público-Privadas (APP) en el Perú: beneficios y riesgos'. Accessed 21 September 2020. https://departamento.pucp.edu.pe/economia/libro/las-alianzas-publico-privadas-app-en-el-peru-beneficios-y-riesgos

Boyle, M. 'Brain Drain in the Health Sector Curbed Says Dr. Waqainabete'. Accessed 26 May 2020. https://www.fbcnews.com.fj/news/health/brain-drain-in-the-health-sector-curbed-says-dr-waqainabete

Bread for the World. 'The Weakest Should Not Bear the Risk'. Accessed 16 February 2020. https://www.brot-fuer-die-welt.de/fileadmin/mediapool/2_Downloads/Fachinformationen/Analyse/Analyse_64_en-The_Weakest_Should_not_Bear_the_Risk.pdf

Brookings Institute. 'What Happens to Health Financing during the Middle-Income Transition?'. Accessed 18 February 2020. https://www.brookings.edu/blog/future-development/2019/12/16/what-happens-to-health-financing-during-the-middle-income-transition

Brooks, B. 'Exclusive: Philips, under Investigation in U.S. and Brazil, Fired Whistleblower Who Warned of Graft'. *Reuters*. Accessed 18 February 2020. https://www.reuters.com/article/us-brazil-corruption-healthcare-exclusiv/exclusive-philips-under-investigation-in-u-s-and-brazil-fired-whistleblower-who-warned-of-graft-idUSKCN1VB0BJ

Bundu, M. J. 'Addax Bio-energy under Fire in Sierra Leone'. Accessed 16 February 2020. https://www.politicosl.com/node/1319

Burke, J. 'Ethiopia: These Changes Are Unprecedented: How Abiy Is Upending Ethiopia Politics'. *The Guardian*. Accessed 20 February 2020. https://www.theguardian.com/world/2018/jul/08/abiy-ahmed-upending-ethiopian-politics

Business Wire. 'Addax Bioenergy Signs Loan Agreement for €258 Million Renewable Energy Project in Sierra Leone'. Accessed 16 February 2020. https://www.businesswire.com/news/home/20110617005346/en/Addax-Bioenergy-Signs-Loan-Agreement-%E2%82%AC258-Million

Callao Salud SAC. 'Quiénes somos: Memoria Corporativa 2016. Complejo Hospitalario Alberto Barton'. Accessed 21 September 2020. https://callaosalud.com.pe/presentacion/quienes-somos

CEFP. 'Las Asociaciones Público Privadas como Alternativa de Financiamiento para las Entidades Federativas'. Accessed 1 May 2020. https://www.cefp.gob.mx/publicaciones/documento/2016/junio/eecefp0032016.pdf

CEFP. 'Proyectos para Prestación de Servicios (PPS)'. Accessed 1 May 2020. https://www.cefp.gob.mx/intr/edocumentos/pdf/cefp/cefp0192007.pdf

CEMDA. 'Admiten amparo contra ampliación del puerto de Veracruz por violar derecho al medio ambiente sano'. Accessed 1 May 2020. https://www.cemda.org.mx/admiten-amparo-contra-ampliacion-del-puerto-de-veracruz-por-violar-derecho-al-medio-ambiente-sano

CESOP. 'El proyecto del tren transístmico'. Accessed 1 May 2020. http://www5.diputados.gob.mx/index.php/camara/Centros-de-Estudio/CESOP/Estudios-e-Investigaciones/Carpetas-Informativas/Carpeta-informativa-No.-119.-El-proyecto-del-tren-transistmico

CGTP. 'GCTP Perú'. *Facebook*. Accessed 21 September 2020. https://es-la.facebook.com/notes/cgtp-per%C3%BA/-plataforma-de-lucha-del-paro-nacional-9-de-julio-cgtp/1726275177599760/?__tn__=H-R

Chamber of Deputies of the Honourable Congress of the Union. 'Ley de Asociaciones Público Privadas'. *Diario Oficial de la Federación* [Official Journal of the Federation]. Accessed 1 May 2020. http://www.diputados.gob.mx/LeyesBiblio/pdf/LAPP_150618.pdf

Christian Aid. 'Who Is Benefitting?'. Accessed 16 February 2020. https://www.christianaid.org.uk/sites/default/files/2017-08/who-is-benefitting-sierra-leone-report-july-2013.pdf

Conteh, S. and Thompson, E. 'Toward a Customary Land Bill in Sierra Leone: A Review of Law and Policy'. Namati, Freetown: Sierra Leone.

Cordiant. 'Development Finance Institutions Announce Financial Close of Pioneering Addax Bioenergy Project in Sierra Leone'. Accessed 16 February 2020. http://intranet.cordiantcap.com/press_release/development-finance-institutions-announce-financial-close-of-pioneering-addax-bioenergy-project-in-sierra-leone

The Council of Governors. 'Senate Proceedings on the Medical Equipment'. Accessed 18 February 2020. https://cog.go.ke/component/k2/item/184-senate-proceedings-on-the-medical-equipment

CNDH. 'Sobre el caso de violaciones a los derechos humanos atribuibles a elementos de los cuerpos de guardias y vigilantes auxiliares de la entonces Comisión Estatal de Seguridad Ciudadana del Estado de México; y del acceso a la justicia en su modalidad de procuración'. Accessed 1 May 2020. https://www.cndh.org.mx/sites/default/files/documentos/2019-11/REC_2019_98.pdf

CNDH. 'CNDH Requests the Federal and State Authorities of Oaxaca and Veracruz to Grant Precautionary Measures before the Consultation on the Project Interoceanic corredor Istmo de Tehuantepec'. Accessed 1 May 2020. https://www.cndh.org.mx/documento/solicita-cndh-autoridades-federales-y-estatales-de-oaxaca-y-veracruz-otorgar-medidas

CONABIO. 'Áreas de Importancia para la Conservación de las Aves (AICA)'. Accessed 1 May 2020. http://avesmx.conabio.gob.mx/AICA.html

CONABIO. 'Estrategia para la Conservación y el Uso Sustentable de la Biodiversidad del estado de Oaxaca'. Accessed 1 May 2020. https://bioteca.biodiversidad.gob.mx/janium/Documentos/15091.pdf

CONABIO. 'Estrategia para la Conservación y el Uso Sustentable de la Biodiversidad del estado de Veracruz'. Accessed 1 May 2020. http://repositorio.veracruz.gob.mx/medioambiente/wp-content/uploads/sites/9/2018/02/ECUSBE-VER-Estrategia-de-Conserv-y-Uso-Sust-de-la-Biodiversidad.pdf

CONEVAL. 'Pobrezaestatal 2018'. Accessed 1 May 2020. https://www.coneval.org.mx/coordinacion/entidades/Paginas/inicioent.aspx

COPASA. 'México confía a Copasa las obras del puerto de Veracruz'. Accessed 1 May 2020. http://www.copasagroup.com/es/colocacion-de-la-primera-piedra-en-edar-orense/

COPASA. 'Programa de Emisión de Pagarés COPASA 2019'. Accessed 1 May 2020. https://www.bmerf.es/docs/docsSubidos/MARF/DIPagar%C3%A9sMARF/DBII_con_Anexos_-_MARF__versi%C3%B3n_web__compressed__1_.pdf

Cordella, T. 'Optimizing Finance for Development'. *World Bank Group*. Accessed 18 February 2020. http://documents1.worldbank.org/curated/en/859191517234026362/pdf/WPS8320.pdf

Corredor Interoceánico del Istmo de Tehuantepec. 'Estatuto Orgánico del Corredor Interoceánico del Istmo de Tehuantepec'. Accessed 1 May 2020. https://www.gob.mx/ciit/documentos/estatuto-organico-del-corredor-interoceanico-del-istmo-de-tehuantepec?idiom=es

Daily News. 'Gvt Suspends Hospitals' Private Partnerships'. Accessed 11 February 2020. https://dailynews.co.zw/articles-2018-01-29-gvt-suspends-hospitals-private-partnerships

DAWN. 'Public-Private Partnerships and Gender Justice in the Context of the 3rd UN Conference of Financing for Development'. Accessed 1 February 2021. https://dawnnet.org/wp-content/uploads/2015/03/Ffd3_Public-Private-Partnerships-and-Gender-Justice.pdf

Deo, R. 'Fiji "Missed Opportunity" to Promote Gender Equality in Budget', interviewed by S. Rench for *Public Finance Focus*. 3 July 2018. Accessed 26 May 2020. https://www.publicfinancefocus.org/news/2018/07/fiji-missed-opportunity-promote-gender-equality-budget1

Department of Information. 'COVID-19: Labasa Hospital to Be an Isolation Facility'. *Fiji Sun*. Accessed 26 May 2020. https://fijisun.com.fj/2020/04/05/covid-19-labasa-hospital-to-be-an-isolation-facility

DfID. 'Annual Review-Summary-Sheet'. Accessed 16 February 2020. https://devtracker.dfid.gov.uk/projects/GB-1-203819/documents

DfID. 'Annual Review-Summary-Sheet'. Accessed 16 February 2020. https://devtracker.dfid.gov.uk/projects/GB-1-203819/documents

DfID. 'Business Case and Intervention Summary'. Accessed 16 February 2020. https://devtracker.dfid.gov.uk/projects/GB-1-203819/documents

Dong, D., Naib, P., Smith, O. and Chhabra, S. 'Raising the Bar: Analysis of PM-JAY High-Value Claims, PM-JAY Policy Brief 1'. Accessed 18 February 2020. https://www.pmjay.gov.in/sites/default/files/2019-10/Policy%20Brief_Raising%20the%20Bar_High%20Value%20Claims_10-10-19_WB.pdf

The East African. 'Kenyan Doctors, Govt Agree to End Strike'. Accessed 18 February 2020. https://www.theeastafrican.co.ke/news/Kenyan-doctors-end-strike/2558-3849516-view-printVersion-rf46rez/index.html

Eiffage. 'L'Observatoire. Accessed 15 February 2020. https://www.autoroutedelavenir.sn/fr/lobservatoire

El Comercio. 'Essalud Nobra a Generentes Investigados Por Corrupción'. June 2018. Accessed 21 September 2020. https://elcomercio.pe/lima/sucesos/essalud-nombra-gerentes-investigados-corrupcion-noticia-529013-noticia

El Universal. 'En Oaxaca se produce el 62% de la energía eólica generada en el país'. Accessed 1 May 2020. https://oaxaca.eluniversal.com.mx/estatal/06-01-2020/en-oaxaca-se-produce-el-62-de-la-energia-eolica-generada-en-el-pais

El Universal. 'Oaxaca, entre los 10 estados con más feminicidios durante enero de 2020'. Accessed 1 May 2020. https://oaxaca.eluniversal.com.mx/seguridad/04-03-2020/oaxaca-entre-los-10-estados-con-mas-feminicidios-durante-enero-de-2020

The Equality Trust. 'Finance Development Not Dividends. Challenging the Rise of PPPs'. Accessed 1 February 2021. https://equalitytrust.org.uk/sites/default/files/finance-development-not-dividends-2019-03-v4.pdf

ESCR-NET. 'Captura Corporativa Definición y Características'. Accessed 1 May 2020. https://www.escr-net.org/es/derechoshumanosyempresas/capturacorporativa/caracteristicas

EsSalud. 'Addendum No. 01. Asociación Público Privada Nuevo Hospital III Alberto Barton – Callao'. Accessed 21 September 2020. http://www.essalud.gob.pe/asociacion-publico-privada-contratos-vigentes

EsSalud. 'Addendum No. 2. Asociación Público Privada Nuevo Hospital III Alberto Barton – Callao'. Accessed 21 September 2020. http://www.essalud.gob.pe/asociacion-publico-privada-contratos-vigentes

EsSalud. 'Annexes. Asociación Público Privada Nuevo Hospital III Alberto Barton – Callao'. Accessed 21 September 2020. http://www.essalud.gob.pe/asociacion-publico-privada-contratos-vigentes

EsSalud. 'Annual Report 2018'. Accessed 21 September 2020. http://www.essalud.gob.pe/memoria-institucional

EsSalud. 'Contracts in Force'. Accessed 21 September 2020. http://www.essalud.gob.pe/asociacion-publico-privada-contratos-vigentes

EsSalud. 'EsSalud presenta Plan Maestro 2013–2021'. Accessed 21 September 2020. http://www.essalud.gob.pe/essalud-presenta-plan-maestro-2013-2021

EsSalud. 'Ficha Ténica Del Proyecto Construcción Del Nuevo Hospital III Callao'. Accessed 21 September 2020. http://www.essalud.gob.pe/transparencia/pdf/publicacion/ficha_contrato_hospt_callao.pdf

EsSalud. 'Hospital Alberto Leonardo Barton Thompson: Publicación de indicadores contractuales July–September 2017'. Accessed 21 September 2020. http://www.essalud.gob.pe/transparencia/pdf/publicacion/HOSPITAL_ALBERTO_LEONARDO_BARTON_THOMPSON.pdf

Ethiopian Energy & Power Business Portal. 'Denmark and Ethiopia Expand Cooperation on Wind Energy'. Accessed 20 February 2020. https://www.ethioenergybuz.com/en/?option=com_content&view=article&id=239&catid=26

Ethiopian Energy & Power Business Portal. 'Ethiopian Council of Ministers Approved the Power Purchase Agreement with CORBETTI Geothermal'. Accessed 20 February 2020. https://ethioenergybuz.com/en/renewables/geothermal/596-ethiopian-council-of-ministers-approved-the-power-purchase-agreement-with-corbetti-geothermal.html

Ethiopian Energy & Power Business Portal. 'Ethiopian Ministry of Finance Approves Five Wind Farm Projects for PPP Investment'. Accessed 20 February 2020. https://ethioenergybuz.com/en/renewables/wind/546-ethiopian-ministry-of-finance-approves-five-wind-farm-projects-for-ppp-investment.html

Ethiopian News Agency. 'Gov't Speeding Up Procurement of 17 PPP Projects'. Accessed 20 February 2020. http://www.ena.et/en/?p=8306

Eurodad. 'History RePPPeated. How Public-Private Partnerships Are Failing'. Accessed 26 May 2020. https://eurodad.org/files/pdf/1546956-history-repppeated-how-public-private-partnerships-are-failing-.pdf

FAO. 'National Gender Profile of Agriculture and Rural Livelihoods: Sierra Leone'. Accessed 16 February 2020. http://www.fao.org/3/I9554EN/i9554en.pdf

FAO. 'Securing Land Tenure Rights for Farmers in Sierra Leone'. Accessed 16 February 2020. http://www.fao.org/in-action/securing-land-tenure-rights-sierra-leone/en

Faye, O. A. 'Baisse des Tarifs De L'Autoroute à Péage'. Accessed 15 February 2020. http://reussirbusiness.com/actualites/baisse-des-tarifs-de-lautoroute-a-peage

FED-CUT. 'Contratos APP Son Lesivos Para Essalud y el País. Informativo 06 CDN FED CUT'. Accessed 21 September 2020. https://issuu.com/fedcut/docs/informativo_cut_06_2015

Fezoua, F. 'Opinion: What to Consider when Pursuing a Public-Private Partnership'. Accessed 18 February 2020. https://www.gehealthcare.com/article/opinion-what-to-consider-when-pursuing-a-public-private-partnership

Fick, M. 'Leaders Cheered as Kenya Binged on Medical Equipment. Did Patients Get Help?'. *Reuters*. Accessed 18 February 2020. https://af.reuters.com/article/idAFKBN2080RV-OZATP\

Fiji Government Media Centre. 'Fiji Bureau of Statistics Release 2017 Census Results'. Accessed 26 May 2020. https://www.fiji.gov.fj/Media-Centre/News/Fiji-Bureau-of-Statistics-Releases-2017-Census-Res

Fiji Ministry of Economy. 'Public Private Partnership 2019'. Accessed 26 May 2020. https://www.fijichamber.com/uploads/content/42631983307521566777429_Public_Private_Partnership_Policy.pdf

Fiji Women's Rights Movement. 'National Budget 2019–2020 Analysis'. Accessed 26 May 2020. http://www.fwrm.org.fj/images/national_budget_analysis.pdf

Fikade, B. 'Interview: Economic Pragmatist'. *The Reporter Ethiopia*. Accessed 20 February 2020. https://www.thereporterethiopia.com/article/economic-pragmatist

Fikade, B. 'Major Power, Highway Projects Valued at USD 6.5 bln Approved for PPP'. *The Reporter Ethiopia*. Accessed 20 February 2020. https://www.thereporterethiopia.com/article/major-power-highway-projects-valued-usd-65-bln-approved-ppp

Fikade, B. 'PPP Approves Six Solar Projects Worth USD 800 Mil'. *The Reporter Ethiopia*. Accessed 20 February 2020. https://www.thereporterethiopia.com/article/ppp-approves-six-solar-projects-worthusd-800-mil

FIT. 'Contrato FIT GARMOP-CHM-N-09-AD-20'. Accessed 1 May 2020. https://compranet.hacienda.gob.mx/esop/guest/go/opportunity/detail?opportunityId=1786749

FIT. 'Fallo FIT-GARMOP-OP-Z-2019-LP'. Accessed 1 May 2020. https://sites.google.com/site/cnetuc/contrataciones

FIT. 'Fallo FIT-GARMOP-S-Z-18-2019-LP'. Accessed 1 May 2020. https://compranet.hacienda.gob.mx/esop/guest/go/opportunity/detail?opportunityId=1772031

Forest Survey of India. 'India State of Forest Report, 2017'. Accessed 18 February 2020. https://fsi.nic.in/isfr2017/chattisgarh-isfr-2017.pdf

Forum for Social Studies. 'Public Dialogue on Privatization'. Accessed 20 February 2020. https://www.fssethiopia.org/index.php/2019/09/23/public-dialogue-on-privatization

Gaceta Parlamentaria (Parliamentary Gazette) number 4372-VIII. 'Iniciativa del ejecutivo federal, con proyecto de decreto por el cual se expide la Ley Federal de Zonas Económicas Especiales y se adicionan el artículo 9 de la Ley General de BIenes Nacionales'. Accessed 1 May 2020. http://gaceta.diputados.gob.mx/PDF/63/2015/sep/20150929-VIII.pdf

Garg, S. and Pande, S. 'Learning to Sustain Change :Mitanin Community Health Workers Promote Public Accountability in India'. Accessed 18 February 2020. https://accountabilityresearch.org/publication/learning-to-sustain-change-mitanin-community-health-workers-promote-public-accountability-in-india/

Ghana Statistical Service. '2015 Labour Force Survey'. Accra: Ghana Statistical Service.

GIZ. 'Diagnostic Study of the TVET Sector in Sierra Leone'. Accessed 16 February 2020. https://www.giz.de/en/downloads/giz2018-de-Diagnostic%20Study%20of%20the%20TVET%20Sector%20in%20Sierra%20Leone.pdf

GIZ. 'Health Insurance for India's Poor: Meeting the Challenge with Information Technology'. Accessed 18 February 2020. https://health.bmz.de/ghpc/case-studies/Health_Insurance_India_New/Health_insurance_for_India_s_poor_-_Long_version.pdf

GoSL. 'An Agenda for Change: Second Poverty Strategy Reduction (PRSP 11) 2008–2012'. Accessed 16 February 2020. https://unipsil.unmissions.org/sites/default/files/agenda_for_change_0.pdf

GoSL. 'Final National Land Policy of Sierra Leone'. Accessed 16 February 2020. http://extwprlegs1.fao.org/docs/pdf/sie155203.pdf

GoSL. 'Legal Framework'. Accessed 16 February 2020. https://ppp.gov.sl/legal-framework

GoSL. 'Sierra Leone Vision 2025: Sweet-Salone'. Accessed 16 February 2020. https://unipsil.unmissions.org/sites/default/files/vision_2025.pdf

GoSL. 'Public Private Partnership Unit Brochure'. Accessed 16 February 2020. https://ppp.gov.sl/wp-content/uploads/2019/12/PPP_BROCHURE.pdf

GoSL. 'The Agenda for Prosperity: Road to Middle Income Status – Sierra Leone's Third Generation Poverty Reduction Strategy Paper 2013–2018'. Accessed 16 February 2020. http://www.sierra-leone.org/Agenda%204%20Prosperity.pdf

GoSL. 'The Public Private Partnership Unit (PPPU)'. Accessed 16 February 2020. https://ppp.gov.sl/

G20 EPG. 'Making the System Work for All: Report of the G20 Eminent Persons Group on Global Financial Governance'. Accessed 18 February 2020. https://www.globalfinancialgovernance.org/assets/pdf/G20EPG-Full%20Report.pdf

Gouvernement de la République du Sénégal. 'Unité PPP-Partenariats Public-Privé. Accessed 15 February 2020. https://www.sec.gouv.sn/unit%C3%A9-ppp-partenariats-public-priv%C3%A9

Government of Jalisco. 'Ley de proyectos de inversión y de prestación de servicios del estado de Jalisco y sus municipios'. Accessed 1 May 2020. https://transparencia.info.jalisco.gob.mx/sites/default/files/Ley%20de%20Proyectos%20de%20Inversion%20y%20Prestacion%20de%20Servicios.pdf

Havnevik, K. 'Responsible Agricultural Investments in Developing Countries: How to Make Principles and Guidelines Effective'. Accessed 16 February 2020. https://www.government.se/49b727/contentassets/45137cb380734c2fbf97717673cef39c/responsible-agricultural-investments-in-developing-countries

Health Policy Project. 'Kenya Country Health Accounts: Summary of Findings from 12 Pilot Countries'. Accessed 18 February 2020. https://www.healthpolicyproject.com/pubs/7885_FINALSynthesisreportoftheCHA.pdf

Heinrich Böll Stiftung. 'From the Washington Consensus to the Wall Street Consensus'. Accessed 18 February 2020. https://us.boell.org/en/2019/10/11/washington-consensus-wall-street-consensus

Hickel, J. 'Apartheid in the Global Governance System'. Accessed 18 February 2020. https://www.globalpolicyjournal.com/blog/05/01/2021/apartheid-global-governance-system

IFC. 'Public-Private Partnership Stories. Fiji: Lautoka and Ba Hospitals'. Accessed 26 May 2020. https://www.ifc.org/wps/wcm/connect/fbec1baa-08ce-45cf-9d3c-a6d1854a4ea6/Fiji-Health-PPP-Story.pdf?MOD=AJPERES&CVID=mSDV5kh

IMF. 'Public-Private Partnerships'. Accessed 26 May 2020. https://www.imf.org/external/np/fad/2004/pifp/eng/031204.pdf

IMF. 'Sierra Leone: Poverty Reduction Strategy Paper – Progress Report'. Accessed 16 February 2020. https://www.imf.org/external/pubs/ft/scr/2005/cr05191.pdf

IMF. 'Sierra Leone: Poverty Reduction Strategy Paper – Progress Report'. Accessed 16 February 2020. https://www.imf.org/external/pubs/ft/scr/2008/cr08250.pdf

IMF. '2017 Staff Guidance Note on the Fund's Engagement with Small Island Developing States'. Accessed 26 May 2020. https://www.imf.org/en/Publications/Policy-Papers/Issues/2018/01/26/pp121117-2017-staff-guidance-note-on-the-funds-engagement-with-small-developing-states

INEGI. 'Estadísticas a propósito del día internacional de la eliminación de la violencia contra la mujer (25 de noviembre). Datos Nacionales'. Acccessed 1 May 2020. https://www.inegi.org.mx/contenidos/saladeprensa/aproposito/2019/Violencia2019_Nal.pdf

Institute of Economic Affairs. 'Kenya's Comparison of Out of Pocket Expenditure on Health with Its Peers'. Accessed 18 February 2020. https://www.ieakenya.or.ke/number_of_the_week/kenyaa-s-comparison-of-out-of-pocket-expenditure-on-health-with-its-peers

Inter-American Development Bank. 'LAC PPP Risk Management Group – LAC PPP RMG'. Accessed 21 September 2020. https://www.iadb.org/es/lacpppgroup

International Finance Corporation. 'A Letter from Jim Yong Kim, World Bank Group President'. Accessed 18 February 2020. https://www.ifc.org/wps/wcm/connect/CORP_EXT_Content/IFC_External_Corporate_Site/Annual±Report±2017/2017-Online-Report/Leadership-Perspectives

Instituto Nacional de Estadistica e Informatica. 'Acceso a Seguro de Salud'. Accessed 2 February 2020. https://www.inei.gob.pe/estadisticas/indice-tematico/access-to-health-insurance/

Irava, W. and Prasad, R. 'A Case Study on the Public and Private Mix of Health Services in Fiji'. Accessed 26 May 2020. https://www.fnu.ac.fj/college-of-medicine/images/chipsr/publications/CHIPSR_case_study_public_private_mix.pdf

Jain, N. 'Rashtriya Swasthya Bima Yojana: A Step towards Universal Health Coverage in India', in *India Infrastructure Report 2013/14: The Road to Universal Health Coverage*, New Delhi. Accessed 18 February 2020. http://www.idfc.com/pdf/report/2013-14/Chapter-10.pdf

Jacobs, T. 'Questions over Hospital Upgrade Motives in Fiji', interviewed by J. Meyer for *Dateline Pacific*. 15 May 2018. Accessed 26 May 2020. https://www.rnz.co.nz/international/programmes/datelinepacific/audio/2018644994/questions-over-hospital-upgrade-motives-in-fiji

JSA. 'Implications of the Interim Union Budget 2019–2020 for Health'. Accessed 18 February 2020. https://phmindia.org/2020/02/15/implications-of-the-union-budget-2020-21-for-health-jsa-press-release/

JSA. 'Implications of the Union Budget 2020–21 for Health'. Accessed 18 February 2020. http://phmindia.org/wp-content/uploads/2020/02/Budget-2020-JSA-Analysis.pdf

JSA Chhattisgarh. 'Report of Chhattisgarh JSA Convention'. Accessed 11 April 2019. https://phmindia.org/category/chhattisgarh/

JSA Chhattisgarh. 'Press note on Chhattisgarh JSA Convention on Right to Health'. Accessed 11 April 2019. http://phmindia.org/wp-content/uploads/2018/04/JSA_chattisgarh_RTH.pdf

Kamau, S. K. 'Kenya's 3 Keys to Success: How to Create an Effective Public-Private Partnership Unit'. *World Bank Blogs*. Accessed 18 February 2020. https://blogs.worldbank.org/ppps/3-keys-success-public-private-partnership-ppp-unit-kenya-and-5-lessons-share

Kaur, S., Jain, N. and Bhatnagar, P. C. 'Early Trends from Utilization of Oncology Services: Insights from Ayushman Bharat Pradhan Mantri Jan Arogya Yojana (PM-JAY)'. Accessed 18 February 2020. https://www.pmjay.gov.in/sites/default/files/2019-11/Working%20paper-4%20%281%29.pdf

Kaur, S., Jain, N. and Desai, S. 'Patterns of Utilization for Hysterectomy: An Analysis of EarlyTtrends from Ayushman Bharat Pradhan Mantri Jan Arogya Yojana'. Accessed 18 February 2020. https://www.popcouncil.org/uploads/pdfs/2019_NHA-HysterectomyPM-JAY.pdf

Kenya Health Workforce Report. 'The Status of Healthcare Professionals in Kenya'. Accessed 18 February 2020. https://taskforce.org/wp-content/uploads/2019/09/KHWF_2017Report_Fullreport_042317-MR-comments.pdf

Kenya, Ministry of Planning and National Development. 'The Vision; Seeing the Vision through'. Accessed 18 February 2020. http://vision2030.go.ke

Korir, M. 'Managed Equipment Services: The Kenyan Story: Good Intentions Aren't All That's Needed for a Successful Medical Program'. *The Pathologist*. Accessed 18 February 2020. https://thepathologist.com/outside-the-lab/managed-equipment-services-the-kenyan-story

Kotze, A. 'How to Fund a Failing Health System'. Accessed 11 February 2020. https://mg.co.za/article/2017-04-06-00-how-to-fund-a-failing-health-system

Kumar, A. 'Three Amputations a Day: Fiji Diabetes Death Rate Worst in the World'. Accessed 26 May 2020. https://www.stuff.co.nz/world/south-pacific/104333879/three-amputations-a-day-fiji-diabetes-death-rate-worst-in-the-world

Lamberti, J. and Rothstein, T. 'Empresas participantes en el proyecto del Nuevo Aeropuerto de la Ciudad de México'. *PODER*. Accessed 1 May 2020. https://www.colaboratorio.org/nuevo-aeropuerto-de-la-ciudad-de-mexico-investigacion-corporativa

Lappin, K. Interview via Skype, May. (See Annex 3 for questionnaire).

Lowy Institute. 'Australia's Foreign Aid'. Accessed 26 May 2020. https://www.lowyinstitute.org/issues/australian-foreign-aid

Lucanivalu, L. 'Increase in Health Ministry Budget Has Been Progressive: Akbar'. *Fiji Sun*. Accessed 26 May 2020. https://fijisun.com.fj/2018/03/10/increase-in-health-ministry-budget-has-been-progressive-akbar

Lutua, K. Personal Interview, 2020.

Lyons, K. 'Australia Slashes Pacific Aid Funding for Health as Region Battles Medical Crises'. *Guardian Australia*. Accessed 26 May 2020. https://www.theguardian.com/world/2020/feb/18/australia-slashes-pacific-aid-funding-for-health-as-region-battles-medical-crises

Mandivengerei, P. 'Zim Doctors Blast Govt Hospital Privitisation Bid'. Accessed 11 February 2020. https://www.newzimbabwe.com/zim-doctors-blast-govt-hospital-privatisation-bid

Martinez, F. 'Veracruz, Primer Lugar en Feminicidios'. *La Jornada*. Accessed 1 May 2020. https://jornada.com.mx/2019/09/26/politica/016n1pol

Masuka, N. 'PPP Model Overview'. Accessed 11 February 2020. https://drive.google.com/drive/folders/1oTp45kJNHdw2gJqAfFrRUBFHbVKy01vo?usp=sharing.

Mbanje, P. 'Health Minister Sees Red over Audit Report'. Accessed 11 February 2020. https://www.newsday.co.zw/2019/12/health-minister-sees-red-over-audit-report

McCaig, E. 'We Do a Lot of Cutting: The Rise of Diabetic Amputations in the Pacific', interviewed by T. Aualiitia for *ABC Pacific Mornings* 11 July 2019. Accessed 26 May 2020. https://www.abc.net.au/radio-australia/programs/pacificmornings/diabetic-amputations/11298552

MEF. 'Marco Macroeconómico Multianual 2020–2023'. Accessed 21 September 2020. https://www.mef.gob.pe/contenidos/pol_econ/marco_macro/ MMM_2020_2023.pdf

MEF. 'National Infrastructure Plan for Competitiveness'. Accessed 21 September 2020. https://www.mef.gob.pe/contenidos/inv_privada/planes/PNIC_2019. pdf

MEF. 'Organization Table'. Accessed 21 September 2020. https://www.mef.gob. pe/contenidos/acerc_mins/doc_gestion/organigrama_2019.pdf

MEF. 'Statistics'. Accessed 21 September 2020. https://www.mef.gob.pe/es/ asociaciones-publico-privadas/estadistica

Michelitsch, R. and Szwedzki, R. 'Una década de alianzas público privadas en América Latina y el Caribe: ¿qué hemos aprendido?'. Accessed 1 May 2020. https://blogs.worldbank.org/es/ppps/una-d-cada-de-alianzas-p-blico-privadas-en-am-rica-latina-y-el-caribe-qu-hemos-aprendido

Ministère De L'Économie et Des Finances. 'Plan D'Actions Prioritaires 2014–2018'.

Ministère De L'Économie et Des Finances. 'Plan D'Actions Prioritaires 2019–2023'.

Ministère de la Femme, De La Famille et De L'Enfance. 'Stratégie Nationale Pour L'Équité et L'Égalité de Genre 2016–2026'.

Ministry of Health, Kenya. 'Demystifying the Managed Equipment Service Scheme (MES) Project in Kenya'. Accessed 18 February 2020. http:// publications.universalhealth2030.org/uploads/MES-BROCHURE.pdf

Ministry of Health. 'Kenya National Health Accounts FY 2015/2016'. *Nairobi Government of Kenya*. Accessed 18 February 2020. http://www. healthpolicyplus.com/ns/pubs/16339-16616_KenyaNHAmainreport.pdf

Ministry of Health. 'Transforming Health: Accelerating Attainment of Universal Health Coverage'. Accessed 18 February 2020. https://www.health.go.ke/wp-content/uploads/2016/03/KHSSP-BOOK.pdf

MINSA. 'Indicadores de Gestión y Evaluación Hospitalaria, Para Hospitales, institutos y DIRESA. Documento de trabajo'. Accessed 21 September 2020. http://bvs.minsa.gob.pe/local/MINSA/2739.pdf

MINSA. *Manual de Indicadoreshospitalarios. Serie Herramientas Metodológicas en Epidemiologia y Salud Pública*, no. 4 (2001): Lima: MINSA, General Office of Epidemiology.

MINSA. 'Norma Técnica de Salud – Categorías de Establecimientos del Sector Salud RM No. 546-2011-MINSA'. Accessed 21 September 2020. https://www. gob.pe/institucion/minsa/normas-legales/243402-546-2011-minsa

MINSA. *Plan Nacional Para La Prevención y Control de Cáncer de Mamas 2017–2021 (RM No. 442-2017-MINSA)*. Lima: MINSA, General Directorate of Strategic Interventions in Public Health, Directorate of Prevention and Control of Cancer.

MoFEP. 'National Policy on Public Private Partnerships (PPP)'. Accessed 26 January 2020. http://www.mofep.gov.gh

MoFEP. 'The Annual Public Debt Report for the 2018 Financial Year'. Accessed 26 January 2020. http://www.mofep.gov.gh

MoHMS and WHO. 'Ministry and WHO Clarify Report On Fiji's Diabetes Rate'. *Fiji Sun*, 19 June 2018. Accessed 26 May 2020. https://fijisun.com. fj/2018/06/19/ministry-and-who-clarify-report-on-fijis-diabetes-rate

Mudyarabikwa, O. and Madhina, D. 'An Assessment of Incentive Setting for Participation of Private for-Profit Health Care Providers in Zimbabwe'. Accessed 11 February 2020. https://shopsplusproject.org/sites/default/files/resources/2415_file_sar15.pdf

Mujeres Del Istmo, las que con amor Cuidan la Tierra. Contra el machismo, la violencia y los desafíos que trae para las mujeres el Corredor Interoceánico (Women of the Isthmus, those who lovingly care for the land. Against machismo, violence and the challenges that the Interoceanic Corridor brings to women). Accessed 1 May 2020. https://istmoresiste.org.mx/serie-de-radio/

Munyuki, E. and Jasi, S. 'Capital Flows in the Health Care Sector in Zimbabwe: Trends and Implications for the Health System'. Accessed 11 February 2020. https://www.equinetafrica.org/sites/default/files/uploads/documents/DIS79pppMUNYUKI.pdf

Mutua, J. and Wamalwa, N. 'Leasing of Medical Equipment Project in Kenya: Value for Money Assessment'. Accessed 18 February 2020. https://www.ieakenya.or.ke/publications/research-papers/leasing-of-medical-equipment-project-in-kenya-value-for-money-assessment

Namati. *Customary Land Rights Legal Review Report*. Namati, Freetown.

Namati. *Model Land Commission Bill*. Namati, Freetown.

Namati. 'Namati Welcomes Sierra Leone's Progressive New National Land Policy'. Accessed 16 February 2020. https://namati.org/news-stories/namati-welcomes-sierra-leones-progressive-new-national-land-policy

Namati. *Summary Model Customary Land Bill*. Namati, Freetown.

Negin, J., Irava, W., Leon, C. and Morgan, C. 'Sustainable Health Financing in the Pacific: Tracking Dependency and Transparency'. Accessed 26 May 2020. http://devpolicy.org/what-constitutes-donor-dependence-20130109/?print=print

Ngumi, N. 'Health for All: A Reflection on the Current State of Healthcare in Kenya'. *The Elephant*. Accessed 18 February 2020. https://www.theelephant.info/features/2018/08/16/health-for-all-a-reflection-on-the-current-state-of-healthcare-in-kenya

NHA. 'Ayushman Bharat Pradhan Mantri Jan Arogya Yojana: Annual Report 2018–19'. Accessed 18 February 2020. https://nha.gov.in/img/resources/Annual-Report-2018-19.pdf

NHSRC. 'Household Healthcare Utilization & Expenditure in India: State Fact Sheets'. Accessed 18 February 2020. http://nhsrcindia.org/sites/default/files/State Fact Sheets_Health care Utilization and Expenditure in India.pdf

NHSRC. 'National Health Accounts: Estimates for India FY 2015–16'. Accessed 18 February 2020. https://main.mohfw.gov.in/sites/default/files/NHA_Estimates_Report_2015-16_0.pdf

NHSRC. 'NRHM in the Eleventh Five Year Plan (2007–2012): Strengthening Public Health Systems'. Acccessed 20 June 2018. http://nhsrcindia.org/sites/default/files/NRHM in 11th five year plan.pdf

Nicholas, I. 'PNG PM Officially Opens Expanded Jackson International Airport'. Accessed 26 May 2020. http://www.pireport.org/articles/2015/07/01/png-pm-officially-opens-expanded-jackson-international-airport

NITI Aayog. 'NITI Aayog Annual Report 2019–20'. Accessed 18 February 2020. https://niti.gov.in/sites/default/files/2020-02/Annual_Report_2019-20.pdf

Nundy, M., Dasgupta, R., Kanungo, K., Nandi, S. and Murugan, G. 'The Rashtriya Swasthya Bima Yojana (RSBY) Experience in Chhattisgarh: What Does It Mean for Health for All?'. Accessed 18 February 2020. https://www.researchgate.net/publication/304525632_The_Rashtriya_Swasthya_Bima_Yojana_RSBY_experience_in_Chhattisgarh_What_does_it_mean_for_Health_for_All

Oakland Institute. 'Understanding Land Investment Deals in Africa: Country Report: Sierra Leone'. Accessed 16 February 2020. https://www.oaklandinstitute.org/sites/oaklandinstitute.org/files/OI_SierraLeone_Land_Investment_report_0.pdf

Obrador, L. and Manuel, A. 'Rehabilitación del Corredor Interoceánico del Istmo y parques industriales impulsarán desarrollo en sur-sureste'. *AMLO*. Accessed 1 May 2020. https://lopezobrador.org.mx/2020/06/07/rehabilitacion-del-corredor-interoceanico-del-istmo-y-parques-industriales-impulsaran-desarrollo-en-sur-sureste-presidente

Office of the United Nations High Commissioner for Human Rights. 'The Right to Health', Fact Sheet no. 31. Accessed 18 February 2020. https://www.ohchr.org/Documents/Publications/Factsheet31.pdf

Okoye, V. 'Street Vendor Exclusion in "Modern" Market Planning: A Case Study from Kumasi, Ghana'. Accessed 18 February 2020. https://www.wiego.org/publications/street-vendor-exclusion-modern-market-planning-case-study-kumasi-ghana

Oltoch, C. 'Managed Equipment Services (MES) – Healthcare for Development: The Kenya MES Experience'. Accessed 18 February 2020. https://docplayer.net/57372467-Managed-equipment-services-mes-healthcare-for-sustainable-development-the-kenya-mes-experience-cynthia-olotch.html

Oqubay, A. 'Breaking Down Ethiopia's Fast-Growing Economy'. *Bloomberg QuickTake*. Accessed 20 February 2020. https://www.youtube.com/watch?v=o5TVk48Z194

Otieno, J. 'Chinese Firm in Medical Gear Probe Says Leasing Expensive'. *The Star*. Accessed 18 February 2020. https://www.the-star.co.ke/news/2019-11-07-chinese-firm-in-medical-gear-probe-says-leasing-expensive

Pacific Islands Forum Secretariat. 'National Economies and Commitments to Benefit from Gender Responsive Budgeting'. Accessed 26 May 2020. https://www.forumsec.org/2017/06/14/national-economies-and-commitments-to-benefit-from-gender-responsive-budgeting

Pacific Island Report. 'India's Apollo Group Plans $44 Million Hospital in Fiji'. Accessed 26 May 2020. http://www.pireport.org/articles/2007/09/27/india%C3%A2%C2%80%C2%99s-apollo-group-plans-44-million-hospital-fiji

PAHO. 'Análisis de las Reformas del Sector Salud en los Países de la Región Andina. 2nd. edition'. Accessed 21 September 2020. https://www.paho.org/hq/dmdocuments/2010/Analisis_Reforma_Sector_Salud-SubRegion_Andina_2002.pdf

PAHO and WHO. 'Documento de posición de la OMS sobre el tamizaje por mamografía. Resumen de recomendaciones'. Accessed 21 September 2020. https://www.paho.org/hq/dmdocuments/2015/SP-Mammography-Factsheet.pdf

Parliament of Kenya, The Senate. 'The Managed Equipment Services (MES) Project, Brief and Suggested Questions'. Accessed 18 February 2020. http://www.parliament.go.ke/sites/default/files/2018-11/MES%20Brief_Nov%202018%20%285%29_%20With%20Suggested%20Questions%20.pdf

Parliament of the Republic of Fiji. 'Budget 2018–2019 Taxation and Other Government Revenue'. *Budget Briefings 2018*. Accessed 26 May 2020. http://www.parliament.gov.fj/wp-content/uploads/2018/07/Government-Revenue-2018-19-FINAL.pdf

Patolwala, M. 'Transforming Kenya's Healthcare System: A PPP Success Story'. *World Bank Blogs*. Accessed 18 February 2020. https://blogs.worldbank.org/ppps/transforming-kenya-s-healthcare-system-ppp-success-story

Perez Orozco, A. 'Subversión Feminista de la Economía. Aportes para un debate sobre el conflicto capital-vida'. *Traficantes de Sueños*. Accessed 1 May 2020. https://www.traficantes.net/sites/default/files/pdfs/Subversi%C3%B3n%20feminista%20de%20la%20econom%C3%ADa_Traficantes%20de%20Sue%C3%B1os.pdf

PHFI. 'A Critical Assessment of the Existing Health Insurance Models in India'. Accessed 18 February 2020. http://planningcommission.nic.in/reports/sereport/ser/ser_heal1305.pdf

PHRN. 'Exploring Health Inequities amongst Particularly Vulnerable Tribal Groups : Case Studies of Baiga and Sabar in Chhattisgarh and Jharkhand States of India Report of a Study by Public Health Resource Network'. Accessed 18 February 2020. https://www.researchgate.net/profile/Sulakshana-Nandi/publication/320903156_Exploring_health_inequities_amongst_Particularly_Vulnerable_Tribal_Groups_Case_studies_of_Baiga_and_Sabar_in_Chhattisgarh_and_Jharkhand_states_of_India-_A_Briefing_Note_By_Public_Health_Resource_Netwo/links/5a01ab6f4585152c9db17eac/Exploring-health-inequities-amongst-

Particularly-Vulnerable-Tribal-Groups-Case-studies-of-Baiga-and-Sabar-in-Chhattisgarh-and-Jharkhand-states-of-India-A-Briefing-Note-By-Public-Health-Resource-Netwo.pdf

PIAPPEM. 'Experiencia mexicana en Asociaciones Público-Privadas para el desarrollo del Infraestructura y la provisión de servicios públicos". Accessed 1 May 2020. https://piappem.org/file.php?id=295

PODER. 'Saltillo: El origen de la privatización de aguas mexicanas'. Accessed 1 May 2020. https://www.rindecuentas.org/reportajes/2019/06/06/saltillo-el-origen-de-la-privatizacion-de-aguas-mexicanas

PODER. 'Tren Maya "como anillo al dedo" para las extractivas'. Accessed 1 May 2020. https://www.facebook.com/214825975198976/posts/3548377661843774

Polo, M. 'United Union of Healthcare Workers Callao Salud'. *Facebook*. Accessed 21 September 2020. https://es-la.facebook.com/pg/Sindicato-Unido-de-Trabajadores-Asistenciales-De-Callao-Salud-163097324448932/posts/?ref=page_internal

Post Courier. 'Medical Board Puts Aspen Medical Services on Notice'. Accessed 26 May 2020. https://postcourier.com.pg/medical-board-puts-aspen-medical-services-on-notice

Pratibha, J. 'Public-Private Partnership Not Privatisation Says Acting PM'. Accessed 26 May 2020. https://fijisun.com.fj/2018/03/13/public-private-partnership-not-privatisation-says-acting-pm

PSI. 'Fiji Nurse Questions Privatisation at World Bank's Annual Meeting in Bali'. Accessed 26 May 2020. http://www.world-psi.org/fr/node/11649

Radio New Zealand. 'Indian Hospital Group Features at Fiji Health Forum'. *Radio New Zealand*, 21 April 2017. Accessed 26 May 2020. https://www.rnz.co.nz/international/pacific-news/329198/indian-hospital-group-features-at-fiji-health-forum

RamPrakash, R. and Lingam, L. 'Publicly Funded Health Insurance Schemes (PFHIS): A Systematic and Interpretive Review of Studies Does Gender Equity Matter?'. Accessed 12 July 2019. http://www.esocialsciences.org/eSSH_Journal/Repository/6N_Publicly Funded Health Insurance Schemes_Rajalakshmi.pdf

RAN. 'Estadística Agraria con perspectiva de género'. Accessed 1 May 2020. http://www.ran.gob.mx/ran/indic_gen/nucag-certynocert-resultados-2019.pdf

Ravindran, T. K. S. 'Universal Access: Making Health Systems Work for Women'. *BMC Public Health*. Accessed 18 February 2020. https://bmcpublichealth.biomedcentral.com/articles/10.1186/1471-2458-12-S1-S4.

RGI. 'Census of India Website'. Accessed 29 May 2018. http://censusindia.gov.in/2011-Common/CensusData2011

RGI. 'Sample Registration System (SRS) Bulletin'. Accessed 18 February 2020. https://censusindia.gov.in/vital_statistics/SRS_Bulletins/SRSBulletin_2018.pdf

Rodríguez Enríquez, C. 'Corporate Accountability and Women's Human Rights: An Analytical Approach to Public-Private Partnerships (PPPs)'. Accessed 15 February 2020. https://dawnnet.org/wp-content/uploads/2021/04/DAWN-Discussion-Paper-31_-PPPs-analytical-framework.pdf

Rodríguez Enríquez, C. 'Corporate Power: A Risky Threat Looming Over the Fulfilment of Women's Human Rights'. in *Civil Society Reflection Group on the 2030 Agenda for Sustainable Development. Spotlight on Sustainable Development 2017. Reclaiming Policies for the Public.* Accessed 15 February 2020. https://www.socialwatch.org/node/17687

Romero, M. J. 'Can Public-Private Partnerships Deliver Gender Equality?'. Accessed 16 February 2020. https://d3n8a8pro7vhmx.cloudfront.net/eurodad/pages/443/attachments/original/1590686869/Can_public-private_partnerships_deliver_gender_equality_.pdf?1590686869

Romero, M. J. 'What Lies Beneath? A Critical Assessment of PPPs and Their Impact on Sustainable Development'. *European Network on Debt and Development.* Accessed 20 February 2020. Brussels: Eurodad. https://www.eurodad.org/what_lies_beneath

Romero, M. J. 'Where Is the Public in PPPs? Analysing the World Bank's Support for Public-Private Partnerships'. Accessed 1 February 2021. http://www.brettonwoodsproject.org/2014/09/public-ppps-analysing-world-banks-support-public-private-partnerships

Romero, M. J. and Ravenscroft, J. 'History REPPPeated: How Public-Private Partnerships Are Failing'. Accessed 16 February 2020. https://eurodad.org/files/pdf/1546956-history-repppeated-how-public-private-partnerships-are-failing-.pdf

Ruiz Caro, A. 'El Proceso de Privatizaciones en el Perú Durante el Perído 1991–2002'. Accessed 21 September 2020. https://repositorio.cepal.org/handle/11362/7273

Samuel, J. 'Bill to Liberalise Investment Laws Reaches Council of Ministers'. Accessed 20 February 2020. https://addisfortune.news/bill-to-liberalise-investment-laws-reaches-council-of-ministers

Sarmiento, M. 'Alianzas público-privada en el sector Salud desatan cuestionamientos al Ejecutivo'. Accessed 21 September 2020. https://redaccion.lamula.pe/2017/07/26/alianza-publico-privada-en-el-sector-salud-desata-cuestionamientos-al-ejecutivo/lumasap

SCT. 'Ferrocarril del Istmo de Tehuantepec, S.A de C.V'. Accessed 1 May 2020. https://www.ferroistmo.com.mx

SEF. 'Construcciones y Maquinaria SEF, S.A de C.V'. Accessed 1 May 2020. http://www.sefcym.com/index.php/nosotros

SEGOB. 'Decreto por el que se abrogan los diversos de Declaratorias de las Zonas Económicas Especiales'. *Diario Oficial de la Federación* [Official Journal of the Federation]. Accessed 1 May 2020. https://www.dof.gob.mx/nota_detalle.php?codigo=5579365&fecha=19/11/2019

SEGOB. 'Decreto por el que se aprueba el Programa Nacional de Desarrollo de las Franjas Fronterizas y Zonas Libres'. *Diario Oficial de la Federación* [Official Journal of the Federation]. Accessed 1 May 2020. http://dof.gob.mx/nota_detalle.php?codigo=4696464&fecha=12/11/1981

SEGOB. 'Decreto por el que se crea el organismo público descentralizado, con personalidad jurídica y patrimonio propio, no sectorizado, denominado Corredor Interoceánico del Ismto de Tehuantepec'. *Diario Oficial de la Federación* [Official Journal of the Federation]. Accessed 1 May 2020. https://dof.gob.mx/nota_detalle.php?codigo=5562774&fecha=14/06/2019

SEI. 'Agriculture Investment and Rural Transformation: A Case Study of the Makeni Bioenergy Project in Sierra Leone'. Accessed 16 February 2020. https://mediamanager.sei.org/documents/Publications/Climate/SEI-PR-2015-09-Makeni-Project.pdf

Seidu, A. 'Public-Private Partnerships in Ghana: Interrogating the Efficacy of a Politically Convenient Practice'. Accessed 20 January 2020. http://library.fes.de/pdf-files/bueros/ghana/16591.pdf

SEMARNAT. 'Ecorregiones terrestres de México'. *Atlas Digital Geográfico.* Accessed 1 May 2020. http://gisviewer.semarnat.gob.mx/aplicaciones/Atlas2015/biod_ETN1.html

SENER. 'Plan Quinquenal de Expansión del Sistema de Transporte y Almacenamiento Nacional Integrado de Gas Natural, 2015–2019'. Accessed 1 May 2020. https://www.gob.mx/cenagas/acciones-y-programas/plan-quinquenal-de-expansion-del-sistema-de-transporte-y-almacenamiento-nacional-integrado-de-gas-natural-2015-2019

Sesay, B. J. 'Effects of Addax Bioenergy Investment on Female Farmers' Rights to Land and Their Livelihoods in Bombali District, Sierra Leone'. Accessed 16 February 2020. http://lup.lub.lu.se/luur/download?func=downloadFile&recordOId=5470857&fileOId=5470859

Seyoum, A. 'Departure from Development State'. *The Report Ethiopia.* Accessed 20 February 2020. https://www.thereporterethiopia.com/article/departure-developmental-state

SHCP. 'Programa para el Desarrollo del Istmo de Tehuantepec'. *Conferencia Binacional de Infraestructura.* Accessed 1 May 2020. https://www.gob.mx/programaistmo/articulos/programa-para-el-desarrollo-del-istmo-de-tehuantepec

SHCP and BANOBRAS. 'Diseño, construcción, operación y mantenimiento de la Infraestructura de transporte del gasoducto Jáltipan, de Veracruz a Salina Cruz'. *Proyectos México.* Accessed 1 May 2020. https://www.proyectosmexico.gob.mx/proyecto_inversion/037-gasoducto-jaltipan-salina-cruz

SIBC Online. 'Engineering Procurement for Tina Hydro Power Project Signed'. Accessed 26 May 2020. http://www.sibconline.com.sb/engineering-procurement-for-tina-hydro-power-project-signed

Sierra Express Media. 'Masethele Village in Important Land Renegotiation with Addax Bioenergy Sierra Leone Limited'. Accessed 16 February 2020. https:// sierraexpressmedia.com/?p=53981

SiLNoRF and BfA. 'Analysis of RSB Certificate March 2013'. Accessed 16 February 2020. https://sites.google.com/site/silnorf/news-1/analysis-of-rsb-certificate-march-2013

SiLNoRF and BfA. 'Final Monitoring Report on the Scale Down of Addax Bioenergy in Makeni, Sierra Leone (July 2014–June 2016)'. Accessed 16 February 2020. https://brotfueralle.ch/content/uploads/2019/03/2016-Monitoring-report-Silnorf.pdf

SiLNoRF and BfA. 'Monitoring Report August 2012'. Accessed 16 February 2020. https://sites.google.com/site/silnorf/news-1/monitoring-report-july-2012

SiLNoRF and BfA. 'Monitoring 2014'. Accessed 16 February 2020. https://sites.google.com/site/silnorf/news-1/monitoring-report-2014

SiLNoRF and BfA. 'RSB Complaint September 2013'. Accessed 16 February 2020. https://sites.google.com/site/silnorf/news-1/rsb-complaint-september-2013

SINAMES. 'Pronouncing'. *Diario Uno*. March 2015. Accessed 21 September 2020. https://issuu.com/impresosdiariounoperu/docs/du22032015/14

SINAMSSOP. 'Document 2010'. Accessed 21 September 2020. http://www.sinamssop.org/pliegos-y-acuerdos-anteriores

SINAMSSOP. 'Minutes 2010'. Accessed 21 September 2020. http://www.sinamssop.org/pliegos-y-acuerdos-anteriores

SINAMSSOP. 'No al ofrecimiento de ESSALUD a empresas británicas APPs'. Accessed 21 September 2020. http://www.sinamssop.org/2017/04/no-al-ofrecimiento-de-essalud-a-empresas-britanicas-apps

SINAMSSOP. 'Press Release No. 004-2014-UG'. Accessed 21 September 2020. http://www.sinamssop.org/2014/12/nueve-sindicatos-de-essalud-constituyeron-frente-de-defensa-del-derecho-a-la-salud-y-la-seguridad-social

SINAMSSOP. 'Statement 008-2010'. Accessed 21 September 2020. http://www.sindicatomedicoperu.org/pdf/comunicado/C-2010/comunicado008.pdf

SinEmbargo, D. B. 'Peña dio a Cusaem, la compañía de seguridad de priistas del Edomex, al menos 3,389 millones en 5 años'. Accessed 1 May 2020. https://www.sinembargo.mx/04-02-2020/3724020

SINESS. 'Gestión de EsSalud busca traspasar a empresas extranjeras el servicio a la salud por el que pagan millones de asegurados'. Accessed 21 September 2020. https://sinesss.org/gestion-de-essalud-busca-traspasar-a-empresas-extranjeras-el-servicio-a-la-salud-por-el-que-pagan-millones-de-asegurados

Singh, R. 'Fiji National Provident Fund', PowerPoint presentation at the PSI/ FES Forum on Pensions and Social Security, Singapore. Accessed 26 May

2020. https://www.world-psi.org/sites/default/files/documents/research/ fiji_national_provident_fund_-_rajeshwar_singh.pdf

Smith, O., Naib, P., Sehgal, P. and Chhabra, S. 'PM-JAY Policy Brief 8: PM-JAY Under Lockdown: Evidence on Utilization Trends'. Accessed 18 February 2020. https://pmjay.gov.in/sites/default/files/2020-06/Policy-Brief-8_PM-JAY-under-Lockdown-Evidence_12-06-20_NHA_WB.pdf

SNA. *Data of PMJAY and MSBY Utilisation from September 2018 to October 2019*. Raipur: Department of Health and Family Welfare, Chhattisgarh.

Solution Africa. 'Private and Financial Sector Development Project'. Accessed 16 February 2020. http://www.southsouthworld.org/component/k2/46-solution/2400/private-and-financial-sector-development-project

State Health Resource Centre Chhattisgarh (SHRC CG). *Study on Pradhan Mantri Jan Arogaya Yojana (PMJAY) in Chhattisgarh State through Household Surveys*. Raipur: SHRC Chhattisgarh.

Sunbird Energy. 'AOG Transfers Ownership of Pioneering Bioethanol and Green Electricity Operation in Sierra Leone'. Accessed 16 February 2020. https://www.sunbirdbioenergy.com/2016/09/30/aog-transfers-ownership-of-pioneering-bioethanol-and-green-electricity-operation-in-sierra-leone-to-sunbird-bioenergy

Sundaram, J. K. and Chowdhury, A. 'World Bank Financialization Strategy Serves Big Finance'. *Inter Press Service*. Accessed 18 February 2020. http://www.ipsnews.net/2019/04/world-bank-financialization-strategy-serves-big-finance

Sunday, F. and Thoronjo, P. 'Report: Billions Wasted in State Medical Project'. *The Standard*. Accessed 18 February 2020. https://www.standardmedia.co.ke/article/2001360362/report-billions-wasted-in-state-medical-project

Swedwatch. 'No Business, No Rights'. Accessed 16 February 2020. https:// swedwatch.org/wp-content/uploads/2017/11/86_Sierra-Leone_171108.pdf

Takoulevu, J. M. 'Sierra Leone: IFC Finances 50 MW Solar Project'. Accessed 16 February 2020. https://www.afrik21.africa/en/sierra-leone-ifc-finances-50-mw-solar-project

Talawadua, F. Interview, 27 May 2020. (See Annex 2 for questionnaire).

Talei, F. 'Fiji Health Minister: Two Doctors Committed Suicide because of Work Stress'. Accessed 26 May 2020. https://fijisun.com.fj/2019/02/14/two-doctors-commited-suicide-work-stress/

Tatukivei, I. T. 'Fiji Nurse Questions Privatisation at World Bank's Annual Meeting in Bali'. Accessed 26 May 2020. http://www.world-psi.org/fr/node/11649

Tilahun, E. 'Workshop Advances Food Fortification'. *Capital Ethiopia*. Accessed 20 February 2020. https://www.capitalethiopia.com/capital/workshop-advances-food-fortification

Tren, R. and Bate, R. 'Despotism and Disease: A Report into the Health Situation of Zimbabwe and Its Probable Impact on the Region's Health'. Accessed 11 February 2020. https://reliefweb.int/report/zimbabwe/despotism-and-disease-report-health-situation-zimbabwe-and-its-probable-impact

UNCTAD. 'Bilateral Investment Treaties 1995–2006: Trends in Investment Rulemaking'. Accessed 18 February 2020. https://unctad.org/en/Docs/iteiia20065_en.pdf

UNDP. 'Human Development Report 2019 – Beyond Income, beyond Averages, beyond Today: Inequalities in Human Development in the 21st Century'. Accessed 18 February 2020. http://hdr.undp.org/sites/default/files/hdr2019.pdf

UNDP. 'Prospects of Public-Private Partnership (PPP) in Ethiopia – Development Brief, UNDP Ethiopia No. 1/2015'. Accessed 20 February 2020. https://www.undp.org/content/dam/ethiopia/docs/Public%20Private%20Partnership%20jan2015updated.pdf

UNICEF. 'Zimbabwe Multiple Indicator Cluster Survey Report 2019'. Accessed 11 February 2020. www.unicef.org.Zimbabwe.reports

Unión European. 'Libro Verde Sobre La Colaboración Público-Privada y el Derecho Comunitario en Materia de Contratación Pública y Concesiones'. Accessed 1 February 2021. https://op.europa.eu/en/publication-detail/-/publication/94a3f02f-ab6a-47ed-b6b2-7de60830625e/language-es

UNOPS. 'Access to Energy: Giving Sierra Leone the Power to Change Lives'. Accessed 16 February 2020. https://www.unops.org/news-and-stories/stories/access-to-energy-giving-sierra-leone-the-power-to-change

Wainiqolo, I. and Shivanjali, S. 'Modelling Fiji's Tourism Arrivals', Economics Group Working Paper, Reservice Bank of Fiji. Accessed 26 May 2020. https://www.rbf.gov.fj/modelling-fijis-tourism-arrivals/

Waradi, T. 'India's Apollo Group Plans $44 Million Hospital in Fiji', interviewed by *The Fiji Times, 26 September 2007*. Accessed 26 May 2020. http://www.pireport.org/articles/2007/09/27/india%C3%A2%C2%80%C2%99s-apollo-group-plans-44-million-hospital-fiji

Waqainabete, I. 'Move Concerns FNA', maiden speech in Parliament, reported by V. Kumar of *The Fiji Times*, 13 December 2018. Accessed 26 May 2020. https://www.fijitimes.com/move-concerns-fna

WBG. 'Gender Equality & PPPs'. Accessed 16 February 2020. https://ppp.worldbank.org/public-private-partnership/ppp-sector/gender-impacts-ppps/impacts-ppps-gender-inclusion

WBG. 'PPIAF Assistance in Sierra Leone'. Accessed 16 February 2020. http://documents.worldbank.org/curated/en/188111468167372625/pdf/758740PPIAF0As00Box374359B00PUBLIC0.pdf

WBG. 'Project Information Document (PID): Appraisal Stage: Western Area Power Generation Project'. Accessed 16 February 2020. http://documents.worldbank.org/curated/en/223741467993762150/pdf/AB7825-PID-P153805-Initial-Appraisal-Box396261B-PUBLIC-Disclosed-5-25-2016.pdf

Whaites, M. 'Questions over Hospital Upgrade Motives in Fiji', interviewed by J. Meyer. *Radio New Zealand*, 15 May 2018. Accessed 26 May 2020. https://www.rnz.co.nz/international/programmes/datelinepacific/audio/2018644994/questions-over-hospital-upgrade-motives-in-fiji

WHO. 'Out-of-Pocket Payments, User Fees and Catastrophic Expenditure'. Accessed 18 February 2020. https://www.who.int/health_financing/topics/financial-protection/out-of-pocket-payments/en

WHO. 'The Abuja Declaration: Ten Years on'. Accessed 18 February 2020. https://www.who.int/healthsystems/publications/abuja_report_aug_2011.pdf?ua=1

WHO, Country Office for India. 'Demand Side Assessment of Primary Healthcare in Chhattisgarh'. Accessed 18 February 2020. https://apps.who.int/iris/bitstream/handle/10665/352601/9789290229209-eng.pdf?sequence=1&isAllowed=y

World Bank. 'Base De Données 2019'. Accessed 15 February 2020. https://data.worldbank.org/country/senegal

World Bank. 'Current Health Expenditure per capita (current US$)'. Accessed 26 May 2020. https://data.worldbank.org/indicator/SH.XPD.CHEX.PC.CD?end=2017&start=2017&view=bar&year=2017

World Bank. 'Ghana's Infrastructure: A Continental Perspective'. Accessed 20 January 2020. https://elibrary.worldbank.org/doi/epdf/10.1596/1813-9450-5600

World Bank. 'Maximising Finance for Development'. Accessed 18 February 2020. https://www.worldbank.org/en/about/partners/maximizing-finance-for-development

World Bank. 'PPP Unit (Sierra Leone)'. Accessed 16 February 2020. https://library.pppknowledgelab.org/documents/3924?ref_site=kl

World Bank. 'PPPs Vital to Improve Infrastructure Quality in Latin America'. Accessed 1 May 2020. https://www.worldbank.org/en/news/press-release/2017/05/04/ppps-vital-to-improve-infrastructure-quality-in-latin-america

World Bank. 'Sierra Leone: Joint Staff Assessment of the Interim Poverty Reduction Strategy Paper'. Accessed 16 February 2020. http://documents.worldbank.org/curated/en/275861468759854663/pdf/multi0page.pdf

World Bank. 'The Migration of Skilled Health Personnel in the Pacific Region: A Summary Report'. Accessed 26 May 2020. https://iris.wpro.who.int/bitstream/handle/10665.1/5501/9290611758_eng.pdf

World Bank. 'Vue D'Ensemble, 2018'. Accessed 15 February 2020. https://www.banquemondiale.org/fr/country/senegal/overview

World Bank. 'World Bank Helps Sierra Leone Improve Operational Performance of the Energy Sector'. Accessed 16 February 2020. https://www.worldbank.org/en/news/press-release/2019/05/17/world-bank-helps-sierra-leone-improve-operational-performance-of-the-energy-sector

World Bank. 'Zimbabwe: Country Profile'. Accessed 24 September 2017. http://databank.worldbank.org/data/Views/Reports/ReportWidgetCustom.aspx?Report_Name=CountryProfile&Id=b450fd57&tbar=y&dd=y&inf=n&zm=n&country=ZWE

World Bank – International Monetary Fund. 'Maximizing Finance for Development: Leveraging the Private Sector for Growth and Sustainable

Development'. Accessed 1 February 2021. https://www.devcommittee.
org/sites/dc/files/download/Documentation/DC2017-0009_
Maximizing_8-19.pdf

Yewondwossen, M. 'Investors Ask to Shed Light on Solar Project'. *Capital
Ethiopia*. Accessed 20 February 2020. https://www.capitalethiopia.com/
capital/investors-ask-to-shed-light-on-solar-project

Index

accountability 13, 27, 37, 53–4, 58–9, 61, 145, 216, 218. *See also* transparency and accountability
Addax Bioenergy Sierra Leone (ABSL) 12, 168, 170–2, 196, 284–6
    background 174–8
    downsizing 184–5
    resistance against 181–2
    socio-economic impact of 182–4
    tax incentives for 176–7
Addis Fortune 51
Africa
    Africa Infrastructure Country Diagnostic (AICD) 28
    African Charter on Human and Peoples' Rights (ACHPR) 21, 71
    African Development Bank (AfDB) 169–71, 177–9, 194
    African Infrastructure Development Index (AIDI) 168
    African Union Agenda 2063 20
Agence Française de Développement (AFD) 28, 80
Agence pour la Promotion des Investissements et Grands Travaux Sénégal (National Agency for the Promotion of Investment and Major Works Senegal, APIX) 74
Agence régionale de développement (Regional Development Agency, ARD) 72
Agencia de Promoción de la Inversión Privada (Private Investment Promotion Agency, PROINVERSIÓN) 89, 113

Agribusiness Investment Task Force (AITF) 173
agriculture sector 172–3
Alberto Barton Hospital III 87, 92, 101–2
Alberto Sabogal Hospital 97
Alexander, N. 5
Ali, A. A. 45–6
All People's Congress (APC) 176
Apollo Group 253
Appiah-Kubi, K. 202
Armed Forces Revolutionary Council (AFRC) 209
Ashurst LLP 256–7
Asia
    Asian Development Bank (ADB) 271–3
    Asia-Pacific Economic Cooperation (APEC) 272
Aspen Medical 255–6, 283
Australian Trade and Investment Commission (Austrade) 254, 282
Autoroute à péage de Dakar-Diamniadio (Dakar-Diamniadio Toll Motorway, APDD). *See* Dakar-Diamniadio highway project
Awo, M. A. 210
Ayah, R. 35
Ayushman Bharat-Pradhan Mantri Jan Arogya Yojana (AB-PMJAY) 12, 146
Azvi Group 125

Ba Hospital 249–50, 254–64, 275–7
Barton, A. 87
Barton PPP 87–8, 90, 104–5
    agreements 94
    contract and participants 92–3

coverage and quality of services 97–100
economic repercussions 96–7
investment and operating resources 95
objective 92
payments and costs 95
resistance 101–2
social organizations 102–4
supervision 95–6
terms 94
transparency 101
working conditions 100
Bebbington, A. 106 n.11
Beijing Platform 71, 238
Belgian Investment Company for Developing Countries (BIO) 194–5
Below Poverty Line (BPL) 81, 145
Bennett, R. A. 185
Berhe, M. G. 48
bilateral investment treaty (BIT) 31–2, 40 n.21
BM3 SALUD consortium 92
Bo-Kenema Power Service (BKPS) 171
Bread for All (BfA) 182–3, 185
Brookings Institution 22
build, lease, transfer (BLT) 120
build-operate-transfer (BOT) 205, 208, 211, 235
Bumbuna Phase II Hydro Power Project 192
Business Operating Permits (BOPs) 207–8

Callao Salud S.A.C. 92–3
Chang, H. -J. 47–8
Chhattisgarh 143–7, 149–58, 285
China New Energy Limited (CNEL) 185
Chronic Renal Disease (CRD) 236
civil society organizations (CSOs) 6, 168, 172, 224
Clinical Establishments Act (CEA) 149

Comisión Nacional de Hidrocarburos (National Hydrocarbons Commission, CNH) 128
Comité national d'appui aux partenariat public-privé (National Committee for Support to Public-Private Partnership, CNAPPP) 76
Committee
Committee for the Promotion of Infrastructure and Health Services (CPISS) 96–7
Committee for the Promotion of Private Investment of EsSalud (CPIP) 103
The Committee on Economic, Social and Cultural Rights (CESCR) 20–1
community health workers (CHWs) 158
compensation 12, 81, 83, 122, 155, 183, 284
Confederación Nacional de Instituciones Empresariales Privadas (National Confederation of Private Business Institutions, CONFIEP) 114
Construction-Exploitation-Transfert (Construction-Operation-Transfer, CET) 79, 84 n.8
contract
contracting 6, 76, 79, 90, 102, 207, 228–30, 232, 236
contractors 176, 203, 211–14, 216, 232, 256
contractual 6–7, 22, 77, 79, 97, 146, 167, 178, 234–5
social 10, 218
Convention on the Elimination of all forms of Discrimination against Women (CEDAW) 21, 71, 238
corporate
accountability (*See* accountability)

capture of states 2–3, 122, 134
corporations 2, 4, 54–5, 127, 133, 174, 279
interests 3, 279, 283, 287, 290
responsibility 21, 68, 78, 81–2, 89, 91, 120, 122, 131, 208, 251, 265, 287
state responsibility 89
Covid-19 pandemic 12, 19, 35, 131–2, 157, 159, 241, 250, 263, 288
CPISS. *See* Committee for the Promotion of Infrastructure and Health Services (CPISS)
crisis 25, 35, 69, 103, 134, 204, 209, 225, 232, 274, 288
CSOs. *See* civil society organizations (CSOs)

Dakar-Diamniadio highway project 68–9, 79–83
debt 25, 46, 50, 54–8, 60–1, 70, 73–5, 83, 184, 189–90, 204, 235, 249, 256, 262, 266, 282
Decreto Legislativo (D.L.) 1012 90, 92, 101
Deo, R. 275
Department for International Development (DfID) 28, 169, 171–2, 191
Department of Health and Family Welfare (DoHFW) 149
Dessallegn H. 45
development
developmental state (DS) 45–52, 54, 60–1
development financial institutions (DFIs) 174, 178–9, 184–5, 194–6
financing 1, 5, 9, 73–4, 271
Development Alternatives with Women for a New Era (DAWN) 68, 146–7, 250
D-Floor 232–5, 238, 240

Direction de l'appui au secteur privé (Private Sector Development Department, DASP) 75
Direction des financements et des partenariats public-privé (Public-Private Partnerships Financing Department, DFPPP) 76
Direction du développement du secteur privé (Private Sector Support Department, DDSP) 75
District Assembly Common Fund (DACF) 207
D.L. 1362 91
Document de politique économique et sociale (Economic and Social Policy Document, DPES) 84 n.5
Document stratégique de réduction de la pauvreté (Strategic Poverty Reduction Document, DSRP) 84 n.5
Draft Guidance 6–7
D.S. No. 144-2009-EF 101

economic growth 11, 27, 38, 45, 49, 52, 60–1, 67, 88–9, 120, 124, 189–90
EDFIs. *See* European development financial institutions (EDFIs)
education 3, 21, 25, 37, 71, 73, 155, 170, 179, 208, 212, 231, 265–6
efficiency 2, 8, 54–5, 78, 88–9, 107, 120, 148, 218
Eiffage Group 80–2
Electricity Distribution and Supply Company (EDSA) 191
Emerging Africa Infrastructure Fund (EAIF) 176, 194
Eminent Persons Group (EPG) 6, 29
energy
for sale 58–60
sector 10, 46, 55, 58–60, 170–1, 186–8, 191–2, 284

Sunbird Bioenergy 184–5
Enquête sénégalaise auprès des
    ménages (Senegalese
    Household Survey, ESAM) 69,
    84 n.4
environment/environmental
    authorization 122, 127, 135n3
    Environmental, Social and Health
        Impact Assessment (ESHIA)
        176
    impacts 76, 81, 119–20
    legislation 122
    relevance 129
    socio-economic 79
equity 23–5, 60, 72–3, 75–6, 83, 147,
    173, 177, 183, 185, 203, 218, 239
EsSalud 87, 90, 92–105, 116
Ethiopia 10, 45–7, 281
    DS 45–52, 54, 60–1
    energy sector 58–60
    Ethiopian Electric Power (EEP)
        56, 58, 60
    Ethiopian People's Revolutionary
        Democratic Front (EPRDF)
        45, 48
    media coverage mirrors 50–5
    SOEs 55–8
    uncertainty 61
Eurodad 15 n.8, 37, 54
European development financial
    institutions (EDFIs) 176–7

Farmer-Based Organizations (FBO)
    180
Farmer Development Programme
    (FDP) 175, 183
The Federation Workers' Union Centre
    of the Social Health Insurance
    of Peru (FED-CUT) 103
feminist 1, 7–10, 14, 19, 37, 38, 46,
    71, 87, 120, 216, 250, 279,
    288–91
Ferrocarril del Istmo de Tehuantepec
    (Tehuantepec's Istmo Railway,
    FIT) 123, 126–7, 131

The Fifth Final Complementary
    Provision of D.L. 1012 90
Fiji 258–60, 263–5
    Apollo Group 253
    donors, role of 254
    economic landscape 250–1
    Fijian dollars (FJD) 252
    Fiji National Provident Fund
        (FNPF) 14, 256–8, 260, 263,
        265, 283
    Fiji National Provident Fund
        Decree 2011 (Decree No. 52)
        257
    Fiji National Provident Fund
        Transition Decree 2011
        (Decree No. 51) 257
    Fiji Nursing Association (FNA)
        13, 250, 259–62, 264
    private sector, role of 255–6
    promotion of PPPs 253–4
    resistance 260–3
Fikade, B. 56
financial markets 6, 29, 73–4, 88
fiscal
    accountability 27
    compression 2
    constraints 9
    hardships 290
    implications 8
    mindedness 203
    policy 291
Fish Harbour and Industrial
    Processing 193
Five-Year Plan 127–8
focus group discussion (FGD) 202–3
foreign direct investment (FDI) 128
Foreign Investment Advisory
    Services (FIAS) 172
Foro de la Sociedad Civil en Salud
    (Civil Society Forum on
    Health, FOROSALUD) 104
Forum for Social Studies (FSS) 55, 57
fragmentation 213
Franc CFA (CFA Franc, FCFA) 77,
    79–80, 82

free, prior and informed consent
(FPIC) 12, 178, 182–3
free trade zones 119–20, 124–5, 132
Frontier Markets Fund Manager
(FMFM) 194
Fujimori, A. 88, 90

Geda, A. 55
gender equality 7–8, 12–13, 21,
71–3, 83, 167–8, 202, 205,
223–4, 226, 231–8, 241, 269,
284
Gender Inequality Index (GII) 22
gender-responsive budget 274–6
The General Confederation of
Workers of Peru (CGTP) 102
General Electric (GE) 31
General Health Law 89
General Sales Tax (GST) 89
Ghana 201–4, 218
financial closure 204–5
local governance in 206–8
market trading in 208–10
global capitalism 279–81
governance 3, 21–2, 29, 37, 70, 72,
145, 147, 149, 169, 195, 205–8,
213, 218, 280, 284, 287, 288,
290, 291
government
Alberto Fujimori 88
and development visions 21–2
of Fiji 249, 256–9, 263
Government of Sierra Leone
(GoSL) 167–74, 176, 184–6
Government of Zimbabwe (GoZ)
224–5
local governance in 206–8
NDA 146
Senegalese 76
The Grand Ethiopian Renaissance
Dam 49
gross domestic product (GDP) 225
gross national income (GNI) 22
Group of Twenty (G20) 5–6, 15 n.5,
29

Hamburg Principles 5
Hauge, J. 47–8
health
Fiji health sector 251–2
Health and Wellness Centres
(HWCs) 156
Health Development Partners
(HDPs) 227
Health Policy Guidelines
1995–2000 89
Kenya health sector 20–8
Ministry of Health (MoH) 26,
251, 260
PPPs in health sector 89–90
primary healthcare (PHC) 224,
227
public health 19, 144–5, 152,
155–6, 158–9, 241, 251
Zimbabwe health sector
224–31
Heavily Indebted Poor Countries
(HIPC) 75
Hendriks, T. D. 210
Hickel, J. 29
Hoag, F. 6
Hospital Alberto Leonardo Barton
Thompson 87
Humala, O. 88
Human Development Index (HDI)
22
Hyundai Engineering Company
Limited (HEC) 272

ICF. *See* Investment Climate Facility
(ICF)
IFC. *See* International Finance
Corporation (IFC)
IFI. *See* International Financial
Institution (IFI)
Independent Evaluation Group
(IEG) 7–8
India 12, 143–4, 146–8, 157, 287–8
Indian Medical Association (IMA)
148
indigenous women 133–5, 286

Industrial Development Corporation (IDC) 195
inequity 146–7, 151
infant mortality rate (IMR) 225
inflation 4, 15 n.9, 227
information and communications technology (ICT) 169
infrastructure
  Infrastructure Council 79
  Infrastructure Crisis Facility Debt Pool (ICF-DP) 195
  sector 46, 78, 168–9
Institute for Economic Affairs (IEA) 32
Instituto Nacional de los Pueblos Indígenas (National Institute of Indigenous Peoples, INPI) 130
Instituto Peruano de Seguridad Social (Peruvian Institute of Social Security) (became EsSalud with Law No. 27056, of 1999, IPSS) 90
insufficient consultation 212
Inter-American Development Bank (IDB) 89, 116
international
  International Covenant on Economic, Social and Cultural Rights (ICESCR) 20
  International Finance Corporation (IFC) 169, 172–3, 178, 191, 253–4, 257, 262–3, 266 n.11
  International Financial Institution (IFI) 5–7, 12, 29, 47, 50, 53–4, 57, 59–61, 167, 185, 202–3, 279–80, 285
  International Monetary Fund (IMF) 23, 29, 50–1, 53, 61, 176, 202, 223, 249, 262–3
  International Trade Centre (ITC) 172
Interoceanic Corridor 11, 119–20, 123–5, 129–31, 133–4
Investment Climate Facility (ICF) 173, 186 n.3

Investor State Dispute Settlement (ISDS) 32
Iseme, Kamau and Maema (IKM) 32
Isthmus of Tehuantepec Corridor 119, 123–33, 280, 283–4

Jacobs, T. 258
Jáltipan-Salina Cruz gas pipeline 119, 123, 127–8
Jan Swasthya Abhiyan (People's Health Movement, JSA) 147, 154, 156–8
Japan International Cooperation Agency (JICA) 171
Jasi, S. 230
Joint Ventures Partnerships Act 227, 242

Kebour Ghenna, A. 55, 57–8
Kenya 10
  Healthcare Budget Allocation 33–4
  history 22–6
  Kenya Health Sector Strategic and Investment Plan (KHSSP) 27
  life expectancy 22
  measures 22
  MES programme 22, 27–35, 37
  OOP payments in 23, 25–6
  SDG Partnership Platform 28
  timeline and equity 23–5
Kenyatta, U. 21
Kissy HFO Project 192
Kumaranayake, L. 239

labour 2, 9, 11–12, 19, 30, 82, 87, 93, 100–2, 124, 132, 143, 145, 168, 172, 178–9, 181–2, 201, 236, 284–6
land reform 173–4
Lappin, K. 262, 277–8
La Red Asistencial Sabogal de EsSalud (Sabogal Healthcare Network of EsSalud) 87–105
Latin America 1, 88, 120, 122, 172, 195

laundry company 232
Lautoka Hospital 249–50, 253–64, 275–7
The Law for the Modernization of Social Security in Health 89
liberalization 10, 47, 49–51, 54, 61, 67–8, 120, 145, 224–5, 228, 241, 281
lockable shops 202, 210–12, 214–16
López Obrador, A. M. 119

macroeconomics
    Multi-year Macroeconomic Framework (MMF) 89, 106 n.3
    policy/policies 10, 19, 30, 46, 50–1, 58
    reforms 51–3, 55, 60
Madhina, D. 233
Managed Equipment Services (MES) programme 22, 27–35, 37
Manifestación de Impacto Ambiental (Environmental Impact Statement, MIA) 130
Manuh, T. 209
Maputo Protocol 21, 71, 238
market
    Dome Market 202, 210–18, 286–8
    financial 6, 29, 73–4, 88
    marketisation 1
    open market sheds/stalls 211
    trading 208–10
Maternal Mortality Ratio (MMR) 226
Maximizing Finance for Development (MFD) 5, 29–30
Mbuya Nehanda maternity hospital 236
MDB. *See* multilateral development bank (MDB)
media coverage 47, 51–4, 58–60, 263
Medical Services Act 228, 233–4, 239
Medium Term Plan (MTP) 21
megaproject 11, 49, 119, 124–8, 130–2, 136 n.9

Member of Parliament (MP) 212
Memorandum of Understanding (MoU) 31, 176, 223
Metals and Engineering Corporations (METEC) 48–9
Metropolitan, Municipal and District Assemblies (MMDAs) 207
Mexico 119–22, 124–5, 127–8, 130, 134, 135 n.1, 280, 283–4, 286
migrants 127
    migrate 252
    migration 70, 143, 183, 252
    migratory 291 n.2
Ministerio de Salud (Ministry of Health, MINSA) 89, 97, 102
Minister of Health and Child Care 241, 245
ministry(ies)
    Ministries, Departments and Agencies (MDAs) 207
    Ministry of Finance and Economic Planning (MoFEP) 205
    Ministry of Health and Child Care (MoHCC) 227–8, 232–6
    Ministry of Health and Medical Services (MoHMS) 251, 273
minority 1, 290
Mkadawire, T. 47
Mnangagwa, E. 226
Model Land Commission Bill 174
Mollinedo, R. M. 124
monetary
    incentives 151, 155
    international monetary institutions 53, 57
    international monetary organizations 53
Mudyarabikwa, O. 233
Mugabe, R. 226
Mukhyamantri Swasthya Bima Yojana (MSBY) 146, 151
multilateral development bank (MDB) 5–6, 13, 14 n.4, 29, 249, 253–4, 266

multi-stakeholder forum (MSF) 183
Municipal Chief Executive (MCE) 213
Munyuki, E. 230
Mylenko, N. 53

Nakuru District Hospital 23
national
    National Airport Corporation
      (NAC) 272–3
    National Bank of Ethiopia (NBE)
      62 n.3
    National Democratic Alliance
      (NDA) 145
    National Gender Policy of
      2013–17 238
    National Health Insurance
      Scheme 12, 145
    National Health Mission (NHM)
      145–6, 156
    National Health Strategy (NHS)
      225, 228, 238
    National Power Authority (NPA)
      171, 175
    National Rural Health Mission
      (NRHM) 144–5
    National Sustainable Agriculture
      Development Plan (NSADP)
      171–2
    National System for the
      Promotion of Private
      Investment (SNPIP) 91
    The National Union of Nurses of
      the Social Health Insurance 103
    National Urban Health Mission
      (NUHM) 145
Negin, J. 252, 274
Netherlands Development Finance
    Company (FMO) 176,
    194
New Patriotic Party (NPP) 215
non-communicable diseases (NCDs)
    251, 273
non-governmental organizations
    (NGOs) 178
Nyazema, N. 226

Oaxaca territory 119–20, 124–5,
    127–30, 132–4
Office of the President and Cabinet
    (OPC) 232
Official Development Assistance
    (ODA) 73–4, 282
Olivier, J. 229–30, 232, 234, 236–7
operating company (OC) 93–4, 96–7,
    100, 102
Órgano de Control Interno (Internal
    Control Body, OCI) 96–7
Oryx Group Limited (AOG) 174, 176
Ouko, E. 34
out-of-pocket (OOP) 23, 25–6, 147,
    153–4, 157–9, 225

Pacific
    Pacific Islands Forum Secretariat
      (PIFS) 274
    Pacific Private Sector
      Development Initiative (PSDI)
      254, 273
pan african 10, 37, 71
PAP. *See* Priority Action Plans (PAP)
PAP2 72, 75, 83
Parirenyatwa Group of Hospitals
    (PGH) 231–9, 242 n.12, 285
Parirenyatwa Hospital Act 231, 245
Parirenyatwa Hospitals Board of
    Governors (PHBG) 231–3,
    237, 245–7
People's Health Movement (PHM)
    157
People's Movement for Democratic
    Change (PMDC) 176
Peru 88, 106 n.2
    civil society 116
    international organizations 114,
      116
    National System for Private
      Investment Promotion 114
    principles in 113
    private enterprises 114–15
    projects in 112
    the state 113

PFHI. *See* publicly funded health insurance (PFHI)
pharmacy 236-7
Philips Medical Systems 30-1
Plan d'action de réinstallation (Resettlement Action Plan, PAR) 81
Plan Nacional de Infraestructura para la Competitividad (National Infrastructure Plan for Competitiveness, PNIC) 89
Plan Sénégal Émergent (Emerging Senegal Plan, PSE) 11, 69-70
poverty 67, 69-70, 74, 76, 81, 84 n.3, 272
poverty reduction strategy (PRS) 167, 170
Pradhan Mantri Jan Arogya Yojana (PMJAY) 12, 144-6, 148-59, 288
Priority Action Plans (PAP) 72, 75, 83
Private and Financial Sector Development (PFSD) 169
The Private Investment Promotion Agency (PROINVERSION) 89, 113
private sector
    discourse and development 2-3
    dynamics 74-5
    entities 30-2
    privatization 56, 88
Projet Équité de genre dans la gouvernance locale (Gender Equity Project in Local Governance, GELD) 73
Protectorate Land Act (1927) 173
Proyectos de Infraestructura Diferidos en el Registro de Gasto (Deferred Infrastructure Projects in the Expenditure Register, PIDIREGAS) 120
Proyectos para Prestación de Servicios (Project for Provision of Services, PPS) 120-2, 125

public health
    Public Health Act 237
    Public Health Resource Network (PHRN) 147
Public Investment Division (PID) 205
publicly funded health insurance (PFHI) 12, 145-7, 158-9
    actors 148-9
    design and implementation 150
    in India 147-8
    regulatory and legal framework 149-50
    for women's 151-7
public-private engagement typology 229
Public-Private Infrastructure Advisory Facility (PPIAF) 167, 171
public-private partnerships (PPPs) 1, 14 n.2
    characteristics 4, 92-6
    classification of 91
    DS transition 47-50
    feminist review 288-91
    financing 68, 70, 75-6, 79, 84 n.8, 218
    geopolitics of 282-3
    for infrastructure 78-9
    legal and institutional framework 76-7
    legal and regulatory framework 90-1, 169
    limitations 77-8
    media coverage 50-5
    multidimensional analysis of 9-10
    narrative 281-2
    overview 3-5
    in practice 7-9
    projects 192-3
    resistance to 101-4, 240-1
    risks 8-9
    trajectory 203-6
Public Private Partnerships Unit (PPPU) 27-8, 169-70

public-private-professionals-people partnerships (PPPPPs) 242
Public Procurement and Disposal Act (PPDA) 169
public sector 4, 6, 12, 15, 23, 27, 37, 56–7, 61, 76, 79, 91, 95, 122, 153, 155, 157–8, 202, 218, 237, 256, 258, 263, 275, 282
public services 2, 7, 11, 23, 25, 30, 37, 55, 61, 76–8, 88–90, 101–2, 104, 113, 116, 143, 204, 249–50, 253, 256, 271, 282, 286

quality of life 69–70, 72, 194

Rashtriya Swasthya Bima Yojana (RSBY) 145–7, 149, 152, 154–5
Regional Assistance Mission to the Solomon Islands (RAMSI) 255
Regional Network for Equity in Health in East and Southern Africa (EQUINET) 224, 228, 233
Remove Administrative Barriers to Investments (RABI) 173
Remuneration
    Remuneration for Investments (RPI) 95
    Remuneration for Operations (RPO) 95
    Remuneration for Service (RPS) 95
renal dialysis services 235–6
The Reporter Ethiopia 53, 56, 58, 60
Reproductive and Child Health (RCH) 156
resistance and re-existence 132–3
rights
    human 1–2, 7, 10–11, 13–14, 19–21, 32–7, 45, 60, 68–9, 72, 78–9, 81–3, 127, 131, 147, 184, 205, 216, 223–4, 237–9, 241, 250–1, 264, 272, 284
    labour 11, 101, 285

land 173–4, 178
    social 78, 91, 284–5
    women's 12, 21, 37, 71, 83, 168, 174, 178–81, 186, 237
Romero, M. J. 54, 57
Roundtable for Sustainable Biomaterials (RSB) 178

SACMAG Group 125
Sahyadri Hospitals 276
SAPs. *See* structural adjustment programmes (SAPs)
scheduled castes (SCs) 143, 148, 152, 157–8
scheduled tribes (STs) 143, 148, 157–8
SDGs. *See* Sustainable Development Goals (SDGs)
Secretaría de Ambiente y Recursos Naturales (Secretariat of the Environment and Natural Resources, SEMARNAT) 127, 130
Secretaría de Energía (Secretariat of Energy, SENER) 128
Secretaría de Hacienda y Crédito Público (Ministry of Finance and Public Credit, SHCP) 123, 130
security
    food 13, 22, 176, 178, 183, 186, 274
    peace and 70, 72
    social 87, 89, 93, 102–3, 145, 205
SEF Group 127
SENAC SA 80–2
Senegal 67–9, 281, 284
    Dakar-Diamniadio highway project 79–83
    economic stability 69–70
    finance development 73–4
    gender policies and social inequalities 70–3
    infrastructure 78–9

legal and institutional framework
76–7
limitations 77–8
private sector, rise of 74–5
unintended consequences 75–6
Sénégalaise des Eaux (Senegalese
Water Board, SDE) 78, 85 n.9
Senghor, L. S. 80
Sierra Leone 167–8, 170–8, 181–2,
185–6, 191–3, 284–5
Sierra Leone Investment and
Export Promotion Agency
(SLIEPA) 172–3
Sierra Leone Network on the
Right to Food (SiLNoRF)
181–3
Sierra Leone People's Party
(SLPP) 176
Sindicato Nacional de Médicos de
EsSalud (Doctors' National
Union of EsSalud, SINAMES)
103
Sindicato Nacional Médico del
Seguro Social del Perú
(National Medical Union
of Social Security of Peru,
SINAMSSOP) 102–3
Sistema de Transporte y
Almacenamiento Nacional
Integrado de Gas Natural
(Integrated National Natural
Gas Transport and Storage
System, SISTRANGAS) 128
Smallholder Commercialization
Programme (SCP) 171
social balance 77–8
social movement 101, 104, 106 n.11
social resistance 285–6
Société nationale des eaux du Sénégal
(Senegalese National Water
Company, SONES) 78
Solar Era 193
State 1–4, 10–13
Ethiopia 47–8, 57

Fiji 256–8
Ghana 207–10
State Nodal Agency (SNA) 149–50
state-owned enterprise (SOE) 47–51,
53, 55–8, 61, 202, 204, 254,
281
Stratégie nationale de développement
économique et social
(National Strategy for
Economic and Social
Development, SNDES)84 n.5
Stratégie nationale pour l'équité et
l'égalité de genre (National
Gender Equity and Equality
Strategy, SNEEG) 71–2
structural adjustment 22–6, 48, 69,
145, 201, 223
structural adjustment programmes
(SAPs) 23, 69, 73–4, 145,
201–2, 207–9, 223, 225, 241,
281–2
Sub-Saharan Africa (SSA) 62 n.2
Sunbird Bioenergy Mabilafu Project
(SBMP) 183–4
Sustainable Development Goals
(SDGs) 5–7, 20, 28–9, 72, 74,
146, 167, 203, 249, 253–4, 266,
271
Swedfund International AB 195
Swiss-based Addax 174

Talawadua, F. 252, 260–2, 276
Tatukivei, I. T. 262, 266 n.21
tax
General Sales Tax (GST) 89, 95
incentive 176–7, 186, 228
taxation 241, 252
taxpayer 3, 30, 34, 235, 260
Taye, B. 55–6, 58
territorial sovereignty 283
Third Party Administrator (TPA)
148
Tina Hydropower Limited (THL)
272

toll motorway project. *See* Dakar-
Diamniadio highway project
Training and Research Support
Centre (TARSC) 224
Transitional Stabilisation Programme
(TSP) 226–7
transparency and accountability
13, 37, 150–1, 203, 214–15,
239–41, 250, 280, 283
Transshipment Container Part
(TIDFORE Project) 193
25 MW Betmai Hydro 193

UN Conference on Financing for
Development (2015) 271
United Nations
The United Nations Conference
on Trade and Development
40 n.21
United Nations Development
Programme (UNDP) 169
United Nations Office for Project
Services (UNOPS) 191–2
United Progressive Alliance (UPA)
145–6
The United Union of Healthcare
Workers Callao Salud
(SUTACAS) 102
Universal Health Coverage (UHC)
22, 146, 227

Veracruz territory 119–20, 124–5,
128–34
Village Vegetable Garden (VVG)
180–1, 183
Voluntary Guidelines on the
Responsible Governance of
Tenure of Land, Fisheries and
Forest (VGGT) 174

Whaites, M. 258
Whyle, E. B. 229–30, 232, 234, 236–7
women 11–13
ABSL PPP on 178–81

access to health services 36–7
Afro-Mestizo 133–5, 286
caesarean sections 155
harassment and abuse 154
high OOP expenditure 153–4
hysterectomies 155
in Kenya (*See* Kenya)
male control 214
OOP expenditure 25
PFHI schemes 151–7
working conditions and impact
100
World Bank (WB) 5–6, 12, 23, 27–9,
32, 50–1, 53, 61, 74, 80, 116,
120, 150, 167, 169, 171, 173,
202–3, 223, 235, 249, 262,
265–7, 271, 279, 281
World Bank Group (WBG) 28, 52,
167, 173, 266, 272
World Health Organization (WHO)
226, 265 n.2

Zimbabwe 223, 241–2, 285
contracting out 230–1
Zimbabwean dollars (ZWD)
226–7
Zimbabwe Coalition on Debt and
Development (ZIMCODD)
239–40
Zimbabwe College of Public
Health Physicians (ZCPHP)
234–5
Zimbabwe Health and
Demographic Survey (ZDHS)
226
Zimbabwe Investment and
Development Agency Bill of
2019 239
Zimbabwe Joint Ventures
Partnerships Act of 2016
239
Zonas Económicas Especiales
(Special Economic Zones,
SEZ) 124, 128